Mothers of Six Cultures

Antecedents of Child Rearing

Mothers of Six Cultures

Antecedents of Child Rearing

❖ ❖ ❖ ❖ ❖ ❖

John Wiley & Sons, Inc.,
New York · London · Sydney

Leigh Minturn

Associate Professor
Department of Psychology
University of Illinois

William W. Lambert

Professor
Departments of Psychology,
Sociology, and Anthropology
Cornell University

❖ ❖ ❖ ❖ ❖ ❖

John and Ann Fischer

Kimball and Romaine Romney

William and Corinne Nydegger

Thomas and Hatsumi Maretzki

Robert and Barbara LeVine

Preface

This book is the result of the efforts of many people. It is a sequel to *Six Cultures—Studies of Child Rearing* edited by Beatrice Whiting, and is based on material from the same field work described in that book. The total project was directed by Irvin Child of Yale, William Lambert of Cornell, and John Whiting of Harvard. The Behavioral Sciences Division of the Ford Foundation financed the field work. The funds for the analysis of the interview material on which this book is based came from the Cornell Social Science Research Center and from Grant Number M-2331 of the National Institutes of Health.

The mother interviews were coded at Cornell under the direction of William Lambert and me. The coding was done by Laura Holmberg, Roz Solomon, Carol Lubow, Eleanor Wardwell, and Denny O'Connor.

William Lambert and I were co-investigators for both grants, and we worked out the overall plan and analysis of this book. William Lambert suggested that we include hypotheses about the antecedents of our factors.

The analysis of the separate societies, which was done at Cornell, is not included in this text, but it formed a basis for the later factor analysis of the combined sample of societies. The factors analysis was done at Illinois and forms the basis of our discussion in this book.

William Lambert read the text and made editorial comments and revisions on the first eight chapters. He helped formulate the hypotheses concerning the cultural antecedents of the child-training factors described in the text and contributed extensively to the introductory and summary chapters.

The cross-cultural test of our hypotheses on data from the HRAF files was done by me at Illinois. The data for this analysis were gathered by an advanced class in "Cross Cultural Perspectives in Child Development" that I taught in the spring of 1963. Dr. Lambert made editorial comments on this chapter and wrote part of the introductory statements of the chapter. His contribution to the chapter is also reflected in some of the hypotheses being tested.

The within-culture tests of our hypotheses, based on the analysis of variance among mothers within each of our six communities, is presented in Chapter 17. This chapter is chiefly the work of William Lambert. The data were compiled from census material on individual families gathered by the field teams. I compiled many of the contingency tables presented in the chapter; others were compiled by William Lambert from census material supplied by Beatrice Whiting. William Lambert did the statistical analysis for the chapter and wrote the text. I revised the text and suggested additional analyses which were also carried out at Cornell.

The book is based on interview data gathered by the field teams of the *Six Cultures* project. The material for the ethnographic summaries in the Introduction and Chapters 10 through 16, which deals with each of the six communities, was derived largely from these interviews and the text of *Six Cultures*. In addition to revising the chapters dealing with the communities in which they did field work, my field team colleagues have helped me to interpret their ethnographic data in terms of our hypotheses about the antecedents of child-training practices, and have supplied me with information about living arrangements and various aspects of income, household economy, and women's roles. Their contribution, therefore, extends throughout the entire book. Without their data and assistance the book could not have been written.

In addition to the authors and the interview coders, a number of other people have assisted us in the production of this text. Alfred L. Baldwin of Cornell has been an invaluable advisor of long standing in the planning and execution of this research. Ledyard Tucker, Henry Kaiser, and Raymond Cattell of the University of Illinois advised me about the procedures for factor analysis. Jim Nunnally, late of the University of Illinois, now at Vanderbilt University, devised our analysis plan of including the data from all societies in our factor analysis and testing for between-society differences on factor scores. Carol Landsea and Sue Weidemann helped with the statistical analyses at Illinois. The manuscript was typed by Mary Thompson and Jean Powell. Marvi Vidmar proofread the manuscript and compiled the index. Irvin Child read a preliminary draft of the text and contributed extensive and helpful comments. John and Beatrice Whiting also read a preliminary draft and made helpful suggestions on analyses and the presentation of reference material. We wish to thank all these people for their advice and assistance.

Finally, the anonymous but most important contributors to this book are the patient women who gave their time and friendship to answer the questions of our interviews, and to provide the material upon which this book is based. We owe them our most grateful thanks. We have tried to tell their story with precision and understanding. We hope we have succeeded.

LEIGH MINTURN

August 1964

Contents

List of Tables

APPENDIX

Introduction

This book reports an adventure in research exploration in an important area of human endeavor: the raising of children. This area is intrinsically interesting, representing as it does the focus of both the major joys and struggles in the families all over the world. From the outset we have approached this intricate matter in a number of manners and with a number of aims, hoping to throw light and to achieve perspective with an approach of many facets since one approach alone might hide something of great importance.

We are reporting a research exploration. Exploration must be seen for what it is or else the reader may have too high an expectation of what we have accomplished. It is one thing to explore with known tools but unfounded hypotheses. The best of physicists have done this. It is equally interesting to explore with founded ideas and unknown tools. This is the daily task of some developmental engineers. Some of the hypotheses and methods used in this research were developed specifically for it, and were therefore untested. Herein lay part of the excitement of this endeavor.

Our theories were, of course, not totally new with us since we leaned heavily on the care and thoughtfulness of many other researchers. But these ideas of learning theorists, personality psychologists, social psychologists, anthropologists, and sociologists had not yet been proven themselves in cross-cultural exploration. Our tools—questionnaires, methods of observation, strategies of research, measurement scales—had been tried before by social scientists in the United States and other countries. But the particular interviews used in this research were especially developed for this research project, even though they were usually based on the results of previous research. The interview that forms the subject matter for the present text is similar to the interview used by Sears, Maccoby, and Levin in their book *Patterns of Child Rearing* (1952).

The most exploratory aspect of our study had to do with whether or not these theories could be interpreted by our measurement devices with the same effects in six different areas of the world. This is the crux of our report. Some experts would say it is impossible in principle to measure the same behavior in six different cultural contexts while others would say that it is possible to do so, but only with great difficulty because the cultural setting determines the meaning of behavior. We knew it would not be easy and it did not prove to be easy, but this book attests to the fact that this aspect of our aim was not totally a failure.

Consider, for example, the problem of aggression training. In most societies parents and other child caretakers do things to keep children from hurting other people. But the parents in these different societies use different methods to prevent such behavior. In some places parents try to stop children from quarreling with relatives, but are not as concerned about quarrels with nonrelatives. In other societies parents are worried about aggression involving girls but not boys. Less commonly, parents may be more tolerant of aggression by girls than aggression by boys. Parents also differ in the extent to which they are concerned about aggression to children as opposed to aggression directed to adults. All these differences in parental behavior and attitudes are influenced by the theories that parents have about the nature of aggressive actions and the motives behind children's aggression. Such theories and ideas differ widely from culture to culture and to a lesser extent from family to family within a culture. The problem of cross-cultural research is to design measures that will reflect this variation without losing the core meaning of the behavior studied that is necessary for meaningful comparisons.

Considerable thought was devoted to this problem before any of the field teams went abroad to gather data. All of the project personnel, the senior investigators, and the field team members met for six weeks to plan the research before the field teams dispersed to their various destinations. The results of the discussions of this meeting were consolidated and published as the *Field Guide for a Study of Socialization in Five Societies* (1963). This guide was sent to all of the field teams and was used by all of them as a basis for organization of their research. The behavior systems (i.e., similar behaviors that tend to occur together, probably stemming from the same motivation) that we planned to investigate are defined in this guide. The behavior systems singled out for special attention are aggression, dependency, obedience, responsibility, achievement, sociability, social control mechanisms, and conscience development. The guide also contains the English version of all the interviews used and instructions for carrying out the research.

In writing the results of the research we focused first upon the problem of describing the cultural context of socialization. This material describing the cultural background of the people in the different societies, along with the generally held beliefs and values about these behavior systems, is to be found in the first book of this series, *Six Cultures—Studies of Child Rearing.* It represents one of our exploration strategies in that it attempts to reflect the overall picture which will assist us in interpreting that part of the story contained in the present book.

The materials from this broader book will assist us to decide in what sense and to what degree we actually measured the same things about these "behavior systems" in all six cultures. If the behavior systems described in each society do not make reasonable psychological and cultural sense in each culture context, then we would worry about whether we had succeeded in defining these systems with sufficient generality and flexibility to permit meaningful definitions within each society and, at the same time, with sufficient theoretical clarity to permit comparisons among societies.

Searching for the "big cultural picture" was only one way we went about our task. We also tried to find comparable behaviors by studying a great deal about a very carefully sampled group of individual children. If a child is punished for hitting someone in the presence of a parent, he may develop a learned avoidance of such behavior in such a situation. This avoidance, if consistently and clearly dealt with and followed up, may become a characteristic of the child's behavior under many social conditions. It may show up in some direct or transformed way in his reports about himself or in his fantasy. These possible effects (to be tested in later reports) provided one basis for our interest in what impinges on the children. We also assumed that if we focused upon what impinged upon children under similar conditions *that these impingements would relate to one another in a similar way wherever we went.* Mothers who ask for many chores to be done may ask that they be done frequently, and may ask for more of them to be done as a child matures— everywhere. Of course, the specific chores may differ in two cultures or from family to family within a culture. But, we argued, if we lived in each place for a while we would note the variations in chores and ask questions in each place about the particular set of possible chores that might be placed upon a child. In America it may involve feeding the dog; in Okinawa it may involve carrying about the baby on one's back; or, in India, it may focus upon carrying water. In each case there is a duty impinging on the child, and he or she must see to it that something gets done: *the child is expected to be responsible.*

If, then, on a collection of questions involving responsible behaviors, the positions of mothers on these requirements *vary in similar ways* from cultural setting to cultural setting, we may have put our fingers on a common dimension of socialization. If, on the other hand, we give a reasonable opportunity for this common pattern of variation of requirement to occur and it does *not* occur, then it would be an area of impingements on a child which would be more difficult to compare from culture to culture. Finally, suppose the discovered variation among such measures as frequency and number of chores and the age of the child do covary similarly in all societies, but this variation does not make good sense in terms of the context, then we would again worry about whether we were measuring comparable behavior.

One way to tap these common pressures on the children of our samples was to have long and full discussions with parents, particularly with mothers, about how they dealt with their children. These interviews, which usually took one to two hours and more than one session, began after the field workers had lived in the community for some months, and after considerable observing and general interviewing had been done. All the field workers started from the same questionnaire and, with the aid of bilingual assistants, worked hard to translate the instrument into the best possible fit to the prototype English questionnaire, altering it only where necessary for the requirements of the cultural setting. This was no easy task. People, as in the Philippines, who do not think in *general* terms of rewards find it difficult to deal with questions like "Do you reward your child for helping around the house?" There are also the many problems involved in gaining rapport and keeping it, with the attendant problems of getting honest answers rather than idealized ones that reflect the cultural values rather than the mother's actual behavior.

The cross-cultural comparison of answers to our questions is meaningful only to the extent that we succeeded in translating our interview questions into terms that were meaningful within the context of each society and still sufficiently faithful to the original meaning of the questions to permit comparison among societies. The material presented in this book indicates that despite the problems inherent in this task we have to a large extent succeeded in this endeavor.

The mothers' answers to the interviews were recorded, typed, and sent to Cornell for analysis. Coders read the interviews and made a number of ratings based upon the total information contained in the interview. They also analyzed the mothers' answers to the "standard questions" and scaled these answers on an *a priori* scale, as will be described in Chapter 1. When the reliability of the work of these raters was assessed, the analysis, which is the core of the present volume, could begin.

Not all the material obtained from the mothers could be used because the decision was made to use a particular model for analyzing the data—the model of factor analysis. It was necessary to leave out some interesting issues that were not investigated in all of our societies, and questions were also dropped that did not show at least some variation from mother to mother within all of the societies.

The reader who is unfamiliar with factor analysis may appreciate some simple words about this demanding method. We shall describe it in the context of three of its virtues in our search for comparable sources of impingement on the children of these cultures. First, a "factor" is itself simply a set of *interrelated issues,* a pattern of behaviors on which mothers tend to have different positions but in consistent ways. If mothers who tend to say "I punish my son for hitting me" also say "I punish my son if he hits his sister," and, if at the same time, other mothers who say "I never punish my son for hitting me" also say "I never punish my son for hitting his sister," then these two behaviors would be good candidates for making up a single factor. In this context a factor is a pattern of behaviors that vary together. A factor is, in effect, an empirically derived behavior system. In the last chapter we shall consider relationships among the behavior systems defined by our factor analysis and those defined in the field guide that formed the organizational basis for the interview.

Second, factor analysis goes a bit further. It helps us recognize that a mother's answer may covary (i.e., vary together) with more than one *kind* of thing. If a mother says "I always punish my son for hitting me," then she may be saying something about her handling of aggression, and *at the same time* something about her expectations regarding her son's obedience. The "analysis" in "factor analysis" can therefore be viewed as involving this matter of more than one meaning in a particular answer—it permits an item in one factor to participate in defining more than one factor. In the jargon of the method, an item such as the answer to a question may have a "loading" on more than one factor.

Third, factor analysis permits us to uncover the *number* of covarying item clusters (factors) which are more or less *independent* of one another, or it can "pick up" for us factors which are related to one another. The value of the first strategy is that with the use of a set of *independent* factors a great many of the things mothers told us could be summarized by a very few statements. Most of the information contained in the long interview could be pared down to the mother's position on a few factors. If the factors so discovered make sense, then this simplification may help us to organize the relevant behaviors in these otherwise complicated matters of child rearing.

To find factors in a factor analysis is not very difficult. But there are "good" factors and "bad" factors. Good factors are clusters of covarying items which capture a great deal of the differences in the answers to questions as one goes from mother to mother or from culture to culture. This is reflected in the percentage of variance of the answers that is explained by a factor or a set of factors. On this score our factors do fairly well as described in Chapter 1.

There is some value in having factors that are independent (or orthogonal) because they permit you to communicate the most information most concisely. Let us say a word more about "independence" or orthogonality of factors. This simply means that as you go from factor one to factor two and report the standing (or scores) of the mothers on each, you are saying something fresh and new each time the mothers' positions on each factor are stated. That is, on the average, a mother's position on factor two cannot be predicted from what she said on the covarying items of factor one, and in turn, neither of these will (on the average) predict her stand on factor three and so on.

Some people like to use the analogy of space: rooms can vary in length (factor one) in a manner which has no relation to how they vary in height (factor two) or depth (factor three). As with rooms, so with rearing children: we can describe a family or culture in terms of its height, width, and depth on a series of "factors" which have names like "aggression training," "warmth of mother," etc. The factors we shall talk about in this book are orthogonal.

There might, of course, have been factors which captured the co-variation of behavior *within* a society but missed the covariation of behavior between societies; or factors might reflect variation between societies but not among the mothers of the same society. Fortunately the factors extracted from the interviews with mothers reflect both kinds of variance. This is "good" for the purposes of the present book because it means that our interviews were sensitive enough to pick up individual differences among mothers in one community and general enough to reflect differences on the same behavior systems between mothers in different societies.

So let us turn to the book which follows. It starts with a more exact statement of the method and aim of the "factor analysis." Then it tells the story of each of the factors, or dimensions, that came out of the analysis. We discuss here the questions that form the basis of the factors and, of much greater interest, how the mothers in the different societies stand on the various issues which compose each factor. These chapters reflect the distilled differences in the opinions of many mothers on the rearing of children. These differences reflect some of the fervor of commitment, the serenity of age-old tradition, or the quandry of indecision that is found in this important component of the human condition.

After describing the mean differences between mothers of our six cultures on their factor scores, we present hypotheses concerning the reasons for these differences. Our hypotheses suggest that differences in living patterns and economic activities account for most of the between-culture differences on mean factor scores.

Having derived these hypotheses from the analysis of the interview data, we conducted an additional study to test them on a larger sample of societies. We utilized material from the Human Relations Area Files for this purpose. A class of students at the University of Illinois rated the available ethnographic material from 76 societies using the same scales that were used to code the mother interviews. Ratings of social structure, living arrangements, and economic variables that had been made by other investigators on these same societies were used as the antecedent variables. Chapter 9 is devoted to the presentation of these data and the evaluation of the hypotheses in terms of the degree to which they are confirmed or refuted by these analyses.

The second half of the book is devoted to a discussion of the factor patterns within each of our six cultures. These latter chapters take up each cultural group in turn and place our cross-cultural factors back into their natural context. Here we have tried to portray the balances and imbalances on these basic matters in the various cultural groups under study. We have tried to show why one group of mothers punish their children for one kind of behavior and reward them for another, while another group puts the pressure on quite different behaviors. We see how (in part, at least) the pressures on the children make sense in terms of the important rights and duties in some diverse parts of the world.

In Chapter 17 we return to our hypotheses and discuss them in terms of within-group variation in living arrangements, family composition, and economic responsibilities. In this chapter we discuss the extent to which the child training practices of individual mothers can be predicted from the same variables that we used to predict the customary societal norms for these same behaviors.

In the last chapter, we summarize our findings in the light of our hypotheses, evaluate our data and interpretations, and discuss our conclusions concerning the probable determinants of the behaviors that have been called socialization practices. Finally, we offer some advice to other researchers concerning the design of future studies of maternal behavior.

The Societies

The book *Six Cultures—Studies of Child Rearing* contains a general description of the physical and social environment and a detailed description of the life of the children in each of our six societies. The reader who wishes to become familiar with the communities described in the following chapters should refer to this book. The information in the following ethnographic sketches, as well as much of the material for the chapters on the individual societies, represents summaries of the fuller text in *Six Cultures—Studies of Child Rearing*. For readers who are not interested in this fuller description, we present a brief description of each of the communities included in this study.

Orchard Town: New England, U.S.A.

In 1954, when our study began, Orchard Town was on the fringe of an area which was becoming suburbanized. A number of families in the town were newcomers, the vanguard of the suburban rush. They had chosen Orchard Town as the place closest to the city where they could still feel that their children would be growing up in a rural atmosphere.

The country around Orchard Town is rolling and rocky. The climate is typical of much of New England. For a few days in the summer, temperatures may go over 90 degrees. In the winter, temperatures fall below freezing much of the time, giving the children chances to skate on a number of small ponds in the town. Snow and rain are not excessive but are sufficient to keep the countryside well watered and green. School is usually canceled for a few days each winter because of heavy snowfalls.

There are three centers of population in Orchard Town, separated by sparsely inhabited areas. For our study we chose one of these, North Village, with a population of about 1000 people. The houses of North Village are spaced more closely together around the central business district, which in 1954 included about a dozen stores, most of them in a single line on one side of the main street. All the stores were small, serving only local people. Houses outside the central area were more widely separated, but even in the center the lawns were sizable, and the general appearance was that of a country town. Some of the houses in the central area were built over a century ago, but others are decorated with the gingerbread of late Victorian architecture. Out on the periphery, smaller, modern-style houses were being built.

Orchard Town was not chosen as a "typical" American town. Although Orchard Town mothers have much in common with mothers in other parts of the country, the town has some special features that limit the degree to which child-rearing patterns can be generalized. For one thing, at the time of our study Orchard Town had a rather narrow range of economic statuses. There were no poverty-stricken families in the sample and few in the village. On the other hand, there were few really well-to-do families and those that there were, as it happened, had no children in the age range that we were studying. Of course, there were recognized gradations in social status, but the town was small enough so that people of different status constantly found themselves thrown together in activities outside the home, such as church, school, PTA, women's clubs, and local politics.

With one exception, the families in our sample consisted exclusively of parents and children. In the exceptional family, the mother's mother was living in the household. In two other families of the twenty four, the mother's mother had lived in the household at some time after the parents were married. In several other families one or the other grandmother was living in another house in the town.

The sample families did not live in Orchard Town by accident. In all cases either the mother or the father were native New Englanders, in most cases both parents were. In the majority of the sample families at least one parent had been born either in Orchard Town or within a ten-mile radius. Where economically practical, there seemed to be a slight bias in favor of living near the wife's relatives. A few of the husbands and wives in our sample had met as children in Orchard Town and had married on reaching adulthood. However, since this study took place not too long after World War II, individual travel had evidently resulted in marriages between individuals from towns somewhat farther apart. Two wives, in fact, were not native New Englanders and had come from much more distant parts of the United States; one of these as the result of a war-time romance. Wives and husbands were not knowingly related by blood in any instance.

Children are very important to the people of Orchard Town, although they make no significant economic contribution to their families. They do, however, contribute to the family reputation by proper behavior. Before adolescence, girls are considered to be easier to raise; after adolescence, boys are said to give less trouble. As a whole, the parents we questioned did not prefer one sex over another in their children and most said they would prefer to have children of both sexes.

School classes group the children by annual age grades but because of the spacious arrangement of the houses in the community and the small average number of children per family, age grade groups often break down outside of school. Families living in the more remote areas of the town at times find their children playing almost exclusively with their own siblings. Mothers, considering this disadvantageous, sometimes transport the children over distances of a mile or so to make other friends.

There are several childhood ceremonies related to age. Entering and leaving grade and high school are important events in the lives of the children. We heard of birthday parties up to about the age of twelve, but rarely thereafter. Ceremonial initiation into adult status does not occur. The break with childhood and with the family would come for some at the time they leave home for college, and for others at the time of marriage.

Although most of the children of Orchard Town contribute little of practical value to the household, a "good" child as he grows older manages to find part-time jobs to get a little extra spending money. Babysitting, mowing lawns, weeding gardens, and picking apples were some of the chores we saw teen-agers performing. However, since the child's future as an adult is thought to depend heavily on his achievement in school, children may earn money only at odd times. A child who had to neglect his schooling for work would be considered to be sacrificing his future welfare.

To care for their children properly, most residents recognized a need to limit the number of children in their families. Families with two or three children were most common and those with more than four were rare.

Throughout most of its history Orchard Town has been mainly a farmer's town, but recently farming has declined greatly. There are now a few local factories, but the number of local people they employed during our study was small. Most of the fathers in our sample either commuted to jobs in the city or its suburbs, or they furnished service to the people of Orchard Town. The men's income was usually sufficient to support the families without the wives earning extra money. One mother in the sample had a hobby of raising animals which occasionally netted a little money, and another mother was a frequent baby-sitter. A few mothers went to work during the harvest season, packing apples.

All but two of the families studied owned or were buying their homes. To own property is a mark of good standing in the village. Renters are likely to be in an inferior status and may be thought to have weaker characters than property owners. Respect for the property of others and caring for one's own property are important values.

Aside from real estate, every family has a vast accumulation of objects, only part of which are in use at a given time. There are various institutionalized ways of periodically putting those objects no longer needed in the family into circulation again, such as the rummage sale and the auction. Or, these objects may be thrown in the town dump, later to be rescued by someone who could use them.

Politically Orchard Town was divided into two factions in 1954. One faction consisted of the old-timers who had been born and raised in Orchard Town. They had little desire for change and would sometimes say proudly, "What was good enough for me is good enough for my children." The other faction was the newcomers. Newcomers felt the town was standing still as a result of the attitude of the old-timers toward change. A newcomer was said to be anyone who had lived in the town less than 40 years. Just before our study began, the old-timers still held formal control in all of the town organizations. In 1953 one of the leaders of the old-timers died, and it became evident that the newcomers would soon become a political majority. As this time approached, considerable tension developed between the two groups. Following the death of this leader, the old-timers entered a period of gradual political decline from which they have no hope of recovering. Both newcomers and old-timers are proud of the town meeting system of government and the principle that everyone has a right to speak and vote.

Informal controls of behavior have probably always been much more important than they would be in a larger city. Avoidance, gossip, and occasional direct criticism are the chief means of informal social control. Although the more conservative people are probably inspired to act at times directly out of a fear of God, we believe there is less emphasis on the idea of God as a punishing or rewarding agent than in small towns in some other parts of the country. A generation ago the "bogey man" used to have some control over young children, but he has now lost his influence in Orchard Town. Occasionally his place might be taken by a stranger or a policeman, but most children see clearly that the adults of the town are the ultimate controllers of their behavior.

The old-timers and the newcomers differed in child-training practices as well as in politics. The old-timers, for example, were staunch believers in strict discipline. Newcomers, on the other hand, were generally trying to adopt a permissive attitude in child training, which was being advocated in the newspaper columns of that time, and which had been earlier adopted in the upper-middle classes of the nearby city.

Orchard Town has always produced a large number of variant adult personality types which the community, with a wry tolerance, refers to as "characters." The widest variation seems to be found among the old-timers. These people are more independent, more insistent on the sacredness of their property rights, and have more the feeling that the individual should go through life doing his work faithfully, according to his own principles, and above all uncomplainingly, in a hard world, relatively without joy. Newcomers have less absolute notions as to what is good and bad. They are more susceptible to the informal social controls. They are eager to please and want their children to grow up to be happy, even if this may sometimes mean that they achieve less. The boundaries of Orchard Town do not encompass the lives of the newcomers as strictly as they do those of the old-timers. If newcomers are dissatisfied with a local institution they are ready to seek satisfaction elsewhere. They are more ready to reform the world actively if it should interfere with the development of individual potentiality. The oldtimers seem to have finally accepted the newcomers as just another of life's hardships, to be borne without complaint.

Juxtlahuaca, Mexico

Santo Domingo barrio is part of the town of Juxtlahuaca in the state of Oaxaca, Mexico. The cultural heritage of the 600 barrio members derives basically from the Mixtec Indians whose culture was flourishing in the area before the time of Christ.

Although priests penetrated the area early in introducing religious changes, the basic subsistence patterns have been little affected. Maize, beans, and chile have remained the basic diet. Even the introduction of oxen and the plow have failed to affect greatly the pattern of land exploitation. Thus, the intrusion of Spanish culture elements in the Mixtec area has involved little change in such features as land usage and subsistence patterns, residence, and certain aspects of village organization.

The state of Oaxaca is divided into 28 *distritos* or districts. Juxtlahuaca is a village or town located in the extreme west central part of the state and is the *cabecera* or head town, roughly equivalent to a county seat, of a district of the same name. The district is approximately 54 miles from north to south and 48 miles from east to west. This 3000 square miles is further divided into *municipios*. These municipios may be thought of as towns together with a large surrounding area inhabited by scattered hamlets and isolated families. Thus there is no land between municipios as all the land and the people living on it belong to some municipio.

Juxtlahuaca with a population of nearly 3600 and Tecomastlahuaca with a population of about 2500, together with eight small villages of less than 500 each, numerous hamlets, and scattered families, bring the population of the municipio to about 30,000, with an average density of about ten people per square mile. Juxtlahuaca and Tecomastlahuaca are mostly Spanish speaking, although each contains a Mixtec-speaking barrio, or community neighborhood. Otherwise, practically all the people in the district speak only an Indian dialect.

Mean temperatures throughout the year vary only slightly owing to the cloud cover in summer and the afternoon winds during the rest of the year. The warmest months are May, June, July, and August with lows of 50°F. and highs of 86°F., and a mean temperature of 60°F.

The hills rise steeply on all sides of the barrio and its fields. Firewood is there for the taking, and families including older children, but not small ones, make semiannual trips during the slack season to gather it. Herds of cattle, belonging to townspeople, and sheep, which some barrio members also own, graze on the hillsides.

Santo Domingo is set off from the rest of the town by a clear geographical boundary. A deep *barranca* through which a stream runs lies at the southern end of the town and separates it from el Centro. Santo Domingo is referred to locally as *the* barrio. The barrio occupies about the same area as the remainder of the town, with the result that one-sixth of the total population lives on one-half the total land.

The moment one crosses the natural boundary, the barranca, the distinctive features of the barrio become apparent. None of the barrio's streets are paved in any way except for an occasional pathway of stones. Two or three of them, those which lead across the barrio toward el Centro, are as wide and flat as a road. The others slope more or less sharply and are narrow, rocky, and cut by gullies. During the rainy season most of these become intermittent, muddy streams, and at planting time, water diverted from the river for irrigation runs down several streets from the hillside.

Santo Domingo barrio is composed entirely of Indians and contains approximately 600 people, as compared to about 3000 for the remainder of the town. They are distinguishable from Spanish-speaking townspeople, though not primarily by physical type since both groups are relatively short and brown-skinned with straight black hair. (The town population does include a few blond and red-haired people, but the Indian population does not.) The basis for the distinction is cultural rather than physical and is most clearly seen in language and dress.

The houses along the streets are separated from each other by occasional cornfields or fields of alfalfa. Although some present a blank, windowless adobe wall, the back of a room which opens on the inner courtyard, most houses in the barrio are set back from the street in a grassy courtyard. The yards have fruit trees, low shrubs, and sometimes flowers. During the dry season the village looks sunbaked, while during the rainy season the corn is in various stages of growth and the vista is green and luxuriant.

Ideally, a group of brothers, together with their wives and families, will occupy separate dwelling units surrounding a common courtyard. We designate this cluster of structures and accompanying courtyard by the term compound. Each nuclear family typically maintains separate sleeping and cooking facilities, and eats apart from the others, while it shares the courtyard and engages in a number of common activities with the other families. There are two distinct structures within a compound, even in those cases where it is occupied by only one family. These two structures are the cook shack and the main room, which is used for sleeping, storage, and visiting. We will refer to the main room as the house and understand that all cooking takes place in the cook shack located adjacent to or near the house.

The arrangement of the compound varies a great deal, but almost always includes a house and cook shack for each family. The women, children, and older people spend most of their time within the compound, while the adult men are usually away at their fields during the day. Children play with and are cared for by their siblings and cousins within the compound, and the majority of their play activity, especially in the early years, is confined to the area. Sometimes, for special reasons, the compound will include families of daughters of the older people, but on the whole, residence is patrilocal.

Mixteco is the first language a barrio child learns and the only language some of the oldest barrio people speak. Most people between these extremes speak Spanish as well, but Mixteco is used at home and in most of the daily routine. Spanish is used when it is required—in dealings with the priest, the nuns, and with merchants in el Centro, none of whom know any Mixteco. Barrio meetings and all the events of the barrio fiestas are conducted in Mixteco; but if a non-Mixteco guest is present, the conversation will be carried on in Spanish as a courtesy. School children are under pressure to use Spanish at school and frequently also use it at play. Children of preschool age, especially those who have no older siblings, hear Spanish much less and do not formally learn it until shortly before they are ready to enter school.   However, young children who spend a great deal of time with an older sister who has learned Spanish begin to learn it from her, for she will often use it, except for expressions of endearment or warnings given under stress.

The typical, conservative costume of barrio men is homemade, of coarse white material.   It consists of a pair of trousers which reach to mid-calf, where they are tied, and which are secured at the waist by wrapping and tying in back.   They have neither buttons nor pockets, but a pocket for carrying money is improvised by tucking a small cotton bag into the waist band.   The long-sleeved, collarless shirt has a concealed pocket on the inside left front in which are carried cigarettes or tobacco, and sometimes folding money.   Huaraches, a locally made leather sandal with a heavy rubber sole, are worn on the feet.   Every man has a sombrero.   A plaid wool blanket or serape, sometimes with an opening cut for the head, is used for warmth outdoors in the early morning or at night.   It also serves as a covering for sleeping.

Indian women wear a hand-embroidered, white cotton blouse and a printed cotton skirt which reaches almost to the ground—both homemade.   They cover their heads and shoulders, as well as carry their infants, with a rebozo, a long dark blue cotton shawl.   This rebozo and the characteristic way that it is draped is the mark of a Mixteco woman throughout this part of the state.   Women are usually barefoot.   They carry money in a cotton bag tucked inside the blouse.   Small loads are carried in locally woven handbaskets, and heavy loads are carried in a *tenate,* or carrying-basket, on a tumpline across the forehead.   Their hair is worn in braids which either hang down the back or are wrapped around the head.   Women's earlobes are pierced for earrings, but not all women wear them.   No makeup of any kind is worn.   Unlike the men's costume, the women's costume is worn by all adult barrio women without exception or alternative.

Indians are different from townspeople and townspeople attach a negative value to this difference.   They look down on the people of the barrio, and barrio people avoid interacting with them whenever possible. Townspeople and barrio members do meet at the market and in the stores of the town.   (The food habits of the two groups are sufficiently different that such encounters are not as frequent as one might suppose. Indians consume no canned goods and buy very little meat, while town diet is varied.)   Here, interaction is limited to the specific act of buying and selling, and the Indian waits until all townspeople have been served. He is sometimes refused service altogether, and is from time to time addressed or referred to in a derogatory way. The prices he pays and the prices he receives for his products are set by the townsperson.

The most important product of this social situation is a sense of solidarity among barrio Indians that is unknown in the town. Membership in the barrio community is highly valued by those inside it.

For the typical barrio adults, the universe is spatially limited to the barrio and their horizon does not extend much beyond the valley they know so well. Most of the men have visited Oaxaca or Pueblo at one time or another, and during the war some even got to the United States as unskilled laborers, although none stayed long enough to learn any English. These outside cities, so briefly visited, are part of the Indian's universe only in a most casual sense. Their local focus and main identifications center around the barrio itself. This localization of identification is even more striking for the women and children. None identify much with the larger town of Juxtlahuaca, let alone with the state or national cultures. If outside the community and asked where they are from, they answer, "barrio Santo Domingo, Juxtlahuaca," or sometimes just, "the barrio," if the questioner is acquainted with the region.

The basic assumption of the Indian about the world in which he lives seems to be that it operates according to certain rules or laws ultimately controlled by that part of the universe which we would call the supernatural. He also believes that the general plan of things is ongoing and immutable, and that therefore man must learn certain patterns of action and attitudes to bring himself into conformity with this scheme of things. If he does these things, he believes that he will receive the minimum amount of punishment and the maximum amount of reward. There is the feeling that some suffering or misfortune is inevitable, but there are certain ways of avoiding it or mitigating it once it has fallen. In the Indian scheme of things in the barrio, the individual seems to be somewhat submerged in the group; that is to say, that the individual exists as a member of a group that is adjusted to nature and by following its pattern, he survives and prospers.

Group decisions are taken by consensus rather than by majority rule or dictatorial fiat. Perhaps it can be said that almost all the patterns of social activity in the barrio lead toward merging with the society rather than individual distinctiveness. The approved way of doing things is to live and let live, and to adjust to other human beings to avoid conflict. This does not mean highly organized cooperation, although men do work together in groups which move from one field to another. However, each family has its own property, and each individual family goes about its business not interfering with others, although cooperating within a wide range of activities such as planting and harvesting, etc.

Tarong, Philippines

The northwest coast of Luzon rises steeply to the rough central mountains, only about six miles from the sea. There is little flat land but the sloping valleys are natural spillways and, when terraced for water control, make excellent rice paddies. Almost all such land is under cultivation and additional paddies have been created by leveling sections of hillsides. The ridges are either left to natural brush and bamboo or are utilized for housing.

Here in the north the rainy season is short, only three months of regular daily downpour followed by another month of gradually decreasing showers. The climate is pleasant; the rainy season is cool but at no time is more than a sweater necessary and the nearness of the ocean moderates the heat of the dry season. The fauna is equally benign. A few small scorpions and centipedes and occasionally a snake, which is assumed poisonous though this is doubtful, are the only dangerous animals.

Far more dangerous are witches and supernatural beings who unpredictably and malevolently bring sickness, cause accidents, and kill. Talismans protect from such forces but the best defense is avoidance of known witches and suspected spirit places. If one suffers a spirit or witchcraft attack, the local medicine men may be able to cure it by propitiation and a wide variety of magical manipulations, but the modern medical doctor from town may also be consulted.

Tarongans are nominally Roman Catholic but attendance at the town church is restricted to baptisms, weddings, and funerals. The cross and santos are considered fine talismans against evil spirits and prayers for the dead are never omitted, but beyond this Christianity is hazy. The malevolent spirits whose work is frequently in evidence and the ancestor spirits who keep watch over house and fields are more immediate and real to the Tarongan.

Rice is the staple of the diet and the basis of the economy, but because of the seasonal rains only one crop can be grown in this area. A variety of dry season crops are possible and at present, eggplant, sugar cane, and tobacco are preferred, providing the only important source of cash. Small quantities of fruits and vegetables for household consumption are raised in plots convenient to the houses and bananas are grown along the paddy dikes. Since there is no portion of the banana plant that is not used in some way, its general utility rivals that of bamboo.

Carabao exclusively are used as farm animals and cows are raised in small numbers for sale. Goats, pigs, and chickens are the mainstay of rural households for quick cash and feast food. The daily diet is largely vegetables and rice, but any mudfish, snails, frogs and such caught in the fields are added. Beef, carabao, and pork can be bought in small quantities at the weekly market in town as can fish, octopus, and shellfish. Because of the depth of the ocean off this coast and the lack of deep-sea fishing equipment, sea foods are scarce and expensive and are not the important part of the diet they are in the south.

Tarong is a typical *barrio* of this area, situated about five miles from the town, a mile from the sea (and the coastal highway), and extending to within three miles of the mountains. It encompasses about two square miles of sloping valleys and ridges and boasts one dirt road. Its population, at the time of the study, was 298. Of the 61 households this figure represents, all but six are descended from the seven families who originally settled this area in approximately 1860.

The barrio is the smallest administrative unit but has little autonomy. Its sole official is an unpaid *teniente*, elected by the barrio to act as its spokesman, but his power is limited to persuasive mediating. All judicial, regulatory, and police functions are retained in the municipality whose seat is the town and whose officials are elected at large. But when barrio boundaries are coterminous with kin group membership, as they often are and as is the case in Tarong, loyalty and unity can be assumed in interbarrio affairs and group control in intrabarrio disputes. Where these conditions are not met, barrios show little cohesion and are no more than an administrative convenience.

The public schools provide the only occasion for interbarrio cooperation. The Tarong school, for example, serves three barrios for the first through fourth grades and six barrios for the fifth and sixth grades, with a total enrollment of about 100 pupils. Much of the construction and maintenance of schools must be provided by their districts, and interbarrio work groups have been created for this purpose but they remain limited to school activities.

Education is highly valued by Tarongans and children complete as many grades as parental resources allow. Almost all children finish fourth grade and two-thirds graduate from sixth grade. To go beyond this level is difficult since this means tuition plus room and board for high school in town. Nevertheless, about a fourth of Tarong's households had sent or were sending a child to this high school, in part because of the social prestige it confers. Eight households had managed to send one or more of their children to a provincial college, generally to obtain teachers' certificates. Unfortunately, jobs are scarce and field work too menial after this much education; those who are forced to return are often bored and bitter.

More important than the barrio in the lives of Tarongans is their *sitio*, the housing cluster to which they belong. Sitios vary as to size; they ranged in Tarong from a few to eighteen households, but five to seven is most common. A sitio contains one or more patrilocal household clusters, occasionally including a few remote relatives whose closer kin have died or who have moved from their own sitio for other reasons. Kinship is reckoned bilaterally and maternal relatives are by no means ignored; in fact, 15 per cent of the households in Tarong were matrilocal, usually because of economic advantages. In either case, sitio membership means being part of a tight-knit kindred which functions as a group in all but the most private affairs.

Marriages are preferred between second cousins or less closely related neighbors, which serves to tie sitios to each other in multiple relationships. Increasing population has now made possible marriages between cousins living in the same sitio, an arrangement considered ideal. Although parental suggestions have considerable influence on choice of spouse, no boy or girl is forced to marry against his or her wishes. Should a poor choice (from the parental point of view) be insisted upon, it is likely that a grudging consent will be obtained in time.

At marriage, the groom's family provides a house, usually in its house cluster, some livestock, and most if not all the land that is to be the son's inheritance. Increasing population and limited land have decreased individual holdings and inflated the price of land. At present, only one-fifth of Tarong's households can supply all their rice from their own land. The rest are forced to tenant land, help harvest or polish rice for shares, engage in petty trade, etc. Approximately one-fifth of the households remain far below a normal rice income. For three or more months each year these families subsist largely on their kinsmen's charity and on roots and other foods growing wild on the hillsides.

Tarongans are all farmers and thus are a part of the general "barrio" or rural class. But movement out of this class is not impossible and has been accomplished by a few Tarongans, notably through college education. Barrio attitudes are basically equalitarian. There are variations in family prominence based primarily on wealth, but prestige is not inherited as is land and leadership must be earned. More important, good fortune and bad alike are most often ascribed to uncontrollable luck, leaving the individual unburdened by pride or shame in his contacts with his neighbors. A social gulf is developing, however, between landowners (of whatever amount) and the landless. The latter have little voice in community affairs and no expectations of obtaining even a little land which would make them "respectable poor."

The land and house given to the new couple at their wedding is symbolic of their autonomy, but usually for many years a couple does not make any important decisions without consulting one or more of the group. In only one area is complete autonomy customary: a woman's kitchen is inviolate. No woman will even enter another woman's kitchen without specific invitation, a rule which serves to reduce mother and daughter-in-law friction.

Sitio living is not conducive to privacy. Houses are clustered close together around common family yards through which the major footpaths pass. Yards range in size from 15 to 25 feet to 35 by 100 feet and are neat, swept, and often tree-shaded. The yards are never empty, for this is where a large part of the daily work is done and where children play.

If it is raining or too sunny, children and adults use the railed porches facing the yard. This is a favorite spot for mothers who are doing work they cannot take out or who are restrained because of an infant. From the porch they can gossip with their sisters-in-law, watch the children at play, check on some of the chores, chat with their husbands if they are not in the fields that day, and get news from each passerby, who must run a friendly gantlet of questions about his destination.

The houses themselves offer little more privacy. Each is two structures, both elevated five to six feet on posts, joined by an open porch. The larger section is the *sala* (living room) and sleeping rooms with movable partitions to separate these areas. Since only woven mats and pillows are in common use, the sleeping area is small.

The kitchen section is usually about a third the size of the other and is used for eating as well as cooking by most families. The walls of both sections are bamboo; the area under the sala is also enclosed. Floors throughout are split bamboo except for the sala where wood planks are used if the family can possibly afford them. The roof is steep and made of layers of carefully tied cogon grass. Windows are generous but well shuttered. These houses are well adapted to the climate and are airy and comfortable. They are certainly not soundproof, but secretiveness is contrary to Tarongan values and a desire for privacy would be interpreted as an admission of wrongdoing.

Tarongan amusements are invariably sociable. Parties are given frequently for birthdays, weddings, baptisms, and so on and provide occasions for relatives and friends from nearby barrios to gather. Here the adults can indulge in their favorite pastime of gossip, news dissemination, and joking while young people, chaperoned by the group, play cards and dance with potential husbands and wives. Impromptu intimate gatherings of this sort, though not always including a dance, occur within the sitio at any time and are usual even at presumably solemn sickbeds, funerals, and wakes. Men enjoy gambling at cards and betting on the weekly cockfights in town, but Tarongan thriftiness ensures that bets are small and indulgence only sporadic.

Family and sitio decision making is a democratic process; all members of the group are expected to contribute their opinions and all are expected to accede to majority decision. Certain family heads, by virtue of their proven good sense and ability, do lead the others, but they have no authority. The most important of these leaders function as sitio representatives in barrio decisions and political affairs, but their leadership here also rests on persuasion. Authority is vested in the group as a whole and is enforced by gossip, economic pressure, and ostracism.

The equalitarian base of Tarongan society is nowhere more apparent than within the nuclear family. All decisions that will affect the family are made in consultation by husband and wife and children nearing adulthood. Family earnings are pooled and children contribute to the savings as do husband and wife. The virtue of thrift is learned by Tarongan children long before adolescence. Since a Tarongan household is a production as well as a consumption unit, a woman's contribution is often large and her opinions are not ignored. Customarily it is the wife who keeps the savings, makes most of the household's expenditures, and gives family members money when they can convince her of their need. In short, although women are less assertive than men in public, they are equals in family affairs.

Tarongan marriages are stable and generally satisfactory to both partners. Although divorce is not recognized, separations do occur, but infrequently. Tarongans are modest and insistent upon a girl's virginity at marriage, but they are far from prudish. Sex attitudes are tolerant, deviance is permissible, and problems of sexual adjustment before or after marriage are very rare. The double standard of sexual behavior is accepted in theory but its practice is limited to the wealthy, since illegitimate as well as legitimate children must be properly supported.

Children are considered an integral part of a marriage and childless couples are pitied; adoptions are usual for such couples, although they are not legalized. There is little concern with the sex of one's children but all Tarongans agree that it is best to have both boys and girls. Children are enjoyed and indulged but Tarongans are concerned that their children grow into proper adults and discipline is far from lacking. To have raised a good family is the major pride of an elderly Tarongan and, having done his duty in regard to his own family, he indulges his grand-children shamelessly.

Second only to his pride in his own family is the satisfaction a Tarongan feels when he knows he has been a dependable, helpful neighbor. Sitio life is the structural response to Tarongans' strong needs for affection, sociability, and acceptance by his group. Tarongans can often recreate these ties and sentiments in new environments, but if this proves impos-sible, they are forced to withdraw. Neighborliness, in this broad usage, is a dominant value of the culture. Its overt manifestations are an easy-going, tolerant attitude toward others (as long as their obligations are met), expressiveness of emotion, and overwhelming nurturance.

Taira, Okinawa

The village in which the Okinawan children were studied lies in the northern, mountainous part of the island. It faces the Pacific Ocean and is surrounded by hills and valleys with higher mountains nearby. In 1954 Taira was just barely recovering from the complete destruction of all houses at the end of World War II. Located in an area which is limited in good quality land for rice growing and farming, this village was then still quite isolated from the central part of Okinawa where contacts with the American military had introduced rapid changes.

The central part of Taira is a clustered village; beyond that houses are spread here and there between the fields. The children we studied lived in the main and central part. Living in a relatively warm climate where temperatures may be in the eighties (Fahrenheit) during summer and rarely below 50 degrees during winters, the houses are built so that air can pass through easily. Few of them were of such solid construction that they would have much chance to withstand, without some damage, the typhoon winds which threaten the islands periodically and cause havoc in residences and fields. The thatch roofs as well as tile roofs of more permanent structures are sufficient to keep out the rains, even though these become heavy during part of the winter months and in May and early June. But the thatch roofs are more efficient in keeping houses cool during hot summers, although these have a drawback: the house rats. The rats are pursued by poisonous snakes (*habu*), this poses one of the real threats in the Taira children's environment.

The houses are simple, whether they are temporary buildings or the permanent structures that have been rebuilt. There is usually a large front living room or two rooms where people congregate during the day. At night family members sleep there on mattresses spread on the floor. Most of the time the sliding doors or panels of these rooms, which usually face south, are kept open all during the day, and residents can watch those passing by or may be watched from the outside, except where foliage has grown back, or where the traditional screens have been erected at the gate to the yard. At night the panels are kept shut to keep cold air and bad spirits out. The ancestral shelf is located in the front room. In the back of the houses there is usually a small room used for sleeping and a kitchen, a simple affair with an open hearth. Although all rooms are raised and have (oftentimes loose) floor boards, part of the kitchen has a dirt floor. Near the house in the courtyard are chicken coops, pig and goat pens, or a small stable for the few horses in Taira.

There is a main road through the village on which lumber trucks and other cars occasionally pass; houses are either located alongside this road, or on one of the side streets or paths. Children play inside yards and on the streets, and in open lots throughout the village so that, in effect, the entire central community serves as a playground. There are some focal points—the two concrete water tanks which are fed by water from the mountains, the village store which belongs to the Cooperative, the village office, and the area near the small village shrine. Each time a vehicle passes through the village large clouds of dust are raised and engulf nearby areas. Children stand at the side of the street, shouting at the passing passengers and running after the cars.

Children who play so freely in all parts of the village are never far from relatives or people they know intimately. The majority of families in the community can trace kinship relations to each other, though some are remote ties and the simple fact of community residence reinforces such ties as much as feelings of kinship. In effect, we may say, the entire central community is like a kinship group in its interpersonal relations. Structurally this can be explained by the marriage system and residence rules. Marriage traditionally has been with a woman from the same community, and even though at the time of our study about half the wives came from elsewhere, their home was never very far away. At least one son, preferably the oldest, remains with his parents after marriage and eventually takes over the house and land. Younger sons may set up a new residence in the community or move to the city. Actually many Taira families have at one time or another taken up residence elsewhere, in Japan or in the South Seas, but the end of the war brought a number of them back to Taira where they immediately became rein-

tegrated.   Even without war it is not uncommon to leave and eventually
to return to the community.

Households are therefore of two kinds: those in which a family and
surviving parents live and those in which there are only the nuclear
family and its children.   Where there are references to grandmothers,
these are usually mothers of a child's father, only occasionally a maternal
grandmother.   For religious purposes, especially the worship of ancestors,
patrilineally related families maintain relationships and meet at regular
intervals at the "main house."   But as our description of marriage indicates, since so many wives are from the same community, there is a great
deal of interrelationship between relatives on both sides, the kindred.
These may function in economic cooperation as well as in social gatherings and other activities.   This is why children are surrounded by relatives and why the boundary lines of kin relationships are not too clearly
drawn.

There are special interest groupings in the village.   Of greatest relevance to this discussion is the Woman's Association which theoretically
includes all women between the ages of 25 and 57.   Locally they represent issues that would tend to relieve some of the heavy work and modify
some of the traditional practices which are burdens in the life of women.
Some modern child-rearing ideas are introduced in this way—although
they did not seem to have had much affect upon the basic tenor of attitudes and practices at the time of the study.

The village, part of a township, is governed by a village headman who
is responsible to a council; both are elected.   In effect, there are a
number of leaders in the village, established more on the basis of their
education and experience than because of other social distinctions, who
assume most of the political responsibilities.   In 1954 village politics
were barely influenced by national politics, and the village government
ran relatively smoothly in this well-integrated community.   Although
there was voting of household heads, most decisions seemed to be ultimately arrived at by consensus of the entire council or village meeting.
There was a tendency to depend heavily on the decisions of village leaders,
but the leaders did not seem to decide counter to village sentiment.

In village affairs, as well as in family affairs, men are formally in
charge, though women *de facto* enjoy a much higher status than a super-
ficial impression would suggest.   It is true that, in the family, boys are
valued more than girls, and that no father would be happy unless he has
at least one, but preferably three boys.   But at the same time, women
have traditionally been the mediators between man and the supernatural,
and this alone has reinforced their importance.   Boys realize that the
society accords them higher status, but they receive their nurturance and

support mostly from women during their childhood. Also, they must certainly be aware of the religious and economic role which women play. All play activities suggest that girls assume their female role positively, even with enthusiasm. Playing house and tending children are activities that girls enjoy, even if their younger siblings are burdens at times.

Making a living in Taira during the mid-1950's was hard work and the rewards were limited. Although nobody was so poor that he could not adequately feed the family, few people seemed to have more than minimum resources, even though a later visit to the village suggested that some saving for new houses was possible even then. People grow two staple foods, rice and sweet potatoes, which take a considerable amount of time during planting and harvesting. Rice can be grown twice a year. Seasonal peaks for harvesting and replanting fall in the early part of the year and midsummer. For cash income which every farmer needs—not only to pay his taxes, but also for many consumer goods—he had a choice of cutting firewood for sale, growing sugar, or doing both. Firewood gathering and preparation of bundles for sale is hard work, but it brings cash quickly. The village cooperative store buys it and pays even before delivery to the customers in town. Sugar, on the other hand, takes more than a year from planting to harvesting and milling. How much sugar a person grows depends on the amount of suitable land he has and his long-range entrepreneurship. All families have some land although the amount and quality vary. Few people grow enough rice for sale, but all families have one other source of income—raising pigs. While the men attend to the sugar fields and do much of the work in the paddies, women share with men the exploitation of forests for firewood, cultivating sweet potatoes, and participating in rice planting and harvesting. Raising pigs is entirely the work of women. A balance of participation in subsistence activities would show that women play as large a role as men.

The village as a whole relies heavily on cooperation. There are various forms of cooperative activities. Some include only family members; others, family and neighbors; still others, whole parts of the community. A few activities are community-wide: those having to do with public construction or with festivities celebrated by the entire village. Historical tradition here explains much about cooperation. Until sixty years ago land was communally owned and family units and the whole community were collectively responsible for taxes and in legal matters. The psychological significance of this pattern emerges in many aspects of Taira life; we have discussed this more fully in the ethnography of Taira child rearing.[1] Cooperation is also still present in another sense. The

[1] "Taira: An Okinawan Village," in Whiting, B. (Ed.) *Six Cultures—Studies of Child Rearing.* New York: John Wiley and Sons, 1963.

store is owned by the all-village cooperative organization, and during the days of our studies it handled the major share of marketing and distributing for residents.

Although agriculture and firewood lumbering are the main sources of Taira's economy, there is some fishing, much of it done by persons who have not become fully integrated with the community. Only one of the families represented in this study belonged to the few fishermen. Nevertheless, women from various houses sold fish occasionally when there was a chance to make some extra money.

There were no very poor or very rich persons in Taira, although there were considerable differences in family income. The postmaster, the village "doctor"—a medical corpsman, one of the farmers, and one or two government officials were better off than most of the other villagers. One or two families were at the bottom of the income groups, usually because they had little land since they were widows or younger sons, who in a few cases lived matrilocally. One of these relatively poor families is represented in the sample of families studied intensively.

Where do Taira people turn if the burdens of life are more than they can individually cope with? They do not participate in any of the major religious systems, although elements of Buddhism are represented in their beliefs and practices, and Christianity is spreading the word in such a way that even in the remote areas children have picked up some concepts. Basically, beliefs are a mixture of ancestral worship and relationships toward animistic spirits, some of which are elevated to the rank of deities. The once nationwide state religion, which was based on worship of animistic deities, has broken down even though the office of the priestess still exists and is occupied in Taira. She functions today mostly as a guardian of the village, worshipping deities which protect the village and its residents. Individual families take care of ancestral worship. Deceased members of the family are represented on the ancestral shelf by small tablets. Their remains rest in large family tombs on the outskirts of Taira. By and large, we may say about Okinawan religion that it is not so much a system of belief and related ethics that characterizes relationship to the supernaturals, including ancestors, but a desire to perform the required rituals for fear that omission would cause supernatural displeasure and lead to misfortune among the living.

Placating rather than worshipping seems to be the essence of religious practices but at the same time, their function is, to draw family and community together. As a result, Taira people tend to search for reasons to explain misfortunes in ritual omissions. For the purpose of learning about the causes of unlucky events they consult a female religious specialist who, is in effect, a shaman. This person has the ability to analyze ritual neglects and to prescribe rituals that should reconcile the supernaturals with the living. People therefore go for advice even though they also consult others; the village "doctor," the Public Health nurse, and eventually physicians in the city. The Shaman, as well as the priestess, and the family priestesses, who are responsible for maintaining ancestor worship, all have a traditional place in village culture and are well integrated with it. Children, however, participate in religious matters merely as spectators and no pressures are put upon them for more. At school they learn that the religious beliefs and practices of their parents are merely "superstitions," but their parents had learned the same thing when they were young, and it remains to be seen how much such learning and the full influence of Christianity changes the religious patterns which are so obviously deeply imbedded in culture and personality.

Not only in religious matters but in others affecting traditions, the school is one of the main sources of modern ideas. When they are 6 years old, children begin to attend the public school which is located in the next village, less than two miles from their home. Here they are exposed essentially to the Japanese school system, and they attend classes at least until the end of junior high school. Some go on to high school and beyond; others who cannot meet the increasingly demanding educational standards of higher grades for their schooling, make their place in the village or seek work elsewhere. Education is highly valued and is the major means of changing life toward a more comfortable existence. This is widely recognized and parents wish nothing more than a good education for their children. Several families make real sacrifices to be able to send their older children through high school. This means for them giving up helping hands at home and maintaining the students during that period when they have to board, since the high school is located in another township. Hopefully, the educated children will some day ease the burden of their parents' life.

At the time of our study it seemed that the children were exposed to two somewhat contrasting influences in terms of personality development. The home environment is lenient and pressures toward achievement are relatively minor. At school, competition and individual achievement striving is stressed. The lack of reinforcement at home is one of the problems of educators, but school efforts to establish autonomy and achievement through individual efforts seemed to be unsuccessful. At least, the parents of the children, except those who were village leaders on the basis of education and autonomy, tended to rely strongly on the emotional support and practical cooperation from other community members. The continued reliance on such religious specialists as the shaman suggests that more deep-seated personality traits in adults change only gradually and have not responded immediately to education.   Even though boys and girls have equal opportunity for schooling, women have retained their ties with the supernatural in Taira according to traditions, with the exception of village leaders, both men and women, who try to introduce "modern" ideas.   They may laugh at the beliefs that take others to the shaman, but most of them have a tolerant attitude toward such beliefs and practices, and when we left Taira in 1955, not even the most enthusiastically modern representative of the Woman's Association would offend or oppose those who continued reliance on long-established customs.   But the children of Taira whom we studied grow up in a different world from their elders because their island is undergoing rapid change.   Perhaps the warmth and protection of a well-integrated community has prepared them to assume a different place in society from their parents without upset, or perhaps the lack of enforcing individual achievement striving will be a burden for their adjustment.   These are questions further studies should answer some years from now.

Khalapur: Uttar Pradesh, India

The Indian study was done in a neighborhood of families of the Rajput caste in the village of Khalapur, which is located about 90 miles north of Delhi on the large alluvial plain and is watered by the Ganges and its tributaries.   The area is one of the most fertile in India and virtually all available land is under cultivation.

The climate is pleasantly temperate in the late fall and winter except for some chilly, raw days during the short winter monsoon.   Monsoon hail storms in March and early April may cause severe damage to the winter crops that are still unharvested.   The weather becomes hot in the spring and there are frequent, severe dust storms caused by the hot, dry wind blowing from the western desert.   During the day temperatures may rise to 110°F. or higher.   In June, thunder and hail storms often precede the heavy summer monsoon which arrives at the end of June and lasts until September.   The summer is hot and humid, but the monsoon rains bring periodic relief from the most intense heat.   Almost all of the 40 inches of average rainfall falls during the summer monsoon so the farmers of this region rely on irrigation for water for their fields.

The villagers harvest a spring and a fall crop.   The fall crop includes corn, rice, several kinds of legumes, cotton, hemp, and some minor produce. The spring crop includes oats, wheat, barley, peas, mustard, and sugar cane which is harvested later than the grains and vegetables. Sugar cane is by far the most important cash crop for most families, although wheat is also sold in some quantity. During the harvest, most Rajput men participate in the work. Many work almost around the clock and live in their fields, both to save time and to protect their crops from thieves. During the winter, work is slack and the men spend their time in politics, marriage arrangements, and leisurely conversations. Most Rajput families employ low-caste field hands who do most or all of the field work, except during harvesting and planting seasons.

Khalapur has a population of 5000 people, making it an unusually large village for the area. Two thousand people are members of the Rajput caste, the largest single caste group in the village. There are two major roads leading into the village. The one that leads to the neighborhood used in the present research crosses a bridge just at the village edge. The study was conducted with families living in one corner of the village. The neighborhood chosen is inhabited exclusively by members of the Rajput caste. The area is not geographically isolated from the rest of the village since all the village houses are built close together. The neighborhood is bounded on one side by a river and on another by a field, so that it is isolated from other houses on two sides. The two interior boundaries are marked by a nonresidential area containing the temple, school, and meeting house on one side; a street occupied by another caste group and in a different political unit is on the fourth side.

Khalapur was founded by Rajput families and their servants, probably during the fifteenth century. The present Rajputs are descendants of these families and still own the great majority of the village farmlands; this makes them the wealthiest caste group and the central group in village economy. They are also the most powerful political faction of the village, and until recently they were in complete control of the village government. The recent introduction of a government-sponsored town council with elected members has enabled other caste groups to exert some influence in village politics. This has caused some tension between the castes, particularly since the second largest caste group in the village is an untouchable caste.

The Rajputs are traditionally the caste of rulers, landowners, and warriors, and they still maintain their princely, martial tradition. Rajput men consider themselves to be bigger and physically stronger than other castes. Although controlled in their tempers, they are proud and easily insulted. Blood feuds between families were common in the past and these traditional hostilities still persist. Men may plot for years to revenge themselves on enemies. Most quarrels are now fought in the courts which are seen as a new battleground rather than a place of justice. However, many Rajput men, particularly those over 40, still go armed with weighted bamboo staffs and may resort to "a conversation of staffs," if their quarrel is not such that it can be taken to court, or if they are displeased with the court ruling. Rightly or wrongly, Rajputs have little faith in the justice of court decisions. They believe that witnesses, if not judges, may be bribed and unfairly influence the outcome. The informal village council of influential men, respected for their wisdom, is still important in settling disputes, although its legal status has largely been replaced by the formal legal structure. When the Rajputs want justice rather than revenge they prefer to take their disputes to a council of their peers.

The women are more openly quarrelsome, but their disputes are less serious and more easily forgotten. However, the disputes of the women, if prolonged, often lead to serious consequences since they produce friction within the family rather than between groups of distantly related kinsman. Such disputes may lead to division of property, despite strong values in favor of preserving family unity.

Besides the Rajputs the village has a number of other castes. Most of them have service occupations, servicing Rajputs and other caste groups. Some of the more important castes are the Brahmins, who perform religious ceremonies, and the barbers who shave, cut hair, have certain ritual functions, and often make initial marriage contracts for their Rajput patrons. Men of an untouchable caste are field hands and untouchable women are essential to high-caste houses to clean latrines and act as midwives since feces and blood are considered unclean. Each Rajput family uses the services of a carpenter who plows and uses other farm equipment; an iron smith who forges plow blades; weavers who make cloth for sheets and sometimes work clothes; and a potter who supplies the water pots and pottery for festival occasions. Most families send their laundry to a member of the washerman's caste and employ water carriers to bring the women water from the wells. Leatherworkers, members of an untouchable caste group, remove dead cattle, tan the hides, supply harnesses, whips, and some shoes to the villagers. The village also has several shops run by members of the business caste; a goldsmith, a flour mill, and several oil presser families, as well as some other groups.

There is a small community of Moslem families living in the village, but most of the villagers are Hindus. The major Hindu temple is dedicated to Shiva, one of the most important Hindu gods. There are a number of minor shrines to local saints and women who have committed sati. There is also a tomb of a Moslem saint which is much older than the Shiva temple. This saint is regarded as the village protector, and is worshipped by the Hindus as well as the Moslems. In general the Rajput men worship the higher gods of the Hindu's religion. Ram, an incarnation of Vishnu, is a particularly important diety for the Rajputs because they claim descent from this great ruler. The women worship not only these major gods but a number of minor goddesses concerned chiefly with disease. Women also worship the ancestors of their husband's family and keep the ancestor shrines that most families have somewhere on their property. Sacred trees and plants also figure in the village worship and some families attend a yearly religious fair held in a town on the Ganges. The most important religious fair for the Khalapur villagers is held in the railroad town four miles away. Although this community is primarily Moslem in population, it has a large temple in honor of a goddess who seems to be a local version of Durga, the wife of Shiva. Villagers from many nearby villages attend this fair every spring. The women look forward to this outing. Most women attend this fair and do a great deal of shopping when they have finished their worship.

The north-east region of India where Khalapur is located was invaded by Moslems from western Asia in the thirteenth century after an era of periodic warfare. These invaders gradually defeated the Rajput rulers of the area and ruled it until they relinquished their power to the British. The Hindus of this area have adopted a number of Moslem customs, notably the seclusion of women of high-caste groups such as the Rajputs. The seclusion of women is a status symbol since the family must be rich enough to dispense with their help in farming. A few of the older Rajput women from poor families help with the field work, but the young married women never venture from the house except on ceremonial occasions such as weddings, birth ceremonies, and the yearly religious fair. Most houses have some latrine facilities so that young daughters-in-law do not have to leave the house even to relieve themselves.

The custom of secluding women exerts a considerable influence on the architecture. Since a married woman must sit immobilized on the floor with her head bowed and her sari pulled over her face in the presence of her husband, or any of her husband's older relatives including older brothers, the women are unable to work when men, particularly older men, are present. Men and women therefore occupy separate households.

The women's houses are close together, built in the manner of row houses in this country, with a single wall separating adjacent living quarters. Each house is built around a separate courtyard, secluded from the street and surrounded by windowless rooms that are used for storage and winter bedrooms. The women spend most of their time in the open, sunny courtyards and most cooking is done outside except when it is raining. Here the women do their work spinning, carding cotton, preparing grain for storage during the harvest, and endlessly preparing food and cooking. The roofs are flat and several adjacent houses share a common roof that is used for additional storage space, work space, and a "high road" for women who can visit from house to house without going into the street.

The windowless wall of these adjacent women's houses often line both sides of the narrow, winding streets. The appearance of the village would be even more mazelike were it not for the men's platforms that usually are set back from the street and face it. These platforms have covered rooms in the rear that serve as storage places and winter bedrooms for the men. In front of these rooms is a raised platform where the men spend most of their leisure hours. The size, height, and construction of these quarters depend upon the number of men who share them and the family wealth. A poor man of a nuclear family may have a mud brick platform only about 10-feet square and a few inches high with a single room behind it. Such platforms are usually directly outside the entrance to the courtyard. A rich man or a group of wealthy brothers will share a platform with their sons. These may be 40-feet square, several feet high, and have several rooms in back. They are usually not connected to the courtyard since the wives of several senior men who share a platform may have separate courtyards. A large brick platform suitable for entertaining large groups of visitors is a necessity for any family with political influence since many informal political decisions are taken by groups meeting in the men's quarters of some wealthy and influential man.

The third type of structure is the cattle compound. This may be a section of the courtyard or a space enclosed by a mud fence near the men's quarters. Since cattle are sometimes stolen, they are always quartered close to some living area.

Rajput men live in the village of their birth throughout their lives. They usually live in their father's house until the death of one or both parents. Some brothers continue to share the same courtyard and living quarters after their parents' death, but frequently they separate when they can afford to build new living quarters or add to present ones.

The Rajput men take wives from several villages where the Rajput subcaste is of lower status than their own and marry their daughters into another group of villages with a higher status subcaste. Thus, preferred marriages are always within caste with the women marrying into families of higher status than their own, and no women marrying within their own village. Women are not confined to the house in the village of their birth either before or after marriage. Women make frequent and extended visits to their families after marriage, particularly while their parents are still living. They look forward to these visits when they are free from household chores and can leave the courtyards to visit with their friends. Marriages are arranged by the families of the bride and groom. The initial contacts for the marriages are made by the bride's family; the marriage arrangements are made by the men of the families, and the couple do not see each other until the ceremony which takes place at the bride's house. Sometimes brothers marry women from the same household on the assumption that they will get along well together, but most wives have no close relatives in their husbands' village.

Mothers-in-law direct the housework of their sons' wives and have authority over them. There is a strong feeling that a son should not take his wife's part in a quarrel with his mother. When the mother-in-law dies the wives of her sons usually begin to quarrel to some extent. If the wives can get along only the food supplies may be divided and each wife cooks on her own hearth. Severe quarrels result in the construction of a wall dividing the courtyard. Quarrels among the wives may spread to their husbands. If these become sufficiently intense the men not only occupy separate living quarters but divide their land and cattle. The older generation prevent these quarrels from disrupting the family structure, thus, the wives of several brothers do not divide the courtyard until after their mother-in-law's death, and brothers seldom divide their land while their father is alive. Since the older generation does prevent household division, most children are raised in extended families with grandparents, aunts, uncles, and cousins as well as parents and siblings. Of the thirty three families studied, twenty seven were extended families. Nine of these included two generations in the same household, eighteen included three generations, and three families had four generations in the same house. Five of the six nuclear families had split off from a larger household within the last few years. This does not mean that these extended families are large. There is considerable variation in household size. The largest household in the sample had twenty five people in it. The average household has three adult women or adolescent girls, four children, and five or six men, and adolescent boys.

The plurality of males is more pronounced among the preadolescent children. There were twice as many boys as girls in the families studied. Hindu families generally have a strong preference for boys. The spiritual welfare of a man who dies without at least one son to perform certain funeral rites is believed to be seriously jeopardized. This preference for boys is particularly strong among high-caste, landed groups who need sons to run their farms and defend the family in interfamily feuds, who must give expensive dowries to their daughters, and who chafe at their subservient status relative to the families of their sons-in-law. These considerations led to widespread female infanticide among the Rajputs which was stopped in Khalapur only after strong government pressure was brought to bear around the turn of the century. Although the practice of killing daughters has now stopped, the inferior medical care given to girls with chronic illnesses in a population, where one-third of the children die before puberty, still results in a plurality of boys.

Differential treatment of boys and girls is also reflected in their schooling. The girls' school has only five grades. Most girls still do not attend, and those who do often drop out after fourth grade when they have learned to read and write. Rajput boys usually attend school through eighth grade, and, if possible, through high school. Poor families may need the elder son to help with field work, but every family tries to educate at least one son so that one man in the family can read and handle family finances and legal matters.

Nyansongo, Africa

The African mothers interviewed are residents of a remote rural area in highland Kenya, 50 miles south of the equator and just east of Lake Victoria. The area is isolated from urban centers and primary lines of communication (the nearest railway station is 75 miles away), but the fertility of its soil and the high rainfall support a dense and growing population of Gusii farmers. The Gusii are a Bantu-speaking people in a region of linguistically unrelated tribes, but they resemble many other East African peoples in the outlines of their culture: an agricultural and pastoral economy, a dispersed settlement pattern rather than compact villages, a formerly stateless political system with strong patrilineal descent groups, polygynous family structure, an ancestor cult, and initiation ceremonies for boys and girls.

Gusiiland is a hilly part of the Kenya highlands, and its altitude of more than 5000 feet gives it a cool climate for the tropics; between 60 and 80 degrees most of the year. The rainfall, which often exceeds 80 inches a year, comes in two seasons: approximately April through June ("the long rains") and September to October ("the short rains"). During the rains it is cool and may go below 60 at night; in the November to March dry season daytime temperatures exceed 80 degrees but the air remains dry. The heavy annual rainfall feeds the streams and swamps surrounding the hills on which Gusii live, and provides their water supply as well as nourishing their crops.

There is one growing season for the staple crops of corn and eleusine (finger millet), with planting before the onset of the long rains and harvesting at the end of the short rains. Many Gusii plant potatoes and other roots during July and August to insure against a crop failure, and a number of vegetables and fruits—beans, tomatoes, and bananas— are also grown Coffee is the major cash crop, but surpluses of corn and eleusine are common and are sold for cash. The bulk of the agricultural labor is contributed by the women, who break ground in fallow fields with hoes, do most of the routine cultivation during the growing season—including the laborious hand-weeding of broadcast eleusine, and harvest the crops. Their husbands, who—as lineage members—own the land, do the heavy but less routine work of clearing the bush in fallow fields, building fences and houses, and such plowing (with oxen) as is done. Men also take care of the coffee, for the most part, grow some food independent of their wives' supply, and help with the hoeing when it is most needed. Most younger men in Nyansongo, the community studied, seek employment in the vicinity or as migrant laborers on plantations and in cities, at least occasionally, to add to their cash income. When the men are away or at their jobs, women and children do the work at home.

Nyansongo—an ethnographic pseudonym—is a group of 18 homesteads (approximately 208 people) in an area of continuous and dense settlement which exhibits no distinct clustering or boundaries. The community is not recognized as a separate political unit, has no headman or former council of its own, lacks a central plaza or other public meeting-place, and rarely takes collective action. Such solidarity as it has is due to cooperation in agricultural work groups, membership in a single clan and narrower interhomestead kin groupings, a few ritual obligations, and opposition to surrounding communities of different clans, with whom Nyansongans intermarry. Loyalties are focused, not on the local community as such, but on the localized patrilineages within it, each of which unite two or more homesteads, and on the location chief (headman of more than 50,000 people) who lives nearby and plays a dominant part in community control. Despite the diffuse organization of the territorial community and the important lineage and other kin ties which Nyansongans have with persons in other communities, there is considerable neighborly interaction: women work together daily, men drink together at frequent beer parties, elders gather ocasionally to consider disputes and other problems of general interest. An unusual event of emergency proportions, like the exorcism of witchcraft from a mentally afflicted person or a difficult childbirth, draws sympathetic adults from the whole community.

Although the Gusii have probably occupied their highland region for over 200 years, Nyansongo is a relatively new community which must be understood in the context of modern conditions. The British conquest of Gusiiland in 1907 began a series of important changes which have affected many areas of life: pacification of the feuding clans and the introduction of chieftainship and courts; abolition of the cattle villages in which young men spent much of their time; introduction of Christian missions and schools, of currency, markets, new crops, consumer goods, and opportunities for employment; and provision of Western medical treatment for epidemics and other disease. Rapid population growth in the past half-century has favored the diminution in cattle-keeping, raised the value of cultivable land, and increased the frequency of land disputes. Nyansongo was begun around 1930 in an area that had formerly been no-man's-land between Gusii and Masai. Its original settlers invited their kinsmen, and it soon filled up to become one of the areas of high population density in Gusiiland.

Many of the contemporary motives and behaviors of Nyansongans are centered about institutions introduced in the past 50 years or their various consequences. The chief and courts have become legitimate authorities with important roles in the settlement of disputes and enforcement of law and custom. Litigation is a major activity of Gusii men, and Nyansongans spend much of their time at the courts or seeing the chief about judicial matters; boundary disputes account for a considerable proportion of the litigation. The desire for Western consumer goods is very strong, and to acquire them Nyansongans seek employment, engage in trade, grow cash crops, and encourage their children to become educated (though less than surrounding communities).

On the other hand, the Gusii as a whole and Nyansongans in particular are notably conservative compared to other sedentary peoples in Kenya. They are wedded to their home country and tend not to remain in the city for long periods. They insist on cattle rather than money as a bride-price. They perform elaborate initiation ceremonies involving circumcision for boys and clitoridectomy for girls, exempting no one from the process. Christianity has had little effect in Nyansongo; divination, sacrifice to the ancestors, and practices associated with witchcraft and sorcery overshadow Christian ritual and belief as well as Western medicine. Polygamy and beer drinking, prohibited by the dominant Seventh Day Adventist mission, are found in most homesteads. It is particularly remarkable that contemparary social tensions, like those over land boundaries, are often expressed in traditional form through witchcraft accusations and sorcery, which appear to have increased in the past half century.

The organizational structure within which Nyansongo socialization takes place still approximates the traditional forms but has been modified by new settlement, increasing population density, labor migration, and superordinate political control. For example the community itself is still comprised of members of one clan, and is therefore exogamous; those born in the community must find their mates elsewhere. Furthermore, the neighborhoods within Nyansongo approximate patrilineages, i.e., groups of men descended in the paternal line from a single ancestor, which constitute the groups holding rights to land and exercising ancestral sanctions over their members. However, in the process of resettlement these lineages have become fragmented and are represented in numerous communities outside of Nyansongo. Many families have close patrilineal kinsmen living several miles away. Thus the descent groups in Nyansongo are not intact but are only representative fragments functioning as if they were whole.

Relations between neighbors have been conspicuously affected by demographic and political changes. In the past communities united militarily for common defense of their land and cattle; since pacification that is no longer necessary. In earlier days land was abundant, which meant that people could be casual about boundaries, could maintain a distance between homesteads which was commensurate with the type of relations prevailing between them, and could move to new land if they did not like their neighbors. Nowadays the higher population density and increased land values mean that neighbors are jealous of boundaries, must live nearer their neighbors, and cannot move away if they do not like them. The simultaneous decrement in the need for cohesion (common defense) and increment in sources of dispute have produced a community life characterized by divisive quarrels and mutual suspicions, expressed most overtly in litigation and witchcraft accusations. Nyansongans depend on the chief and courts to contain these tensions.

Problems surrounding the care of cattle epitomize the effects of changing conditions on the immediate environment of the child. In the past, cattle were herded communally by initiated young men who acted to protect them from raiding as well as caring for them. These men milked the cattle, and children had to fetch the milk, since women were barred from the cattle villages. Nowadays, not only are there no cattle villages but too many men are away in employment to be depended upon for cattle care. Women do all the milking, and uninitiated children, who formerly herded only sheep and goats, herd the cattle. Overcrowding of the land and increased cultivation make cattleherding more difficult than before, because if the herdboys are not vigilant, the cattle are certain to trespass in a neighbor's garden and eat his crops. When this happens, litigation and bad feelings inevitably result, and such cases are very frequent. Parents put pressure on the young boys to be more responsible herders than their inclinations would lead them to be, and punish them for the costly infractions. The generally irritable attitude of neighbors stemming from cattle trespass and boundary disputes make them less tolerant of the mischief of each other's children; they are quick to threaten litigation if the children get into a fight or pilfer. The same attitude makes parents defensive and equally quick to resort to litigation should a neighbor slap their misbehaving child. Parents attempt to train their children to refrain from fighting children from other homesteads and from giving offense to neighboring adults, for fear of lawsuits. The neighbors on their part would rather make a fuss verbally or legally about children's misbehavior than administer the slap which was traditional among closely related kinsmen, in order to avoid becoming defendants in court. Thus labor migration, overcrowding, and the role of judicial authorities can be seen as factors in the decay of neighborly trust as it affects the life of the child.

Family structure in Nyansongo is more intact than that of larger units. Despite the increase in sexual and marital deviations such as rape and elopement, the traditional outlines of marriage and family life have been retained. Married men remain at their fathers' homesteads where their wives, who must come from outside the community and clan, join them. Although she begins as a stranger, the wife has her own house, and fields are allocated for her use in growing staple crops. If a man has more than one wife, as many Nyansongans do, he must build a house for each one, attempting to space them sufficiently so that the co-wives can keep their distance if they want to. The homestead may also contain houses for the older uninitiated boys as a group and a bachelor hut for each initiated but unmarried man. When a man dies, his widows continue to live where they did before, although each one may be "inherited" by a kinsman of the deceased, often a brother residing nearby. Within the polygynous family, the wife tends to form a unit with her married sons and their wives, who take care of her in her old age.

The head of a homestead, particularly if he is a polygynist, has considerable authority over his wives, married sons, and any other persons living there. Although contemporary economic conditions, particularly employment of the sons, have eroded this authority somewhat, it is still recognized in many areas of behavior. He controls the allocation of land and cattle and represents the homestead in meetings with lineage elders and other external authorities as well as in sacrifices to the ancestors. Filial piety is stressed, and sons may not openly contradict their fathers or take independent decisions on matters of marriage and property.

A crucial feature of the Gusii family is the system of intergenerational avoidance. Even though he may be head of the homestead, a father may not enter the house of his married son, and the latter may not proceed beyond the alcove in his mother's house. Persons of adjacent generations may not shake hands, see each other bathing, or discuss sexual matters. The rules are somewhat stricter between men and women of adjacent generations than for same-sex interaction, and somewhat weaker as they move out from real parent and parent-in-law relationships to those of uncles and aunts. An example of the degree of sexual restraint involved is that a man may not directly tell his father that his wife is pregnant. These rules are adhered to quite strictly in Nyansongo, and their accidental violation causes intense embarrassment, especially to those of the junior generation who are held responsible for any breach. Nyansongans regard this system of avoidance as contributing to marital fidelity and respect to the elder generation; they are shocked by its absence among non-Gusii, whom they view as sexually immoral. Gusii do in fact appear to have stricter prohibitions on sexuality and a higher degree of marital fidelity than many neighboring peoples.

Growing up in the environment described above, the Nyansongo child lives with his mother in her house, is inducted at an early age into the domestic economy which she manages, and develops—especially if he is a boy—a lifelong loyalty to his mother. He is likely to adopt her attitudes to her co-wives; thus, if she gets on poorly with them, he may have little to do with their children though they are in the same homestead. In this arrangement, the father has a less intense relationship with his children because he apportions his time among several wives, is absent working part of the time, and disdains a role in child care. Some widows raise their children without any father surrogate present. When the father is present, he is important as a disciplinarian, and every child learns to respect and even fear his father. In addition, the child must learn to abide by the rules of respect and restraint between generations which become enforced upon him after initiation, and even more after marriage. As he moves about in the community, he learns to refrain from giving offense not only to elders but also to any neighbors who might bring lawsuits against his parents.

Nyansongo parents try to raise children who are obedient, respectful, and restrained with respect to sex and aggression. They hope for advantageous marriages for the girls and some degree of material success for the boys. As the link between schooling and material success becomes clearer to them, they are coming to emphasize education in their aspirations for the boys. Finally, it must be stated that Nyansongo parents are particularly concerned about their boys as the source of support in old age.

SECTION ONE

❖ ❖ ❖ ❖ ❖ ❖

The Factors

1 ❖ The Factor Analysis

Research Aims

The aims of this research are to discover pancultural factors in child-training practices and to use these to describe the similarities and differences in the six cultures we have studied. There are a number of reasons why a search for pancultural scales is useful. Many of the variables that are used in our present researches in child development may be "culture bound" in the sense that they are important only in particular cultural contexts. Malinowski's classic critique of Freud's description of the Oedipus complex as being tied overmuch to the kinds of families found in Europe is a case in point. Even if the variables themselves are present and important in a variety of settings, their influences may differ from society to society, and the interactions among variables may certainly not be the same in all societies. Although findings which only pertain to a particular group are useful within the limited context, a general system of behavior analysis should be applicable to all humans.

The delineation of pancultural factors may assist future researchers by suggesting some simplification for studies of child-training practices by focusing the researcher's attention on some major sources of differences in mothers' statements regarding their practices (and possibly on differences in the actual practices themselves). To the extent that the factors extracted are psychologically and statistically clear, and are determined by differences between mothers from several cultures rather than by cultural differences alone, the factors can be used as dimensions in the direct comparison of practices in different societies or cultural contexts. Factors that have these properties may assist in the formulation of more relevant theories having to do with the general description and function of socialization practices.

Field Investigation

As we outlined in our introduction, field teams were trained together in common procedures and sent to six culture areas of the

Table 1.1   Number of Children

Society	Girls		Boys	
	3–6 yrs.	7–10 yrs.	3–6 yrs.	7–10 yrs.
United States	6	6	6	6
Mexico	6	5	6	5
Philippines	6	6	5	6
Okinawa	6	6	6	6
India	6	6	6	6
Africa	4	4	4	4

world: the Philippines, Okinawa, India, Mexico, Africa, and North-eastern United States. Each team settled in a community and worked intensively with the people of a particular neighborhood. Since a major aim of the research was to investigate differences in child-training practices *between* societies, effort was made to obtain a representative homogeneous group of people within each community in order to minimize the differences in practices *within* each place. Descriptions of the life in these communities, with emphasis on the socialization practices and behavior of the children, are published independently in the volume *Six Cultures—Studies of Child Rearing* (1963).

In addition to the general cultural data gathered through informal observation and interviewing, each team gathered specific material on a small sample of boys and girls ranging in age from 3 to 10 years. The age and sex composition of this sample in each society is presented in Table 1.1. Each child came from a different nuclear family. None of the sample children had any major physical or mental abnormality. An attempt was made to counterbalance the birth order of the sample children. Each of these children, except for some too young to respond, was interviewed and given a verbal projective test. All of the children were observed during a number of 5-minute periods and their behavior was recorded. In this way an attempt was made to obtain a random sample of the childrens' behavior. The mothers, or in the absence of a mother, the principal female caretaker, of each of the sample children was interviewed about her child-training practices.

The Interview

The analysis of this book is concerned with data derived from the interviews conducted with the mothers or mother substitutes of these children.   These interviews were concerned with various areas of child behavior and the policies and practices of the mothers, with respect to these behaviors.   Each team worked from a standard English version of the interview, which was then translated into the native language.

In some cases the questions were altered in order to fit the concepts and practices of the individual cultural settings.   The answers of the mothers (or mother surrogates) of the carefully sampled group of children were recorded verbatim.   There were twenty-one classes of questions, with an average of four subquestions per class.   The total number of mothers interviewed was 133.

The problems involved in such a procedure are many, and not all of them will be dealt with here.   There are issues of the degree to which what mothers reported as their practices are in fact their practices; there are issues relating to the relationship of intracultural factor structures to the pancultural factors reported here; and there are problems of the adequacy of translation of the questionnaire into six languages and of the translation of the answers back into English, etc.   It is difficult to measure the success with which sensitive and systematic translation procedures can place questions into the correct corners and crevices of the meaning "spaces" of people in six cultures.   When preparing the translated versions of the interview, we translated back and forth until the specific meanings of the English standard interview could be recovered from the translated form by translators who knew both languages.   This does not mean that the questions would occur in the same *context* in all six cultures, but it was just these differences in context which we wished to study.   A Mexican mother might report to us that she punished her son when he hit his cousin because she is afraid of bad relations developing in the family.   An American mother may report the same policy, but because she is trying to keep the son from picking on his sibling.   In such ways "cultural meanings" may make for similarity or differences in answers, as do personal meanings.   These are our interests: the ways in which culturally shared or personal meaning contexts make for similarities and differences in the pressures which are reportedly placed on children.   The main problem is to capture through clear translation and sensitive interviewing whatever common dimensions of *differences in pressures* exist across six such diverse cultures.

It was impossible to use all of the information obtained from the mother interviews in the factor analysis, therefore a selection of the mothers' answers was made on the following bases: (*a*) most mothers in all six cultures answered the question; (*b*) the field teams reported that the answers made reasonably good sense in the cultural context, and that they generally appeared to reflect the mother's behavior; (*c*) the coders at Cornell agreed with one another in putting the mothers' answers on a scale; and (d) the answers were theoretically relevant to our general research aims, including the relevance of the answers to past researchers which employed the method of factor analysis on similar material. It was not possible, of course, to maximize all these considerations. The scales finally retained for the factor analysis are listed in Table 1.2. It can be seen from this table that the scales tap a number of aspects of socialization practices: the handling by socializing agents (particularly the mother) of a number of different behavior systems, aspects of caretaking, forms of discipline, some kinds of rules, and the ap-

Table 1.2   Scales Used in Factor Analysis

1. Degree to which mother, when busy, responds to child's requests for help.
2. Degree to which mother is positive when child fights with other children.
3. Degree to which mother is positive or nonpunishing when child becomes angry while being scolded.
4. Proportion of caretaking done by mother.
5. General warmth of mother.
6. Mood variation of mother's warmth.
7. General hostility of mother.
8. Mood variation of hostility.
9. Degree that mother's warmth is contingent upon child's actions.
10. Degree that mother's hostility is contingent upon child's actions.
11. Amount of communication of rules.
12. Consistency of aggression rules.
13. Amount of praise.
14. Consistency of mother's follow-through on nonroutine demands for obedience.
15. Frequency and intensity of physical punishment.
16. Degree to which privileges and gifts are contingent upon child's behavior.
17. Reward for retaliatory aggression to peers.
18. Degree to which mother is aggressive when child is angry or aggressive.
19. Amount of time that mother cares for child.
20. Amount of time that the mother cared for child when child was baby.
21. Amount of time adult other than the mother cared for child when child was a baby.
22. Age at which child began to dress self.
23. Age at which child began to play away from the house.
24. Total frequency of chores.
25. Total number of chores.
26. Degree to which mother expects immediate obedience.
27. Sex of child.
28. Age of child.

parent or reported communication of these rules, as well as the sex and age of the child.

Three types of scales are included in Table 1.2. Scales one through three represent a placement of the mother's verbatim answer to questions put to her into a category implied by the following anchor points of a 9-point scale: (1) Mother (or surrogate) physically punishes or deprives of privileges; (3) Mother reprimands or teaches; (5) Mother withholds approval or ignores; (7) Mother gives approval or gives emotional support; (9) Mother gives reward or gives active help. The answers of the mothers were placed on intermediate points of this scale when necessary, and if the mother's answer indicated that her response encompassed items on two points of the scale (e.g., "Sometimes I scold him; sometimes I just ignore it"), the answer would be an average of the two: the example would be coded 4 on the 9-point scale.

The second type of scale in Table 1.2 involves the scales numbered 4 through 18, which are 7-point rating scales, which the coders at Cornell rated on the basis of reading the entire verbatim protocol of the mother's interview. Point 7 represents the high rating and point 1 the low rating of each scale as named in Table 1.2.

The third class of scales are those numbered 19 through 28, which contains a variety of scales (age, time, frequency, etc.) which were based on answers of the mothers to individual questions. The definition of the scale used in each case is fairly obvious from the name given it in Table 1.2. The coding varies from scale to scale. The codings of the individual scales will be described in the chapters describing the factors defined by the scales.

Not all mothers answered all questions in such a way that their answers could be placed on all of the scales, and this raised problems for the computing machine, which cannot conveniently handle such omissions. This problem was overcome by entering the average coders' rating of all the responses given by all the other mothers in the given culture in the place of a particular mother's "no answer."

Not all coders made all judgments; sometimes one of the coders would leave out a judgment, having overlooked something in the mother's recorded answer, or having decided that what he read in the answer was not enough to provide the basis for a judgment. In such a case it was necessary (to make the computing machine happy) to put that coder's average judgment on that issue for that particular culture in the otherwise empty place of the overlooked judgment.

The reliability of the codings and ratings is reported in Table 1.3. A fairly random sample of protocols (from different societies) was coded by two trained coders at Cornell; the number of cases in the sample in-

Table 1.3   Data Regarding Scale Reliability

Scale Number	Total Number of Entries	Number of Single Answers	Percentage of Disagreement Greater than One Point	Correlation Coefficient between Two Raters
1	19	1	0	.77
2	6	2	50	.53
3	9	0	1	.68
4	17	0	24	.49
5	17	1	19	.55
6	16	3	14	.59
7	16	4	13	.74
8	17	5	17	.67
9	17	2	30	.49
10	16	1	18	.47
11	17	6	3	.81
12	17	1	6	.54
13	17	1	19	.45
14	17	2	13	.67
15	17	0	8	.49
16	17	0	13	.53
17	17	0	5	.51
18	17	4	7	.61
19	23	0	26	.73
20	23	0	39	.71
21	23	0	35	.85
22	22	0	0	1.00
23	21	2	0	.29*
24	23	0	0	.96
25	23	0	0	.98
26	23	0	56	.65
27	23	0	0	1.00
28	23	0	0	1.00

* If computed using double entries, only $r = 1.00$.

volved being given in the second column of Table 1.3 opposite the relevant scale number. The next column reports the number of times only one of the coders entered a judgment (which is, of course, a form of error). The next to last column contains the percentages of disagreement which exceeded one point on the relevant scale. The final column contains a measure of agreement—the Pearson correlation coefficient—

between the two raters' judgments. The highest possible coefficient is +1.00, the lowest, −1.00.

The divergence of these coefficients from 1.00 reflects the errors due to the facts that one rater made a judgment and the other did not, that some mothers failed to answer a question, and that the coders sometimes disagree in their judgments. In evaluating these we should bear in mind that it is possible in Table 1.3 for one of the coders (or even both) to have judged only a very small sample from a given society, and to have had his society value (only a mean of 3 or 4 items) substituted for a missing datum. The table can only underestimate the important reliability, which is the agreement for both judges where each did a full analysis of all cases. On the basis of these considerations it was felt that the coder reliability was adequate for the task.

The Factors

The scores of all mothers on all the scales listed in Table 1.2 were intercorrelated, each with the other. The Pearson correlation coefficients which resulted are presented in Table 1.4. Since the total sample of mothers from all societies was used in computing this matrix, it is based on an N of 133 cases. With this sample size a correlation coefficient of .17 is significant at the 5 per cent level, one of .22 is significant at the .1 per cent level, and a coefficient of .28 is significant at the .1 per cent level. Since the matrix has considerably more high coefficients than would be expected by chance, we can conclude that there are some meaningful relationships among these variables.

The correlations of all the scales (i.e., the intercorrelation matrix) was analyzed in order to uncover all the independent ways that the mother's answers on the various scales "hung together" with one another in the form of factors.[1] Twelve such independent factors were found, but two of them were so weak that they were ignored. The remaining ten factors were further analyzed (or rotated) by a computer procedure called the Varimax program. Such rotation of factors assures independent scores, i.e., orthogonal simple structure. In short, ten ways appeared in which the differences in pressures on our 133 children could be described. And the pressures on a child in any *one* of these ways could not, in principle, be predicted from knowing his pressures on any of the other nine, or any of them in combination. The loadings of the original scales on these ten rotated factors are presented in Table 1.5.

[1] The reader who has not been initiated to factor analysis should read the Introduction for a simple statement of these issues.

Table 1.4 (Continued) *Correlations among Interview Scales*

Scale Number	1	2	3	4	5	6	7	8	9	10	11	12
1												
2	−.05											
3	.12	−.02										
4	−.11	.14	−.07									
5	−.04	.16	−.11	.04								
6	.17	.17	−.11	.25	.05							
7	−.10	.12	.04	.06	−.30	.27						
8	−.04	.10	−.17	.07	−.03	.74	.46					
9	−.11	.06	−.14	−.11	−.08	.19	.31	.27				
10	−.06	−.06	.12	−.20	−.04	−.15	.00	−.23	.22			
11	−.06	.12	−.12	.17	.10	.06	−.02	.01	.05	.04		
12	−.04	−.08	.18	−.05	−.05	−.07	−.08	−.19	.18	.23	.17	
13	.02	.02	−.09	.03	.44	−.03	−.22	−.10	.14	.04	.15	.05
14	.02	.07	−.16	.04	.08	.06	.01	−.01	.25	.02	.27	.20
15	−.06	.03	−.15	−.08	−.33	.18	.50	.29	.47	.08	.07	.09
16	−.07	.13	−.33	−.18	−.05	−.14	.04	−.07	.19	.20	.14	.08
17	.04	.06	−.00	.17	.15	.06	.09	.09	−.21	−.20	−.10	−.62
18	.02	−.10	.43	−.02	−.07	.17	.25	.18	.19	.03	.22	.07
19	.02	.07	−.01	.43	.01	.27	.07	.22	.04	−.18	.04	−.17
20	.03	.06	.12	.08	−.03	−.03	.04	−.07	−.06	−.11	−.21	−.19
21	.02	.01	.01	−.10	.05	−.11	−.03	−.11	.01	.12	.11	.06
22	−.11	.01	.10	−.05	−.06	−.05	.06	.06	−.17	−.01	.02	.04
23	.13	.17	−.28	.10	.03	−.00	−.07	−.02	−.02	−.08	−.10	−.12
24	.17	.06	−.22	.03	−.11	.06	−.03	−.02	−.02	.08	.04	−.05
25	−.02	.02	−.17	−.00	−.14	−.07	−.06	−.12	.13	.05	.07	.05
26	−.04	−.03	−.04	−.05	−.07	−.00	−.01	.00	.04	−.02	.08	.20
27	−.07	.16	.02	−.03	.16	.02	−.02	−.04	−.02	.10	.11	.03
28	.12	.12	.11	.10	−.02	−.01	−.02	−.04	−.16	−.03	.10	.07

Table 1.4 (*Continued*) *Correlations among Interview Scales*

Scale Number	13	14	15	16	17	18	19	20	21	22	23	24	25	26	27	28
1																
2																
3																
4																
5																
6																
7																
8																
9																
10																
11																
12																
13																
14	.01															
15	−.18	.22														
16	.09	.19	.28													
17	−.03	−.26	−.19	−.23												
18	.02	.22	.39	.20	−.15											
19	−.02	−.01	−.03	−.11	.25	.09										
20	−.29	.03	−.04	−.14	.18	−.10	.15									
21	.17	.01	.07	.03	−.13	.12	−.09	−.36								
22	.00	−.00	−.13	−.01	−.12	.09	−.08	.01	.05							
23	−.08	.18	.08	.14	−.01	.17	.03	.14	−.11	−.11						
24	−.12	.10	.10	.17	−.04	.22	.13	.12	.07	.06	.26					
25	−.04	−.02	−.01	.12	−.05	.12	−.05	−.11	−.01	.05	.13	.43				
26	−.04	.26	.09	.08	−.18	−.04	.06	.08	.07	−.04	.01	.01	−.02			
27	.06	.02	−.02	−.06	.07	−.05	−.05	−.03	.05	.11	.06	−.03	.10	.01		
28	.01	.07	−.10	−.15	−.03	−.08	−.03	.12	.00		.22	.31	.39	.08	−.03	

Table 1.5   Rotated Centroid Factors

Scale Number	1	2	3	4	5	6	7	8	9	10
1	.14	.06	− .06	.04	− .09	− .02	.09	− .08	− .08	− .52
2	.11	.00	− .05	.07	.06	.03	.14	.02	.48	.15
3	− .15	− .16	.08	.02	− .06	− .76	− .17	.05	.11	− .27
4	.06	.03	− .02	.04	.74	− .02	.06	.03	.07	.11
5	− .18	.61	− .09	− .07	.03	.09	.04	− .02	.32	− .05
6	− .02	− .05	.02	− .04	.27	.01	.74	− .10	.08	− .17
7	− .11	− .69	− .09	− .02	− .01	.05	.34	− .02	.14	.10
8	− .08	− .20	.07	.03	.10	.10	.91	− .01	.01	− .02
9	− .18	− .21	.25	− .03	− .14	.17	.26	− .50	.12	.19
10	.07	− .10	.16	− .22	− .29	− .09	− .21	− .29	.07	.08
11	.04	.03	.24	− .29	.21	.22	− .05	.03	.28	− .02
12	.04	.02	.70	− .21	− .03	− .17	− .09	− .09	− .07	− .04
13	− .11	.52	− .03	− .31	− .10	.09	.06	− .13	.15	.12
14	− .05	.00	.49	.09	.03	.36	.00	− .04	.23	− .09
15	− .04	.58	.18	.04	− .11	.33	.19	− .29	.05	.10
16	.11	− .08	.14	− .09	− .22	.39	− .11	− .17	.05	.28
17	− .10	.03	− .68	.16	.24	− .03	− .01	.03	.16	− .09
18	.03	− .28	.11	− .28	.05	.64	.09	− .02	− .14	− .20
19	− .02	− .02	− .09	.12	.54	.04	.15	− .10	.01	− .02
20	.01	− .07	− .03	.72	.08	− .02	− .10	.03	.07	− .12
21	.01	.05	.03	− .46	− .08	.04	− .06	.02	− .10	.05
22	.03	− .04	.11	− .02	− .13	− .01	− .02	.53	− .00	.14
23	.29	.02	.01	.15	.04	.36	.00	.09	.23	− .12
24	.64	− .05	.02	.14	.05	.24	− .02	− .22	− .04	− .12
25	.69	− .05	− .01	− .16	.00	.08	− .09	.06	.01	.07
26	− .02	− .03	.37	.11	.03	.06	− .01	.07	.02	.01
27	.01	.06	− .01	− .10	− .00	− .04	− .03	− .03	.35	− .01
28	.56	.05	.12	.10	.01	− .12	.04	.22	.21	− .17

These loadings reflect the degree to which the variations of the mothers' original answers correlate with the factors, and thus help to define the factors.   The higher the loading, the more the scale defines the factor.

Before discussing the interpretation of these factors, some of their structural characteristics may be considered.   We should first note, however, that once we have discovered the factors which are implied by the intercorrelations among the mothers' answers, we can give each mother a "factor score" for each factor.   That is, we can arrive at a score which, for each factor, reflects the pattern of the particular mother's position in answer to the items (or scales) that go to define a factor.   Using these

Table 1.6   Amount   of   Variance Accounted for by Factors and Determinants of Factor Variance

Factor	Percentage of Extracted Variance	Percentage of Total Variance
1	11.1	5.2
2	12.7	6.0
3	12.1	5.7
4	9.5	4.5
5	9.4	4.5
6	13.1	6.2
7	13.3	6.3
8	6.9	3.2
9	6.3	3.0
10	5.4	2.6
Total	99.8	47.2

Factor	Percentage Within-Society Variance	Percentage Between-Society Variance
1	95.4	4.6
2	83.1	16.9
3	67.2	32.8
4	92.6	7.4
5	73.4	26.6
6	52.9	47.1
7	76.4	23.5
8	90.5	9.5
9	76.0	24.0
10	89.0	11.0

factor scores certain vital questions can be asked. First, how much of the variance (or difference in the mother's answers) in the data is attributable to these factors? Table 1.6 shows the amount of such variance that is accounted for by each of the ten factors. That is, the numbers in the table reflect the degree to which a mother's score on a *factor*, her "factor score," is correlated with her original answers (thus "accounting" for them statistically). The first column shows the amount of the total variance which is accounted for by *all ten factors,* that is, attributable to each of the *particular* factors.   The second column shows how much of the total variance of the original correlation matrix (that is, the total difference in all the answers given by the mothers) is accounted for by each factor.   All ten of the factors extracted account for 47 per cent of the total matrix variance.   The remaining variance may be due either to error or to factors which are specific to particular societies, or to other factors which are too weakly measured in our questionnaires to become clear in our analysis.

Since the sample upon which this factor analysis is based includes mothers from six different countries, the question arises as to how much the variance of (or difference among) the factor scores of the mothers is due to differences between *mothers* in the same society, and how much of the variance is due to differences between mothers in different *societies.*   In short, is the factor, by its very nature, reflective only of differences among "unique cultural meaning contexts," or is it reflective of some more human-wide differences in "nonunique cultural, or personal meaning contexts"?   It would be quite possible for factors in such an analysis to be due primarily to between-society differences.   In such a case, the factors could not properly be considered pancultural because the differences would be based mainly on cultural norms which are shared by the mothers in the particular cultures, and only by those mothers.

In order to check this possibility, the sources of variance of the mothers' factor scores was analyzed.   Columns 3 and 4 of Table 1.6 show the percentage of the factor score variance that is due to variance within societies (that is, to individual differences in mothers or children) as compared to variance between societies (due to differences in the cultural means).   It is important to note that the variance is preponderantly determined by within-society variance in all cases.   Only in the case of Factor 6 does the between-society variance approach the magnitude of the within-society variance.   This is evidence that we are dealing with factors which have pancultural meaning and which may be useful in more than one societal context for the study of socialization processes.   We have discovered some common dimensions or clusters of items which apparently reflect pancultural meanings (or personal contexts) that are present across some very diverse cultures indeed.

The interpretation of these factors may now be considered, which rests upon the risky basis of naming the independent patterns of items which vary in similar ways.   For purposes of defining the factors, an arbitrary cutting point of .40 has been chosen; only scales with loadings this great or greater in Table 1.5 have been considered in *naming* the factor. However, scales with loadings of less than .40 may be considered in augmenting the description of the factor, particularly when such loadings seem to be consistent in meaning with higher loadings. Loadings of .30 to .40 are particularly considered for such purposes.

Factors 8, 9, and 10 are statistically weak and somewhat difficult to interpret. Therefore, they will be simply described in this chapter and will not be included in the factor score analyses presented later in the text. The factors are described here in the order of their presentation in subsequent chapters, but they are numbered in the order of their extraction as listed in Table 1.5.

Factor 2: Warmth of Mother. The second factor is a measure of the warmth of the mother's relationship with her child, and the extent to which she uses praise rather than physical punishment as a method of control. Mothers at the warm end of this factor are characterized by:

High general warmth (scale 5, +.61)
Low general hostility (scale 7, —.69)
Frequent use of praise (scale 13, +.52)
Infrequent use of physical punishment (scale 15, —.58)

These scales are consistent in meaning that mothers who score high on this pattern of items are warm rather than hostile with their children, and that they control them through praise rather than through punishment and threat of punishment. The only other scale that approaches an interesting level of loading is number 18, with a loading of —28. This scale has to do with the degree to which the mother is aggressive when the child is himself angry or aggressive, which is certainly consistent in tone with the other scales on the factor.

Factor 7: Emotional Instability. This factor has high loadings on two scales. Mothers who rank high on this factor are characterized by:

High mood variation of hostility (scale 8, +.91)
High mood variation of warmth (scale 6, +.74)

The lower loading of +.34 on scale 7, "general hostility of the mother" broadens the meaning of the factor a bit more. Clearly, the factor is primarily a measure of the degree to which mothers shift (probably unpredictably) from friendly to hostile moods. Since the ratings were made in the context of an interview concerning child training practices, they refer particularly to the mothers' emotional moods while interacting with her children. This kind of factor may be very important in socialization because a mother with this internal emotional shifting may provide a difficult "target" for identification or an aggressive role model. The study of these persons may provide clues to familial and even cultural sources of stress.

Factor 4: Proportion of Time That Mother Cared for Baby. This factor is simply a representation of the proportion of time that the mother (as compared to some other person) spent with the child during its first year or two of life. The factor is defined by two scales.

> Amount of time that mother cared for baby (scale 20, +.72)
> Amount of time that some adult other than the mother cared for baby (scale 21, —.46)

This factor is clearly involved with caretaking. Mothers who score high on this factor can be characterized by the fact that the mother did a higher proportion of the care of her child when he (or she) was a baby, and that other adults spent relatively less time at this activity.

There are a number of other scales that have low, but suggestive, loadings on this scale. It would appear that there is some tendency for mothers high on Factor 4 to be "flat" or neutral in their emotional reactions to their children since they are less aggressive when the child is angry or aggressive toward them (scale 18, —.28) and they use praise less (scale 13, —.31). It is also possible that these mothers who spend more time with their babies come to be able to predict more about their child's behavior because they do less communicating of rules (scale 11, —.29), they have less consistent aggressive rules (scale 12, —.21), and their own hostility is somewhat less contingent upon the behavior of the child (scale 10, —.22) than mothers who share the task of baby tending with other adults (whose multiple mothering may make the child's behavior more variable).

Factor 5: Proportion of Time That Mother Cares for Baby. This factor represents the amount of time that the mother, in contrast to some other socializing agent, spent with the child at the time of the interview. Mothers with high positive loadings on this factor have two characteristics.

> High proportion of the caretaking of the child is done by the mother (scale 4, +.74)
> Mother spends a relatively large amount of time with the child (scale 19, +.54)

There are only two low loadings with this factor, and evidently they tend to touch upon the harassment aspect of the effect of caretaking upon at least some mothers. The heavy caretakers tend to have more variation in warmth due to mood (scale 6, +.27), and to have hostility which is not contingent upon the child's performance (scale 10, —.29).

It should be noted that scale 19 (which is loaded on Factor 5) and scales 20 and 21 (loaded on Factor 4) are relative in nature. They represent measurements of the amount of time that the mother, *as opposed to some other caretaker,* spends with the child, not the total amount of *time* that the mother spends with the child. The scales are based on the questions, "Who usually cares for your child?" and "Who did this when he was a baby?" The ratings were made on a scale running from never to always. Because of their relative nature, a high rating on the scale does not necessarily imply that the mother devotes a great deal of time and attention to the child. For this reason it is not so surprising that Factors 4 and 5 are relatively independent of loadings on scales measuring the personality characteristics of the mothers. Factors 4 and 5 reflect the mothers' structural role vis-à-vis their children rather than the expressive aspects of the role behavior.

Factor 1: Responsibility Training. This first factor is easily interpreted as it has to do with responsibility demands on the child. The ratings include not only the chores assigned to the child by the mother, but also those assigned by others. Therefore this factor deals with the general pressures on children for doing things to help the family get its work done. Some students of groups would not be surprised that this "task orientation" should emerge at once from a factor analysis of socialization processes. The factor may have relevance, then, to group processes as well as to personality development, as is true of most of the factors below. The factor is defined in terms of the age of the child, his frequency of performance of chores, and the number of chores he performs. Since chores which are assigned by members of the family *other* than the mother are included in the ratings, this factor, unlike the others, represents some of the behavioral characteristics of the *child,* as reported by the mother, rather than the characteristics of the mother herself or of only *her* pressures on the child. Children with high "scores" on this factor have the following pattern of characteristics.

They are relatively old (scale 28, +.56)
They do chores frequently (scale 24, +.64)
They do a relatively large number of chores (scale 25, +.69)

These are the only scales with loadings greater than .30, but it is interesting that scale 23, which relates to the age at which children begin to play away from home, has a loading of +.29 in Factor 1. Perhaps because chores take a child away from home early, he is given (to some extent) greater freedom in play as well. It seems quite clear, therefore, that in all the six cultures studied children vary on the number of chores they are expected to perform. The factor also indicates that, as might be expected, older children are counted on to perform more chores and to do them more frequently than are younger children.

Factor 6: Aggression Training, Mother-Directed Aggression. Factor 6 is primarily a measure of the mother's reactions to aggression directed at herself. Certain disciplinary techniques are correlated with characteristic reactions. Mothers with high scores on the nonpermissive end of this factor have the following characteristics.

> High punitiveness when child becomes angry while being scolded (scale 3, —.76)
> High aggressiveness when child is angry with her (scale 18, +.64)

These defining scales suggest that mothers with high scores on this factor tend *not* to be positive or nonpunitive when the child becomes angry when scolded, and that they tend to become aggressive when the child is angry or aggressive with them.

There are four scales with low loadings which help to define this factor. These loadings suggest that mothers who are high on this factor tend to have consistent demands for nonroutine obedience (scale 14, +.36), they tend to use physical punishment more frequently and intensely (scale 15, +.33), they control the child in part through making gifts and privileges contingent upon his good behavior (scale 16, +.39), and (for some reason) they permit play away from home at a relatively late age (scale 23, +.36). It would seem that mothers who are strict and aggressive about such expressions of anger, also use what Sears, Maccoby, and Levin (1957) have referred to as "object-oriented discipline"; e.g., manipulation of gifts and privileges and/or physical punishment, rather than "love-oriented" discipline. Like the mothers who are punitive about peer aggression, they emphasize obedience (scale 14), although not prompt obedience (scale 26). This emphasis on obedience seems to be a sort of connecting link between the two independent aggression-control factors, since it appears again in factor three.

Factor 3: Aggression Training, Peer-Directed Aggression. The third factor indicates a general relationship between a nonpermissive attitude toward peer-directed aggression and high emphasis on obedience training. Mothers with high score patterns are characterized by:

> Consistent rules about aggression (scale 12, +.70)
> Low reward for retaliation (scale 17, —.68)
> Consistent follow through on nonroutine demands for obedience (scale 14, +.49)

It is consistent that these mothers also tend to expect immediate obedience (scale 26, +.37) from their child.

There is no inconsistency in finding two low *positive* loadings in scale 11 (+.24), reflecting the amount of communication of rules in general by the mother (certainly aggression rules are a component of this scale), and in scale 9 (+.25), contingency of mother's warmth. A mother who had rules in the areas of aggression and obedience, and followed up on them, would be reasonably expected to make her warmth at least somewhat dependent upon the child's obedience and his nonretaliatory behavior to peers.

In defining this factor, in which the loading on reward for retaliation (toward peers) looms so large, it is interesting that scale 2, "Degree to which mother is positive when child fights with other children," has essentially a zero loading on this factor, but defines (if anything does) Factor 9. This may suggest a distinction between retaliating when one has been picked on as compared to starting a fight (or, more vaguely, just "being in a fight"). We might expect these to differ, but it is surprising to find them orthogonal. Although scales 17 and 2 are similar in meaning the correlation between them (see Table 1.4) is only .06.

It is also interesting that the mother's reaction to her child's retaliation to peers is not correlated with her own reaction to the child's aggressiveness while being scolded (scale 3), or to the degree to which she herself uses aggression as a reaction to the child's aggressiveness (scale 18). These last two scales *define* Factor 6 and are, therefore, orthogonal to Factor 3.

The existence of these two factors certainly suggests that a number of important dimensions of aggression exist which must be parceled out in cross-cultural analyses. If this is in fact the case, and to the degree that one entertains learning theory hypotheses regarding personality development, then these distinctions suggest that the *peer* aggression displayed by a child may be somewhat independent of the amount of aggression a child directs toward those in authority.

The remaining three factors are less well defined than are the seven discussed above. The loadings are relatively low, and they account for relatively little of the variance. These factors should be viewed as very tentative indeed, but we shall discuss them to the extent that sense can be made from them. Since they are tentative we will not give them formal names.

Factor 8. This factor is defined by two scales, which suggest that mothers who score high tend to give warmth to the child which is not contingent upon his good performance (scale 9, —.50), and that the children of these mothers are able to dress themselves at a relatively later age (scale 22, +.53). This suggests that we are dealing with a weak factor suggestive of "mothering," or of "noncontingent nurturance." The weak loadings are consistent with such an interpretation, suggesting that the mother keeps the child from responsibility (scale 24, −.22) dealing with total frequency of chores, and that she does not try to use punishment to control behavior (scale 10, −.29), suggesting low contingency of mother's hostility, and (scale 15, −.29) showing low tendency to use physical punishment in socialization.

Factor 9. This relatively weak factor may be an artifact of some kind because, though it deals with parental attitudes toward peer aggression, it is not loaded on scale 17, "reward for retaliation" directed toward peers. There may, however, be some sense to this factor if it is viewed as "peer aggression permissiveness" (scale 2, +.48) reflecting the "degree to which mother is positive when child fights other children," tied somewhat to girls (scale 27, +.35). It is interesting that the only other loading above .30 is the "general warmth of the mother" (scale 5, +.32), which gives a picture of an expressive, positive mother who permits her girl to be expressive as well. This may turn out to be a "mutuality of aggression expression" pattern, shared by mother and child. This interpretation would account for the somewhat surprising finding that some mothers permit girls to express aggression more freely than boys. This suggestion can be checked from other data gathered by the project which is not reported here.

Factor 10. This weak factor has only one defining scale (scale 1, −.52), reflecting the fact that this mother does not give help to the child when she is busy. This relationship should probably be ignored. However, it may be of some value for the future to put forward an interpretive hunch: this may be a factor which weakly defines attempts by the mother to keep the child out of her way. There is a weak loading on scale 3 (−.27) which suggests that this mother tends to be punitive when the child is angry when scolded, and on scale 16 (+.28), showing that she gives gifts and privileges contingent on the child's good behavior, suggesting that these mothers bribe children and are impatient about insubordination. Considering the troubles many mothers face in socializing their offspring it would only be justice if our last factor in the present context should reflect harassment.

Comparison with Other Studies

It may be useful to try to relate our pancultural findings to some of the other literature in the field. This is difficult for a number of reasons. First, all the analyses available are intracultural rather than cross-cultural. Second, researchers in this area have not been uniform in their choice of scales used in their studies. Resemblance of factors, then, sometimes rests on one or two scales in another study. Third, there is diversity in the types of statistical analysis used. Baldwin et al. (1949), for instance, analyzed their results by means of what is called a "cluster analysis," whereas Sewell et al. (1955) used what is called the "multiple group method" in extracting their factors, and they also chose to extract correlated factors by this method. Schaefer and Bell (1957) used the centroid factor analytic procedure (as was done in this study), but they used only a nonindependent or oblique rotation. Zuckerman, et al. (1958) describe unrelated factors and compare their results to unrotated factors obtained by Schaefer and Bell (1958). The studies that follow the complex model in analyzing data use more global variables than were used in this study. As Schaefer points out, studies using the score and Whiting approach do not usually obtain data that fit the circumplex model (Schaefer 1959). Milton (1958) used a procedure most comparable to ours, that is, centroid analyses and orthogonal rotation. Finally, comparison of factors obtained on different samples must be to some extent subjective, despite the endeavors of Ahmavaara (1957) and others, since there is as yet no definitively precise method of comparing factorial results obtained on different samples.

However, since there seems to be some similarity of factors across various American samples, it seems reasonable, despite the difficulties involved, to consider which of these factors have some pancultural basis. We shall, therefore, engage in some brief comparisons between our results and those of other investigators.

The factors which have commonly emerged in studies of American samples have been versions of warmth factors and permissive-restrictive factors. It is not surprising, then, that our warmth factor (F2) and restriction factors (F3, F6) are the ones which have the most comparability with the results of other studies.

Factor 2 (warmth of mother) in the present study has a positive loading on maternal warmth and a negative loading on maternal hostility. Mothers high on this factor also praise their children and tend not to use physical punishment. Milton (1958) also distinguishes a warmth factor (FC) which includes, among other scales, affectionate demonstrativeness and praise for table manners. Like our warmth factor, Milton's is orthogonal to his permissiveness factor. Zuckerman et al. (1958), and Schaefer and Bell (1958) find a hostile rejection factor in their unrotated area, which might be considered the opposite end of a warmth factor in his cluster analysis. Becker et al. (1962) found a warmth factor in the interview responses of both mothers and fathers. One of these factors remains when the data are reordered to a circumplex model (Becker and Krug, 1964).

In our study we have isolated two (possibly three) factors concerned with aggression training. One (F3) is concerned with restrictions on aggression to peers and obedience training, the other (F6) is concerned with restrictions on aggression directed at the mother. Milton (1958) finds one aggression factor (FE) which includes treatment of aggression directed at peers *and* at parents. He finds that the factor loading for permissiveness toward peer aggression is correlated with punishment of aggression to parents. We find them to be independent, appearing, as they do, on separate factors. The comparison with Milton's data is further complicated by the fact that he also finds a permissiveness factor, broader in scope than aggression training and obedience, but including these scales. Thus, in Milton's analyses, the scales measuring restrictions on aggressive behavior appear in two factors, but always together, whereas in our data they appear in two separate factors.

Becker et al. (1962) find two permissiveness factors that include a scale on aggression to parents. Schaefer and Bell (1957) find a factor which they call over-possessiveness and Zuckerman et al. (1958) find one called authoritarian control, both include a scale on restrictions on aggression. Baldwin et al. (1949) find a general restrictiveness cluster and Sewell et al. (1955) find a rather diverse factor, which they leave unnamed (F7) and which includes strict obedience training. Although these findings have only tangential resemblance to our aggression training factors, they do seem to be generally concerned with dimensions of strictness of discipline.

Our emotional instability factor (F7) also has some parallels in other studies. Schaefer and Bell (1957) find a factor called "Hostile Rejection of the Homemaking Role," and Zuckerman et al. (1958) find a hostility-rejection factor, both of which include a scale of irritability. Baldwin et al. (1949) also find an emotionality cluster. Milton's (1958) "General Family Adjustment Factor," which includes hostility of the father and the mother's child-rearing anxiety, may represent a related pattern.

The only other similarity between our findings and those of others that may be worth mentioning is that Sewell et al. (1955) found a factor which they called "Non-Punitive Treatment" that includes ignoring the child's neglect of jobs. This might be similar to our first factor, which is concerned with responsibility training.

Finally, none of the studies we reviewed include scales on the proportion of caretaking that is done by the mother. Therefore, we find no factors comparable to our Factors 4 and 5 which deal with this area. These scales differ from most scales in our study, and the other studies reviewed here in that they do not purely represent either attitudes toward child-rearing practices or personality variables. However, such factors may certainly be related both to attitudes of the parents and to behavior of the child. The variable of time spent with the child has been extensively investigated with institutional children and the children of working mothers. It seems rather odd, in view of the great importance attributed to maternal presence in this vast body of literature, that this topic has not been more frequently included in the type of analyses we have cited here. Since these caretaking scales emerge so clearly as factors in our study we hope this kind of measurement will be included in future investigations of this kind.

Placing Mothers on the Scales

We have, then, discovered seven well-defined pancultural factors or scales; five of which appear to have their counterparts in other, single-culture studies. It now remains for us to compare each factor within each culture (to discover patterns of special emphasis), to compare the special emphasis patterns which cultures display, and to interpret these comparisons either by bringing up old or new hypotheses which explain them, or by referring ourselves to the special conditions of a culture which may cast light.

Before we can proceed with an analysis, some technical matters must be considered. If we are to place mother on each of the factor scales, we must compute what are called "factor scores" for each mother.[2] This means that we must take into consideration the mother's position on each of the separate items which define a factor, and arrive at the best possible estimate of her score on each total pattern of such items. This can only be an estimate, but it is possible to evaluate how good our estimate of each mother's factor score is by perusing the S_x's, Table 1.7. These "sigmas" can be interpreted as correlations which reflect the fit between our estimates and the (mathematically) true scores. Since all of these correlations are greater than .80, we can feel fairly sure that our estimates of the mothers' scores are good ones.

With this assurance in mind, we can now look at Table 1.7, which is important from a substantive point of view as well as technically. It

[2] These scores were computed by what is referred to as the "method of least squares regression" (Harmon, 1960). The scores obtained by this method are only estimates of the true factor scores since these scores cannot be computed exactly.

Table 1.7   *Means and Sigmas of Factor Scores*

		Society						
Factor Number*	Factor Title	United States n = 24	Mexico n = 22	Philippines n = 23	Okinawa n = 24	India n = 24	Africa n = 16	Total
2	Maternal Warmth							
	$\bar{X}$	−.01	−.34	.18	.62	−.48	.00	.00
	S_x	.78	.83	.58	.75	1.09	.88	.89
7	Maternal Instability							
	$\bar{X}$	.10	.14	−.57	−.38	.02	1.02	.00
	S_x	1.08	1.00	.58	.81	.89	.41	.95
4	Proportion of Time that Mother Cares for Baby							
	$\bar{X}$	.48	.01	−.18	−.12	−.09	−.15	.00
	S_x	.63	.80	.78	.77	1.10	.88	.85
5	Proportion of Time that Mother Cares for Child							
	$\bar{X}$	.69	−.03	−.58	−.14	−.27	.46	.00
	S_x	.61	.76	.81	.91	.72	.40	.84
1	Responsibility Training							
	$\bar{X}$	.09	.01	.18	−.12	−.32	.24	.00
	S_x	.86	.72	.64	.95	1.06	.90	.87
6	Aggression Training: Mother-Directed Aggression							
	$\bar{X}$	−.13	.28	.50	−.08	−1.13	.89	.00
	S_x	.74	.83	.56	.57	.82	.23	.91
	Aggression Training: Peer-Directed Aggression							
	$\bar{X}$	−.98	.61	.11	.07	.20	.07	.00
	S_x	.79	.52	.55	1.08	.58	.60	.86

* Factors are numbered in order of their extraction but listed in order of their presentation in text.

Table 1.8 *Chi-Square Analysis of Factor Scores*

Factor Number	Factor Title		United States	Mexico	Philippines	Okinawa	India	Africa	Total	χ^2	p
						Society					
2	Warmth of Mother	+	13	9	16	18	7	11	74	14.48	<.02
		−	11	13	7	6	17	5	59		
7	Emotional Instability	+	14	12	4	5	11	16	62	37.55	<.001
		−	10	10	19	19	13	0	71		
4	Proportion of Time That Mother Cares for Baby	+	19	9	10	12	10	5	65	11.99	<.05
		−	5	13	13	12	14	11	68		
5	Proportion of Time That Mother Cares for Child	+	22	12	6	12	9	13	74	28.60	<.001
		−	2	10	17	12	15	3	59		
1	Responsibility Training	+	13	12	14	10	8	8	65	5.25	<.50
		−	11	10	9	14	16	8	68		
6	Aggression Training: Mother-Directed Aggression	+	10	16	19	12	2	16	75	49.85	<.001
		−	14	6	4	12	22	0	58		
3	Aggression Training: Peer-Directed Aggression	+	2	20	13	15	15	10	75	37.01	<.001
		−	22	2	10	9	9	6	58		

displays to us the average position $(\overline{X})$ of the mothers in each culture on each of the seven strong factors. It also contains some information that reflects the degree to which the mothers vary from one another within each of the communities studied (the sigmas, or σ's, in the table). We will not discuss these differences here, since they will be a focus of our discussion in chapters that follow.

Table 1.8 reflects intersociety differences on the factor scores. The last column in Table 1.8 tells us that on Factor 1 there are very few, if any, differences in the way mothers distribute themselves, whereas there are important differences to be found in the other factors. Responsibility training pressures tend to be distributed in a similar way in our six cultural communities, but this is not true for the other factors.

It should be noted at once that what we have just said is true for the *factor scores,* which are in a sense a summary of the mother's position on a number of particular items. In the comparisons to follow we shall often ignore this composite, and fall back on particular items for comparison purposes where this appears meaningful.

So much for this technical issue. One more remains before we begin our comparisons in detail. As we suggested in our introduction, there is no heaven-sent reason for factors to be independent or orthogonal with regard to one another. In fact, the contrary might well be expected; mothers who require much responsibility might, in the nature of things, also tend to squash aggression. In order to check this possibility we have also analyzed all our mothers' answers in such a way that the factors could come out correlated with one another. This is called an "Oblimax oblique rotation of factors with the placement of factors corrected visually," and both the statistical sophisticate and the neophyte might find the results interesting, as presented in Appendix I. We have relegated this analysis to the Appendix to avoid confusion, and because there is a striking similarity between the results of the Oblimax analysis and what we have already said. We will not use the Oblimax factors in the rest of the book. We might have done so if the factors were greatly different or if they had taken their opportunity and turned out to be highly correlated with one another. There are some significant correlations between them (for example, it is interesting to note that mothers who spend a high proportion of their time caring for children are somewhat more unstable in their emotional reactions to their children than are mothers who do not have such exclusive responsibility) but they are few and are uniformly low, the highest being —.37.

We enter upon our detailed comparisons, then, with the assurance that our factors are clear and definite from more than one point of view.

Summary

The data used in this analysis consist of responses to interviews with mothers about their socialization practices. These interviews were conducted in six rural communities in the Northeastern United States, North India, the Philippines, Okinawa, an Indian community in Mexico, and Kenya, Africa. Each sample was selected from a small, culturally homogeneous rural or semirural community.

Selected scales from the mother interviews were factor analyzed, using a centroid method of analysis. The factors were rotated to orthogonal simple structure. Twelve factors were extracted, seven of which were named. The first ten factors account for 47 per cent of the total matrix variance. For every factor the within-group variance is greater than the between-group variance, indicating that the factors are pancultural.

The first seven factors have been named as follows:

1. Responsibility Training
2. Warmth of Mother
3. Aggression Training: Peer-Directed Aggression
4. Proportion of Time Mother Cared for Baby
5. Proportion of Time Mother Cares for Child
6. Aggression Training: Mother-Directed Aggression
7. Emotional Instability of Mother

Despite the fact that the within-society variation is greater than the between-society variation on all factors, there are significant between-society differences on all factors except the first, responsibility training. These differences will be analyzed in subsequent chapters.

In addition to the orthogonal rotation the factors were rotated obliquely. The factors of the oblique rotation are similar to the orthogonal factors. Training of mother-directed aggression appears as two factors in the oblique rotation, but these two could be combined. The same factors appear in both rotations with the exception that the tenth factor of the orthogonal rotation does not appear in the oblique rotation. This factor is weak and badly defined in the orthogonal results. Despite the fact that there are a number of statistically significant correlations among factors, the correlations are generally low, the highest being —.37. In view of this fact the results of the orthogonal rotation will be used in the further analysis.

2 ❖ Maternal Warmth

Factor Definition

The factor to be discussed in this chapter is the second one extracted after rotation. It appears as F2 in Table 1.5 and is defined by four scales:

General warmth of mother (scale 5, +.61)
General hostility of mother (scale 7, —.69)
Amount of praise (scale 13, +.52)
Frequency and intensity of physical punishment (scale 15, —.58)

This factor is a measure of the relative warmth or hostility of the mothers' behavior toward their children. Such a factor might be called either maternal warmth or maternal hostility, depending upon which end of the scale we chose to name. We have chosen to name the factor after the "warm" or positive end of the dimension. Mothers whose scores are near the positive pole of this factor are rated as being relatively warm and relatively *not* hostile in their interactions with people, particularly their children. They praise their children frequently and seldom use physical punishment to chastise them. When they do use physical punishment, it tends to be mild, rather than severe. Mothers on the negative pole of the factor have the opposite characteristics.

The warmth and hostility of the mothers were rated on 7-point scales, on the basis of the tone of the entire interview. They represent, therefore, global ratings rather than scores derived from particular questions. Despite the nonspecificity of the reference for these ratings, the variables themselves are carefully defined.

The dimension of maternal warmth was defined as follows.

This scale measures the amount of warmth shown by the mother to her child and other members of her family, friends, and neighbors. Warmth may be manifested by playing with her child, enjoying him, doing things to please the child and others, demonstrating affection in words and action. Routine caretaking and amusing the child as part of a schedule, or as a matter of felt duty or responsibility, are not to be considered as automatically indicating emotional warmth. The use of reward and praise as techniques of inculcation is also not relevant to the scale *per se*. Signs of affection which are spontaneous with the mother should weigh more heavily in this rating than affection which comes only as a result of the child's or other people's solicitations.

The dimension of hostility was defined in this fashion. "The mother is considered hostile when she expresses much anger and irritableness with others. Often nags, scolds, fights with others." Derogatory comments about the children, husband, relatives, or neighbors and complaints about the children's demands, etc., are considered in making this rating.

The ratings of amount of praise and frequency and intensity of physical punishment might also be based on comments throughout the interview, but specific questions about child training practices, including questions focused around the use of praise and physical punishment, provided most of the information for these ratings.

Praise was defined as follows.

This scale (amount of praise) measures the degree to which the mother indicates by actions or comments that she is pleased with the child. This includes statements of praise made directly to the child, statements of praise made to others in the presence of the child, behavior such as smiling in admiration made directly to the child, or appreciative winks and smiles made to others who are called upon to notice the actions of the child.

Physical punishment was defined more simply. A mother high on this scale is one who "frequently controls deviant behavior of the child by use of painful physical punishment, e.g., frequently whips or beats child."

The correlations among the raw scores of these four variables are not outstandingly high, but they all have probabilities of less than 5 per cent, 5 out of 6 of them have probabilities of less than 1 per cent and 4 out of 6 have probabilities of less than .1 per cent. These correlations, taken from Table 1.4, are as follows:

Table 1.4 Excerpt: Intercorrelations of Defining Scales for Factor 2

Scale Number	Scale Number		
	5	7	13
7	− .30**		
13	+ .44**	− .22*	
15	− .33**	+ .50**	− .18

* = $p < .01$.
** = $p < .001$.

Variation on Factor Scores

Within the design of this study, it is possible to isolate three possible sources of variation in the factor scores. These are the society of the mother and the age and sex of her children. An analysis of variance of the factor scores for this and subsequent factors was computed to estimate the relative importance of these sources of variance. The results of this analysis on the factor scores for Factor 2 are presented in Table 2.1.[1] An analysis of variance of age, sex, and society was computed on the factor scores for Factor 2 to check this possibility. The results of this analysis are presented in Table 2.3. Variance due to society is the only main effect that contributes significantly to variance among means. This variation is occasioned largely by the low position of the Mexican and Indian samples on this factor. Neither the age nor the sex of the children is an important source of variance. This result is predictable from the low loadings of age and sex on this factor.

Table 2.1   Mean Factor Scores for Age and Sex Groups and Analysis of Variance Table on Factor 2: Warmth of Mother

	Boys		Girls		
Society	Young	Old	Young	Old	*Total Group*
Okinawa	.34	.65	.81	.68	.62
Philippines	−.21	.34	.41	.11	.18
Africa	−.52	.21	−.27	.44	.00
United States	.06	.27	−.22	−.16	−.01
Mexico	−.34	.14	−.68	−.40	−.34
India	−1.29	−.71	.28	−.18	−.48

Source	*df*	*p*
Sex	1	NS
Age	1	NS
Society	5	.001
Sex × Age	1	.001
Sex × Society	5	.001
Age × Society	5	.001
Sex × Age × Society	5	.001

---

[1] The results of this analysis should be interpreted with some caution, since Bartlett's chi square indicates that the variation of the factor scores is not homogeneous for all societies on this factor.

There is, however, a significant interaction between age and sex due to a tendency in several societies for mothers to be warmer with older boys than they are with younger boys but not as warm with older girls than they are with younger girls. There is a significant interaction between sex and society because mothers tend to be warmer to girls in the African and Indian samples, and warmer to boys in the other communities. The interaction between age and society appears to be due largely to the fact that the mothers of the African community are considerably warmer with older children than they are with younger ones. Differential treatment of age and sex groups in the different societies leads to a significant interaction between age, sex, and society.

Before proceeding to a consideration of variation on the scales that define Factor 2, let us consider more closely the between-society differences that form the only significant main effect in the analysis of variance.

There is a significant intersociety difference in the placement of mothers on this factor. This is indicated by the chi-square value for intersociety differences in the number of cases above or below the overall median presented in Table 1.8 ($p = .02$), and by the significant effect of society in Table 2.1. However, these differences are not large. Only 17 per cent of the variance of this factor is attributable to differences between culture groups.

The ranking of societies in terms of the percentage of cases above the mean (i.e., the percentage of positive cases) is presented in Table 2.2. Mann-Whitney U tests (Siegel, 1956) were computed for those societies of adjacent rank having the largest percentage differences between them.

It is necessary to be conservative in carrying out this analysis since a number of significant differences would be expected by chance alone, if all possible pairs of societies were tested for each factor. We shall, therefore, test only for those pairs of societies which are adjacent to each

Table 2.2   Analysis of Significant Gaps Among Societies on Factor Scores Grouping of Societies on Factor 2: Maternal Warmth

Rank	Society			Percentage of + cases
1	Okinawa			75
2	Philippines	$\chi^2 = 2.63$	$p > .30$	70
3	Africa			69
4	United States			54
		$Z = 1.40$	$p < .16$	
5	Mexico	$\chi^2 = 0.70$	$p > .30$	41
6	India			29

other with respect to their percentage of deviation from the overall mean of zero. In order to do this we compute the percentage of positive factor scores for each society on the factor. The societies are then ranked; rank "one" being assigned to that society having the largest percentage of positive scores, and rank "six" to that society having the smallest percentage of positive scores. A Mann-Whitney U test (Siegel, 1956) is then computed on the societies of adjacent rank which have the largest gap between their above-mean percentages. After societies differing significantly from their ranked neighbor have been eliminated, chi squares for the remaining societies are computed to determine whether or not the factor scores of these societies come from the same population.[2] This analysis shows that the only two societies of adjacent rank with substantially different distributions are the United States and Mexico ($p < .16$). Chi-square analyses show that the mothers of Mexico and India are generally less warm than the mothers in other societies, while mothers of the Okinawan, Philippine, African, and United States samples form a group without substantial between-society differences on maternal warmth.[3]

Intersociety Differences on Scales

Is the ordering of societies on the scales that make up the material warmth factor the same as their ordering on the composition factor scores? The answer to this question is presented in Table 2.3. The scores have been divided as close as possible to the overall median. Chi-square analyses show that there are significant intersocietal differences on the scales for "general hostility of mother," "amount of praise," and "frequency and intensity of physical punishment." The chi-square value for "warmth of mother" has a probability of greater than 10 per cent, indicating that all of the societies belong to the same population with respect to this variable.[4]

[2] The sophisticated reader will note that this same analysis could have been done by computing a T test between the cultural means. We have chosen to use a nonparametric test, in preference to a T test to avoid making any assumptions about the distribution of factor scores for particular societies. The total sample of factor scores for all societies is distributed approximately normally, since the scores have been standardized. The distribution of factor scores for any particular society, however, may be far from normal.

[3] The differences between the Mexican and African samples does not reach conventional levels of significance. However, the probability that the two groups of societies that result from this division are drawn from the same population is reasonably high ($P < .30$).

[4] In this and subsequent analyses the scores have been divided as close as possible to the median of the entire sample, and the chi-square analyses have been computed

The Mexican and Indian mothers, who are significantly less warm than the others as measured by their placement on the factor, tend to fall in the expected positions on the individual scales, but with some exceptions. The Indian mothers as would be expected are lowest in warmth of mother and amount of praise, and are in the high group for frequency and intensity of physical punishment; but they have an intermediate position on the hostility-of-mother scale. The Mexican mothers, while highest in hostility and use of physical punishment, are intermediate in amount of praise and, surprisingly, second highest on the warmth-of-mother scale. The Okinawan sample, ranked first on the warm end of the factor, maintains an extreme position on each of the four scales that is consistent with its factor position; it is in first place on the scales of warmth of mother and amount of praise, last place on the hostility-of-mother scale, and next to the last rank on the physical-punishment scale. The ordering of the societies that are intermediate in rank on their placement on the factor varies on the scales, but they tend to have intermediate ranks.

The overall placement of the societies on the scales is, then, about what we would expect from their placement on the factor; but the magnitude of the differences between societies is not as great on the scales as on the factor. On the maternal-hostility scale, the Mexican and Okinawan samples, at opposite ends of the ranking, are almost equally deviant from the remaining societies. However, the probability of the difference between Okinawa and its neighbor, the Philippines, is less than 30 per cent, while the probability of the difference between the Mexican and United States samples (not shown in the table) is less than 50 per cent. When the Okinawan sample is removed, the probability of the chi-square value among the remaining societies is less than 20 per cent and greater than 10 per cent. Therefore, although the Okinawan sample does not

---

to determine whether or not there are between-society differences in distribution on the scales. The societies are ranked in terms of the percentage of cases above the median. When the overall chi-square analysis reveals significant intersociety differences, chi-square analyses are computed for those societies, of adjacent rank, having the largest differences between their above-median percentages. Deviant societies are than withdrawn from the sample and chi squares for the remaining societies are computed to determine whether or not these societies come from the same population. The logic of this procedure is the same as that used to determine intersociety differences on the factor score distributions. The only difference is that chi-square analyses are substituted for Mann-Whitney U tests to determine the significance of the differences between societies of adjacent rank. The reason for this procedural change is that the Mann-Whitney U test is based on the rank order of the scores. Since all of the raw data scores are based on a limited scale (1 to 7 points or 1 to 10 points) there are too many scores of the same number to permit such a ranking.

Table 2.3   Maternal Warmth Scales: Intersociety Differences

Warmth of Mother

Rank	Society	Low	High	χ^2	p	Percentage of high scores
1	Okinawa	6	14			70
2	Mexico	9	12			57
3	Africa	7	9			56
4	United States	13	11			46
5	Philippines	12	9			43
6	India	14	7			33
	Total	61	62	7.62	<.20	

Hostility of Mother

Rank	Society	Low	High	χ^2	p	Percentage of high scores
1	Mexico	4	15			79
2	United States	8	15			65
3	Africa	7	9	6.52	<.20	56
4	India	8	9			53
5	Philippines	9	7	1.11	<.30	44
6	Okinawa	16	6			27
	Total	52	61	14.46	<.02	

Amount of Praise

Rank	Society	Low	High	χ^2	p	Percentage of high scores
1	Okinawa	4	20			83
2	Africa	6	10	2.22	<.20	63
3	Mexico	10	12			55
4	Philippines	13	10	5.20	>.20	43
5	United States	15	9			38
6	India	16	8			33
	Total	64	69	16.71	<.01	

Frequency and Intensity of Physical Punishment

Rank	Society	Low	High	χ^2	p	Percentage of high scores
1	Mexico	2	20			91
2	Africa	2	14	2.83	>.20	88
3	India	6	18	1.79	<.20	75
4	Philippines	10	13	2.55	<.20	57
5	Okinawa	16	8	.40	=.50	33
6	United States	18	6			25
	Total	54	79	33.55	<.001	

differ significantly from its ranked neighbor, its removal lowers the chi-square value for the remaining societies to a probability level which indicates that their scores are drawn from the same population.

A similar situation pertains to the scale, amount of praise. The Okinawan sample is the only one that differs substantially from the others. The probability of the difference between this sample and the African sample, ranked 2 on this scale, is less than 20 per cent but greater than 10 per cent. When the Okinawan sample is removed the chi-square value for intersocietal differences among the remaining societies has a probability of between 30 and 20 per cent, indicating that these societies do not differ significantly in their distribution on this scale.

On the physical-punishment scale, the Philippine sample, with a rank of 4, differs substantially from groups of societies with more extreme ranks. The probability of the differences between the Philippine sample and those of both societies adjacent to it is less than 20 per cent. The probability of the differences among the top three samples on this scale, Mexico, Africa, and India, is greater than 20 per cent, whereas the probability of the difference between the Okinawan and United States samples is approximately 50 per cent.

In summarizing the results of Table 2.3, we can say that the intersociety differences are consistent with the intersociety differences on factor scores, but that they are not as large. Although there are significant intersociety differences on three of the four scales with high loadings on Factor 2, as measured by a chi-square analysis of *all* the societies, no societies of adjacent rank have significantly different distributions on any of the scales.

Age and Sex Differences on Scales

Sex and age of children do not contribute independently to variation of the factor scores for Factor 2. It is possible, however, that there are age or sex differences in particular societies on some of the scales that make up the factor. To check on this possibility, the distributions of scores for each of the warmth scales were divided in terms of age and sex of the children. These data are presented in Tables 2.4 and 2.5.[5]

[5] The data are divided as closely as possible to the median of the total sample. When the median of a particular society is different from the median for the total sample, the division on the basis of the society's median is shown in parentheses. The contingency probabilities for analyses involving individual societies were obtained from the tables computed by Finney (1948) and Latscha (1953). These tables give the exact probabilities for 2×2 contingency tables with a total N of less than 40. These tables were used to assess probability levels for all tables involving age and sex differences in this and subsequent chapters.

Table 2.4   Maternal Warmth Scales: Age Differences

Society		Maternal Warmth		General Hostility	
		Low	High	Low	High
Okinawa	Young[1]	3	7	8	3
	Old[2]	3	7	8	3
Philippines	Young	6	3	4	3
	Old	6	6	5	4
United States	Young	6	6	3	9
	Old	7	5	5	6
Africa	Young	4	4	2	6
	Old	3	5	5	3
Mexico	Young	5	7	2	8
	Old	4	5	2	7
India	Young	5	5	4	4
	Old	9	2	4	5
Total	Young	29	32	23	33
	Old	32	30	29	28

Society		Amount of Praise		Frequency and Intensity of Physical Punishment	
		Low	High	Low	High
Okinawa	Young	3[9]	9[3]	8	4
	Old	1[7]	11[5]	8	4
Philippines	Young	6	5	5	6
	Old	7	5	5	7
United States	Young	7	5	9	3
	Old	8	4	9	3
Africa	Young	3	5	0[0]	8[8] **
	Old	3	5	2[6]	6[2]
Mexico	Young	6	6	0[4]	12[8]
	Old	4	6	2[6]	8[4]
India	Young	8	4	3	9
	Old	8	4	3	9
Total	Young	33	34	25	42
	Old	31	35	29	37

[1] Young = 3–6 years.
[2] Old = 7–10 years.
** $p < .01$.

Table 2.5 Maternal Warmth Scales: Sex Differences

Society		Maternal Warmth		General Hostility	
		Low	High	Low	High
Okinawa	Boys	4	6	9	3
	Girls	2	8	7	3
Philippines	Boys	6	4	4	4
	Girls	6	5	5	3
United States	Boys	8	4	5	6
	Girls	5	7	3	9
Africa	Boys	4	4	4	4
	Girls	3	5	3	5
Mexico	Boys	4	7	2	8
	Girls	5	5	2	7
India	Boys	11	0***	2	6
	Girls	3	7	6	3
Total	Boys	37	25	26	31
	Girls	24	37	26	30

*** = $p < .001$.

Society		Amount of Praise		Frequency and Intensity of Physical Punishment	
		Low	High	Low	High
Okinawa	Boys	3[8]	9[4]	9	3
	Girls	1[8]	11[4]	7	5
Philippines	Boys	8	3	5	6
	Girls	5	7	5	7
United States	Boys	8	4	9	3
	Girls	7	5	9	3
Africa	Boys	3	5	0[2]	8[6]
	Girls	3	5	2[4]	6[4]
Mexico	Boys	3	8	1[6]	10[5]
	Girls	7	4	1[4]	10[7]
India	Boys	9	3	1	11
	Girls	7	5	5	7
Total	Boys	34	32	25	41
	Girls	30	37	29	38

The data on age differences are presented in Table 2.4. There are no age differences in treatment on any of the four warmth scales for the total sample. The only significant difference in treatment of elder children versus younger occurs in the African sample. For this sample, younger children are disciplined by means of physical punishment more frequently than older children. This practice has cultural sanction in the belief that it is improper to whip children after they are circumcised.

The data on sex differences are presented in Table 2.5. Again there are no differences in treatment for the combined sample. There is, however, an interesting sex difference in the Indian sample.

The mothers of the Indians are more hostile to boys than to girls. Mothers of boys, as contrasted to mothers of girls, are rated less warm, more hostile, and more likely to use physical punishment. The probability of the sex difference is .1 per cent for the maternal warmth scale and 10 per cent on the maternal hostility and physical punishment scales. This hostility towards boys is particularly interesting since sons are greatly preferred to daughters in Khalapur, as well as elsewhere in India. The implications of this difference in the treatment of boys versus girls will be discussed in more detail in the chapter dealing with Khalapur.[6]

Hypotheses

The intersociety differences on the maternal warmth factor are smaller than they are for most of the other factors of the study. Evidently maternal affection is more dependent upon individual personality factors than upon cultural determinants. Nevertheless, a cultural division does emerge, in which the Mexican and Indian samples are distinguished from the others. As we shall see, this similarity of the Indian and Mexican samples appears in other factors.

On the maternal warmth factor, these two groups of mothers are, in general, less warm than the mothers of the other samples. Their placement on the individual scales that comprise Factor 2 differs. The Mexican mothers are rated as being both warmer and more hostile than those of the Indian sample, as well as being more generous in their use of both praise and punishment, but none of these differences has a probability that approaches statistical significance.

The Mexican and Indian communities are characterized by the fact

[6] Quotations from interviews for this and subsequent chapters may be found in Appendix 2.

that, in both places, brothers and their families live in dwellings that surround a common courtyard, where their children play with their siblings and first cousins. These living arrangements afford a minimum of privacy. People living in such close quarters can easily irritate each other. Emotional control is therefore essential if the group is to survive. This controlled personality is evidently communicated to the children in the form of a certain coldness, which trains them, in turn, to the same pattern.

The placement of the mothers on the scales suggests that this emotional control is more pronounced in the Indian mothers, who are strangers to each other when they marry and who are confined by the custom of secluding women to their courtyards, than it is for Mexican mothers who have frequently grown up together and can, if necessary, leave the courtyard until tempers cool down. These conditions probably account for their ability to become somewhat less emotionally controlled than the Indian mothers. The lack of warmth of the Indian mothers consists, in large part, of not catering to the temper tantrums or fussiness of children, or to their excessive demands for attention. The necessity of training children early to be somewhat stoic is probably the basis of this unresponsiveness. The reaction of one Indian mother to her child's temper tantrum was the remark, "Do you think you are the only child in this house to be making such a fuss?" In houses where children of several sets of parents must grow up together this attitude is highly functional.

The mothers of the African and Philippine communities are intermediate in their expressions of warmth and their scores on this factor are virtually identical. These women usually live in groups of single family houses that surround, or partially surround, a work area that is used by themselves and the women of other families. These women are co-wives, and perhaps the mother-in-law in the Gusii community and relatives of the husband in Tarong. This work area is not enclosed and may be entered freely by friends, neighbors, and passersby. These societies, therefore, might be characterized as yard societies; they are a type of living arrangement more intimate than courtyard living, but less intimate than isolated single family dwellings. It is not surprising then, in the light of our hypothesis, to find that these two groups of mothers are intermediate on warmth.

Our hypothesis predicts that the Okinawan and New England mothers should be the warmest groups of mothers in the study, since they have the most privacy. The Okinawan mothers are, indeed, the warmest group. They deviate from the mothers of the other groups in their infrequent hostility and their high use of praise. They and the New England mothers use less physical punishment than the mothers of the other groups.

The New England mothers are, however, lower than would be predicted in their placement on this factor. These mothers, as we shall see, spend more time with their children than any other group. Possibly this burden of being the sole caretaker leads these mothers to be controlled in their emotions, both to prevent sibling rivalry for expressions of affection and to prevent themselves from being excessively irrascible from constant supervision of their children. Whereas the courtyard mothers may mitigate emotional expression to avoid friction with their children's cousins and their children's aunts, the New England mothers may do so to prevent friction among siblings and between themselves and their children. If this is the case, then the relationship between maternal warmth and privacy of living arrangements is, in fact, curvilinear, with the warmest mothers being the ones with intermediate privacy.

The suggestion that the extended family structures of Khalapur and Juxtlahuaca necessitate a coolness and lack of affection in the mother-child relations contrasts somewhat with the findings reported by Whiting (1961) that high indulgence of infants occurs in extended family households. It is, however, not unreasonable to suppose that the same excess of personnel that makes for prompt attendance upon infants, also leads to training in emotional control for older children.

Summary

The warmth-of-mother factor is defined by four scales: general warmth of mother, general hostility of the mother, amount of praise used by the mother, and the frequency and intensity of physical punishment used by the mother. The intersociety differences for this factor are not large. The mothers of the Mexican and Indian samples appear to express less warmth, as measured by this factor, than the mothers of the other samples. It is suggested that the conditions of living in a household with other families necessitate a training for emotional control that acts as a damper to spontaneous expression of emotion. The warmth-of-mother factor appears to be a measure of this lack of affect in the mother-child relationship.

The sex and age of children do not affect the warmth of their mothers in a uniform fashion in all six societes. There are, however, important interactions between the age and sex of children, their age and society, and their sex and society that affect the warmth of maternal treatment. There is no substantial relationship between the age of the child and any of the scales that make up the factor except in the African sample, which shows that the African mothers are more likely to use physical punishment with younger children than with older children. There is no relationship between the sex of the child and any of the warmth scales except in the Indian sample. The Indian mothers are generally more hostile, less warm, and more likely to use physical punishment with boys than with girls.

3 ✤ Maternal Instability

Factor Definition

This emotional instability factor is listed as Factor 7 in Table 1.5. It is a measure of the extent to which the mothers' moods are variable and unpredictable. It is defined by two scales:

Mood variation of hostility (scale 8. + .91)
Mood variation of warmth (scale 6. + .74)

Mothers who score high on this factor are subject to wide, frequent, and unpredictable shifts in mood. In the context of the interview upon which the data are based, these shifts of temperament are reported by the mother in the context of her behavior while interacting with her child. Probably these temperamental mothers show similar behavior in other social contexts as well.

The definitions of these two variables reflect both variability and unpredictability of mood. Both scales are defined in terms of their high and low points (ratings of 7 or 1). The end points of the variation of hostility scale are defined as follows.

7—Mother's hostility is extremely variable and due to the mother's impulses rather than any other reason.
1—Mother's hostility does not depend on her moods. Either she does not show her dissatisfaction or her variability is contingent upon the particular situation.

The variation of warmth scale is similarly defined.

7—Mother's warmth and affection are extremely variable and due to the mother's impulses rather than any other reason.
1—Mother's warmth does not depend on her moods. Either she shows little variability in warmth or her variability is contingent upon the situation.

We would expect these two variables to be related to each other. It is difficult to imagine a person whose hostility varies but whose warmth does not,- or vice versa. Table 1.4 shows that there is a correlation between these two scales of +.74.   Since a correlation coefficient of .28 has a probability of .1 per cent for this sample, the probability that a correlation of .74 is due to chance is rare indeed.

There are several indications that unpredictable variation in hostility is a more important determinant of emotional instability than is unpredictable variation in warmth.   Scale 8, mood variation of hostility, has a higher loading on the factor than does scale 6, mood variation of warmth.   Scale 11, general hostility of the mother, has a loading of +.34 on the factor, indicating that emotionally unstable mothers tend somewhat to be generally hostile.   Finally, the two contingency scales, 9 and 10, load differentially on the factor; scale 9 contingency of mothers' warmth, has a loading of +.26 while scale 10, contingency of mothers' hostility, has a loading of −.21.   Although these loadings are low, they do suggest that even emotionally unstable mothers tend to make their warmth contingent upon their child's actions, but that their expressions of hostility do not have such a logical basis.   In view of the volatile nature of aggressive responses it is not surprising that they are important contributors to what we have named "emotional instability."

Variation on Factor Scores

Table 3.1 shows the results of an analysis of variance for age, sex, and society on the factor scores for Factor 7.   The results indicate that differences among societies are the only significant source of variance among the group means.   Table 3.2 shows that this intersociety variance is due largely to the unusual instability of the mothers of the African sample and the unusual stability of the mothers of the Okinawan and Philippine samples.   The African sample, in which 100 per cent of the mothers are more than usually unstable, is ranked first on the factor.   The African sample differs from the United States sample in which 58 per cent of the mothers are above the pancultural mean for instability and which is ranked second on the factor ($p = .006$).   The mothers of the United States, Mexican, and Indian samples do not differ substantially from one another and hold an intermediate position on the factor.   At the low end of the factor are the Okinawan and Philippine mothers, who are significantly more emotionally stable than mothers of other societies ($p = .04$).

Intersociety Differences on Scales

The distribution of the societies on the two scales that define this factor are presented in Table 3.3.   The ratings on scales 6 and 8 are

Table 3.1   Mean Factor Scores for Age and Sex Groups and Analysis of Variance Table for Factor 7: Maternal Instability

	Boys		Girls		
Society	Young	Old	Young	Old	Total Group
Africa	1.00	1.02	1.01	1.04	1.02
United States	.14	.12	.15	.01	.10
Mexico	.01	.49	.43	−.42	.13
India	−.19	.67	−.15	−.27	.02
Okinawa	−.40	−.63	−.01	−.46	−.38
Philippines	−.53	−.70	−.62	−.42	−.57

Source	df	p
Sex	1	NS
Age	1	NS
Society	5	.001
Sex × Age	1	NS
Sex × Society	5	NS
Age × Society	5	NS
Age × Sex × Society	5	NS

Table 3.2   Analysis of Significant Gaps among Societies on Factor Scores

Factor 7: Emotional Instability of Mother

Rank	Society				Percentage of + cases
1	Africa ↕	$Z = 2.78$	$p < .006$		100
2	United States ⎫				58
3	Mexico ⎬	$\chi^2 = .84$	$p > .50$		55
4	India ⎭				46
	↕	$Z = 2.10$	$p < .04$		
5	Okinawa ⎫	$\chi^2 = .09$	$p < .80$		21
6	Philippines ⎭				17

divided as close as possible to the median for the entire sample. Chi-square analyses indicate that there are intercultural differences on both these variables. These between-society differences have probabilities of less than .1 per cent for both variation of maternal warmth and for variation of maternal hostility.

Table 3.3   Emotional Instability Scales: Intersociety Differences

Mood Variation of Hostility

Rank	Society	Low	High	χ^2	p	Percentage of high scores
1	Africa	0	16			100
			↕	4.20	< .05	
2	Mexico	6	14 ⎫			70
3	United States	7	15 ⎭	.016	= .90	68
			↕	2.27	< .20	
4	India	9	7 ⎫			44
5	Okinawa	12	6 ⎬	.53	> .70	33
6	Philippines	11	5 ⎭			31
	Total	45	63	23.38	< .001	

Mood Variation of Warmth

Rank	Society	Low	High	χ^2	p	Percentage of high scores
1	Africa	2	14			88
			↕'	6.45	< .02	
2	United States	12	11 ⎫			48
3	Mexico	11	8 ⎭	.137	= .70	42
			↕	1.39	< .30	
4	India	13	4 ⎫			24
5	Philippines	13	4 ⎬	1.20	> .50	24
6	Okinawa	16	2 ⎭			11
	Total	67	43	28.22	< .001	

The African sample differs from all of the others on both scales ($p < .05$ for hostility variation and $p < .02$ for warmth variation). These are the only intersociety differences that are large enough to reach the probability level, conventionally accepted as indicating that two samples are not drawn from the same population. However, if only the African sample is removed, the overall chi-square value for the remaining five societies still has a probability of less than 5 per cent for variation of hostility and less than 10 per cent for variation of warmth. These low probabilities indicate that substantial intercultural differences are still present. Therefore, the chi-square values for those societies, of adjacent rank, having the second largest gap in their above-mean percentages were computed. These societies are the United States and India for the mood variation of hostility scale and Mexico and India for the mood variation of warmth scale. The probabilities of the differences between these pairs of samples are approximately 20 per cent and 30 per cent, respectively. When these divisions are made there is little doubt that the remaining groups of societies are drawn from the same population.

A comparison of the rankings in Tables 3.2 and 3.3 shows that the rank order of the societies on the two scales which "define" Factor 7 is very similar to their rank order for the factor scores. The African sample is outstandingly high on all three rankings. In all three rankings the United States, Mexican, and Indian samples hold the intermediate ranks. On the factor score ranking, the Indian sample falls in the intermediate group while it is included in the low group for the rankings on both scales. However, the differences between the Indian sample and the United States or Mexican samples are not statistically significant for either scale. The Philippine and Okinawan mothers are the lowest in emotional instability, both in the rank order of the factor scores and the rank order of the ratings themselves.

Age and Sex Differences on Scales

The scales measuring the age and sex of the children are not loaded on Factor 7. It is possible, however, that mothers in particular samples may be consistently more or less emotionally unstable with boys versus girls, or with younger versus older children. Tables 3.4 and 3.5 present the scores on variation of warmth and hostility for each sample of mothers, and the total sample, divided in terms of the age and sex of the children. The division of scores has been made as close as possible to the median of the total sample; the division of scores that is optimal for a 50–50 split for that sample is shown in parentheses.

Table 3.4 shows the data on age differences. The contingency tables for the *total* sample show that there are no differences on emotional instability between mothers of children who are 3 to 6 years old and mothers of children who are 7 to 10 years old.

Turning to the individual societies we find three exceptions to this pancultural finding. The Okinawan mothers are more likely to be variable in their expression of warmth with younger children ($p = .04$). Inspection of the Okinawan distributions indicates that mothers of young children may be either variable or predictable in their expressions of warmth, but mothers of older children are consistently predictable.

Table 3.4   *Emotional Instability Scales: Age Differences*

Society		Mood Variation of Hostility		Mood Variation of Warmth	
		Low	High	Low	High
Africa	Young[1]	$0^{(3)}$	$8^{(5)}$	$1^{(4)}$	$7^{(4)}$
	Old[2]	$0^{(6)}$	$8^{(2)}$	$1^{(7)}$	$7^{(2)}$
United States	Young	$3^{(7)}$	$9^{(5)}$	5	6
	Old	$4^{(7)}$	$7^{(4)}$	7	5
Mexico	Young	1	9	6	4
	Old	5	5	5	4
India	Young	5	3	$7^{(6)}$	$1^{(2)}$
	Old	4	4	$6^{(2)}$	$3^{(7)}$
Okinawa	Young	4	5	$7^{(5)}$	$2^{(4)}$
	Old	8	1	$9^{(9)}$	$0^{(0)}$
Philippines	Young	6	1	$6^{(5)}$	$1^{(2)}$
	Old	5	4	$7^{(5)}$	$3^{(5)}$
Total	Young	19	35	32	21
	Old	26	29	35	22

[1] Young = 3–6 years.
[2] Old = 7–10 years.

Table 3.5   *Emotional Instability Scales: Sex Differences*

Society		Mood Variation of Hostility		Mood Variation of Warmth	
		Low	High	Low	High
Africa	Boys	$0^{(5)}$	$8^{(3)}$	$1^{(6)}$	$7^{(2)}$
	Girls	$0^{(4)}$	$8^{(4)}$	$1^{(5)}$	$7^{(3)}$
United States	Boys	$4^{(8)}$	$8^{(4)}$	6	5
	Girls	$3^{(6)}$	$8^{(5)}$	6	6
Mexico	Boys	2	7	2	7
	Girls	4	7	4	7
India	Boys	3	5	$7^{(5)}$	$2^{(4)}$
	Girls	4	7	$6^{(3)}$	$2^{(5)}$
Okinawa	Boys	7	2	$9^{(8)}$	$0^{(1)}$
	Girls	5	4	$7^{(6)}$	$2^{(3)}$
Philippines	Boys	6	3	$6^{(5)}$	$3^{(4)}$
	Girls	5	2	$7^{(5)}$	$1^{(3)}$
Total	Boys	22	33	31	24
	Girls	23	31	31	25

Okinawan mothers also tend to be more variable with young children in expressions of hostility ($p < .10$). The other exception is that the Indian mothers of older children, unlike their Okinawan counterparts, are more likely to be variable in their expression of warmth than are Indian mothers with young children ($p = .04$). This difference does not hold for the expression of hostility.

The distributions of scores, divided by the sex of the children, are presented in Table 3.5. There are no differences between the emotional instability of mothers of boys and mothers of girls for any society in the sample, or for the combined sample. Evidently boys and girls are equally capable of upsetting their mothers.

Hypotheses

The variance due to differences among societies on the maternal instability factor appears to reflect variation in the stressfulness of the mother's role, caused by prolonged association with the children and responsibility for the care of older children.

The rank order of the societies on maternal instability is approximately the same as their rank order on the factor measuring the amount of time that mothers are responsible for child care (Table 5.2). The United States and African samples are high, the Philippine sample low, and Mexican mothers ranked third, on both factors. The Indian and Okinawan mothers reverse their fourth and fifth place ranks on Factor 7 to fifth and fourth, respectively, on Factor 5. The following excerpts of correlations from Table 1.4 indicate that variation of maternal temperament is correlated with responsibility for the care of older children, but not with responsibility for baby care.

Table 1.4   Excerpts: Intercorrelations of Temperament Scales and Responsibility-for-Child-Care Scales

	Scale Number	Care of Older Children		Care of Babies	
		4	19	20	21
Warmth variation	6	.25**	.27**	−.03	−.11
Hostility variation	8	.07	.22**	.07	−.11

** $p = .01$

It is somewhat surprising that temperamental variation is not associated with responsibility for baby care since this would seem to be as tiring a chore as the care of older children. The picture becomes clearer if we add the factor of confinement of the mothers in addition to her child care responsibilities.

The mothers of the African sample are confined to their homes by virtue of their economic responsibilities. These mothers not only have almost complete responsibility of the care of children, but must, with the help of their children, farm the gardens and care for the herds allotted to them by their husbands. They are, as a group, the busiest and most harassed of all the mothers in our study. This harassment is evidently reflected in their temperamental instability.

Suspicious of their hostile co-wives, whom they often view as witches, and their husbands' relatives, who may be their own families' enemies, overburdened with work in their fields, which they do without their husbands' help, plagued with the responsiblity of keeping their own children out of trouble with their neighbors and with the necessity of being hypocritically friendly with people they may hate, these mothers are extremely irritable and unpredictable with their children. They frequently cane children, particularly the younger ones; they expect instant obedience but may ignore disobedience if their children absent themselves until their anger is abated.

It is interesting that both the Filipino and African mothers, at opposite ends of the instability factor, have cooperative work groups. In the Philippines they function smoothly but among the African Gusii they are fraught with arguments.

The mothers of the New England sample are confined to their homes with preschool children by virtue of their isolation from an extended kin group and the fact that older children are in school and therefore unavailable to care for younger children.

The New England mothers are intermediate on both warmth and stability. These mothers are very conscious of their children's moodiness and more permissive about bad temper than mothers in other samples. Isolated from other families and with only their own children to cope with, these mothers can afford to respond to individual differences and temporal variations in their children's personalities. However, their sympathy is checked by their constant contact with their children, by their exclusive and often trying responsibility for them, and sometimes by their own personal ambitions and preferences. Their behavior vascillates between self-conscious warmth and sympathy and impatience born of the fatigue of being constantly "on duty" and the frustration of personal desires.

The Mexican and Indian mothers live in houses or rooms around a common courtyard which they share with their sisters-in-law. They are living in closer contact with other women and their children than are the mothers in any other group, and must do their work in constant contact with the children of their husbands' brothers as well as their own. Most of the Mexican children do not go to school. In the Indian sample many girls do not attend school and young boys only go for half the day. Even though this makes the older children available to help with the care of younger children, it also adds to the congestion of the courtyard. Further, the 6- to 8-year-old children, who are too young to be of much help in household chores, are at home rather than in school. The result is that the minor confusion which usually accompanies the activities of groups of children is confounded by the larger number of children in the house. This situation calls for considerable tact and self-control to avoid quarrels. Emotional display and moodiness cannot be tolerated.

The mothers in the Philippines and Okinawa have both privacy and help with child care. Unlike the mothers of the African and Mexican samples, they live close to an extended group of relatives with whom they are usually on friendly terms. Grandmothers, aunts, or neighbor women help with the care of children when mothers are busy or must leave home. Okinawan mothers spend several hours a day working away from home and leave young children with a grandmother or older child. Unlike the mothers in Mexico and India, however, the Philippine and Okinawan mothers do not share their living quarters with their kin. Most nuclear families have their own houses, surrounded by a yard. Although women may work together they may also retire to their own homes when they want to be away from their neighbors. Most of the children in the Philippine and Okinawan communities go to school, so they are away from the mothers' working areas during part of the day. When home from school, older children often carry babies, providing their mothers with additional baby-care help.

Before leaving this discussion, a negative finding of some interest should be noted. Temperamental instability is not generally related to the degree to which mothers have responsibilities other than child training, particularly those which take them away from home. Although the African mothers, the most temperamental of the group, do have the most extensive economic tasks, the data of the other groups suggest that it is the necessity of coercing children into helping with the chores, rather than the mothers' own work, that leads to instability. The New England mothers must do their housework without help, but the majority of them do not work outside their homes, and do not need to farm or process raw food products. The Mexican and Philippine mothers go to markets to sell produce; yet the Mexicans are fairly temperamental, while the Philippine mothers are the most stable of the groups studied. The Okinawan mothers work away from home cutting firewood, a long and tiring task, but they are the equals of the Filipino mothers in their good natures. Finally, the Rajput mothers of the Indian sample are prevented by the custom of seclusion from ever working outside their courtyards. Although they have much to do within their courtyards, their tasks are almost never such that they cannot be set aside to care for children; yet these mothers are medium, not low, in emotional instability. In short, the data does not lend itself to the popular interpretation that role conflict increases friction between mothers and their children. It may be that few tasks are as harassing as caring for small children, and the increased responsibility of other duties is compensated for by the respite from child care.

The interpretation that the observed variation in maternal temperament is the result of structural factors inherent in the cultures is strengthened by the fact that the stability of the mothers does not vary with the sex of the children and seldom varies with the children's age. The two exceptions to invariance of mothers' temperament with childrens' age are interesting. The Indian mothers have more trouble controlling children as the children grow older and spend more time outside the courtyards where their mothers cannot follow them. In Okinawa, on the other hand, it is the younger children who, in curtailing the time the mother spends away from home collecting firewood to sell, evoke the greatest impatience.

Summary

The emotional instability factor is defined by two scales, mood variation of hostility and mood variation of warmth. Loadings of other scales on the factor indicate that emotionally unstable mothers tend to be generally hostile and that their hostility is more unpredictable than their warmth.

The African mothers are, as a group, more unstable emotionally than the mothers of other societies. They are more unpredictable than other groups both in their expression of hostility and in their expression of warmth. The mothers of the New England, Mexican, and Indian samples are more stable than the African mothers, but less stable than the Okinawan and Philippine mothers. Analysis of intersociety differences on the two scales that define the factor indicates that the New England, Mexican, and Indian mothers maintain this intermediate position on both scales but do not differ significantly from the Okinawan or Philippine groups in terms of the distribution of their raw scores.

Maternal instability is, for the most part, unrelated to the age of the child. Exceptions to this rule occur in Okinawa, where mothers of young children are often more variable in their expression of warmth and hostility than are the mothers of older children, and in India, where the mothers are less consistent in their expressions of warmth with older children than with younger children. The emotional instability of the mothers is not systematically related to the sex of the child in any of the communities included in the study.

The factors determining between-group differences in maternal instability appear to be the degree to which mothers are responsible for the care of older children and the degree to which they are in constant contact with their children.

4 ❖ Mother's Responsibility for Baby Care

Factor Definition

Factor 4 in Table 1.5 is defined by two scales.

Proportion of time that mother cared for baby (scale 20, $+.72$)
Proportion of time that other adult cared for baby (scale 21, $-.46$)

Let us make clear that neither of these scales refers to the actual amount of *time* spent *with* the baby, but rather to the proportion of time that the mother versus some adult other than the mother or father is in *charge* of the infant. Both scales are rated on a dimension from "never" to "always." The points of scales 20 and 21 are defined as follows:

1—Never
3—Sometimes
5—Half the time
7—Usually
9—Always

Thus, mothers with high scores on Factor 4 were the primary caretakers when their children were babies, that is, during the first year or year and a half of the children's lives. A high score does not imply that the mother necessarily spent a high proportion of her time nurturing, fondling, or playing with the infant. It is worth noting that the loading on scale 20, proportion of time that mother cared for baby, is considerably higher than the loading of scale 21, proportion of time that other adult cared for the baby. It is variation in the proportion of baby-tending responsibility assigned to the *mothers* that is of primary importance for this factor. The correlation between scales 20 and 21 is $-.36$. Although probability of occurrence by chance of this size correlation is less than .1 per cent, it is considerably lower than some other correlations in Table 1.4 that have been described in connection with other factors.

93

Since Factor 4 represents a measure of the delegation of responsibility for babies and not time actually devoted to caring for them, it is not surprising that personality characteristics of the mothers are relatively unrelated to it. However, some scales which measure characteristic maternal behavior do have moderate loadings on the factor. Three of these scales indicate that mothers who are the primary caretakers of their babies tend to be more bland but also less predictable in their emotional reactions when their children are older than mothers who had less baby-care responsibility, that is, they tend not to praise their children (scale 13, —.31) or to respond aggressively when the children become angry (scale 13, —.28). However, their hostility is not contingent upon their children's behavior (scale 13, —.31), which would indicate that they may be (from the child's view) unpredictably aggressive. In short, they may be expressing their own emotional needs or frustrations which arise from other aspects of their roles. Furthermore, these mothers with high factor scores are neither coherent nor consistent about stating and enforcing rules. They do not communicate rules well (scale 11, —.29), and they are inconsistent concerning rules about the aggressive behavior of their children (scale 12, —.21). Because all these practices refer to behavior directed to the children when they are older, and since the responsibility for baby tending is independent of responsibility for the care of older children, we must interpret these findings cautiously. But it seems not unreasonable that mothers who must be the primary or only responsible overseers of their babies would learn to control their aggression. Since these mothers are probably more accustomed to their children's characteristic behavior than mothers who share baby care with others, it is also not unreasonable that this familiarity might make them sparing of their praise and informal about their rules. It is possible that these mothers feel a "oneness" with their children due to a sense of knowledgeable control of the children, or because the mothers become more identified with them, that makes explicit rules unnecessary.

Variation on Factor Scores

The results of an analysis of variance by age, sex, and society are presented in Table 4.1. The results show that the society to which the mother belongs is the only main effect of significance. The effect is due largely to the high position of the United States sample on this factor (see Table 4.2).

The probability of the difference between the United States sample and the Okinawan sample, which is ranked second, is 1 per cent. The

Table 4.1   Mean Factor Scores for Age and Sex Groups and Analysis of Variance Table for Factor 4: Proportion of Time That Mother Cared for Baby

Society	Boys		Girls		Total Group
	Young	Old	Young	Old	
United States	.85	.54	.52	.01	.48
Okinawa	−.39	−.03	−.01	−.07	−.12
Philippines	−.45	−.02	.12	−.42	−.18
India	.39	.43	−.78	−.39	−.09
Mexico	−.75	.28	.12	.48	.01
Africa	−.47	−.37	−.43	.68	−.15

Source	df	p
Sex	1	NS
Age	1	NS
Society	5	.05
Sex × Age	1	NS
Sex × Society	5	.01
Age × Society	5	NS
Age × Sex × Society	5	NS

Table 4.2   Analysis of Significant Gaps among Societies on Factor Scores

Factor 4:
Proportion of Time That Mother Cared for Baby

Rank	Society			Percentage of + cases
1	United States			79
	↕	$Z = 2.60$	$p = .01$	
2	Okinawa			50
3	Philippines			43
4	India	$\chi^2 = 1.69$	$p > .70$	42
5	Mexico			41
6	Africa			31

factor scores of the remaining five societies belong to the same population
$(p > .70)$.

Because neither the age nor the sex of the children had high loadings
on this factor, we would not expect these variables to contribute independently to between-mean variance. There is a significant interaction
between society and the sex of the child which is occasioned by the fact
that the United States and Indian mothers spend more time with baby
boys while the Mexican and African mothers spend more time with
baby girls, and the Okinawan and Philippine mothers spend approximately equal amounts of time with babies of either sex.

Intersociety Differences on Scales

Our data include two scales concerning caretaking agents of infants
that were not included in the factor analysis, proportion of time that
father cared for the baby and proportion of time that a child cared
for the baby. These ratings were made on the 9-point scale previously
described. The reason for excluding these judgments from the factor
analysis is that their variance is small. As one can see from Table 4.2,
97 out of 134 children, or 72 per cent, were *never* cared for by an
older child, leaving relatively few cases distributed over the remaining
points on the scale. Fifty-one out of 132 fathers, or 39 per cent, *never*
care for the baby. This percentage is not particularly high, but of the
fathers who do care for the baby, 56 per cent received a rating of 3,
indicating that they did this "sometimes." Therefore, 95 per cent of
the fathers were included on only two points of the scale.

Data from these scales are presented in Tables 4.3 and 4.4 since these
data are relevant to the general topic of caretakers and their variability
is adequate for a simple dichotomous analysis. The reliability of the
scale proportion of time that father cared for the baby is .80, and the
reliability of the scale proportion of time that a child cared for the
baby is .84, as measured by Pearson r correlation coefficients.

In Table 4.3 we see the distribution of societies on the four scales
measuring baby-tending responsibility: the two scales that define the
factor (i.e., the proportion of time that the mother or some adult other
than the parents cared for the baby), and the two additional scales
reflecting the proportion of time that the father or an older child cared
for the baby. Inspection of the overall chi-square values indicates
that there are significant intersociety differences on all four scales.

The distribution of societies on scale 20, proportion of time that
mother cares for baby, is virtually the same as their distribution on the
factor scores. The mothers in the United States sample have a significantly heavier burden (or joy) of baby care than the mothers in any

other society $(p < .01)$. Ninety-two per cent of the United States mothers usually or always care for their babies; one-third of these mothers did all the care of their babies. The remaining societies do not differ substantially from one another and are ranked in the same order as their ranking on the factor scores. The minor exception is that the Mexican and Indian samples, ranked fourth and fifth respectively on the factor scores, are ranked fifth and fourth respectively on scale 20. Since this is the only scale with a really high loading on Factor 4, we would expect that the distribution of scores in this scale would conform to the distribution of factor scores.

The distribution of scores on the other three scales in Table 4.3 is much less similar to the factor scores distribution. Despite the fact

Table 4.3   Caretaking of Baby Scales: Intersociety Differences

Proportion of Time Mother Cared for Baby

Rank	Society	Never to half the time	Usually to always	χ^2	p	Percentage of high scores
1	United States	2	22			92
			↕	7.11	< .01	
2	Okinawa	10	14			58
3	Philippines	12	12			50
4	Mexico	11	11	1.83	> .70	50
5	India	13	11			46
6	Africa	10	6			38
	Total	58	76	15.66	< .01	

Proportion of Time Other Adult Cared for Baby

Rank	Society	Never	Sometimes to always	χ^2	p	Percentage of high scores
1	Philippines	4	20			83
			↕	2.31	< .20	
2	Mexico	8	14			64
3	Okinawa	11	13			54
4	United States	14	10	6.76	> .10	42
5	India	14	9			39
6	Africa	12	4			25
	Total	63	70	16.03	< .01	

Table 4.3 (Continued)   Caretaking of Baby Scales: Intersociety Differences

Proportion of Time Father Cared for Baby

Rank	Society	Never	Sometimes to half the time	χ^2	p	Percentage of high scores
1	Philippines	4	20⎫			83
2	United States	5	19⎬	0.55	> .70	79
3	Mexico	5	17⎭			77
			↕	2.18	< .20	
4	Okinawa	10	13			56
			↕	2.19	< .20	
5	India	15	8⎫	0.42	> .30	35
6	Africa	12	4⎭			25
	Total	51	81	26.60	> .001	

Proportion of Time Child for Baby

Rank	Society	Never	Sometimes to usually	χ^2	p	Percentage of high scores
1	Africa	5	11			69
			↕	2.88	< .10	
2	Mexico	13	9⎫			41
3	Philippines	18	6⎪			25
4	India	19	5⎬	6.41	> .10	21
5.5	United States	21	3⎪			12
5.5	Okinawa	21	3⎭			12
	Total	97	37	25.86	< .001	

that the *overall* chi-square analyses reveal significant intersociety differences, there are no significant differences between societies of adjacent ranks on any of these *single* scales. In the adjacent-rank analysis of Table 4.3, the societies are presented in the minimum number of groups that permit societies included within one group to have no less than a 10 per cent probability that the differences between them are due to chance. In two instances, the probability that societies included in a subgroup are actually drawn from the same population is less than 20 per cent.

Table 4.4 *Caretaking of Baby Scales: Sex Differences*

Society		Proportion of Time Mother Cared for Baby		Proportion of Time Other Adult Cared for Baby	
		Never to half the time	Usually to always	Never	Sometimes to always
United States	Boys	2	10	8	4
	Girls	0	12	6	6
Okinawa	Boys	5	7	5	7
	Girls	5	7	6	6
Philippines	Boys	7	5	2[7]	10[5]
	Girls	5	7	2[7]	10[5]
India	Boys	5	7	8	4
	Girls	8	4	6	5
Mexico	Boys	8	3	4	7
	Girls	3	8	4	7
Africa	Boys	4	4	6	2
	Girls	6	2	6	2
Total	Boys	31	36	33	34
	Girls	27	40	30	36

Society		Proportion of Time Father Cared for Baby		Proportion of Time Child Cared for Baby	
		Never	Usually to half the time	Never	Sometimes to usually
United States	Boys	2	10	11	1
	Girls	3	9	10	2
Okinawa	Boys	5	7	11	1
	Girls	5	6	10	2
Philippines	Boys	3	9	9	3
	Girls	1	11	9	3
India	Boys	8	4	9	3
	Girls	7	4	10	2
Mexico	Boys	2	9	4	7
	Girls	3	8	9	2
Africa	Boys	7	1	3	5
	Girls	5	3	2	6
Total	Boys	27	40	47	20
	Girls	24	41	50	17

On the other factor-defining scale (scale 21), proportion of time that some other adult cared for baby, the Philippine sample is deviantly high ($p < .20$), although not significantly so. When the Philippine sample is removed the probability of differences among the remaining societies is approximately 20 per cent.

The Philippine sample is also ranked first on the percentage of fathers who care for babies. However, on this scale the Philippine sample does not differ from the United States and Mexican communities ($p > .70$). In all three communities over three-fourths of the fathers sometimes care for babies. These three samples differ somewhat from the Okinawan sample, where 56 per cent of the fathers care for babies ($p < .20$). The Okinawan sample differs, in turn, from the Indian and African samples where a minority of fathers act as baby tenders ($p < .20$). The Indian and African samples do not differ from each other ($p = > .30$). In no society does any father tend to the baby more than half the time.

The African sample is the only one in which a majority of the babies are sometimes cared for by an older child. This society differs from the others ($p < .10$), while the remaining societies form a relatively homogenous group ($p > .10$).

Age and Sex Differences

Table 4.4 shows the breakdown of the baby caretaker scales by the sex of the child cared for. Inspection of the contingency tables for the total sample shows again that there is no pancultural relationship between the sex of the child and who cares for it. Only the significant relationships appear in Table 4.4, both in the Mexican sample. The Mexican mothers are more likely to act as primary caretaker if the baby is a girl ($p = .04$), while baby boys are, more frequently than girls, placed in the care of older children ($p = .04$).

Hypotheses

It seems fairly clear that the intersociety differences on the baby care factor are due primarily to the availability of alternate caretakers. The mothers of Orchard Town, living as they do in nuclear family households isolated from their kinsmen, spend more of their time in charge of their children than the mothers of any other group. This isolation from a kin group not only means that other women are not around to help with baby care, but that the number of older children who may help is also less, since child caretakers may be cousins as well as siblings. This isolation of the New England mothers is enhanced by the fact that their older children are in school and their husbands work away from home. The New England fathers are not unusually high in the degree to which they care for babies, despite the fact that they are the only group of adults who can relieve the mothers of their baby-tending chores. As we shall see, they are more helpful with older children.

The New England mothers are unusual in their isolation. The factor scores of the mothers of the other groups appear to be drawn from the same population, with respect to their responsibility for baby care. The differences among societies in the scales that measure the extent to which persons other than the mothers care for children are also small, and we will comment on them only briefly.

The African sample is unusual in the degree to which older children care for babies. This probably reflects the autonomy of the mother-children household that is peculiar to polygynous societies where each wife has her own living unit. Fathers in the African and Indian samples seldom care for children. This isolation of the father from his family is primarily a function of polygamy among the Gusii and the seclusion of women among the Rajputs. The unusual degree to which the Philippine mothers help each other with baby care appears to be related to their geographical proximity to a group of women who are relatives by both blood and marriage. The Mexican mothers, who are also related and living close together, are ranked second on the scale measuring baby care by nonparental adults. We might expect them to be even higher on this scale. Evidently the greater tendency of the Mexican mothers to use older children, who unlike the Philippine children are not in school, as baby tenders lowers their use of other women for this purpose. This difference will become more apparent when we examine the data on the care of older children.

The New England group is the only one that deviates in terms of the factor scores. The differences among societies on the individual scales do not clearly differentiate them into separate groups. This may suggest that, given the availability of some kin group who can act as potential "baby sitters," the extent to which they actually do fulfill this service depends more upon the interpersonal relationships and kinship ties of particular individuals than upon the number of potential mother substitutes in the group as a whole.

Summary

Factor 4, the proportion of time that mother is responsible for the care of the baby, is defined by two scales: scale 20, proportion of time that mother cared for the baby, and scale 21, proportion of time that an adult other than the parents cared for the baby. These scales do not measure the time spent actually caring for babies, but rather the relative importance of the mother's responsibility for the baby as opposed to others' responsibility. Moderate loadings on other scales indicate that mothers who are the primary or only caretakers of their babies are fairly "flat" in their emotional reactions to their older children. They do not respond aggressively when the children are angry with them, or make their hostility contingent upon their children's behavior. They praise infrequently. They are also fairly informal about rules since they do not communicate them well and are inconsistent about their enforcement.

The United States sample is the only one that is significantly deviant from the others on this factor. Orchard Town mothers take more of the responsibility for their babies than the mothers of any other community in the study. They have, as a group, the highest factor scores and the highest ratings on scale 20. The Philippine sample is deviantly high on the proportion of babies cared for by adults *other* than the parents.

Two scales concerning caretaking agents, which, because of low variance, were not included in the factor analysis are included in the chi-square analyses of this chapter. These are proportion of time that *father* cared for baby and proportion of time that a *child* cared for baby. In the Philippines, the United States, and Mexico a majority of the fathers sometimes care for babies. These societies differ from the Okinawan sample where about half of the fathers sometimes care for infants. The Okinawan sample differs in turn from the Indian and African samples, where a minority of fathers ever care for infants. The African sample is deviant in that it is the only sample where a substantial majority of babies are cared for by older children. The other societies form a relatively homogenous group on this last variable.

An analysis of variance shows that, in addition to a significant effect due to society, there is an interaction between society and the sex of babies occasioned by mothers in different societies spending unequal amounts of time with male versus female babies. The only relationships between identity of caretakers and the sex of the children cared for occur in the Mexican sample where baby boys are more likely to be cared for by older children, while baby girls are more likely to be cared for by their mothers.

The order of the societies is tentatively interpreted as being based primarily on the degree to which the mothers are living near to relatives who can serve as substitute caretakers.

5 ❖ Mother's Responsibility for Child Care

Factor Definition

Factor 5 is a surprise. Why, in short, should *two* independent factors appear which deal with such *apparently* related facets of child training? This factor exists, however, and it is defined by two scales that represent two measures of the same variable: the proportion of time that the mother cared for her *child at the time of the interview,* i.e., when the child was 3–10 years old.

> Proportion of caretaking done by mother (scale 4, +.74)
> Proportion of time mother spends with child (scale 19, +.54)

Scale 4 is a rating on a 7-point scale based on the entire interview. The points of this scale are defined as follows:

> 7—Mother takes complete care of the child
> 4—Mother shares care equally with others
> 1—Mother does none of the caretaking

Scale 19 is rated on the same 9-point scale described earlier, where 1 represents "never" and 9 represents "always." The rating was based on specific questions concerning the identity of caretakers. The correlation between scale 4 and scale 19 is +.43.

Mothers with high factor scores on this factor are the chief caretaking agents for their children, who may be anywhere from 3 to 10 years old. Like the scales described in relation to the factor dealing with *baby* care, these scales do not measure the amount of time that the mother actually spends caring for the *child,* but only the *proportion* of time that she is responsible for his care.

No additional scales have loadings of greater than .30 on this factor, although several scales have loadings a bit lower. It is most interesting that these scales seem to indicate that mothers who have the primary responsibility for the care of *older children* have personality characteristics that are in some ways similar, and in some ways quite the opposite of those mothers who are the primary caretakers for their *babies*. Like the mothers who have heavy baby-care responsibilities, mothers who are the primary caretakers of older children seem to tend to be unpredictable in their emotional expressiveness. Their warmth tends to be variable (scale 6, +.27), and their hostility, although not variable (scale 8, +.10), tends not to be contingent upon the behavior of their children (scale 10, −.29). Whereas the baby-tending mothers tended *not* to praise their children, the *child-tending* mothers tend not to manipulate gifts and privileges to control them (scale 16, −.22). Unlike the mothers with high scores on Factor 4, who did not communicate rules well and were inconsistent about aggression rules, mothers with high scores on Factor 5 *do* communicate rules clearly (scale 11, +.21) and also tend to reward their children for peer-directed aggression (scale 17, +.24).

Since babies are helpless, cannot be aggressive, and cannot understand complex communication, it seems possible that mothers who must bear the burden of caring for such infants generalize the behavior that is necessarily appropriate to the babies to their older children, and hence fail to communicate with them clearly or to encourage them to be aggressive. Mothers who must deal with older children, on the other hand, probably learn that clear rules and the encouragement of aggressive self-reliance diminish the burden of their task.

Variation on Factor Scores

Table 5.1 shows the results of the analysis of variance for age, sex, and society on the factor scores for Factor 5. The significant main effect of between-society differences is due largely to the high position of the United States and African mothers on this factor (see Table 5.2). Variations in treatment of younger versus older girls and boys from society to society leads to an interaction between age, sex, and society. The tendency for the United States and Mexican mothers to spend more time caring for older girls than for younger girls appears to be the most obvious cause of this interaction.

Intersociety Differences on Scales

In addition to the ratings of the times that mothers spend as caretakers, ratings were made on the proportion of time that the father, adults other than the mother and father, and older children spend as caretakers. These ratings were made on the same 9-point scales which were described earlier, and which were used for scale 19. Be-

Table 5.1   Mean Factor Scores for Age and Sex Groups and Analysis of Variance Table for Factor 5: Proportion of Time That Mother Cares for Child

	Boys		Girls		Total Group
Society	Young	Old	Young	Old	
United States	.79	.53	.69	.75	.69
Africa	.54	.38	.72	.20	.46
Mexico	.24	−.07	−.44	.16	−.03
Okinawa	−.11	−.34	−.27	.15	−.14
India	−.37	−.38	.14	−.47	−.27
Philippines	−.12	−.84	−.84	−.45	−.58

Source	*df*	*p*
Sex	1	NS
Age	1	NS
Society	5	.001
Sex × Age	1	NS
Sex × Society	5	NS
Age × Society	5	NS
Sex × Age × Society	5	.05

Table 5.2   Analysis of Significant Gaps among Societies on Factor Scores

Factor 5:
Proportion of Time That Mother Cared for Child

Rank	*Society*			Percentage of + cases
1	United States	$\chi^2 = 0.95$	$p > .30$	92
2	Africa			81
		$Z = 2.29$	$p = .02$	
3	Mexico			55
4	Okinawa	$\chi^2 = 4.60$	$p > .10$	50
5	India			38
6	Philippines			26

cause of their low variability these judgments were not included in the factor analysis. They are, however, included in the remaining tables of this chapter, along with the judgments on scales 4 and 19. The reliability of the judgments of the proportion of time that the father cares for the child is .87; for "other adult" it is .90. The reliability of the judgments on the proportion of time that the child was cared for by another child is considerably lower, only .41. This low reliability coefficient is due, in part at least, to the fact that 78 per cent of the total number of sample children are *never* cared for by an older child, so that most of the judgments on this scale are "1."

Table 5.3 shows the results of analyses of intersociety differences on the five separate scales which measure the proportion of time that various

Table 5.3   Caretaking of Child Scales: Intersociety Differences

Proportion of Caretaking Done by Mother

Rank	Society	Low	High	χ^2	p	Percentage of high scores
1	Africa	2	14	0.00	=1.00	88
2	United States	3	20			87
				4.09	<.05	
3	Mexico	9	13	0.38	>.50	59
4	Okinawa	12	12			50
				1.41	<.30	
5	India	16	7	0.00	=1.00	30
6	Philippines	16	7			30
	Total	58	73	28.09	<.001	

Proportion of Time Mother Cares for Child

Rank	Society	Low	High	χ^2	p	Percentage of high scores
1	United States	2	22			92
				3.49	<.10	
2	Africa	5	11			69
				1.38	<.30	
3	Okinawa	12	12			50
4	Mexico	13	9			41
5	India	17	6	5.80	>.10	26
6	Philippines	19	5			21
	Total	68	65	32.17	<.001	

Table 5.3 (Continued) Caretaking of Child Scales: Intersociety Differences

		Proportion of Time Other Adult Cares for Child				
Rank	*Society*	Low	High	χ^2	p	Percentage of high scores
1	Philippines	3	21	0.01	> .90	88
2	Mexico	3	19			86
				6.41	< .02	
3	India	12	11			48
4	Africa	11	5	4.86	> .10	31
5	United States	18	6			25
6	Okinawa	18	5			22
	Total	65	67	42.10	< .001	

		Proportion of Time Father Cares for Child				
Rank	*Society*	Low	High	χ^2	p	Percentage of high scores
1	United States	1	23			96
				4.18	< .05	
2	Philippines	6	18			75
3	Okinawa	7	16	0.47	= .80	70
4	Mexico	8	14			64
				1.14	< .30	
5	India	12	11	0.41	= .80	48
6	Africa	10	6			38
	Total	44	88	20.67	< .001	

		Proportion of Time Child Cares for Child				
Rank	*Society*	Low	High	χ^2	p	Percentage of high scores
1	Mexico	10	12			55
				5.15	< .05	
2	Okinawa	18	5			22
3	Africa	13	3			19
4	Philippines	20	4	2.85	> .60	17
5	India	20	3			13
6	United States	22	2			8
	Total	103	29	16.56	< .01	

caretakers are in charge of the children. The overall chi-square values show that there are significant between-society differences on all five scales. The United States and African samples are high on the proportion of time that mothers care for the children. On scale 4, the proportion of caretaking done by mothers, these societies do not differ from each other ($p = 1.00$) but they do differ from the remaining four communities ($p < .05$). The remaining four communities fall into two groups: (1) Mexico and Okinawa, where from 50 to 59 per cent of the scores are high; and (2) India and the Philippines where 30 per cent of the scores are high. The probability of a difference between the Okinawan and Indian samples is less than 30 per cent.

On the scale, proportion of time that mother cares for child, the United States and African samples are again higher than the other societies, but they also differ from each other ($p < .10$). The probability of the difference between the African sample, which is ranked second, and the Okinawan sample, which is ranked third, is only 20 per cent. However, if the African sample is included in this "low" group the probability of intersociety differences is less than 2 per cent; without it the probability is greater than 10 per cent.

The Philippine and Mexican samples are high on the proportion of children who are cared for by an adult *other* than the parents. These communities do not differ from one another on this variable ($p > .90$), but they do differ from the other societies ($p < .02$). The probability of intercultural differences among the remaining four societies on this variable is greater than 10 per cent.

The United States sample ranks first on the proportion of *fathers* who sometimes care for children. This New England sample differs from the Philippine sample, which is ranked second on this variable ($p < .10$). In the Philippine, Okinawan, and Mexican samples a majority of the fathers sometimes care for children, while in the Indian and African communities, a minority do so.

The proportion of children who are cared for by another child is highest in the Mexican sample. This is the only community where a majority of children, 55 per cent, are sometimes placed in the care of other children. The Mexican sample differs from the others ($p < .05$). The scores of the remaining societies seem to be drawn from the same population ($p > .60$).

Age and Sex Differences on Scales

Tables 5.4 and 5.5 show the results of analyses of these scales in terms of the age and sex of the children. Inspection of the contin-

Table 5.4   Caretaking of Child Scales: Age Differences

Society		Proportion of Time Mother Cares for Child		Proportion of Caretaking Done by Mother	
		Never to half the time	Usually to always	Low	High
United States	Young[1]	0	12	1	10
	Old[2]	2	10	2	10
Africa	Young	1	7	0	8
	Old	4	4	2	6
Mexico	Young	7	5	7	5
	Old	6	4	2	8
Okinawa	Young	6	6	6	6
	Old	6	6	6	6
India	Young	9	3	6	5
	Old	8	3	10	2
Philippines	Young	9	3	8	3
	Old	10	2	8	4
Total	Young	32	36	28	37
	Old	36	29	30	36

Society		Proportion of Time Other Adult Cares for Child		Proportion of Time Father Cares for Child	
		Never	Sometimes to always	Never	Sometimes to always
United States	Young[1]	9	3	0	12
	Old[2]	9	3	1	11
Africa	Young	4	4	4	4
	Old	7	1	6	2
Mexico	Young	3	9	5	7
	Old	0	10	3	7
Okinawa	Young	8	4	4	8
	Old	10	1	3	8
India	Young	4	5	7	4
	Old	8	6	5	7
Philippines	Young	2[6]	10[6]	2	10
	Old	1[7]	11[5]	4	8
Total	Young	30	35	22	45
	Old	35	32	22	43

[1] Young = 3–6 years.
[2] Old = 7–10 years.

Table 5.4 (Continued)   *Caretaking of Child Scales: Age Differences*

Proportion of Time Child Cares for Child

Society		Never	Sometimes to always
United States	Young[1]	11	1
	Old[2]	11	1
Africa	Young	7	1
	Old	6	2
Mexico	Young	6	6
	Old	4	6
Okinawa	Young	10	2
	Old	8	3
India	Young	9	3
	Old	11	0
Philippines	Young	12	0
	Old	8	4
Total	Young	55	13
	Old	48	16

[1] Young = 3–6 years.
[2] Old = 7–10 years.

Table 5.5   Caretaking of Child Scales: Sex Differences

Society		Proportion of Caretaking Done by Mother		Proportion of Time Mother Cares for Child	
		Low	High	Never to half the time	Usually to always
United States	Boys	2	10	0	11
	Girls	1	10	2	11
Africa	Boys	1	7	2	6
	Girls	1	7	3	5
Mexico	Boys	3	8	7	4
	Girls	6	5	6	5
Okinawa	Boys	6	6	6	6
	Girls	6	6	6	6
India	Boys	9	3	9	3
	Girls	7	4	8	3
Philippines	Boys	8	3	9	3
	Girls	8	4	10	2
Total	Boys	29	37	34	33
	Girls	29	36	35	32

Table 5.5 (Continued)   *Caretaking of Child Scales: Sex Differences*

Society		Proportion of Time Other Adult Cares for Child		Proportion of Time Father Cares for Child	
		Never	Sometimes to always	Never	Sometimes to usually
United States	Boys	9	3	0	12
	Girls	9	3	1	11
Africa	Boys	7	1	5	3
	Girls	4	4	5	3
Mexico	Boys	2	9	6	5
	Girls	1	10	2	9
Okinawa	Boys	10	1	2	9
	Girls	8	4	5	7
India	Boys	6	6	6	6
	Girls	6	5	6	5
Philippines	Boys	2[9]	10[3]	4	8
	Girls	1[4]	11[8]	2	10
Total	Boys	36	30	23	43
	Girls	29	37	21	45

Society		Proportion of Time Child Cares for Child	
		Never	Sometimes to usually
United States	Boys	12	0
	Girls	10	2
Africa	Boys	6	2
	Girls	7	1
Mexico	Boys	3	8
	Girls	7	4
Okinawa	Boys	8	3
	Girls	10	2
India	Boys	10	2
	Girls	10	1
Philippines	Boys	11	1
	Girls	9	3
Total	Boys	50	16
	Girls	53	13

gency tables for the total sample indicates that there are no systematic pancultural relationships between identity of caretaking agents and sex or age of the children for whom they care.   Only two significant relationships appear in these two tables, both are in the data from the Philippine sample.   In this sample the older children are more likely to be cared for by another child than are younger children, and girls are cared for more frequently than boys by an adult other than the parents.

Hypotheses

It is somewhat surprising to find that the mothers' responsibility for the care of older children is largely independent of her responsibility for the care of babies.   It becomes more surprising in view of the fact that the main determinant of between-society differences appears to be the same for both factors, namely the availability of substitute caretakers.   Although a number of other factors, some of them specific to particular societies, appear to be influencing the degree to which mothers care for older children, the relative importance of substitute caretakers is still of paramount importance.

An inspection of the scales concerned with the caretakers of babies and older children indicates that the ordering of societies on the scales for baby care is not entirely independent of their ordering on the scales for child care.   The New England sample is deviantly high on both scales, while the Okinawan, Indian, and Mexican mothers maintain middle positions on both scales.   The African and Philippine mothers shift in their responsibility for children as the children become older. Let us look more closely at these comparisons.

The New England mothers maintain exactly the same position on the scale for child care that they held on the scale for baby care; 92 per cent of the mothers are above the pancultural mean on both scales, placing them in first position on both scales.   The heavy responsibility of these mothers for child care continues as the children grow older, despite the fact that the New England fathers help with the care of older children, more than with the care of babies.   Indeed all but one of the New England fathers sometimes help with child care.   They are the only deviant group on the scale measuring paternal care of children, and they join their wives in their unusually high position on this variable. The exclusive responsibility of the parents for child care is further emphasized by the fact that only 25 per cent of the older children are sometimes cared for by a nonparental adult and only 8 per cent of them are ever cared for by another child.

Living in nuclear families isolated from their relatives and with all their older children in school most of the day the New England mothers spend more time in charge of both babies and older children than any other group.   They are the only mothers who must sometimes resort to hiring an unrelated person to care for their children.   The exclusiveness of the responsibility of the American mothers is reinforced by their self-consciousness about their maternal role and their distrust of other people's methods for handling children.   Some mothers are reluctant to let grandparents care for children and may not give grandparents the authority to punish children even when they are allowed to act as caretakers.

The mothers of our African sample shift dramatically from the lowest rank in proportion of time they care for babies to second place, below the New England mothers but higher than any other group in the proportion or time they care for older children.

Apparently the African mothers make heavy use of other children in the care of their babies, but make less use than other cultures do of older children in the care of the child when he has reached a reasonable age.   Other adults are sometimes available to take some responsibility for the child from the African mothers, but the fathers, who are so often absent, still cannot help.   It appears, then, that in Africa the mother takes over greater care of her offspring when he gets old enough to help in the economy; the increased care includes carefully overseeing her children in their care of the baby, as well as in their active work in heavy chores.   This indicates that the low position of the African mothers on the responsibility for babies factor is perhaps deceptive; the children are caring for babies but the mothers are closely supervising the child caretakers, with little assistance from their husbands, co-wives, or in-laws.

The African mothers spend more time in charge of older children than the mothers of the above four groups.   These mothers live in mother-child households and often have co-wives as their nearest neighbors. They may not be on good terms with their co-wives because of jealousies and suspicions.   Grandparents care for children if they are around, but they have too many grandchildren to give extensive help.   Older children are placed in official charge of babies but mothers are usually in charge of older children, although they may simply "keep an eye" on these children while they tend to their domestic chores.   Fathers are rather distant and authoritarian and do little to care for children except to guide their sons when the latter come to help them work.

The Mexican, Okinawan, Philippine, and Indian mothers are relatively low in the proportion of time they care for both babies and older children.   In all of these societies women are living near to their sisters-in-law and mothers-in-law. The Philippine, Okinawan, and Mexican mothers may also be living near their own blood relatives, since all of these communities are partially endogamous. Grandmothers and aunts help with children in all these societies, particularly in the Philippines and Mexico. The Okinawan mothers spend several hours a day away from home and leave young children with a grandmother or older children when they are not in school. Older children are also used to care for younger children, particularly in Mexico where they seldom go to school. Indian girls are also unlikely to attend school but their status of "guests" in their own homes makes mothers reluctant to burden them with extensive baby care duties. Fathers may help care for children in Okinawa and in the Philippines where they are expected to take over when their wives are confined from childbirth. The Indian fathers sometimes take their sons with them to work or to the men's quarters but seldom care for older girls or babies.

Adult female relatives appear to be particularly helpful as caretakers for older children. If we compare the percentage of time that mothers care for babies as opposed to older children, we note that the United States and African mothers are the only ones who spend a greater proportion of their time caring for older children than they do caring for babies. The mothers of all other groups spend less time caring for older children than for babies.

This difference is greatest for the mothers of the Philippine example. Whereas 50 per cent of these mothers usually care for babies, only 21 per cent of them usually care for older children. This decline in the mothers' responsibility for child care is not accompanied by a commensurate increase in the responsibility of other caretakers. These mothers continue to be unusual in the degree to which they rely on other women to help them with their children, since nonparental adults are even more important in the care of older children than they were with babies. However, fathers and older children have less responsibility for older children than they had for babies. Evidently the care of these children is diffuse. Mothers appear to be willing to leave older children to their own devices, secure in the knowledge that anyone of their neighbors would see that they did not get into trouble.

The shift of responsibility of the Indian mothers is only slightly less than that of the mothers of the Philippine community. Forty-six per cent of the mothers of the Indian sample usually care for their babies, while 26 per cent of them usually care for older children. In the Indian case, however, the slack is taken up specifically by other women in the family and by fathers who sometimes care for boys who are helping with the farmwork, although they still care for boys infrequently relative to fathers in other groups.

The Mexican and Okinawan mothers drop only slightly in their responsibility for older children. In Mexico other women and children take over the responsibility relinquished by the mothers. In Okinawa fathers and older children act as substitutes. Other women are less often caretakers of older children than of babies in Okinawa. The analysis of child-care responsibility seems to indicate that availability of other caretakers is the chief factor determining the extent to which this duty falls to the mothers.

Why then are there two factors for child care, when the antecedents seem to be the same? The answer to this puzzle will have to await further research. It may well be that a more extensive analysis may reveal only one child-care factor. However, two things should be considered in interpreting the present findings.

First, it must be remembered that the factor structure is not influenced by the scales measuring the extent to which fathers and older children act as caretakers, or by the scale measuring the amount of care of older children done by adults other than the parents, since these scales were not included in the factor analysis. Their importance lies in clarifying what happens to children when their mothers are not caring for them.

Second, each factor is based on the loadings of all the scales in the analysis, not just those which we have used to define it. It will be remembered that several scales with moderately high loadings presented somewhat different pictures of the variables related to the care of infants as opposed to older children. Mothers who have heavy baby-tending duty do not communicate rules well, while mothers who chiefly care for older children emphasize clear rules. Baby-tending mothers are low in use of praise, while child-tending mothers are low in use of privileges. Evidently these two groups of mothers have rather different methods of child rearing. It may be that the independence of the factors stems from these subsidiary characteristics.

Summary

Factor 5, proportion of time that mother cares for child, is defined by two scales that are similar measures of the same variable: scale 4, proportion of caretaking done by mother, and scale 19, proportion of time that mother cares for child. These scales measure the time that the mother is in *charge* of her child, not the time she actually spends interacting with him. Moderate loadings on other scales indicate that mothers who are primarily responsible for the care of their children are variable in their expressions of warmth and do not gear their hostility to the behavior of their children. In this respect they are similar to the mothers who have the primary responsibility of caring for their babies. However, unlike the mothers who are the primary caretakers for babies, the mothers who are the primary caretakers of older children communicate the rules clearly and tend to reward their children for peer-directed aggression. They also tend not to control their children through the manipulation of gifts and privileges.

The United States and African samples are high on Factor 5. Although there are substantial intersociety differences among the remaining societies, there are no further significant differences between societies of adjacent ranks on the factor score distribution.

Three scales which were not included in the factor analysis have been added to the chi-square analyses presented in this chapter. These are the proportion of time that the children were cared for by their fathers, by older children, or by adults other than the parents. The United States sample is high, not only in the proportion of time that mothers are responsible for their children, but also in the proportion of fathers who sometimes care for children. The Philippine and Mexican samples are high in the number of children who are cared for by adults other than the parents, and the Mexican sample is also high on the number of children who are cared for by older children.

There is significant interaction between society and the age and sex of children on this factor. The only significant relationships, for a particular society, between the age or sex of children and the identity of their caretakers occurs in the Philippine sample, where older children are more likely to be cared for by another child than are younger children, and girls are more likely to be cared for by an adult other than the parents.

Our tentative interpretation of the cultural orderings on this overall factor refers the ordering to the degree to which the alternate caretakers are trusted to replace the parental socializing agent. This appears to be very much the case in the Philippines and in India, but not to be the case in New England or in Africa.

6 ❖ Responsibility Training

Factor Definition

The factor that has been called "Responsibility Training" is defined in terms of three scales: the child's age, the frequency with which he or she performs chores, and the number of types of chores that the child performs. This factor differs from the others in that it represents behavior of the child, rather than the mother. Furthermore, since chores assigned by persons other than the mother were included in the ratings, the factor measures the mother's report about other people's behavior, as well as her own. This is not true of the other factors.

The factor is defined by three scales:

Total frequency of chores (scale 24, +.64)
Total number of chores (scale 25, +.69)
Age of child (scale 28, =.56)

The variable frequency of chores is rated on a 7-point scale ranging from never to several times daily. The variable number of chores is scored from 1 to 10. The score for each child on this scale represents the sum of the number of types of chores listed in Tables 6.3 and 6.4, plus a miscellaneous category that the child performs. Thus, a boy who gathers wood, feeds an animal, and runs errands would receive a score of 3 on this dimension. The age of the children is scored from 3 to 10 years old.

The correlations among the raw scores of these variables are presented in Table 1.4. They are as follows.

Table 1.4   Excerpt: Intercorrelations of Defining Scales for Factor 1

Scale Number	24	Scale Number 25
25	.43**	
28	.31**	.39**

** $p < .01$

These three scales are the only ones with loadings of greater than .30 on this factor. It seems clear that the factor measures the extent to which children share in the responsibility of carrying out the families' daily routine tasks. The loading on age indicates that, as might be expected, older children are expected to do more chores and to do them oftener than younger children.

Variation on Factor Scores

Table 6.1 shows that the age of children is the only significant contributor to variation among means for this factor. An inspection of the group means indicates that in all societies older children of both sexes are expected to be more responsible than younger children. The analysis of between-society differences in factor scores presented in Table 6.2 confirms the finding that there are no significant differences between societies on the responsibility training factor ($p > .30$).

Table 6.1   Mean Factor Scores for Age and Sex Groups and Analysis of Variance Tables for Factor 1: Responsibility Training

Society	Boys		Girls		Total Group
	Young	Old	Young	Old	
Philippines	−.10	.50	−.42	.62	.15
Mexico	−.23	.16	−.28	.51	.04
United States	−.42	.53	−.45	.87	.13
Africa	−1.02	1.07	−.53	.52	.24
Okinawa	−.92	.81	−.62	.27	−1.15
India	−.82	.34	−1.20	.41	−.32

Source	df	p
Sex	1	NS
Age	1	.001
Society	5	NS
Sex × Age	1	NS
Sex × Society	5	NS
Age × Society	5	NS
Sex × Age × Society	5	NS

Table 6.2   Analysis of Societal Ranks on Factor Scores

Factor 1: Responsibility Training

Rank	Society	Percentage of + cases
1	Philippines	61
2.5	Mexico	54
2.5	United States	54
4	Africa	50
5	Okinawa	42
6	India	33

Intersociety Differences on Scales

Although there are no significant intersociety differences on the factor scores for Factor 1, there are intersociety differences on the two scales that define the factor. This rather odd result is evidently caused by the minor but cumulative loadings of other scales on this factor that negate the societal differences on assignment of chores.

Table 6.3 shows the analysis of intersociety differences on the frequency with which children do chores and the number of types of chores they perform. The first part of the table presents the data on the total frequency and number of chores, e.g., two of the three scales that define Factor 1. The latter part of the table presents the data for the individual chores that were added to construct the total frequency and number scales.

The scale total number of chores refers to the variety of chores that children are expected to perform in terms of the classification of chores in the latter part of the table. The data are divided between one chore and more than one chore, a division that is as close as possible to the median of the overall sample. The analysis shows that the mothers of the Mexican, Philippine, and African samples expect their children to do more chores than do the mothers of the United States, Okinawan, and Indian samples.

The data on the total frequency of chores is divided into three groups: less than daily, daily, and several times daily. The overall chi square has a probability of less than 1 per cent, so there are between-society differences on this scale. The societies are ranked in terms of their percentage of high scores, following the procedure of the tables in preceding chapters. In this case the classification is somewhat misleading, since the only significant intersociety difference is between the United States and India, societies that have tied ranks on their percentage of high scores. An inspection of the table shows that this differences is occasioned by the fact that fewer children in the Indian sample do chores daily.

If the societies are divided, as indicated by the analysis of total fre-

Table 6.3   Responsibility Scales: Intersociety Differences

		Total Number of Chores				
Rank	Society	0–1	2–6	χ^2	p	Percentage of high scores
1	Mexico	2	20			91
2	Philippines	3	20	2.66	>.20	87
3	Africa	4	12			75
				4.31	<.05	
4.5	United States	14	10			42
4.5	Okinawa	14	10	0.53	>.50	42
6	India	16	8			33
	Total	53	80	31.05	<.001	

		Total Frequency of Chores					
Rank	Society	Less than daily	Daily	Several times daily	χ^2	p	Percentage of high scores
1	Africa	5	2	9			56
2	Philippines	8	4	11			48
3	Mexico	5	9	8			36
4.5	United States	6	12	6			25
4.5	India	14	4	6			25
6	Okinawa	11	10	3			13
	Total	49	41	43	24.11	<.01	
	Africa + Mexico + Philippines	18	15	28			
	United States + India + Okinawa	31	26	15	9.48	<.10	

Table 6.3 (Continued)   Responsibility Scales: Intersociety Differences

Care of Siblings

Rank	Society	No	Yes	χ^2	p	Per cent Yes
1	Okinawa	16	8			33
2	Philippines	16	7			30
3	Mexico	17	5			23
4	India	19	5			21
5	Africa	13	3			19
6	United States	22	2			8
	Total	103	30	5.90	>.30	
	Total %	77%	23%			

Help Cook

Rank	Society	No	Yes	χ^2	p	Per cent Yes
1	Africa	10	6	1.56	>.30	39
2	Philippines	17	6			26
3	Mexico	17	5	1.84	<.20	23
4	Okinawa	22	2			8
5	United States	22	2	3.13	>.20	8
6	India	24	0			0
	Total	112	21	13.64	<.02	
	Total %	84%	16%			

Clean House

Rank	Society	No	Yes	χ^2	p	Per cent Yes
1	United States	3	21			88
2	Okinawa	12	12	7.85	<.01	50
3	Mexico	13	9			41
4	Philippines	16	7	3.58	>.30	30
5	India	18	6			25
6	Africa	16	0	3.11	<.10	0
	Total	78	55	29.14	<.001	
	Total %	59%	41%			

Carry Water

Rank	Society	No	Yes	χ^2	p	Per cent Yes
1	Africa	4	12	.005	>.90	75
2	Mexico	8	14			64
3	Philippines	18	5	8.09	<.01	22
4	India	21	3	4.96	>.20	12
5	Okinawa	21	3			12
6	United States	24	0			0
	Total	96	37	39.20	<.001	
	Total %	72%	28%			

Table 6.3 (Continued)   Responsibility Scales: Intersociety Differences

Gather Wood

Rank	Society	No	Yes	χ²	p	Per cent Yes
1	Philippines	14	9			39
2	Africa	10	6	1.32	>.50	38
3	Mexico	17	5			23
4	Okinawa	23	1	3.49	<.10	4
5	United States	24	0	.004	>.98	0
6	India	24	0			0
				25.10	<.001	
	Total	112	21			
	Total %	84%	16%			

Feed and Water Animals

Rank	Society	No	Yes	χ²	p	Per cent Yes
1	Mexico	15	7			32
2	Philippines	16	7			30
3	India	19	5			21
4	Okinawa	19	5			21
5	Africa	13	3			19
6	United States	22	2			8
				4.33	>.50	
	Total	104	29			
	Total %	78%	22%			

Pasture Animals

Rank	Society	No	Yes	χ²	p	Per cent Yes
1	Philippines	15	8			35
2	Africa	14	2	2.46	<.20	13
3	Mexico	21	1			5
4	India	23	1	2.69	>.50	4
5	United States	24	0			0
6	Okinawa	24	0			0
				26.24	<.001	
	Total	121	12			
	Total %	91%	9%			

Help in Fields and Gardens

Rank	Society	No	Yes	χ²	p	Per cent Yes
1	Africa	8	8			50
2	Mexico	18	4	4.34	<.05	18
3	Philippines	19	4			17
4	India	21	3	9.56	>.05	13
5	United States	24	0			0
6	Okinawa	24	0			0
				28.20	<.001	
	Total	114	19			
	Total %	86%	14%			

Table 6.3 (Continued) *Responsibility Scales: Intersociety Differences*

Run Errands

Rank	Society	No	Yes	χ^2	p	Per cent Yes
1	Mexico	8	14			64
			↕	8.85	< .01	
2	Philippines	16	7 ⎞			30
3	India	18	6 ⎟			25
4	United States	19	5 ⎬	3.07	> .50	21
5	Africa	13	3 ⎟			19
6	Okinawa	22	2 ⎠			8
	Total	96	37	11.28	< .05	
	Total %	72%	28%			

quency of chores, and a chi square computed on the difference between the combined distribution of the Mexican, Philippine, and African samples versus the United States, Okinawan, and Indian samples, we find that the chi square for this analysis is 9.48 with a probability of less than 10 per cent.

This division is fairly faithfully reflected in the distributions of the societies on the number of children who are expected to perform the various chores included in the number of chores scale. An inspection of the latter half of Table 6.2 shows that the Mexican, African, and Philippine children are in the top ranks (in some order) in the chores of cooking, carrying water, gathering wood, pasturing animals, and helping in fields and gardens. Further, two of these three societies are in the top three ranks for all other chores except cleaning house. It seems clear that the children of these three communities are expected to do more varied chores than the other children of the study.

Before accepting this conclusion, however, it should be noted that when, as in some societies, no children in the sample do certain chores, such total absence of assignment may indicate either that children are believed to be too young for that particular task or that the job does not exist in that society. In the latter case it is not, of course, a valid measure of responsibility for that group.

Care of younger children, cooking, cleaning house, feeding and watering animals, and running errands are jobs that must be done in all societies. Girls are not asked to cook in the Indian community because the task is considered to be too hard for them. Housecleaning in the African community is a relatively light job and always done by mothers. All groups have some gardens, although not all families have gardens in New England. In New England and in Okinawa children do not help with gardening. All of these cases represent real nonassignment of a possible task.

Sometimes, however, this is not the case. The United States is the only society where none of the children ever carry water. The absence of this chore in the United States is due to the presence of running water in the homes which makes the task unnecessary.

Children never gather wood in the United States or Indian samples, and only one child has the chore of gathering wood in Okinawa. In the United States sample wood was not generally used as fuel for either heating or cooking. Such wood as was used was usually purchased. In India cow dung cakes are the staple fuel for cooking. Wood is scarce since virtually all of the land is under cultivation. Such wood as was used for kindling was obtained by stripping branches from trees owned by the family. This work was done by the men. In Okinawa firewood represents the major source of cash income. There has been heavy depletion of the trees near the sample village of Taira. Because of this depletion the villagers must walk about a mile uphill to reach the area where trees are still available. The Maretzkis report that adults of both sexes and some children over the age of 12 clear trees. It is not a task for younger children.

No children pasture the animals in the United States and Okinawa. The American families do not have grazing animals. In Okinawa few families have horses and cattle are not used for plowing; goats are raised, but they are never left to graze.

In one instance the New England children are scored as perhaps more responsible than they really are. Eighty-eight per cent of these children are scored as helping with the housework, significantly more than in any other group. For the Orchard Town sample the job of picking up toys was coded as housecleaning. Since the children in other societies have very few toys relative to the American children this particular task was seldom mentioned by any other mothers. American children may also be expected to tidy up their own rooms, put away their clothes, etc. As the children in most other societies do not have rooms of their own, this task also appears much less frequently in interviews with mothers not from the United States. It might be argued that, since in both these tasks the children are only cleaning up after themselves, this should not be given as much weight as when children help with the general housework. If picking up toys and putting away clothes is coded as housecleaning, then we find that only four girls and four boys actually help with the housecleaning. The boys' contribution to housework mainly consists of wiping dishes, although one boy empties wastebaskets and one helps make the beds. This recount moves the United States to rank 3, between Mexico and the Philippines, and makes Africa, where no children clean house, the only society which differs significantly from the others on this variable.

Therefore, three of the chores, carrying water, gathering wood, and pasturing animals do not exist in the New England neighborhood and not all families have gardens. Two chores, gathering wood and pasturing animals, are not possible for children in Okinawa, and one, gathering wood, does not exist in the Indian sample. The low position of the New England children certainly seems to be at least partially due to the technological development that makes their services unnecessary.

Since all chores are present in the Mexican, Philippine, and African samples, the high position of these societies on the scale measuring the total number of chores is somewhat exaggerated. However, if we take only those chores that are necessary in all of the samples, caring for young children, cooking, cleaning house, feeding and watering animals, helping in the fields and running errands, we find that the Mexican children are in the first three ranks on all of them, and the Philippine children are in the first three ranks on all but one of them, i.e., cleaning house. The African sample is high on only two of these chores, cooking and helping in the fields. However, their low position on three of these scales appears to be due to errors of the interview and scoring. The African children do not usually care for other children who are old enough to get around themselves. On the other hand, Table 3.2 shows that 69 per cent of them do care for babies. Evidently the mothers interpreted this question to refer to older children. The African boys do pasture animals, since they usually take the herd to pasture by a river there is no need for separate watering. Furthermore, these children rank first in frequency of chores. All things considered, it seems that the children of these three groups do more work than the other children in the study.

Age and Sex Differences on Scales

An obvious question that might be asked about this factor is whether or not the positive relationship between relatively advanced age, increased frequency, and number of chores holds in all the societies of the sample. Is it always the case that older children have more chores to do and do them more frequently than younger children?

Data pertaining to this question are presented in Table 6.4 in the form

Table 6.4   Frequency and Number of Chores: Age Differences

		Total Frequency of Chores			Total Number of Chores	
		Less than daily	Daily	Several times daily	Low 0–1	High 2–6
Okinawa	Young[1]	10	1	1***	10	2*
	Old[2]	1	9	2	4	8
Philippines	Young	5	3	3	3[9]	8[2]
	Old	3	1	8	0[3]	12[9]
India	Young	10	0	2*	10	2
	Old	4	4	4	6	6
United States	Young	3	7	2	10	2*
	Old	3	5	4	4	8
Mexico	Young	4	3	5	1[9]	11[3]
	Old	1	6	3	1[6]	9[4]
Africa	Young	4	1	3	4	4
	Old	1	1	6	0	8
Total	Young	36	15	16***	38	29***
	Old	13	26	27	15	51

		Take Care of Siblings		Help Cook		Clean House		Carry Water	
		No	Yes	No	Yes	No	Yes	No	Yes
Okinawa	Young[1]	9	3	11	1	9	3*	12	0
	Old[2]	7	5	11	1	3	9	9	3
Philippines	Young	7	4	11	0**	8	3	10	1
	Old	9	3	6	6	8	4	8	4
India	Young	11	1	12	0	9	3	11	1
	Old	8	4	12	0	9	3	10	2
United States	Young	11	1	12	0	1	11	12	0
	Old	11	1	10	2	2	10	12	0
Mexico	Young	10	2	10	2	6	6	5	7
	Old	7	3	7	3	7	3	3	7
Africa	Young	6	2	8	0***	8	0	3	5
	Old	7	1	0	8	8	0	1	7
Total	Young	54	13	64	3***	41	16	53	14
	Old	49	17	46	20	37	29	43	23

* $p < .05$.
** $p < .01$.
*** $p < .001$.
[1] Young = 3–6 years.
[2] Old = 7–10 years.

Table 6.4 (Continued) Frequency and Number of Chores: Age Differences

		Gather Wood		Feed and Water Animals		Pasture Animals	
		No	Yes	No	Yes	No	Yes
Okinawa	Young[1]	12	0	11	1	12	0
	Old[2]	11	1	8	4	12	0
Philippines	Young	7	4	9	2	9	2
	Old	7	5	7	5	6	6
India	Young	12	0	11	1	12	0
	Old	12	0	8	4	11	1
United States	Young	12	0	12	0	12	0
	Old	12	0	10	2	12	0
Mexico	Young	9	3	8	4	12	0
	Old	8	2	7	3	9	1
Africa	Young	7	1	6	2	8	0
	Old	3	5	7	1	6	2
Total	Young	59	8	57	10	65	2*
	Old	53	13	47	19	56	10

		Help in Fields or Gardens		Run Errands	
		No	Yes	No	Yes
Okinawa	Young[1]	12	0	11	1
	Old[2]	12	0	11	1
Philippines	Young	11	0	5	6**
	Old	8	4	11	1
India	Young	11	1	11	1
	Old	11	1	8	4
United States	Young	12	0	10	2
	Old	12	0	9	3
Mexico	Young	11	1	3	9
	Old	7	3	5	5
Africa	Young	7	1***	6	2
	Old	1	7	7	1
Total	Young	64	3**	46	21
	Old	51	15	51	15

* $p < .05$.
** $p < .01$.
*** $p < .001$.
[1] Young = 3–6 years.
[2] Old = 7–10 years.

of chi-square analyses. The first entry the table presents the associations between age and frequency of chores. The frequency with which children may do chores was originally rated on a 7-point scale. For the purpose of these analyses the scale has been condensed to three parts, which as nearly as possible divide the cases into three equal divisions: less than daily, daily, and several times a day. The chi-square value for the total sample has a probability of .1 per cent, as would be expected from the loadings of these variables on the factor.

Among the individual societies, however, the chi-square value reaches a probability of less than 5 per cent in Okinawa and India only, although the trend in all societies is for older children to perform chores more frequently than younger children. This tendency is least pronounced in the United States, largely because of the fact that children under the age of 6 are usually expected to pick up their toys and straighten their rooms.

The second entry in Table 6.4 shows the relationship between age of the child and the number of kinds of chores that he is expected to do. Again the chi-square value for the overall sample has a probability of .1 per cent. The relationship between age and number of chores is positive for all societies except Mexico, and has a probability of less than 5 per cent in the Okinawan and Indian samples.

The Philippine and Mexican samples present a problem in this analysis because the break between one chore or none and two chores or more is not the best breaking point for these societies since virtually all children have at least two chores. In parentheses are presented the chi-square analysis where the cases have been divided as close as possible to their own median for number of chores. The dividing line for the Philippine sample is between two and three chores, and for the Mexican sample between three and four chores. When this is done the relationship between number of types of chores and age becomes positive for the Mexican sample, although not significantly so. For the Philippine sample, the association has a probability of less than 5 per cent.

In summary, the positive relationship between age and frequency of performing chores and the positive relationship between age and number of types of chores are consistent for all societies in the study. Both these relationships attain acceptable levels of significance for the Okinawan sample. The positive association between age and frequency of doing chores is also significant for the Indian sample. The positive association between age and the number of kinds of chores performed has a probability of 5 per cent or less for the Okinawan, Philippine, and United States samples.

The latter half of Table 6.4 presents the data on age differences in the performance of individual chores. An inspection of the table shows that the chores of caring for younger siblings, carrying water, gathering wood, and feeding and watering animals are assigned with little regard for age, within the age range of the study, in all six societies. There are no age differences in the total sample for the chores of cleaning house and running errands, but older children are more likely to clean house in Okinawa, and younger children are more likely to run errands in the Philippines.

In general older children are more likely than younger ones to help cook, pasture animals, and help in the field. These age differences are significant for the overall sample and there is no society in which these relationships are reversed. However, the differential assignment of these chores by age is not pronounced in most societies. Younger children are never asked to cook in the Philippines or Africa, and only one young child helps in the fields in Africa. So few children in any group pasture animals that this trend does not reach significance for any single group.

The sex of the child is not a scale that has a high loading on the responsibility factor. In general boys and girls are assigned about the same number of chores and expected to do them with about the same frequency. This finding is somewhat contrary to the results found by Barry, Bacon, and Child (1957) in a cross-cultural study of differences in socialization as related to the sex of the child. These authors found that responsibility training is usually emphasized most strongly in the training of girls. However, of the types of behavior studied by these authors, responsibility showed the most variation among societies in the relative emphasis for boys versus girls.

Table 6.5 presents the relationship of the sex of the child to frequency of doing chores and the number of chores assigned for the separate samples in our study. It may be that the type of relationship which Barry et al. found exists in some of the societies of our study.

The chi-square analysis for the total sample shows that, as would be expected from the factor loadings, there is no relationship between sex and responsibility training for the overall sample. There is no relationship between sex and the number of chores assigned for any of the society samples. In each of the communities in this study boys and girls do approximately the same number of chores. It is not always true, however, that they do them with the same frequency. In the United States sample, half of the girls and none of the boys do their chores several times a day. This represents a difference in frequency of assignment of chores that has a probability of only 2 per cent. This is the only society where there is a significant difference in the frequency with

Table 6.5   *Frequency and Number of Chores: Sex Differences*

		Total Frequency of Chores			Total Number of Chores	
		Less than daily	Daily	Several times daily	Low 0–1	High 2–6
Okinawa	Boys	6	4	2	6	6
	Girls	5	6	1	8	4
Philippines	Boys	4	0	7	1 [6]	10 [5]
	Girls	4	4	4	2 [6]	10 [6]
India	Boys	6	0	6	9	3
	Girls	8	2	2	7	5
United States	Boys	4	8	0*	8	4
	Girls	2	4	6	6	6
Mexico	Boys	2	4	5	1 [8]	10 [3]
	Girls	3	5	3	1 [7]	10 [4]
Africa	Boys	3	2	3	2	6
	Girls	2	0	6	2	6
Total	Boys	25	18	23	27	39
	Girls	24	21	22	26	41

		Take Care of Siblings		Help Cook		Clean House		Carry Water	
		No	Yes	No	Yes	No	Yes	No	Yes
Okinawa	Boys	7	5	12	0	9	3*	10	2
	Girls	9	3	10	2	3	9	11	1
Philippines	Boys	9	2	8	3	10	1*	8	3
	Girls	7	5	9	3	6	6	10	2
India	Boys	10	2	12	0	12	0**	11	1
	Girls	9	3	12	0	6	6	10	2
United States	Boys	11	1	12	0	2	10	12	0
	Girls	11	1	10	2	1	11	12	0
Mexico	Boys	9	2	11	0**	8	3	5	6
	Girls	8	3	6	5	5	6	3	8
Africa	Boys	7	1	6	2	8	0	3	5
	Girls	6	2	4	4	8	0	1	7
Total	Boys	53	13	61	5	49	17***	49	17
	Girls	50	17	51	16	29	38	47	20

*$p < .05$.
**$p < .01$.
***$p < .001$.

Table 6.5 (Continued) *Frequency and Number of Chores: Sex Dif-*
ferences

		Gather Wood		Feed and Water Animals		Pasture Animals	
		No	Yes	No	Yes	No	Yes
Okinawa	Boys	11	1	7	5*	12	0
	Girls	12	0	12	0	12	0
Philippines	Boys	6	5	6	5	5	6
	Girls	8	4	10	2	10	2
India	Boys	12	0	7	5*	12	1
	Girls	12	0	12	0	11	0
United States	Boys	12	0	10	2	12	0
	Girls	12	0	12	0	12	0
Mexico	Boys	9	2	5	6*	10	1
	Girls	8	3	10	1	11	0
Africa	Boys	7	1	6	2	6	2
	Girls	3	5	7	1	8	0
Total	Boys	57	9	41	25***	57	10*
	Girls	55	12	63	4	64	2

		Help in Fields or Gardens		Run Errands	
		No	Yes	No	Yes
Okinawa	Boys	12	0	11	1
	Girls	12	0	11	1
Philippines	Boys	10	1	8	3
	Girls	9	3	8	4
India	Boys	10	2	9	3
	Girls	11	1	9	3
United States	Boys	12	0	11	1
	Girls	12	0	8	4
Mexico	Boys	7	4	4	7
	Girls	11	0	4	7
Africa	Boys	4	4	7	1
	Girls	4	4	6	2
Total	Boys	55	11	50	16
	Girls	59	8	46	21

*$p < .05$.
**$p < .01$.
***$p < .001$.

which girls versus boys do chores. The direction of relationship between frequency of doing chores and sex is not always in favor of greater responsibility for girls. In Africa girls tend to do chores more often than boys, but in the Philippines and India boys work somewhat more frequently than girls.

Our responsibility indices, then, do not show the same consistency of emphasis on female responsibility training that was reported by Barry, Bacon, and Child. Since this study includes only six societies, this finding cannot be interpreted as a refutation of the previous result. Furthermore, we get the impression from the content of the mothers' reports that, although the frequency with which boys and girls perform chores is about the same, the chores of the girls are sometimes more time consuming.

Although the sex of the child is not a measure that is related to the total number of chores that a child does, or to the frequency with which he or she does them, we might expect that certain kinds of tasks would be assigned more frequently to boys, while others would be assigned to girls. Data pertaining to these questions are presented in the latter half of Table 6.5. The types of chores are listed across the top of the table in the same order of presentation as in Table 6.4.

The chores of caring for siblings, carrying water, gathering wood, helping in the fields, and running errands are assigned without regard for the sex of the children. Children below the age of 10 are rarely asked to cook in any of our samples. When this task is assigned, it tends to be assigned to girls, particularly in Mexico. Girls are also chosen to clean house more often than are boys, particularly in Okinawa and in India. Boys are usually assigned to the tasks of feeding and pasturing animals, when they are cared for by children. In Okinawa, India, and Mexico, feeding and watering of animals is definitely a boy's task. Subtle differences are apparent in the approach of both mothers and children to learning of responsibility: the enthusiasm of Okinawan girls, the versatility of the Philippine children, the careful codification of rules by the American mothers. In all societies, however, the same basic trend defined by the factor appears, a gradual increase as the child grows older in the variety of chores he is expected to perform and the frequency with which he is expected to perform them.

Hypotheses

Since the between-society differences on this factor are small and appear only on the scales and not on the factor scores, any hypotheses about them must be tentative. The intersociety differences on the variety of chores done by children and, to a lesser extent, the frequency with which they do them seem to be related to the degree to which the mothers contribute independently to the families' finances.

The African mothers, with their children's help, support themselves and their children and, with their other co-wives, contribute to their husbands' food supply. The Mexican and Philippine mothers go to market regularly to sell or barter produce. These three groups of women expect their children to contribute more help in the running of the household than do the others in the sample.

The Okinawan mothers gather firewood along with their husbands and, at the end of the day, the wood of the entire family is sold together, so that their financial contribution is not separate. In New England some of the mothers work, but most are housewives who contribute only labor to their families. In India the restrictions of seclusion prevent any of the mothers from working outside their homes and restricts the labor contribution that they make to the family work. These mothers probably expect less from their children than any other group.

The expectations of mother concerning responsible behavior in children appear to be related to beliefs about the age at which children become responsible.

There is considerable cross-cultural uniformity of beliefs about the age at which children are thought to be capable of being instructed and responsible for their own actions in the absence of adults. In most samples children are believed to achieve this capacity at about the age of 6 or 7.

Mothers in our African sample begin to train responsible behavior earlier than other mothers. They begin to send their children on errands when they are 2 years old. However, they do not expect the process of responsibility training to be complete until initiation, which takes place for girls when they are 7 to 8 years old and for boys when they are 10 to 12. Between the ages of 2 and 8 children learn to do most adult tasks. They are excluded only from those jobs which would greatly tax their strength. Boys between the ages of 8 and the time they are initiated are usually not introduced to new responsibilities, but spend their time herding cattle and helping in the fields, as they did in younger years.

The designation of the age of responsibility is most explicit in the Mexican and Okinawan samples. The Mexican mothers believe that children gain "awareness" at the age of 2, at which time they become capable of learning by imitation. At the age of 6 or 7 they acquire the ability to reason and are thereafter teachable until the age of 18 when their character is "set." In Okinawa children are "godlike" until the age of 6. This "godlike" nature is senseless and untrainable. When they reach 6 years of age they outgrow this personality and become responsible and trainable.

The Philippine belief, although less explicit, is very similar to that of the Okinawan mothers. Children are believed to begin to have "sense" at the age of 4, when they begin to be trainable, and are expected to be sufficiently responsible to do chores without being asked by the time they are 6 years old.

The samples of India and the United States have the latest estimates of the age of responsibility. Children in Khalapur are not considered ready to be taught their adult roles until they are 12 years old, although, like Mexican children, they are considered capable of learning through imitation as soon as they learn to talk, at about 2 years of age. The New England mothers do not trust children to care for younger children without supervision until they are 12 years old, but in evaluating this belief it should be noted that the children-caretakers in other samples have more adults around than in New England. Certainly mothers of both groups expect considerable help from children under 12 years of age, and in both groups children start school at about the age of 6, indicating that their parents believe they can absorb instruction at that time. The Indian mothers sometimes explicitly distinguish between capacity to be instructed in school work and capacity to learn adult tasks and roles, which they believe develop later.

It would seem then, that mothers who encourage responsibility tend to encourage early responsibility, while those who expect relatively little responsible behavior from their children also delay responsibility training until a later date. Our hypothesis is that the degree of encouragement of responsible behavior is related to the mothers' economic contribution to the family.

Tangential evidence for this interpretation of these data is provided in the next chapter dealing with the analysis of maternal reactions to the mother-directed aggression of their children. We shall delay further interpretation of the responsibility analysis until the discussion in Chapter 7.

Summary

The responsibility training factor is defined by three scales: frequency of chores, number of chores, and age of child. The positive loading of the age of child scale on the factor indicates that, in general, older children are expected to do more chores and to do them more frequently than younger children. However, analysis of the individual societies shows that, while there is a tendency in all societies that is consistent in direction with this general correlation, the relationship between age and increased responsibility is not universally a strong one. In general there is no relationship between the amount of work expected from a child and the sex of the child. The one exception in our data to this generalization is that the Orchard Town mothers expect girls to do chores more frequently than boys.

Analysis of particular types of chores shows that although there are no significant differences among societies in their placement on the factor itself, there are differences in the variety of chores that children in various societies perform, and a lesser difference in the frequency with which they do them. In general the Mexican, Philippine, and African children are more responsible than are the New England, Okinawan, and Indian children.

Analysis of the age and sex differences in the performance of particular chores indicates that certain chores are "sex typed." Housecleaning is done primarily by girls, while feeding, watering, and pasturing animals tends to be boys work. Despite the overall relationship between age and responsibility, cooking and pasturing animals are the only particular chores that are usually done by older rather than younger children. Particular societies sometimes exhibit relationships between age or sex and particular types of chores that are not generally present in other societies or in the combined sample.

It is suggested that the degree of responsibility training is related to the degree to which the mothers must make independent contributions to the family income, as well as fulfill her child-rearing role. Further explication of this hypothesis will be presented in the next chapter.

7 ❖ Aggression Training: Mother-Directed Aggression

Factor Definition

Let us now turn our attention to Factor 6, which is defined by two aggression training scales that concern the mothers' reactions to the aggression of the child that is directed toward *her*. These scales are:

> Degree to which mother is positive or nonpunishing when the child becomes angry while being scolded (scale 3. — .76)
> Degree to which mother is aggressive when the child is angry or aggressive toward her. (scale 18 —.64)

Mothers with high scores on Factor 6 react aggressively and punitively to anger and aggression on the part of their children that is directed specifically to them. Scale 3 is a measure of the mother's reaction to aggression in the specific situation where the child is being scolded. Scale 18 is a more general measure.

Scale 3 represents a judgment made of the mothers' answers to a specific question. The question read as follows in the original version.

> Sometimes children get angry at their parents when they are being criticized or scolded. How do you handle this with _____?

The name of the child who was the subject of the interview was inserted into the blank. The judgments of the responses to this question were coded on a 9-point scale where point 1 was defined as mother physically punishes or deprives of privileges, and point 9 was defined as mother gives reward or active help. (See Chapter One for a further description of this coding procedure.)

Scale 18 is a rating on a scale that could be based on remarks made in any part of the interview. The information most relevant to the rating comes from the above question, and another, "What (would you do) if your child should kick or strike you?" The points of scale 18 are defined as:

7—Mother retaliates with extreme aggression.

5—Mother spanks or gives other formatized punishment.

3—Mother scolds mildly.

1—Mother never aggresses to child under these conditions; nurtures or distracts.

The correlation between scale 3 and scale 18 as shown in Table 1.4 is —.43. This correlation has a probability of occurrence by chance of less than .1 per cent.

Although these two aggression training scales are the only ones with loadings of greater than .40 on Factor 6, there are several additional scales that have moderately high loadings on this factor. Scale 14, consistency of mother's follow-through on nonroutine demands for obedience, has a loading of +.36. This scale is also important in Factor 3 which dealt with peer-directed aggression. Evidently mothers who discourage hostility, either toward themselves or toward other children, also emphasize obedience.

Two scales which measure specific disciplinary techniques have moderately high loadings on Factor 6. They are scale 15, consistency and intensity of physical punishment (+.33), and scale 16, degree to which gifts and privileges are contingent upon the child's behavior (+.39).

Sears, Maccoby, and Levin (1957), in their study of New England mothers, also find evidence for a connection between emphasis on aggression control training and emphasis on obedience, but they do not find the same independence in the relationship between maternal reaction to *peer*-directed and to *mother*-directed aggression. The factor analysis of their data produced two factors concerned with aggression training. One they call "permissiveness-strictness." Mothers at the strict end of this factor set high standards for strict obedience and do not permit their children to display aggression to other children or to the parents. This factor combines both of the attributes that are found in the two aggression training factors of this study. The other factor the authors call "aggressiveness and punitiveness." Mothers who are high on this factor encourage their children to be aggressive to other children but punish them for aggressing against the parents. These "punitive" mothers also make frequent use of physical punishment as a disciplinary technique, but there is no relationship between aggression training and the use of rewards and privileges. It is somewhat confusing to find that in one factor punishment of peer-directed aggression is positively associated with punishment of mother-directed aggression and in another their relationship is negative. The results of the present study, in which punishment of peer-directed aggression varies independently of punishment of mother-directed aggression, are more clear.   However, the connection between strict aggression training, emphasis on obedience, and the use of physical punishment appears in both studies.

Scale 23, age at which the child begins to play away from the house, has a loading of +.36 on Factor 6, indicating that mothers who punish aggression directed to themselves also insist that their children stay close to home until they are relatively old.   The reason for this relationship is not very clear.   It may represent a correlation between emphasis on obedience and reluctance to let children be independent.   In view of the fact that the total frequence of chores has a loading of +.24 on the factor, the reluctance to let children leave home may also reflect a desire on the part of the mothers to keep the children at home so that they can help her with her work.

Variation on Factor Scores

Table 7.1 shows the results of an analysis of variance on the factor scores for Factor 6.   Society is the only significant source of between-mean differences on this factor.   Neither the age nor the sex of chil-

Table 7.1   Mean Factor Scores for Age and Sex Groups and Analysis of Variance Table for Factor 6: Aggression Training: Mother-Directed Aggression

Society	Boys		Girls		Total Group
	Young	Old	Young	Old	
Africa	.84	.89	.98	.86	.89
Philippines	.40	.68	.43	.48	.50
Mexico	.39	.27	.48	−.10	.26
Okinawa	.05	−.06	−.25	−.06	−.08
United States	−.06	−.32	−.32	.16	−.13
India	−.61	−1.49	−1.28	−1.12	−1.13

Source	df	p
Sex	1	NS
Age	1	NS
Society	5	.001
Sex × Age	1	NS
Sex × Society	5	NS
Age × Society	5	NS
Age × Sex × Society	5	NS

Table 7.2 *Analysis of Significant Gaps among Societies on Factor Scores*

Factor 6: Mother-Directed Aggression

Rank	Society			Percentage of + cases
1	Africa			100
		$Z = 2.17$	$p = .02$	
2	Philippines	$\chi^2 = 0.64$	$p > .30$	83
3	Mexico			73
		$Z = 1.62$	$p = .10$	
4	Okinawa	$\chi^2 = 0.33$	$p > .50$	50
5	United States			42
		$Z = 3.90$	$p < .0001$	8
6	India			

dren has any substantial effect on their mothers' treatment of mother-directed aggression.[1]

Table 7.2 shows that there are three significant gaps between societies on this factor.[2] In the African sample, 100 per cent of the cases are above the mean of the combined sample. The African mothers are more punitive when their children become angry with them than the mothers of any other community in the sample. The chance probability of the difference between the African sample and the Philippine sample, ranked second on the factor, is .02. The scores of Philippine and Mexican mothers do not differ from one another ($p > .30$); mothers in both groups are usually above the pancultural average. The mean of the Okinawan mothers on Factor 6 is —.08, very close to the pancultural mean of zero. Fifty per cent of the Okinawan mothers have scores above zero and 50 per cent have scores below zero. The United States mothers are also close to the average, with a mean of —.13 and 42 per cent of the mothers with high scores. The Okinawan and United States mothers form an intermediate group, differing from both the Philippine and Mexican mothers on the one hand ($p = .10$), and from the low-scoring Indian mothers on the other

[1] Bartlett's chi square shows that the variation of the factor scores from society to society is not uniform for Factor 6. The results of this analysis of variance must, therefore, be interpreted with caution.

[2] Table 1.8 shows that the chi-square value for between-society differences is 49.85, with a probability of .1 per cent. Differences between societies account for 47 per cent of the variance on this factor; more variance is accounted for by cultural differences on this factor than on any other factor in the study.

($p < .0001$), but not from each other ($p > .50$). The mothers of the Indian community are decidedly more permissive about mother-directed aggression than any of the other groups. Only 8 per cent of these Indian mothers have scores that are above the pancultural mean.

Intersociety Differences on Scales

With the exception of the Mexican sample, the placement of societies on scale 3 (the degree to which the mother rewards the child's anger) is comparable to the distribution of their factor scores (see Table 7.3).

Table 7.3   Mother-Directed Aggression Scales: Intersociety Differences

Reward for Child's Mother-Directed Anger

Rank	Society	Low	Middle	High	x^2	p	Percentage of high scores
1	India	1	2	14			82
				↕	6.89	$< .05$	
2	Mexico	6	2	8			50
				↕	3.92	$< .20$	
3	United States	5	9	8	1.38	$= .50$	36
4	Okinawa	2	11	6			32
				↕	9.81	$< .01$	
5.5	Philippines	8	8	0			0
				↕	10.67	$< .01$	
5.5	Africa	16	0	0			0
	Total	38	32	36	63.94	$< .001$	

Retaliation to Child's Mother-Directed Anger

Rank	Society	Low	High	x^2	p	Percentage of high scores
1	Africa	1	15			94
2	Philippines	4	18	1.52	$> .30$	82
3	Mexico	3	13			81
			↕	4.27	$< .05$	
4	India	10	9			47
5	Okinawa	13	11	0.00	$= 1.00$	46
6	United States	13	10			43
	Total	44	76	21.88	$.001$	

The scores in this scale have been divided into low, middle, and high categories. All the African scores fall into the low category. These mothers are less likely to be lenient when children are angry with them than the mothers of any other sample ($p < .01$). The Indian mothers, on the other hand, are likely to be more permissive about mother-directed aggression than any other group of mothers ($p < .05$). The Philippine mothers are tied with the African mothers for last place on the ranking, which is based on the percentage of high scores. However, none of the Philippine scores fall into the high category, but half of them fall into the middle category. For this reason the distribution of the Philippine sample differs from that of the African sample ($p < .01$), and is similar to the moderately extreme position that the sample holds on the factor score distribution. The Mexican sample, however, although moderately high on the factor score distribution, indicating that these mothers generally discourage mother-directed aggression, moves to second place on the reward for child's anger ranking. The Mexican, United States, and Okinawan mothers represent intermediate positions on this scale, with the Mexican group being highest.

Only two groups of societies emerge from the analysis of the scale, retaliation to mother-directed aggression. In the African, Philippine, and Mexican communities a majority of the mothers report that they retaliate when their children become angry with them. In the Indian Okinawan, and New England communities, a minority of mothers retaliate under these conditions. The difference between the Mexican sample, lowest of the "high" group, and the Indian sample, highest of the "low" group, has a probability of less than 5 per cent.

Age and Sex Differences on Scales

Table 7.4 shows the distribution of the two mother-directed aggression scales in terms of the age of the children. The only association of these scales with age occurs in the Mexican sample where the mothers are more likely to retaliate aggressively to younger than to older children. The only association between these variables and the sex of the child (see Table 7.4) occurs in the Okinawan sample where mothers are more likely to retaliate to the anger of boys than to the anger of girls.

Hypotheses

A comparison of Tables 6.2 and 7.2 reveals that the rank order of societies on responsibility training and punishment of mother-directed aggression is similar. The African, Philippine, and Mexican groups

Table 7.4   Mother-Directed Aggression Scales: Age Differences

Society		Reward for Child's Mother-Directed Anger	
		Low	High
India	Young[1]	$1^{(4)}$	$8^{(5)}$
	Old[2]	$0^{(3)}$	$8^{(5)}$
Mexico	Young	$4^{(5)}$	$5^{(4)}$
	Old	$2^{(3)}$	$5^{(4)}$
United States	Young	$1^{(5)}$	$10^{(6)}$
	Old	$4^{(9)}$	$7^{(2)}$
Okinawa	Young	$1^{(6)}$	$9^{(4)}$
	Old	$1^{(7)}$	$8^{(2)}$
Philippines	Young	3	4
	Old	5	4
Africa	Young	$8^{(8)}$	$0^{(0)}$
	Old	$8^{(7)}$	$0^{(1)}$
Total	Young	18	36
	Old	20	32
Total		38	68

Society		Retaliation to Child's Mother-Directed Anger	
		Low	High
India	Young	6	4
	Old	4	5
Mexico	Young	$1^{(2)}$	$8^{(7)}$ *
	Old	$2^{(6)}$	$5^{(1)}$
United States	Young	8	3
	Old	5	7
Okinawa	Young	6	6
	Old	7	5
Philippines	Young	$1^{(9)}$	$9^{(1)}$
	Old	$3^{(7)}$	$9^{(5)}$
Africa	Young	$0^{(4)}$	$8^{(4)}$
	Old	$1^{(6)}$	$7^{(2)}$
Total	Young	22	38
	Old	22	38
Total		44	76

[1] Young = 3–6 years.
[2] Old = 7–10 years.
* $p < .05$.

are high, and the United States, Okinawan, and Indian groups are low on both dimensions. This suggests the following hypothesis: When mothers are expected to make independent economic contributions to the family finances, either by the supervision of the running of a herd and garden in a mother-child household, as in the African community, or by marketing their produce or handiwork, as in the Philippines and Mexico, they expect children to help them with their daily chores. These mothers have sufficient status to enforce these expectations and they react severely when children challenge their authority. They are, therefore, more severe in their punishment of aggression to themselves than are mothers who do not have this economic independence. These relationships among a degree of economic independence of the mothers, their expectations of responsible behavior from the children, and their punishment for insubordination are probably rooted both in the social structure that necessitates this behavior and the mother's personality that results from her relatively favored position.

This hypothesis suggests that there should be a positive correlation between the scales that define the responsibility and mother-directed aggression factors, even though the two factors are independent of one another. Table 1.4 shows that this is indeed the case.

Table 1.4   Excerpt: Intercorrelations of Defining Scales for Factors 1 and 6

Scale	3 Degree That Mother Is Positive When Child Is Angry	18 Degree That Mother Is Aggressive When Child Aggresses to Her
24. Total Frequency of Chores	$-.22**$	$+.22**$
25. Total Number of Chores	$-.17*$	$+.12$
		$*p < .05$
		$**p < .01$

We are, then, justified in assuming that mothers who expect children to be responsible also punish children who defy them. We shall now look more carefully at the economic situations of the mothers in these six communities.

The most independent group of mothers is the African sample. Since their marriages are polygynous, these women depend less upon the assistance of their husbands than the mothers of the other communities. Each wife has her own house, garden, and herd of cattle. She and her

Table 7.5   Mother-Directed Aggression Scales: Sex Differences

Society		Reward for Child's Mother-Directed Anger	
		Low	High
India	Boys	1[4]	8[5]
	Girls	0[3]	8[5]
Mexico	Boys	4[4]	2[2]
	Girls	2[4]	8[6]
United States	Boys	3[6]	7[4]
	Girls	2[8]	10[4]
Okinawa	Boys	0[7]	11[4]
	Girls	2[6]	6[2]
Philippines	Boys	5	3
	Girls	3	5
Africa	Boys	8[7]	0[1]
	Girls	8[8]	0[0]
Total	Boys	21	31
	Girls	17	37
Total		38	68

Society		Retaliation to Child's Mother-Directed Anger	
		Low	High
India	Boys	4	5
	Girls	6	4
Mexico	Boys	2[4]	6[4]
	Girls	1[4]	7[4]
United States	Boys	8	3
	Girls	5	7
Okinawa	Boys	4	8*
	Girls	9	3
Philippines	Boys	1[8]	10[3]
	Girls	3[8]	8[3]
Africa	Boys	1[6]	7[2]
	Girls	0[4]	8[4]
Total	Boys	20	39
	Girls	24	37
Total		44	76

* $p = .05$.

children largely support themselves from their herd and garden and the mother is responsible for the economic production of her household. These mothers are the least permissive about aggression directed at themselves.

The Gusii mothers of Nyansongo punish aggression to themselves more severely than the mothers of any other group. Gusii society has strong centralized authority that extends in a hierarchy from the chief through the men of individual families. Teaching children to respect this authority is the job of their mothers. Since the mothers believe that the basis of this respect begins with teaching children to respect them, they react with righteous indignation to defiance by their children. They interpret such aggression as an insult to their authority, "I am one of the parents," and they punish it by withholding the food upon which that authority is based, "I refuse her food for five days."

The economic importance of these African women is recognized explicitly in the custom of the bride-price. A man must pay the father of his bride several head of cattle to compensate him for the loss of his daughter's services before the marriage is recognized.

The Philippine and Mexican mothers do not farm (they form the mid-high group on this factor) independently but they go to market regularly and sell produce or handicraft. Thus they bring a supplementary cash income to their families, which they can, in part, use for themselves. Together they form a middle-high group on this factor.

The Okinawan and New England mothers form the mid-low group on Factor 6. As a rule these mothers do not make independent contributions to their families' incomes. The Okinawan women gather firewood with their husbands and sell it to a vendor, but the wood of a family is sold as a unit and the cash is usually paid to the husband. Half of the New England mothers contribute some money to the family finances, but none are self-supporting. Like most American women, it is socially possible for them to work if necessary. Furthermore, since the United States families must hire baby-sitters to replace maternal services, the potential financial value of the mothers' services is more apparent than it is in communities where relatives can provide free mother substitutes.

The Indian mothers are prohibited from working by the custom of seclusion that confines them to their courtyards. Since they live in extended households and their services can be easily performed by other women of the household, the only substantial contribution of the Indian women to their husbands' families is their dowries. These are paid by the bride's father to the father of the groom. The transactions, therefore, are through men, although dowries consist in part of goods made by the women of the bride's family. Furthermore, divorce is impossible among the Indians and the dowry is not refundable.

The Rajput dowry system contrasts sharply with the bride-price of the Gusii. Among the African Gusii a woman is an economic asset and commands a payment from her husband to her father. Among the Indian Rajputs, it is the bride's family who must pay to have their daughter married.[3]

The mothers of the Indian sample are more permissive about aggression to themselves than any other group. They frequently comfort children who get angry while being scolded, thereby undermining their own authority. The contrast between the behavior of these mothers and those in the African sample who are most punitive about defiance of their own authority is particularly interesting in view of the fact that both are training children to adjust to a society that is highly authoritarian and very aggressive. Both groups had blood feuds, which have in frequent years been replaced by frequent litigation in the courts. Adults, both male and female, are frequently hostile and suspicious of their neighbors in both communities. The political and social structure is based on hierarchial authority in both places. The fathers are distant and stern, and when dealing with their children they are chiefly concerned with discipline.

We should also add a more theoretical note. From the perspective of considerations of human learning, Factor 6 represents more a stopgap measure for the immediate control of action than a long-range strategy for training children to be less aggressive toward parents in the long run. Mothers who score high strike out against signs of anger directed at them. Taken by itself, such a tactic might have a number of long-range effects which would surprise the practitioner. The mother might be avoided by the child when he was angry, and such avoidance due to conditioned anxiety might become a more generalized avoidance.

Summary

Factor 6 is a measure of the mothers' reaction to aggression by the children that is directed against them. The factor is defined by two scales: degree to which mother is positive when the child becomes angry while being scolded and degree to which mother is aggressive when the

---

[3] Paradoxically, some Rajput men who were too poor to obtain wives with dowries had to pay the families of their wives to obtain a bride. When this occurred the bride brought a small dowry that consisted of goods and part of the bride-price money.

child is angry or aggressive to her. Mothers with high loadings on this factor punish their children for aggressing against them by being, in turn, aggressive to the children. Mothers with high scores also tend to follow through on nonroutine demands for obedience. They discipline by physical punishment and the manipulation of gifts and privileges.

The six communities of the study fall into four groups on Factor 6. The African mothers stand alone at the high end of the factor, being more punitive to mother-directed aggression than the mothers in any of the other communities. All the African factor scores on Factor 6 are above the pancultural mean for the factor. The Philippine and Mexican mothers form a second group. Most, but not all, the mothers in these communities have factor scores that are higher than the pancultural mean. The Mexican and Philippine mothers differ, in turn from the mothers in Okinawa and the United States, where approximately half the scores fall above, and half below, the pancultural mean. The Indian mothers are at the low end of the factor. They are generally less punitive about aggression directed at them than other mothers. The Indian sample is the only one in which a fair proportion of the mothers regularly reinforce at least minor outbreaks of anger by consoling the children when they become angry. They do this even when the children become angry while being scolded. Since not all Indian mothers follow this nurturant course, this sample has greater variability of scores than any other.

The distribution of the societies on scale 3, degree to which the mother is positive when the child becomes angry while being scolded, is comparable to their distribution of the factor scores, with the exception that the Mexican sample moves from a position representing moderately high punitiveness on the factor score distribution to one representing relatively low punitiveness on scale 3. On scale 18, the measure of maternal retaliation to attacks, the societies fall into two groups; the African, the Philippine, and the Mexican samples are high on this scale and the Indian, the Okinawan, and the United States samples are low.

The reaction of mothers to mother-directed aggression is unrelated to either the age or sex of the children with but two exceptions. When a child is angry with them, Mexican mothers are more likely to retaliate if the child is younger than 7 years old, and Okinawan mothers are more likely to retaliate if the child is a boy.

A hypothesis of an underlying dimension of economic independence of the mothers was suggested to explain the cultural ordering. Theoretical considerations point up some possible uncomfortable by-products of the tactics involved in this factor.

8 ❖ Aggression Training:
Peer-Directed Aggression

Factor Definition

In Chapter 7 we discussed the handling of aggression directed to the mothers. How do these same mothers handle aggression directed to other children? Factor 3 is defined by three scales.

Consistency of aggression rules (scale 12, +.70)
Reward for retaliatory aggression to peers (scale 17, —.68)
Consistency of mother's follow-through on nonroutine demands for obedience (scale 14, +.49)

The consistency of aggression rules scale refers to the degree to which the mother's rules regarding aggression are the same in all settings or situations in which the child behaves. That is, does she require the same aggressive behavior in any situation, or do the rules change with the situational changes? Since, in practice, mothers do not encourage children to be aggressive in all situations, a high rating on this scale indicates that the mother generally discourages aggression. In fact, the end points of the consistency of aggression rules scale are defined as follows:

Score 7: Rules concerning aggression are the same in all settings, never fight under any circumstances.
Score 1: Rules concerning aggression are very specific and change with different situations.

The scale, reward for retaliatory aggression to peers, reflects the extent to which the mother encourages her child to defend himself in quarrels with his playmates. The points on this scale are defined as:

Score 7: Mother would go out of her way to punish retaliation to peers.
Score 4: Mother would "let it go."

Score 1: Mother would go out of her way to reward retaliation to peers.

Mothers with high scores on Factor 3 are those who discourage peer-directed aggression by articulating rules that forbid the expression of aggression in almost any situation and by punishing their children for fighting with other children.

Since the loadings of these two aggression training scales are considerably higher than the loadings of the third defining scale which involves obedience training, the latter has not been included in the naming of the factor. However, the consistency with which mothers enforce their nonroutine demands has a loading of +.49 on Factor 3, well above the .40 cutting point. This indicates that mothers who discourage peer-directed aggression in their children also insist that the children be obedient. Nonroutine demands are those which are non-repetitive and are dependent upon a particular situation, such as washing hands or sitting still, as opposed to chores that the child is required to perform regularly. The end points of scale 14 are defined as follows.

Score 7: Mother always enforces demands and always sees to it that the child performs them.
Score 1: Mother never enforces demands and pays no attention to whether or not the child complies.

Scale 26, degree to which mother expects immediate obedience, has a loading of +.37 on this factor, indicating that the mothers with high scores not only enforce their demands upon their children but expect the children to respond to them promptly.

The correlations among these four scales, taken from Table 1.4, are given below.

Table 1.4 Excerpt: Intercorrelations of Defining Scales for Factor 3

Scale	Scale Number		
Number	12	17	14
17	−.62**		
14	+.20*	−.26**	
26	+.20*	−.18*	+.26**

*$p > .05$.
**$p < .01$.

All these correlations have probabilities of less than 5 per cent, indicating that none of them are due to chance. The correlation between the two aggression scales (Nos. 12 and 17) is much higher than the other correlations as would be expected from their content and from their high loadings on the factor.

This factor is interesting theoretically. Mothers who have high scores would appear to be attempting not only to teach children rules for role behaviors involving aggression, but also to actually hold down the occurrence of the behaviors themselves. Few students of the control of behavior would doubt that the mothers who are high on the items of this factor would achieve control over the frequency of occurrence of this class of behavior in peer interaction, at least as it occurs *in the presence* of the parents. They give low reward (or active punishment) to the occurrence of retaliation. A child is punished if he strikes back even when he has been picked on. They follow through (with sanctions) when demanding obedience on such a rule. They maintain consistent rules and enforce the demands which are consistent with such rules. Such behavior on the part of a socializing agent should have effects upon children to help them develop a concept of the rules as well as (through anxiety learning) control on peer aggression. It reads as if the parent were watching the frequency of the behaviors involved and behaving in a way which would empirically lower the frequency. The research of Sears, Maccoby, and Levin (1957) suggests that these techniques may not, in fact, be very effective.

Variation on Factor Scores

Table 8.1 shows the results of the analysis of variance for the factor scores on Factor 3.[1] The only main effect of any importance is due to society. This difference is due largely to the high position of the Mexican sample and the extremely low position of the United States sample on this factor. Table 8.2 shows that the mothers of the Mexican sample discourage peer-to-peer aggression more than any other group ($p < .002$) and the mother of the United States encourages such aggression more than any other group ($p < .00003$).

Table 8.1 also shows that there is an interaction among society, age, and sex of children that affects maternal treatment of peer-to-peer aggression. This interaction appears to be caused by a few exceptions

[1] Bartlett's chi square indicates that the variance of the factor scores is not uniform across societies, so the results of this analysis should be interpreted with caution.

Table 8.1 Mean Factor Scores for Age and Sex Groups and Analysis of Variance Table on Factor 3: Aggression Training: Peer-Directed Aggression

| Society | Boys | | Girls | | Total Group |
	Young	Old	Young	Old	
Mexico	.44	.54	.80	.63	.60
Okinawa	−.26	.20	−.19	.52	.07
India	.26	.44	−.06	.16	.20
Africa	.08	−.35	.20	.35	.07
Philippines	.11	.08	−.15	.35	.11
United States	−1.42	−.58	−1.16	−.75	−.98

Source	df	p
Sex	1	NS
Age	1	NS
Society	5	.001
Sex × Age	1	NS
Sex × Society	5	NS
Age × Society	5	NS
Sex × Age × Society	5	.05

Table 8.2 Analysis of Significant Gaps among Societies on Factor Scores

Grouping of Societies on Factor 3: Peer-Directed Aggression

Rank	Society			Percentage of + cases
1	Mexico			91
	↕	$Z = 2.26$	$p < .02$	
3	Okinawa ⎫			63
3	India ⎬	$\chi^2 = 0.18$	$p > .98$	63
3	Africa			63
5	Philippines ⎭			57
	↕	$Z = 4.34$	$p < .00003$	
6	United States			8

to the general tendency of the mothers to be stricter with older children's quarrels than with those of younger children. The exceptions are that the African mothers are more strict about peer-to-peer aggression with young boys; the Philippine mothers are equally strict with old and young boys; and the Mexican mothers are stricter with younger than with older girls.

Intersociety Differences on Scales

Table 8.3 shows the distribution of our communities on the two aggression training scales and the two obedience training scales that comprise Factor 3. Scale 26 has been included in the analysis because its loading is so close to the .40 cutoff point, and its meaning so in accord with scale 14 that it seems wisest to consider it along with the other three scales.

Table 8.3 shows that the Mexican and United States samples are at, or near, the extremes of the ranking on all four scales. The Mexican mothers, who are, as a group, the most strict about peer-directed aggression as well as about obedience training, rank fifth on reward for retaliation and second on expectation of prompt obedience. The United States mothers, who are the most permissive about both peer-directed aggression and obedience, are ranked last on consistency of aggression rules, first on reward for retaliation, and fifth on both of the obedience scales. This is the sort of placement we would expect from the placement of these societies on the overall factor score distribution.

In terms of significant gaps, the distribution of the individual scales are not the same as the distribution of the overall factor scores. In the consistency of aggression rules scale, only the United States sample differs from the others ($p < .01$) in the direction of having situationally specific rather than overall rules governing aggression.

The distributions of scales 17, reward for retaliation, and 14, follow-through on obedience demands, have been divided into three sections instead of two because many cases fell on one intermediate point, making three "natural" groups. This complicates the analysis of these scales, but they have been ranked in terms of the percentage of cases in the "high" category in order to make the basis of their ranking consistent with that of the other scales. On reward for retaliation, the United States sample provides more reward for retaliation than the Okinawan sample which is ranked second ($p < .001$). The probability of the difference between the Okinawan mothers and the (rank 3) Indian mothers is less than 5 per cent. When the Okinawan sample is not included, the chi-square value for the remaining four societies that are

Table 8.3 Peer-Directed Aggression and Obedience Training Scales: Intersociety Differences

Consistency of Aggression Rules

Rank	Society	Low	High	x^2	p	Percentage of high scores
1	Mexico	3	18			86
2	India	4	12			75
3	Philippines	8	15	8.22	<.10	65
4	Okinawa	10	12			54
5	Africa	8	8	8.89	<.02	50
6	United States	22	2			8
	Total	55	67	30.55	<.001	

Reward for Retaliation

Rank	Society	Low	Middle	High	x^2	p	Percentage of high scores
1	United States	1	3	20	17.78	<.001	83
2	Okinawa	11	7	5	4.33	<.05	22
3	India	9	13	2	7.16	<.10	8
4	Africa	5	10	1			6
5	Mexico	13	6	1			5
6	Philippines	13	9	1			4
	Total	52	48	30	77.98	<.001	

Expectation of Prompt Obedience

Rank	Society	Low	High	x^2	p	Percentage of high scores
1	Africa	0	16			100
2	Mexico	5	17	2.36	<.20	77
3	Okinawa	9	15	2.81	<.30	63
4	India	9	12			57
5	United States	19	5	6.28	<.02	21
6	Philippines	19	4	0.09	<.80	17
	Total	61	69	40.46	<.001	

Consistency of Obedience Training

Rank	Society	Low	Middle	High	x^2	p	Percentage of high scores
1	Mexico	2	5	12			63
2	Philippines	5	7	9	14.43	<.01	43
3	Okinawa	13	1	10			42
4	Africa	2	8	6			37
5	United States	12	4	5	8.12	<.01	24
6	India	11	5	4	0.45	=.50	20
	Total	45	30	46	29.53	<.001	

ranked low in reward for retaliation is greater than 30 per cent. That is, no significant differences are left when the Okinawan group is dropped.

The African mothers expect their children to obey more promptly than do the mothers of any of the other societies ($p < .20$). The Mexican, Okinawan, and Indian mothers form an intermediate group on this scale, while the United States and Philippine mothers give children the most leeway for obeying orders ($p < .02$).

On the consistency of obedience scale, the United States and Indian mothers are unusually low as compared with the mothers of the other communities ($p < .02$). The United States and Indian mothers do not differ from each other on this scale ($p = .50$). The differences among the remaining four societies are due to the fact that the Okinawan sample, ranked three, has an unusually high number of cases in both the "high" and the "low" categories and only one case in the middle category. When this sample is removed, the probability of differences among the Mexican, Philippine and African mothers is greater than 10 per cent.

Age and Sex Differences on Scales

Table 8.4 shows that the behavior of mothers with respect to the scales that are important for Factor 3 is generally not affected by the age of the child. There is no association between age and any of the scales for the *combined* sample. Possibly the greater aggressiveness-permissiveness for boys has been overestimated by other researchers. Another possibility is that the fathers are the important socializing agents for aggression in boys, while mothers react the same way to children of either sex. In the United States and Okinawan samples there is some indication of differential aggression training for older boys versus older girls. Although all children under the age of 7 tend to be rewarded for peer-directed aggression in these societies, boys above this age are usually not so rewarded, while girls usually are. This trend does not, however, reach conventionally accepted probabilities of statistical significance in either society. It is particularly surprising that the reward for retaliation should be greater for girls. Possibly the greater aggressiveness of boys makes such encouragement unnecessary. Table 8.5 shows that sex is sometimes relevant to obedience training. The Mexican mothers expect girls to obey more promptly than boys ($p = .02$). The African mothers, on the other hand, expect boys to obey more promptly than girls ($p = .06$). Barry, Bacon, and Child (1957) find that in most societies where there is a sex difference in obedience training, girls are taught to be more obedient than boys. However, there was

Table 8.4   Peer-Directed Aggression and Obedience Training Scales: Age Differences

Society		Consistency of Aggression Rules	
		Low	High
Mexico	Young[1]	$1^{(8)}$	$10^{(3)}$
	Old[2]	$2^{(8)}$	$8^{(2)}$
Philippines	Young	5	6
	Old	3	9
Okinawa	Young	5	5
	Old	5	7
Africa	Young	3	5
	Old	5	3
India	Young	2	6
	Old	2	6
United States	Young	$12^{(8)}$	$0^{(4)}$
	Old	$10^{(5)}$	$2^{(7)}$
Total	Young	28	32
	Old	27	35
Total		55	67

Society		Reward for Retaliation	
		Low	High
Mexico	Young	8	3
	Old	5	4
Philippines	Young	8	3
	Old	5	7
Okinawa	Young	4	8
	Old	7	4
Africa	Young	2	6
	Old	3	5
India	Young	4	8
	Old	5	7
United States	Young	$0^{(1)}$	$12^{(11)}$
	Old	$1^{(6)}$	$11^{(6)}$
Total	Young	26	40
	Old	26	38
Total		52	78

[1] Young = 3–6 years.
[2] Old = 7–10 years.

Table 8.4 (Continued)   *Peer-Directed Aggression and Obedience Training Scales: Age Differences*

Society		Consistency of Obedience Training	
		Low	High
Mexico	Young[1]	6	5
	Old[2]	1	7
Philippines	Young	6	3
	Old	6	6
Okinawa	Young	8	4
	Old	6	6
Africa	Young	7	1
	Old	3	5
India	Young	7[3]	2[6]
	Old	9[5]	2[3]
United States	Young	8[6]	2[5]
	Old	8[6]	3[4]
Total	Young	42	17
	Old	33	29
Total		75	46

Society		Expectation of Prompt Obedience	
		Low	High
Mexico	Young	4[3]	7[2]
	Old	1[2]	10[9]
Philippines	Young	10[9]	2[2]
	Old	9[4]	3[8]
Okinawa	Young	6[8]	6[4]
	Old	3[4]	9[8]
Africa	Young	0[2]	7[5]
	Old	0[2]	8[6]
India	Young	5	6
	Old	4	6
United States	Young	11[7]	1[5]
	Old	8[5]	4[7]
Total	Young	36	28
	Old	25	40
Total		61	68

[1] Young = 3–6 years.
[2] Old = 7–10 Years.

Table 8.5   Peer-Directed Aggression and Obedience Training Scales: Sex Differences

Society		Consistency of Aggression Rules	
		Low	High
Mexico	Boys	2[10]	9[1]
	Girls	1[6]	9[4]
Philippines	Boys	3	8
	Girls	5	7
Okinawa	Boys	5	6
	Girls	5	6
Africa	Boys	4	4
	Girls	4	4
India	Boys	1	6
	Girls	3	6
United States	Boys	11[8]	1[4]
	Girls	11[5]	1[7]
Total	Boys	26	34
	Girls	29	33
Total		55	67

Society		Reward for Retaliation	
		Low	High
Mexico	Boys	7	3
	Girls	6	4
Philippines	Boys	5	6
	Girls	8	4
Okinawa	Boys	7	5
	Girls	4	7
Africa	Boys	3	5
	Girls	2	6
India	Boys	5	7
	Girls	4	8
United States	Boys	0[5]	12[7]
	Girls	1[2]	11[10]
Total	Boys	27	38
	Girls	25	40
Total		52	78

Table 8.5 (Continued)   *Peer-Directed Aggression and Obedience Training Scales: Sex Differences*

Society		Consistency of Obedience Training	
		Low	High
Mexico	Boys	3	6
	Girls	4	6
Philippines	Boys	7	3
	Girls	5	6
Okinawa	Boys	7	5
	Girls	7	5
Africa	Boys	4	4
	Girls	6	2
India	Boys	6[5]	3[4]
	Girls	10[6]	1[5]
United States	Boys	9[7]	2[4]
	Girls	7[5]	3[5]
Total	Boys	36	23
	Girls	39	23
Total		75	46

Society		Expectation of Prompt Obedience	
		Low	High
Mexico	Boys	4[9]	7[2] *
	Girls	1[2]	10[9]
Philippines	Boys	9[4]	2[7]
	Girls	10[9]	2[3]
Okinawa	Boys	5[6]	7[6]
	Girls	4[6]	8[6]
Africa	Boys	0[0]	8[8]
	Girls	0[4]	7[4]
India	Boys	3	8
	Girls	6	4
United States	Boys	10[5]	2[7]
	Girls	9[7]	3[5]
Total	Boys	31	34
	Girls	30	34
Total		61	68

* $p = <.05$.

less sex differentiation on obedience than any of the other variables that they studied because in 62 per cent of their societies there was no difference on obedience training. Our African sample seems to be an exception to this general trend.

Hypotheses

Within-group peer aggression is a potentially disruptive force in all societies for no society can survive long without some degree of mutual trust and cooperation among its members. All the mothers show some degree of concern for the quarrels of their children; but the Mexican mothers are more concerned, and the New England mothers less so than the mothers of other groups. Why? The most obvious explanation is that the relative anxiety about peer-group aggression is related to the intimacy of social and economic bonds among members in the community, and to the degree to which children can disrupt these adult relationships.

The Mexican sample represents the high extreme of interdependence among the groups in the sample. The Santo Domingo barrio studied by the Romneys contains only 600 Indians in a town with a total population of 3600. This group of Indians is poor and low in status, relative to their Spanish-speaking neighbors. Relations between the two groups are characterized by hostile avoidance. The Indian community is 90 per cent endogenous so kinship ties are very close. Poverty makes it difficult for married people with families to leave the community. The living pattern also leads brothers and their families to live around a common courtyard where the children play. Child care is largely communal and older cousins are more likely to substitute for caretakers than are older sisters. Relatives also look to each other for help with their work and for financial assistance, an important service for a group so poor.

The Mexican mothers are more punitive about aggression among children than any other group. They use physical punishment to punish physical aggression, more than for any other deviation. To prevent their children from getting into fights they keep close to home and sometimes do not send them to school, where they are bullied by the more aggressive children of the town. They successfully teach their children to be unaggressive and to fear aggression from outsiders as they do themselves. They prefer to have their children play alone, although most of them, in fact, play with their close relations.

The living arrangements in the Indian sample are similar to those in

Mexico. Brothers and their families also live around a common courtyard. The Indian Rajputs however, are exclusively exogamous, so
that wives within the courtyard are not usually related. They are at
the top of the social hierarchy of the Khalapur village, whereas the Mixte-
can-speaking Indians are the lowest group on the Juxtlahuaca social
ladder. The Rajputs are also fairly wealthy and can afford to divide
their living quarters if quarrels make this necessary. Their social ties,
therefore, are not as intimate as they are in Juxtlahuaca.

The reaction of the Indian mothers to peer-to-peer aggression is also
tempered by their belief that young children are incapable of anger.

The Indian and African mothers are very similar in the severity with
which they punish peer group aggression; and they do not differ from
the Philippine and Okinawan samples in their placement on this factor.
The Gusii mothers, however, attribute highly aggressive motivations to
their children, while the Rajput mothers feel that serious aggression occurs only among adults. The Gusii mothers interpret attacks of preadolescent boys on girls as sexual in nature, a sort of attenuated rape.
They also believe that older children may kill newborn babies by their
jealousy. The Rajput women, on the other hand, sometimes expressed the belief that children are too young to be really angry. Anger
for them is a long-term motivation. Since the fights of children are
quickly over they are not considered serious. Unlike the Gusii mothers
Rajput mothers do not feel they must interfere in their children's
quarrels. This difference in attitude probably also affects these mothers'
reactions to their children's aggression to themselves. The Gusii
mothers are reacting to defiance that they see as based on strong and
evil motivation, and Rajput mothers are reacting to defiance that they
view as childish and transitory.

Finally, the Khalapur Rajputs are traditionally a warrior caste. Men
train their sons to defend their rights. Although the mothers do not
participate directly in such training their sense of this warrior tradition
no doubt influences their reactions to quarrels among their sons. The
combination of these factors is probably sufficient to lower the concern
of the Rajput mothers from what we might expect from their living
arrangements, to a level comparable to that of the Okinawan, African,
and Philippine samples.

The people of the Okinawan, African, and Philippine samples are
also more or less related, and depend upon each other for help and
financial assistance. They do not, however, share their living quarters.
The mothers, who usually come from outside the community, have
more privacy in these three communities, and the children of each
nuclear family have some space to play that they share only with sib-

lings. Under these circumstances the quarrels of children are probably not as likely to disrupt adult relationships, although this is still a grave concern among the mothers of our Okinawan and African communities.

The New England families are the only group whose members are not living next door to their relatives, and whose livelihood does not depend upon the support of their neighbors. This situation has dual implications regarding sociability among adults. On the one hand, the New England mothers can ignore their neighbors if they do not get along with them. On the other hand, they have no claims of kinship to cement relationships with neighbors if they do want to be friends. Their insistence that their children stand up for themselves may be seen both as a lack of concern with maintaining constant friendships, "If you can't get along with them, play with somebody else; there are lots of people in this world," and a reluctance to complain to their neighbors on behalf of their children, "You couldn't go to the parents and tell them." These two situations are peculiar to the United States sample. In all the other samples there are a limited number of friends available to children, but mothers can complain to other mothers and expect some cooperation if these friendships are disrupted.

It should be noted that, although New England mothers do reward peer retaliation more than any other group, this reward is highly differential. Mothers punish children if they are the instigators of aggression or if they attack younger children, even when provoked. More than any other group of mothers, they are concerned that children learn the rules of "fair fighting" and the occasions that justify retaliation. African mothers also try to fix responsibility for children's quarrels and they also have a concept of just retaliation. But they usually do not trust their children to settle their disputes and get involved themselves when quarrels come to their attention. The New England mothers, on the other hand, expect children themselves to behave fairly in their fights and they avoid getting involved in them, unless some child habitually violates their rules for fair aggression. When this happens their concerns for their children's safety, or their fear of paying doctor bills for neighbor's children, makes them abandon their "neutral corner." It is notable that, in general, the New England children do fight fairly and seldom injure one another, while the Gusii children, who are far more suppressed in their aggression, may hit each other hard enough to make visible scars or bruises when they do exchange blows.

This same problem appears among the Okinawan children. The Okinawan mothers rank second in the severity with which they discourage aggression among peers, and their children are generally sociable and friendly. When Okinawan boys do fight, however, they may throw rocks at one another, and their parents, like the Gusii parents, are often fearful of being sued for injuries inflicted by their children. It may be that the New England parents, by permitting limited aggression, are more effective in training for aggression control than are mothers who attempt to suppress all expressions of hostility.

Summary

The two scales with the highest loadings on the peer-directed aggression factor are scale number 12, consistency of aggression rules, with a loading of +.70 and scale number 17, reward for retaliatory aggression to peers, with a loading of —.68. Scale 14, consistency of mother's follow-through on nonroutine demands for obedience, has a loading of +.49 on Factor 3; this is considerably lower than the loadings of the two aggression scales but is above the .40 cutoff point. Scale 26, degree to which mother expects prompt obedience, has a loading of +.37 on the factor and has been included in the analysis. Mothers with high scores on Factor 3 discourage aggression in most situations, do not reward their children for retaliation to peers, consistently see to it that the children obey their orders, and expect them to obey promptly.

The mothers of the Mexican sample discourage peer-directed aggression and emphasize obedience more than the mothers in other societies of the study. At the other extreme, the mothers of the United States sample encourage retaliation to peers and are generally more lenient in their expectations of obedience than the mothers of other societies. Analysis of intersociety differences on the four scales that define the factor indicates that the Mexican and United States mothers are at, or near, the expected extremes on all four scales, although the African mothers are lowest in expectation of prompt obedience and reward for retaliation, and the Indian mothers are the most inconsistent in obedience training.

There is an interaction between society, sex, and age on the factor scores. None of the four scales are related to the sex or age of the children when the entire sample is considered. There are some relationships between the mothers' behavior on these variables and the sex or age of the children in particular societies. The mothers of Mexico expect girls to obey them more promptly than boys and older children to obey more promptly than younger ones. The Okinawan mothers also expect prompter obedience from older children. The mothers of Africa expect boys to obey more promptly than girls, an unusual expectation by cross-cultural standards. Somewhat surprisingly, there is no relation between training of peer-directed aggression and sex in any of the societies in our sample.[2]   The only relation between such aggression train-ing and age is that the New England mothers are more likely to re-ward the retaliation of younger children than of older ones.

The hypothesis is advanced that structural relationships with neigh-bors may be stronger and more demanding in those societies which rank high or intermediate on this factor, whereas the low-scoring American community has few such ties to deter competition and mild aggression between childhood peers.

[2] The scales of Factor 9 suggest that some mothers reward the retaliation of girls more strongly than that of boys. However, the loadings on this factor are too low to warrant its serious consideration.

9 ❖ The Antecedents of Child Training: A Cross-Cultural Test of Some Hypotheses

In the first part of this book, we discussed how our samples of mothers from the six cultures placed themselves on our seven factor dimensions. At that time we also put out some suggestions as to the determinants of these modal or average differences on the various scales. Some of these interpretations as to the antecedents of child-training practices were reasonable extensions of findings from other cross-cultural studies, but others merely represented our *post-hoc* interpretations as to why the groups ranked or differed as they did. As in the case with all *post-hoc* hypotheses these must be considered as highly tentative until they have been tested. Six groups are a minimal number for tests of between-group differences that use a societal mean rather than individual differences as the cases. It would be necessary for the rank-order correlation of the societal means on two variables to be virtually perfect before the relationship could be regarded as anything more than a chance phenomena. The fact that the group means of societies of adjacent ranks are usually not significantly different from each other renders the analysis of between-group differences even more tentative. Finally, it is impossible to test a hypothesis on the same sample from which it was derived.

In order to know whether our hypothesized relationships can be regarded as generally useful principles, it is necessary to test them on a larger sample of societies. We are forced, therefore, to test all of these hypotheses by taking them to another court of empirical judgment. This is a large sample or group of societies on which ratings of the variables or attributes involved in our hypotheses are present, so that we can test systematically whether our hypothesized relationship holds when culture or tribes are used as the unit of analysis.

In principle this is a good strategy, but we must face the fact that we

164

are not always able to find the information which will be most directly in our own hypotheses in the existing ethnographic literature. In this chapter we will report our attempt in this direction, however, because, among other things, it will bring to the attention of some students of child rearing a potentially powerful tool which can help to resolve the equivocal status of our hypotheses when our independent replications have been either too few or too unreliable.

In order to test our hypotheses, the scales used for rating the mother interviews were given to the students in an advanced class in cross-cultural studies of child-rearing practices. The students formed teams and divided the scales topically. We chose a sample of 76 societies that had adequate material on child training from the Human Relations Area Files. This list of societies was divided among the students on each team and each student read the relevant ethnographic material for the societies assigned to him and, if sufficient information was available, rated each society on the scales assigned to his team. (See Table 9.1 for a complete list of the societies used in this study.) Certain societies of the sample, varying in the amount of material available on children, were chosen for reliability judgments. Table 9.2 shows the names of the scales rated and the percentage of reliability obtained for each scale. The reliabilities are based on a sample of societies with two or three

Table 9.1   Geographical Distribution of Sample Societies

Africa		Insular Pacific	North America	South America	East Eurasia
Azanda	Rwala	Alorese	Commanche	Abipone	Ainu
Bambara	Siwan	Aranda	Copper Eskimo	Auracanians	Andamese
Bemba	Somali	Balinese	Crow	Aymara	Bhil
Chagga	Wolof	Ifugao	Cross Ventre	Callinago	Chuckchee
Fang		Kapauka	Mandan	Cuna	Kachin
Ganda		Marquesans	Navajo	Jivaro	Karyak
Katab		Marshall	Ojibwa	Nambicuara	Lepcha
Kikuya		Pukapuka	Papago	Siriono	Maori
Mbunda		Samoa	Pawnee	Tapirapi	Monguor
Mende		Tikopia	Tarahumara	Timbira	Okinawa
Mongo		Trobriand	Yakut	Tucuna	Samayed
Ngohi		Wogeo	Yurak	Tupinambu	
Nuer		Wollcian	Zuni	Yahgan	
Nupe		Yapese			
Nyakyusa					

Table 9.2 Reliability of Class Ratings

Scales	Percentage of Double Entries	n	Percentage of Agreement	n
Warmth of mother	67	30	89	9
Hostility of mother	70	27	75	12
Amount of praise	65	11	100	2
Frequency and intensity of physical punishment	73	15	92	12
Reward for peer-to-peer aggression	65	14	88	8
Mood variation of warmth	67	27	75	8
Mood variation of hostility	67	27	67	12
Amount of time mothers care for babies	89	9	100	8
Amount of time fathers care for babies	82	9	100	7
Amount of time other adults care for babies	60	10	67	6
Amount of time older children care for babies	90	8	67	7
Amount of time mothers care for children	100	21	67	9
Amount of time fathers care for children	82	14	89	9
Amount of time other adults care for children	75	12	83	6
Punishment for mother-directed aggression	85	26	90	10
General permissiveness	80	15	73	11
Total number of chores for boys	84	34	73	30
Total number of chores for girls	100	36	67	36
Total frequency of chores for boys	89	38	75	32
Total frequency of chores for girls	100	40	90	40
Frequency of food gathering for boys	65	20	75	8
Frequency of food gathering for girls	65	24	75	8
Regularity of food gathering for boys	65	20	75	8
Regularity of food gathering for girls	67	24	75	8
Regularity of school attendance	67	18	75	8
Other chores—Girls	100	10	90	10
Other chores—Boys	100	10	90	10

students reading the material for the reliability check. The percentage of double entries refers to the percentage of ratings where both students made any rating, as opposed to the times that only one student in the pair made a rating. The percentage of agreement column refers to the percentage of times that the ratings of both students agreed to within one point. All of the ratings except those involving responsibility training were made on 7 point scales (see Appendix 3).

Some judgments were eliminated from the analysis because of their unreliability. The rules for excluding judgments were: double judgments were eliminated if they did not agree to within one point and single judgments were eliminated if they were marked doubtful.

We have used two kinds of analysis to test our hypotheses: Pearson r correlation coefficients and chi-square analysis. When chi-square analysis was used, the data were divided as closely as possible into equal segments.

Maternal Warmth. Variation in maternal warmth appears to be largely an individual matter, since the differences among societies are not large. Nevertheless, the low warmth of the Mexican and Indian mothers suggests that sharing an enclosed courtyard with members of other nuclear families leads to more controlled emotions than does living in more private houses.

This hypothesis was tested by comparing the ratings of the four scales defining the maternal warmth factor (general warmth of mother, general hostility of mother, frequency of praise and frequency of physical punishment; for reliability see Table 9.2) with ratings collected by Murdock on family and household composition (*Ethnology*, Vols. 1 and 2, 1963, 1964). Murdock lists several kinds of extended family houses. The largest groupings are communal households, where all or a substantial portion of families of a community occupy a large dwelling, and extended families, consisting of at least two siblings or cousins in two adjacent generations. Smaller extended families consist of two families in the junior generation and one senior person, or two related families of adjacent generations. Polygamous families, where co-wives occupy a common dwelling, form a fifth type of extended family. We would like to analyze small and large extended families separately, but unfortunately our sample included only one case of a communal family dwelling and four cases of large, extended families. We therefore found it necessary to combine all four types of extended families. For the purposes of our analysis we considered both nuclear family dwellings and mother-child households to be single family dwellings. One case of a polygamous society where co-wives occupy the same dwelling if they are sisters and separate dwellings if they are not sisters was excluded from the analysis, since there seemed to be no clear criterion for classifying them.

The results of the chi-square analysis of the relationships involved in the hypothesis appears in Table 9.3. None of the relationships are significant. Furthermore, their direction suggests that any relationship between maternal behavior and household structure may be somewhat different than the single factor of warmth would indicate. Mothers in multiple family dwellings tend to be both less warm and less hostile than mothers in single family dwellings. They also use less praise and

Table 9.3   Comparison of Maternal Warmth and Household Composition

Scales		Percentage of Multiple Family Dwellings	Percentage of Single Family Dwellings	n
Warmth of mother	High	59	74	23
	Low	41	26	12
Hostility of mother	High	37	48	17
	Low	63	52	22
Frequency of praise	High	57	63	26
	Low	43	36	17
Frequency of physical punishment	High	39	53	25
	Low	61	47	28
General permissiveness	High	66	55	34
	Low	37	45	24

less physical punishment than mothers in single family dwellings. The direction of these relationships certainly suggest that mothers who raise their children in the presence of other women and children are more controlled in their emotions and sparing in their use of both reward and punishment than mothers who live in private homes.

However, the last entry in Table 9.3 raises some doubts about the interpretation of the first four entries. Mothers in societies characterized by multiple family dwellings tend to be rated as more permissive than mothers in societies with nuclear or mother houses. In the light of this relationship we might view the relative absence of both warmth and hostility and praise and punishment that characterizes life in multiple family dwellings as indicative of a policy of laissez faire, rather than emotional control. This latter interpretation is more compatible with the Whiting finding that infants are indulged more in extended family houses.

A definitive choice between these two interpretations must await a much more careful field investigation of this variable in a selected sample of societies, and probably a more detailed and sophisticated definition of the behaviors that may be considered to be indices of warmth.

Table 9.4 shows the correlations among the class ratings of the four warmth variables. The pattern of relationships among these variables is approximately the same as the pattern of the factor analysis study, but the magnitude of the correlation varies. It is interesting that, despite the high negative correlation between warmth and hostility and between

Table 9.4   Correlations among Warmth Scales

Scales	Warmth of Mother	Hostility of Mother	Frequency of Praise
Hostility of mother	−.29*		
Frequency of praise	.18	−.33*	
Frequency of physical punishment	−.07	.20	−.37*

*$p = .05$.

punishment and praise, all four variables have the same direction of relationship when compared with household structure. This does appear to indicate that they are being independently measured and may therefore be considered as independent tests of the hypothesis.

Aggression Training: Peer-Directed Aggression. We have hypothesized that severe punishment for peer-directed aggression occurs in societies where adults must maintain close-knit interpersonal relationships. There are several kinds of influences that might produce such conditions, but the presence of multiple family dwellings is certainly one of the most compelling. If we view punishment for peer-directed aggression as part of a process of training in emotional control, this hypothesis may be considered an extension of the hypothesis concerning the relationship between maternal warmth and family composition.

Some confirmation for this hypothesis has been reported by Whiting who found in a previous study that 92 per cent of the societies with extended family households have severe aggression training, while only 25 per cent of the societies with nuclear family households had severe aggression training. The probability of the difference between these two groups is .001, using Fisher's exact probability test. The polygynous and mother-child households fell between these two extremes and were not significantly different from either (Whiting, 1959). It should be noted that we failed to replicate this result with our scale of reward versus punishment for peer-directed aggression. However, the variance on this scale is very low due to the infrequent occurrence of rewards for peer-to-peer aggression.

When considering the results involving household composition, it should be noted that not all families of a society have the same type of household structure. Societies with predominately nuclear families will have some small extended families. More important, societies with extended families will have family groupings that vary considerably in size. Some houses have several nuclear families residing in them, thus fulfilling the criterion of a large, extended family; others have small extended families and still other houses are nuclear. Similarly, a substantial percentage of households in polygynous societies will be monogamous houses at any given time. Therefore, a thorough test of this hypothesis would necessitate much more careful census data on residence patterns.

Maternal Responsibility for Infant and Child Care. We have suggested that the amount of time that mothers spend caring for children is a simple, inverse function of the amount of time other caretakers spend in the same task. In order to test this hypothesis, members of the class rated our sample of societies on the amount of time that mothers, fathers, nonparental adults, and older children spend in charge of younger children and babies. The rating of the amount of time that older children spend caring for other children, exclusive of infants, was not reliable and had to be excluded. The reliabilities of the other ratings are shown in Table 9.2.

Table 9.5 shows the intercorrelations of the amount of time that mothers spend with infants and children and the amount of time that

Table 9.5 Comparison of the Time That Mothers versus Other Caretakers Spend with Infants and Children

Time that Babies are Cared for by Mothers			Time that Children are Cared for by Mothers		
	r	n		r	n
Fathers	− .40†	57	Fathers	+ .22*	62
Nonparental adults	− .06	51	Nonparental adults	− .37†	56
Children	− .56‡	54			

Time That Children are Cared for by Mothers Time that babies are cared for by			Time That Babies are Cared for by Mothers Time that children are cared for by		
	r	n		r	n
Fathers	.19	55	Fathers	.10	60
Nonparental adults	.06	51	Nonparental adults	− .18	54
Children	− .18	51			
Mothers	.40†	59			

*$p < .05$.   †$p < .01$.   ‡$p < .001$.

other caretakers spend with infants and children. The amount of time that mothers spend with babies is negatively correlated with the amount of time that fathers and older children spend caring for children, but is unrelated to the amount of time that nonparental adults spend caring for their children. The time that mothers spend caring for older children is negatively correlated with the amount of time nonparental adults care for children. Evidently, other women are helpful with older children, but not with infants. Perhaps the reason behind this is that the mothers must be available to nurse infants. Surprisingly, the time that mothers spend with older children is positively correlated with the time that fathers spend with older children.

Further examination of the data indicates that the positive correlation between the time that mothers and fathers care for children is relatively consistent across extended, mother-child, and nuclear families. Evidently it is a fairly general relationship. Since the time that fathers care for children has a low negative correlation of —.10 with the time that other adults care for them, this may represent a tendency for parents to care for children to the exclusion of other relatives. The lack of correlation between the time that mothers and other adults care for babies may be somewhat influenced by household structure. These two variables are relatively unrelated in extended families and mother-child households, but our small sample of eight nuclear household societies with ratings on these variables shows the expected negative relationship between the time that mothers versus other adults spend with babies.

Table 9.5 also shows that the time that mothers spend caring for either infants or older children is independent of the amount of time that other caretakers spend with other children in a different age group. Only the time that mothers spend with babies is positively correlated with the amount of time that they themselves must spend with older children. The independence of caretaking across age groups tends to support our finding that the care of infants and older children are separate factors.

In general, our hypothesis that mothers spend less time caring for their offspring when they have other people to help is confirmed; with the qualifications that the relationship is specific to age groups of children, the presence of other women does not affect the time that mothers spend with infants, and mothers spend more time in charge of older children, if fathers also care for them.

Maternal Instability. On the basis of a comparison of the child-care data and the maternal instability data of the *Six Culture* study, we hypothesized that mothers are more unstable when they must spend large

Table 9.6   Comparison of the Amount of Time That Mothers Care for Infants and Children and Maternal Instability

	Time Mothers Care for Babies		Time Mothers Care for Children	
	r	*n*	*r*	*n*
Variation of warmth	− .04	41	− .08	38
Variation of hostility	− .21	39	− .19	37

amounts of time caring for children. Table 9.6 shows the results of this same analysis using the larger sample. All of the correlations are low and they are actually negative in their direction. This hypothesis, therefore, is definitely not confirmed by the additional data. Instability is not related to extended versus nuclear families. We have no alternative hypothesis to propose at the present time.

Aggression Training: Mother-Directed Aggression. We have suggested that mothers who contribute to the family income, and who therefore have extensive duties other than child care, are less permissive about insubordination from their children than are mothers who are less burdened with chores that are unrelated to their children. Unfortunately we have no direct measure of the extent to which women contribute independently to the family economy.

We have used a scale suggested by Judith Brown measuring women's participation in subsistence activities to test this hypothesis (1963). Brown's method is a modification of an earlier scale developed by Heath (1958, 1959). It consists of multiplying the importance of a number of subsistence activities (animal husbandry, fishing, shellfishing, marine hunting, hunting and gathering, agriculture) with the degree of participation of women in each of the subsistence activities. The ratings are taken from the ethnographic atlas in *Ethnology*. The resultant index is a measure of the importance of women in the food production activities of the society. We assume that women who contribute heavily to the basic economy make more financial contributions to their families than women who are economically unimportant.

This index was compared with the class ratings of the degree of punishment for mother-directed aggression and with a rating of general permissiveness. These two measures are not highly correlated with each other ($r = .19$), but the general permissiveness scales seem to be measuring a similar conceptual variable as the scale of punishment, specifically for mother-directed aggression. Since the raters were able to include

Table 9.7   Comparison of Punishment for Mother-Directed Aggression, General Permissiveness, and Responsibility Training with Importance of Women in Subsistence Activities

	Amount of Punishment for Mother-Directed Aggression			General Permissiveness			Responsibility* for Boys			Responsibility* for Girls		
	Low	*High*	*n*	*Low*	*High*	*n*	*Low*	*High*	*n*	*Low*	*High*	*n*
High (145+)	55%	45%	11	75%	25%	12	38%	62%	13	58%	42%	12
Medium high (108–144)	10%	9%	19	60%	30%	21	39%	61%	23	39%	61%	23
Medium low (73–107)	50%	50%	14	57%	43%	21	38%	62%	13	38%	62%	13
Low 72–	50%	50%	10	50%	50%	14	47%	53%	15	64%	36%	14
Total *n*			54			68			64			62

* Responsibility = Total frequency of chores plus total number of chores.

more societies in this rating of general permissiveness, it was decided to include this scale in the analysis.

Table 9.7 shows the results of these two comparisons. The scale measuring punishment for mother-directed aggression is unrelated to the importance of female labor in subsistence activities, but the general permissiveness scale shows a consistent trend in the predicted direction; as the importance of women in subsistence activities increases, they become less permissive with their children. This trend is not statistically significant, largely because importance of women in subsistence activities is not predictive of permissiveness for those societies where women are unimportant in the economy. Evidently some other variable is necessary to predict whether or not women who do not have extensive food production duties will be permissive with their children.[1] These data certainly do not confirm our specific hypothesis. They do, however, provide some support for a general negative relationship between permissiveness and the degree to which women must work to produce food.

Responsibility Training. Our final hypothesis is that mothers who have extensive duties besides those of child training will require children to be

[1] One possible variable that would predict this relationship is the number of roles that are related neither to the subsistence activities, nor to child care that women must perform (e.g., doctor, magician, religious leader). However, the only scale of this dimension available at present does not consider the percentage of women who may hold these roles. This scale is not related to our measures of general permissiveness or punishment for mother-directed aggression.

more responsible than mothers who can devote themselves more exclusively to their children. The latter part of Table 9.7 shows the relationship between a combined responsibility training index and the degree of participation of women in the economy. There seems to be virtually no relationship between participation of women in the economy and responsibility training of children, although there is a suggestive trend for girls.

Table 9.8 shows the intercorrelations of the responsibility training scores and the scores of general permissiveness and punishment for mother-directed aggression. The scales of total frequency of chores and total number of chores represent summations across the frequency ratings of different types of chores (see Appendix 3). These scales are not related to either general permissiveness or punishment for aggression to mothers. Some of the individual scales, however, are correlated with these scales and these present a most intriguing picture. The regularity with which both boys and girls gather food is positively correlated with permissiveness; that is, mothers are more permissive when their children have extensive duties gathering food than when this is not the case. The same relationship holds for regularity of school attendance. Mothers are more permissive when their children attend school regularly.

The amount of punishment for mother-directed aggression is positively correlated with the frequency and regularity of performance by girls of a group of miscellaneous chores, consisting primarily of handicraft, weaving,

Table 9.8   Comparison of Responsibility Training and Permissiveness

Responsibility Training	General Permissiveness		Amount of Punishment for Aggression	
Boys	*r*	*n*	*r*	*n*
Total frequency of chores	.10	60	− .11	52
Total number of chores	− .03	60	.10	52
Regularity of food gathering	.41	27	.27	24
Girls	*r*	*n*	*r*	*n*
Total frequency of chores	.10	60	− .16	53
Total number of chores	.00	60	.03	53
Regularity of food gathering	.35*	23	.24	23
Frequency of other chores	.06	40	.45†	35
Regularity of other chores	.01	48	.49†	35
Regularity of school attendance	.35*	22	− .22	21

*$p < .05$.   †$p < .01$.

sewing, and making baskets, mats, or pots. This group of chores appears to require more skill than the others. It may be that mothers punish insubordination when they must teach their daughters difficult tasks. Unfortunately our sample has too few cases that overlap with the Barry, Bacon, and Child (1957) sample to permit a meaningful comparison of our punish-for-mother-directed-aggression ratings and their measures of achievement training.

SECTION TWO

✤ ✤ ✤ ✤ ✤ ✤

The Societies

10 ❖ Introduction: Factor Patterns between Societies

In Section One we described the factors extracted from the responses of the mothers of our six cultures to interviews concerning some of their child-rearing practices. We also discussed some between-culture differences in child-training practices, as measured by mean differences of factors scores for seven factors. We presented some hypotheses concerning the social circumstances that lead to these cultural differences and some data from a larger sample of societies that are relevant to these hypotheses.

In the following chapters we shall describe the child-training practices of each of our groups of mothers in greater detail, drawing from the ethnographic data to interpret the behavior of each group of mothers within the context of their culture. We have drawn heavily, for this second section, from the material presented in the first volume of this series, *Six Cultures—Studies of Child Rearing*. In the concluding chapter of this section we shall consider our hypotheses in the light of individual differences among the mothers of each of our communities.

Before turning to a detailed consideration of the socialization practices related to our factors of each of our groups, let us consider the relationships among these factors for each of our six communities. The factor analysis of the interview data was conducted on the data of all the samples simultaneously. The factors were rotated in such a way that they are orthogonal to each other when all of this data is considered. It is, however, possible that the factor structure might not be orthogonal for a particular society.

In theory the best way to investigate this possibility would be to compute the factor analysis for each society. However, this procedure might produce somewhat different factors which would complicate the problem. Further, our samples of from 16 to 34 mothers in each society are much too small to do an adequate factor analysis. An approximate estimate of the factor structure within each society may be obtained by examining the distributions for the factor scores of each factor against every other factor, for each of the six samples of mothers. This can be done most easily through the use of the chi square. Tables 10.1 to 10.6 present the results of these chi-square analyses. The factor scores have been dichotomized at the mean for each particular society, rather than the pancultural mean of zero. These contingency tables show that there are no significant relationships between factors for the mothers of the Mexican and African samples. The proportion of time that mothers care for older children is positively associated with punishment for mother-directed aggression in the United States sample. Punishment for peer-to-peer aggression is negatively associated with the proportion of time that mothers care for babies in the Philippines, positively associated with maternal warmth in Okinawa, and positively associated with emotional instability in the Indian community.

It might be argued that there is some tendency for the aggression-training factors to be related to other factors in particular communities. However, we would expect one or two relationships to be significant at the 5 per cent level for each group of 36 contingency tables. The operation of random variation would lead to this proportion of "significant" relationships. Since there is no more than one significant relationship per society between the factor scores of different factors, and since none of these relationships reaches the 1 per cent level of significance, it seems safe to assume that these factors are independent of each other within each of our samples as well as for the entire sample of the responses of all the mothers.

This result simplifies our analysis of these factors in their cultural contexts as well as our analysis of individual differences among the mothers of particular societies. We can proceed with both of these analyses on the assumption that we are dealing with independent entities in each of our seven factors.

In the preceding section we considered each factor separately, and in terms of our hypothesized determiners. We can also consider these factors in terms of similarity of their content areas. When they are considered in this manner six of the seven factors form three sets of pairs. There are two factors that describe personality characteristics of the mothers themselves: warmth and instability. Two factors are concerned with the mothers' overall responsibility for child; care one of these describes responsibility for babies, the other describes responsibility for older children. Two factors describe policies of aggression training; one describes maternal reactions to aggression by children that is directed against them, the other describes reactions to aggression by children that is aimed at other children.

Table 10.1 *Chi-Square Test of Independence of Factor Scores: Orchard Town Mothers*

Factor Number	Factor Title	Factor 2	Factor 7	Factor 4	Factor 5	Factor 1	Factor 6	Factor 3
2	Warmth of Mother		+ | +5 8 −6 5	+ | +6 7 −3 8	+ | +6 7 −5 6	+ | +7 5 −6 6	+ | +7 6 −5 6	+ | +6 7 −6 5
7	Emotional Instability			+ | +6 6 −5 7	+ | +3 6 −8 7	+ | +6 6 −5 7	+ | +5 7 −6 6	+ | +6 6 −5 7
4	Proportion of Time That Mother Cares for Baby				+ | +5 7 −6 6	+ | +3 9 −6 6	+ | +6 6 −6 6	+ | +6 6 −3 9
5	Proportion of Time That Mother Cares for Child					+ | +7 5 −4 8	+ | +7 2 −5 10 $p = .045$	+ | +5 7 −6 6
1	Responsibility Training						+ | +6 6 −6 6	+ | +7 5 −5 7
6	Aggression Training: Mother-Directed Aggression							+ | +6 6 −6 6
3	Aggression Training: Peer-Directed Aggression							

+ = Greater than Orchard Town mean.
− = Less than Orchard Town mean.
United States sample, $n = 24$.

Table 10.2 Chi-Square Test of Independence of Factor Scores: Juxtlahuaca Mothers

Factor Number	Factor Title	Factor 2	Factor 7	Factor 4	Factor 5	Factor 1	Factor 6	Factor 3
2	Warmth of Mother		+ − +7 6 −3 6	+ − +6 7 −3 6	+ − +7 6 −5 4	+ − +5 5 −8 4	+ − +8 5 −3 6	+ − +6 7 −4 5
7	Emotional Instability			+ − +5 4 −5 8	+ − +4 8 −6 4	+ − +3 7 −7 5	+ − +3 8 −7 4	+ − +4 6 −6 6
4	Proportion of Time That Mother Cares for Baby				+ − +4 5 −8 5	+ − +4 6 −5 7	+ − +5 4 −6 7	+ − +4 6 −5 7
5	Proportion of Time That Mother Cares for Child					+ − +7 3 −5 7	+ − +6 6 −5 5	+ − +5 5 −7 5
1	Responsibility Training						+ − +4 6 −5 7	+ − +4 6 −6 6
6	Aggression Training: Mother-Directed Aggression							+ − +6 4 −5 7
3	Aggression Training: Peer-Directed Aggression							

+ = Greater than Juxtlahuaca mean.
− = Less than Juxtlahuaca mean.
Mexican sample, *n* = 22.

Table 10.3 Chi-Square Test of Independence of Factor Scores: Tarong Mothers

Factor Number	Factor Title	Factor 2	Factor 7	Factor 4	Factor 5	Factor 1	Factor 6	Factor 3
2	Warmth of Mother		+ − +7 5 −5 6	+ − +4 8 −6 5	+ − +5 7 −6 5	+ − +6 6 −6 5	+ − +8 4 −6 5	+ − +6 6 −7 4
7	Emotional Instability			+ − +4 6 −8 5	+ − +7 4 −5 7	+ − +8 4 −4 7	+ − +6 8 −6 3	+ − +7 6 −5 5
4	Proportion of Time That Mother Cares for Baby				+ − +3 7 −8 5	+ − +5 7 −5 6	+ − +4 6 −10 3	+ − +3 10 −7 3 $p = .033$
5	Proportion of Time That Mother Cares for Child					+ − +4 8 −7 4	+ − +6 5 −8 4	+ − +8 5 −3 7
1	Responsibility Training						+ − +8 4 −6 5	+ − +6 6 −7 4
6	Aggression Training: Mother-Directed Aggression							+ − +8 5 −6 4
3	Aggression Training: Peer-Directed Aggression							

+ = Greater than Tarong mean.
− = Less than Tarong mean.
Philippines sample, n = 23.

Table 10.4 *Chi-Square Test of Independence of Factor Scores: Taira Mothers*

Factor Number	Factor Title	Factor 2	Factor 7	Factor 4	Factor 5	Factor 1	Factor 6	Factor 3
2	Warmth of Mother		+ − +7 4 −4 9	+ − +7 3 −6 8	+ − +6 4 −6 8	+ − +5 9 −5 5	+ − +3 7 −10 4	+ − +8 2 −5 9 p = .040
7	Emotional Instability			+ − +6 7 −5 6	+ − +4 8 −7 5	+ − +6 8 −5 5	+ − +6 7 −5 6	+ − +5 8 −6 5
4	Proportion of Time That Mother Cares for Baby				+ − +6 7 −6 5	+ − +7 7 −6 4	+ − +5 8 −8 3	+ − +7 6 −6 5
5	Proportion of Time That Mother Cares for Child					+ − +8 6 −4 6	+ − +7 5 −6 6	+ − +7 6 −5 6
1	Responsibility Training						+ − +6 8 −7 3	+ − +8 6 −5 5
6	Aggression Training: Mother-Directed Aggression							+ − +6 7 −7 4
3	Aggression Training: Peer-Directed Aggression							

+ = Greater than Taira mean.

− = Less than Taira mean.

Okinawan sample, $n = 24$.

Table 10.5 Chi-Square Test of Independence of Factor Scores: Khalapur Mothers

Factor Number	Factor Title	Factor 2	Factor 7	Factor 4	Factor 5	Factor 1	Factor 6	Factor 3
2	Warmth of Mother		+ − +4 6 −7 7	+ − +3 7 −8 6	+ − +5 5 −7 7	+ − +4 3 −6 11	+ − +3 7 −7 7	+ − +6 4 −6 8
7	Emotional Instability			+ − +5 6 −6 7	+ − +6 6 −5 7	+ − +3 4 −8 9	+ − +3 7 −8 6	+ − +8 4 −3 9 p = .050
4	Proportion of Time That Mother Cares for Baby				+ − +5 6 −7 6	+ − +2 5 −8 9	+ − +7 4 −3 10	+ − +7 5 −4 8
5	Proportion of Time That Mother Cares for Child					+ − +2 5 −10 7	+ − +3 9 −7 5	+ − +7 5 −5 7
1	Responsibility Training						+ − +3 4 −7 10	+ − +4 3 −8 9
6	Aggression Training: Mother-Directed Aggression							+ − +3 9 −7 5
3	Aggression Training: Peer-Directed Aggression							

+ = Greater than Khalapur mean.
− = Less than Khalapur mean.
Indian sample, n = 24.

Table 10.5   Chi-Square Test of Independence of Factor Scores: Nyansongo Mothers

Factor Number	Factor Title	Factor 2	Factor 7	Factor 4	Factor 5	Factor 1	Factor 6	Factor 3
2	Warmth of Mother		— +4 7 −2 3	— +3 8 −3 2	— +5 6 −4 1	— +5 3 −6 2	— +5 6 −2 3	— +7 4 −3 2
7	Emotional Instability			— +2 4 −4 6	— +2 7 −4 3	— +3 5 −3 5	— +4 3 −2 7	— +5 5 −1 5
4	Proportion of Time That Mother Cares for Baby				— +3 3 −6 4	— +3 5 −3 5	— +3 3 −4 6	— +5 5 −1 5
5	Proportion of Time That Mother Cares for Child					— +3 5 −3 5	— +4 5 −3 4	— +5 5 −4 2
1	Responsibility Training						— +4 4 −5 3	— +5 3 −5 3
6	Aggression Training: Mother-Directed Aggression							— +4 6 −3 3
3	Aggression Training: Peer-Directed Aggression							

+ = Greater than Nyansongo mean.
− = Less than Nyansongo mean.
African sample, *n* = 16.

The factor that deals with responsibility training is the only one that describes mothers' reports of their children's behavior, rather than their own behavior. This factor has no logical pair in the present study.

In order to facilitate the description of the behavior of each group of mothers we have grouped the factors into the pairs described above. At the beginning of each of the chapters dealing with particular societies we shall present a figure that represents a graphical presentation of the mean of the sample of mothers of a particular society for each of the factors, on scales representing the possible range of the distribution of factor scores from plus 1 to minus 1. When interpreting these figures the reader should remember that the pancultural mean for each group of factor scores is always zero. These figures therefore are a simple, visual representation of the mean positions of each group of mothers on the six factors that make up our factor pairs.

We have also computed the difference between the position of each group of mothers for each of the factor pairs. The differences between positions of the mothers of a sample for the factors of a factor pair were computed by means of the Wilcoxsin matched-pairs signed-ranks test (Siegel 1956).[1]

We could, of course, compute the difference between any two factor means. However, it does not seem particularly meaningful to ask: "Do mothers care for babies more than they emphasize responsibility," or "Are mothers more warm than they punish children for peer-to-peer aggression?" It does seem meaningful to compare the position of these groups of mothers on the three pairs of factors that are linked by content area. That is what we have done in the tests, for differences between means on the pairs of factors.

With these tests we have, in effect, asked three questions:

1. Are mothers more warm than unstable, or more unstable than warm?
2. Is the responsibility of mothers for child care greater for babies or for older children?
3. Do mothers react more severely to aggression by children when it is directed against themselves, or when it is directed against other children?

---

[1] This test is similar to the Mann-Whitney U test that was used in the chapters of Section One to test for between-society differences on a single factor. The Mann-Whitney test is designed for comparisons between sets of scores obtained from different people. The Wilcoxsin test is designed for comparisons between sets of scores obtained from the same people.

Each of these comparisons appears meaningful and these three appear to be the only meaningful comparisons of this nature that are possible for this group of factors. They are, therefore, the only comparisons of between-mean differences within each cultural sample that have been computed.

We now turn to a consideration of these socialization factors in their various cultural contexts.

11 ❖ The Mothers of Orchard Town, New England

Figure 11.1 shows the mean position of the Orchard Town mothers on the factors measuring temperament, responsibility for child care, and aggression training.

The mothers of the Orchard Town sample are intermediate in warmth. Their mean on the "warmth" factor is —10, almost at the pancultural mean of zero. They rank fourth of a high group of four societies on the percentage of cases above the pancultural mean (Table 2.1). They rank fourth on the scale, warmth of mother, a scale that shows no significant intercultural differences. They rank second on hostility of mother but are not substantially different from five other samples. They rank fifth on amount of praise, but again are not reliably different from five other samples. Only on their use of physical punishment are they somewhat unusual. On this scale they rank last and, with the Okinawan mothers, report using substantially less physical punishment than any of the other groups (Table 2.2). Their affectionate expressiveness is approximately the same for children regardless of age after the child is no longer an infant and for both sexes (Tables 2.3 and 2.4).

These mothers also hold an intermediate position on emotional stability. They rank second on the emotional instability factor and, with the mothers of the samples in Mexico and India, form a middle group on this dimension (Table 3.1); with Mexico they form a middle group on variation of both hostility and warmth (Table 3.2). Their position on the two factors is approximately equal (Figure 11.1, scale 1). These mothers are about as warm as they are stable.

The warmth of the New England mothers seems to waver between sensitive concern for their children's needs, both physical and emotional, and anxiety about their own willingness to and capability for meeting these needs. Since Orchard Town is not occupied by related kin groups who agree upon a single set of norms, these mothers worry much more

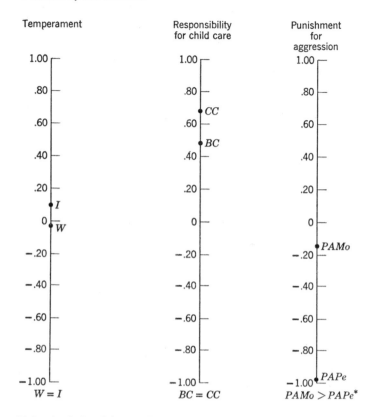

Figure 11.1   Analysis of intrasociety differences on mean factor scores: Orchard Town.

* $p < .01$, W = warmth of mother, I = instability of mother, BC = mother's responsibility for baby care, CC = mother's responsibility for child care, $PAMo$ = punishment for aggression to mother, $PAPe$ = punishment for aggression to peers.

than other mothers about the correctness of their own behavior and that of their children. Although most mothers were, unlike those in other samples, aware that the investigators were "professionals" and anxious to make a good impression, they frequently expressed doubts about their ability to raise their children well. Their success in this maternal role was most important to them since children's character is believed to be shaped largely by their mothers.

Children are thought to possess various potentials which, although based on heredity, are heavily influenced by training. It is the responsibility of parents to recognize and understand the child's potential and then to reinforce and guide it. Since different children have different potentials, parents cannot decide in advance the nature of a given child's potential. Either too little or too much pressure on a child may harm the development of his natural potential. Too little discipline is thought to make children lazy; too much discipline makes them nervous.

Mothers must, therefore, choose a middle ground in discipline and many are anxiously unsure of where this middle ground should be. Mothers are expected to place the development of their children above their own convenience and not indulge in practices that might inhibit such development. Since the mother is the chief caretaker, she is primarily responsible for the development of children's character. Most mothers recognized this responsibility and take it very seriously.

On the other hand, since alternate roles are available to women in American society, some mothers feel their children to be burdens who are limiting their lives and preventing the fulfillment of their personal ambitions. These attitudes may be accentuated when wives feel that their husbands are not taking their fair share of child-tending duties. Wives are sometimes bitter with their husbands for such neglect and some displace their resentment to the children.

This conflict of desires, to raise children well and give them an abundance of affection and to maintain some autonomy and privacy, is accompanied by several beliefs about practices that "spoil" children which do not occur in most other samples. Some of these beliefs have the ring of rationalizations. Mothers' responses to their infants' crying depends upon their interpretation of the infant's needs. It is considered dangerous to spoil children by picking them up when they are crying only for companionship. Furthermore, letting infants "cry it out" is considered good occasionally both for character and lungs. Children are weaned early panculturally speaking, most are weaned before the age of 18 months. Allowing children to have bottles after they are walking is also thought to "spoil" them. Bedtime is fixed fairly rigidly until children reach their teens. The rationale for this is that children need their sleep, but the practice also frees the mothers for the evening. Playing outside in all but the most inclement weather is good for children's health, and also gets them out of mother's way. Children who come running home to mothers with their problems instead of settling them themselves are also "spoiled" and it is felt that they should be more independent, and bother their mothers less.

One good reason for this conflict, perhaps the most important one, is the fact that the New England mothers have very little help in caring for their children. They are significantly higher than any other group on the proportion of time they are in charge of babies (Tables 4.1 and 4.2) and, with the African mothers, higher than other groups on the proportion of time they care for older children (Tables 5.1 and 5.2). The proportion of time that they spend caring for the infants is approximately the same as the proportion of time they spend caring for older children (Figure 11.1).

The factors that contribute to this isolation are inherent in American society. In Orchard Town all families are nuclear, consisting of a man and his wife and children, although a widowed parent of either spouse may sometimes live with them. Families like to live near the wife's parents if possible, but many families have few if any relatives living nearby. The fathers work away from home in jobs which, for the most part, do not permit them to take their sons along. Older children are all in school; this takes them away from home but leaves the mother alone with preschool children.

Some fathers help take care of children during the times that they are home. They may amuse the children while their wives get dinner, and let their sons come with them when they work around the house on weekends. Fathers usually help most when the family has several preschool children, but they are less likely to care for babies than they are to care for children over 2 years old. Seventy-nine per cent of the fathers sometimes cared for babies. This proportion is not too unusual, since it places them between the Philippine and Mexican fathers in a group that is higher on this scale than other samples (Table 4.2). The time these fathers spend in caring for older children is more deviant. Ninety-six per cent of the Orchard Town fathers sometimes care for older children, a substantially higher proportion than in any other sample (Table 5.2).

Persons other than the parents seldom care for children except at times when it is necessary for parents to leave for a specific purpose. Older children may be placed in temporary charge of younger ones while the mother goes shopping. Some women share such child-tending duties with their neighbors. Children may be left with relatives, usually grandparents, when the parents go on vacation. When parents go out in the evening they must often hire an unrelated person to stay with the children. The paid baby-sitter, an ubiquitous American phenomenon, is the end result of the American family's isolation.

None of these caretakers are used very frequently. Only 12 per cent of the Orchard Town children care for babies (Table 4.2) and only 8 per cent of them care for older children (Table 5.2). They are lower than other samples on both of these dimensions, although not significantly lower than most other groups. Adult caretakers, other than the parents, are also relatively infrequent. Forty-two per cent of the Orchard Town babies and 25 per cent of the older children are sometimes cared for by such adults (Tables 4.2 and 5.2). Although these figures do not place the sample unusually low, the extent of care by these adults is low, as evidenced by the fact that the mothers have so great a share of the care-taking responsibilities.

Unavailability of adult caretakers is perhaps the chief reason why they are not used, but not the only one. Child-rearing norms are unclear in Orchard Town. Since neighbors are unrelated, their values may be different and many mothers do not trust their neighbors' judgment with their children. Value conflicts may occur even within the family. Some mothers resent correction of their children by grandparents. The wisdom of the aged is not respected as much here as in other societies, and grand-parents sometimes are not given the authority to reprimand their charges. When parents are present their word takes precedent over that of the grandparents. Many grandparents are reluctant to care for their grand-children, and are therefore unavailable except in emergencies. This lack of clarity of norms, distrust of other people's judgment, and great concern that children be raised well, leads some mothers to avoid other caretakers even when they are available. Mothers sometimes brag that no one else has ever fed their children or put them to bed. Thus, the values of the mothers as well as their physical isolation makes them assume almost exclusive care of their children.

In general the Orchard Town children do not have as many chores as children in the other samples. This sample is ranked either five or six on the percentage of children doing chores for every task except running errands and helping to clean house. The sample ranks fourth on the percentage of children who run errands, only 21 per cent of the Orchard Town children were reported to do this. In sharp contrast to these low ratings, the sample ranks first in the percentage of children (88%) who help clean house, and is significantly higher than any other society on the percentage of children doing this one chore (Table 6.2). Girls do chores more frequently than boys ($p < .02$) but do not have more varied chores to do (Table 6.4).

These results are due in part to the greater technological development of American society as compared to the other societies in the sample and to the greater wealth of the Orchard Town families as compared to the families of other samples. Some of the chores assigned to children in other countries, such as gathering wood and carrying water, are totally absent in Orchard Town because of inside plumbing and central heating. Others, such as caring for animals and helping in fields, are rare or absent because the Orchard Town families are not farmers. Some of the families have gardens but they contribute only a small portion of their total food and reportedly none of the children in the sample age range help in them, although some teenagers do so occasionally.

The educational requirements of the American school system keep older children away from home most of the day. The children eat lunch at school and have homework in the evening. After school and on weekends many children spend some time away from home taking special lessons, such as music lessons, or participating in scout meetings or other club activities. Since education is required for both boys and girls neither are available for baby tending or cooking during the day. The high school standards expected of the children lead many parents to excuse them from work around the house. This unavailability is reflected in the finding that only 8 per cent of the children care for younger siblings or help cook. The equality of treatment of both sexes is reflected in the absence of sex differences in task assignments.

The only chore that the Orchard Town children are more likely to do than other children is clean house. This result is due in large part to the frequent reports that children must pick up their toys. This in turn reflects the relative wealth of the Orchard Town families. Picking up toys is not a chore for children in the other samples because the children own few if any toys. The frequency of this particular task probably also accounts for the somewhat unusual finding that although the younger children have fewer chores to do than older children they do them almost as often (Table 6.3). Picking up toys is required of almost all the children (Table 6.2), and the children, whether young or old, are required to do this every day.

Technology and wealth are not, however, the whole story. The age at which children are thought to be responsible is somewhat later here than in some other societies. Children are discouraged from taking charge of younger siblings because children are considered irresponsible and incapable of coping with the irrationality of younger children. Babysitting is considered to be more burdensome than in other places. Not until the age of 12 are children judged to be responsible caretakers. This attitude stems in part from the great concern of these mothers that they raise their children properly, a concern that causes them far more anxiety than the mothers of any other sample. In part, it comes from a desire to treat children equally regardless of their age. To some degree, however, it reflects genuinely low expectations for responsible behavior.

The low level of expectancy is also reflected in the absence of strict training in obedience (Table 8.2). Mothers expect to remind their children about doing chores and often do not follow through on their requests. Some mothers are concerned about becoming "nags" by too frequently repeating their requests. They also do not require prompt obedience. Finally, although these women consider that their status is roughly equal to their husbands', the husband has the entire responsibility for discipline, when he is around, in eight of the twenty-four families studied. This practice seems calculated to reduce obedience to mothers when they are alone. In any case the data show that the Orchard Town mothers rank fifth in both consistency obedience training and expectation of prompt obedience, and are significantly lower than most other societies on both these scales.

Consistent with this laxness in obedience training is the unique position of these mothers on the factor measuring punishment for peer-directed aggression.

Figure 11.1 shows that the mean of the Orchard Town mothers for the peer-directed aggression factor is at the extreme low end of the scale; it is, in fact, —.98. This low position is reflected in the position of the Orchard Town mothers relative to the mothers of other societies on this factor.

The Orchard Town sample is lower than any other group on the factor measuring severity of training in peer-directed aggression ($p < .00003$, Table 8.1). They are lower than any other sample on consistency of rules about such aggression ($p < .01$) and higher than any other on reward for retaliation ($p < .001$) (Table 8.2). The extent to which these mothers reward retaliation is particularly striking. Eighty-three per cent of the Orchard Town mothers report that they encourage their children to retaliate when attacked by a peer.

The mothers of this group are not nearly so permissive about aggression directed to themselves as they are about quarrels among children. Figure 11.1 shows that the mean of the Orchard Town sample for mother-directed aggression is —.13, close to the pancultural mean of zero. The Mann-Whitney U test shows that these mothers punish aggression to themselves more strongly than aggression to peers ($p < .01$). Table 7.2 shows that this group ranks third on the mother-directed aggression factor and, with the Taira mothers, forms a middle group, relative to the other societies.

We have suggested that punishment for aggression among peers is related to the degree to which families share their living quarters with their relatives, and that punishment for aggression to the mothers is related to the economic importance of the mothers. Since the Orchard Town mothers have a high degree of privacy and do not usually work, the discrepancy between these two aspects of aggression training is consistent with our interpretation.

It should be clearly recognized that the relative lack of punishment for peer-directed aggression does not mean that Orchard Town mothers permit uncontrolled aggression among children. The distinction between fair and unfair fighting is taught early. Mothers punish infants for biting, although they will permit them to hit or howl. If a child persists in biting even into early childhood, parents will not let their children play with the offender. One 3 year old was shunned by the neighbors for this reason. Throwing rocks or using sticks is also prohibited. These rules are enforced by parents who consider such practices unfair and are also concerned that they may have to pay the doctor's bill for an injured child. Furthermore, children are not encouraged to start fights, only to defend themselves if wrongfully attacked. Mothers do not comfort a child who is not, in their opinion, in the right.

Conflict is also channeled into competition. Unlike the children in Tarong who are too "ashamed" to perform in public, Orchard Town children are encouraged to show off to overcome their supposedly innate shyness. This training starts in the home and is reinforced in the early grades in school when teachers encourage children to volunteer information. The success of this encouragement makes enthusiastic hand waving a problem for teachers in the later grades, who must discourage the more enthusiastic children.

The children soon learn the rules of fighting fairly. By the time they have reached the age of 7 mothers need not reward retaliation as much as they did in younger years ($p = .06$, Table 8.3). Boys are expected to be more aggressive, at least physically, than girls. The tendency to reward retaliation less in boys than girls seems to be due to the perception that boys are sufficiently aggressive, while some girls must be encouraged to stand up for their rights. The encouragement of aggressive needs in girls seems to be partly due to a desire to treat girls equally and not have them intimidated by their male playmates. The perception of males as the more aggressive sex is tempered by the belief that the fights of boys will diminish with increasing age while the cattiness of girls gets worse as they grow up.

Indirect aggression such as cattiness is frowned upon, as is displaced aggression, particularly to animals. Although mothers in other societies punish aggression to other children but permit children to hurt animals, the Orchard Town mothers are far more concerned about their children's cruelty to pets than they are about their fights with neighbors' children. Why should these mothers be so deviant in peer aggression? The difference may be due in part to the fact that neighbors' children are not relatives as they are in many other samples. If real unfriendliness occurs families can sever their relations and, if necessary, move. This alternative does not exist in the other communities of the study. Furthermore, the families of this sample are independent of each other economically, therefore competition can be emphasized at the expense of cooperative behavior. The requirements for success in self-support in this society require initiative and self-assertion. The concern that boys, particularly, "stick up for themselves" is no doubt training for their future roles. Finally, the democratic values of American society require respect for the rights of individuals. Unlike the societies where close kin ties make group solidarity more important than abstract considerations of justice, the issues of an argument are paramount in Orchard Town. Children are taught to respond in terms of issues, respecting both their interests and the rights of others. The accusation "he hit me first" is seldom heard in other samples, but is an accepted justification for aggression in Orchard Town.

This respect for children's legitimate complaints modifies the reactions of mothers to defiance of their authority, as well as quarrels among children. Mothers are usually patient with the outbursts of small children.

They may simply hold the hands of young children who strike them and even laugh if they are not hurt, but during the preschool period most mothers begin to teach their children self-control. Some mothers try to prevent aggression by avoiding frustrations and distracting their children when they see conflict approaching. When outbursts do occur, aggression to the parents, either physical or verbal, as well as temper tantrums are discouraged. Often verbal aggression elicits only scolding, while physical aggression brings spanking in return. However, the Orchard Town mothers are more sensitive than others to moodiness in children and may ignore aggression if they believe the child to be in a "bad mood," particularly if the upset has some reasonable cause. Mothers are also reluctant to punish children publicly and may stand for more aggression when strangers are present than they would tolerate alone. As children grow older they are expected to confine themselves to verbal expressions of hostility and not hit their mothers. Within these limits the same respect for issues that leads the mothers of Orchard Town to encourage justified retaliation to peers makes them accept some complaints from their children.

The New England fathers seem, in general, to share the values of their wives about aggression. Men do not want their sons to become sissies and encourage them to fight in self-defense. They also think that it is better to let children get their anger "out of their systems" than to harbor hostilities against their parents. One man allowed his son to hit him at certain designated times because he thought this would be good for the child.

Delinquency in Orchard Town is limited mostly to property damage. Such damage as occurs is usually to public property, although occasionally a child arsonist sets fire to a home. New England mothers train their children rather early in respect for property and it may be that aggression against parents is the unconscious motivation for the property damage which occurs.

Summary

The mothers of Orchard Town are unusual in that they are relatively isolated and spend much of their time alone with their children and in exclusive charge of them. Their belief that they must guide their children's development along proper channels, their anxiety about conforming to ideal norms that are culturally unclear, and their conviction that no one else can adequately substitute for a mother makes them reject alternate caretakers even when they are available. The relatively high emotional instability of these mothers appears to be due, in part, to the large amounts of time they spend in charge of children.

These mothers are also unusual in the degree to which they encourage aggression among children. The very isolation that binds them to their homes and children enables them to be less concerned about relations with their neighbors than the mothers of other groups.

Mothers want their children to be independent; a necessary goal in a society that requires it of adults. They also consider principle to be sometimes more important than group solidarity. As part of their child training they encourage children to "stand up for their rights" and, if necessary, fight back when attacked by other children. The extent to which these parents encourage such aggression is unusual, compared to other samples. The training is accompanied by rules for "fair fighting" that are rigidly enforced, so children are seldom injured in a fight.

It is perhaps this same concern for the right of individuals as well as a desire to be democratic and not suppress their children's emotional development that makes these mothers lenient about obedience and permissive about aggression to themselves. They hesitate to nag their children or interfere too much with their activities. Many also feel that it is healthier to let children "blow off steam" than harbor suppressed hostility.

The position of the Orchard Town mothers on the other factors of our study is not extreme. Responsibility requirements are moderate. Older children are required to be in school for most of the day, and are therefore not available for chores. When they come home they often have to study. Some chores that must be done in other places are unnecessary in the

New England sample. The concern about proper techniques of child training made mothers reluctant to put younger children in the care of older ones, who might be too impatient. Most children picked up their own toys and many helped to clean their rooms. They also helped wash dishes. All of these tasks are coded as "clean house," the one kind of chore on which these children are described as unusually high.

Finally these mothers are distinguished by their awareness and comprehension of the purposes of the investigation. They were often more self-conscious with the researchers than the mothers of other samples. They gave more complete responses to the interviews than any other group, perhaps because they were more aware of the purposes of the investigation.

12 ✤ The Mixtecan Mothers of Juxtlahuaca, Mexico

Figure 12.1 shows the position of the Juxtlahuaca mothers on pairs of factors. The figure shows that these mothers are below average on warmth and about average on emotional stability. They are more unstable than warm ($p < .05$). These mothers are very close to the pancultural mean in the extent to which they care for children and have similar means on the factors measuring time spent in the care of babies and of older children. They are above average in their concern for aggression, particularly aggression among children.

The analysis of factor scores indicates that the mothers of the Mexican and Indian samples are colder than the mothers of any other group ($p < .06$, Table 2.2). The analysis of scales shows that 57 per cent of the Juxtlahuaca mothers are rated high on warmth, while 79 per cent of them are high on hostility; 55 per cent are high on the amount of praise they use, while 91 per cent are high on their use of physical punishment (Table 2.2). This coldness is accompanied by intermediate stability. Fifty-five per cent of the Mixtecan mothers have factor scores above the pancultural mean of the emotional instability factor, placing them in the middle of a middle group of three. Seventy per cent of these mothers are rated high in variation of hostility, and 48 per cent of them are rated high in variation of warmth, placing them in a middle group of two on both these variables.

The amount of warmth expressed to children decreases when they reach the second stage of childhood, at about 2 years, and are weaned. Before this time, as they are thought to be senseless, they are comforted when they are unhappy or hurt. After the age of 2, children are ridiculed if they hurt themselves because, since they are now "children who know," they are expected to avoid such accidents.

Weaning seems to mark the transition from the consistent nurturance of infancy to the non-nurturance of older childhood. During weaning children become fussy and may cry frequently. The mothers' sympathy

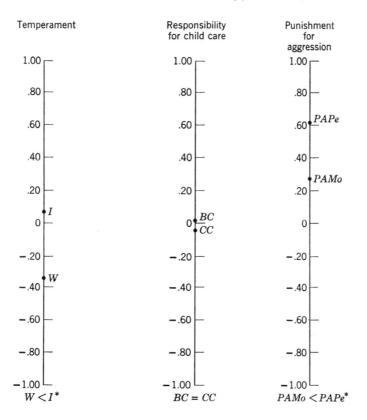

Figure 12.1 Analysis of intrasociety differences on mean factor scores: Juxtlahuaca.

* $p < .05$, W = warmth of mother, I = instability of mother, BC = mother's responsibility for baby care, CC = mother's responsibility for child care, $PAMo$ = punishment for aggression to mother, $PAPe$ = Punishment for aggression to peers.

for such outcries is unpredictable, they may or may not comfort crying weanlings, depending upon their activity at the time, their mood, and other factors. Often mothers encourage older siblings to take care of crying weanlings, thus helping to shift the toddler's dependence from themselves to other members of the family. The weaning process also marks the end of the time that mothers habitually carry children in their shawls. Weaning in Juxtlahuaca is a withdrawal of nutrition, physical contact, and emotional support.

After children are weaned response to their demands is less immediate, particularly when they have no apparent need. Mothers still respond to children fairly promptly when there is some cause for their discomfort, but will usually scold or beat children who "cry without reason," a behavior that they believe increases after weaning. As children reach and pass the "age of reason" nurturance continues to decrease, as demands for responsible behavior increase. Although the mothers badger older children with frequent requests, they seldom praise them for a job well done. When children do not want something from their mothers, or are not wanted by them to do some chore, their mothers usually leave them to their own devices. Neither women nor men enjoy playing with children, so their free time is largely spent apart from adults.

In early infancy, children spend a good deal of their time with their mothers. Mothers care for babies almost exclusively for the first 40 days of their lives, and are the primary caretakers of infants, particularly for the first 4 or 5 months. After these first months the mothers begin to seek help in caring for their infants. When they go to barter at the market, they may take their older children with them, who must then sit quietly for several hours. But mothers leave their nursing babies with female friends or relatives who are also lactating and can nurse them. The most common substitute caretakers when mothers go to do work or visit close to home are older daughters, who are left in charge of younger children when mothers leave the house.

With daughters, mothers-in-law, and sisters-in-law to help them, these mothers rank fifth on the amount of time they spend with children, as measured by the factor score analysis (Table 4.2). They rank fourth on the scale measuring the proportion of time they care for babies, while both children and nonparental adults rank second on their comparable scales (Table 4.3). Mothers are more likely to care for baby girls themselves ($p = .04$, Table 4.4), while older boys are more likely to care for infants than older girls ($p = .04$, Table 4.4). This finding is probably an artifact of family composition where it just happened that several of the mothers with infants had boys of caretaking age but no daughters.

Seventy-seven per cent of these fathers are reported to sometimes care for babies, placing them third in a high group of three on this scale. The amount of care given by these Mixtecan fathers is remarkably consistent; the seventeen fathers who do some baby-sitting are all rated four on the scale, e.g., more than sometimes but less than half the time. Actually, almost the only baby-sitting chore of the fathers of this sample is to mind babies occasionally during the night or early morning or when their wives and daughters take siestas.

Although the factor score analysis shows that the rank of three of the Mixtecan mothers on the child-care factor (Table 5.2) is higher, relative to other societies, than their rank of five on the infant care factor (Table

4.2), the actual proportion of time that these mothers spend in charge of children decreases as they grow older. Fifty per cent of the Mixtecan mothers are rated high on the proportion of time they care for infants (Table 4.3), while only 41 per cent are rated high on the proportion of time they care for older children (Table 4.3). Furthermore, the original, uncondensed ratings on these scales show that seven of these mothers always cared for their infants, while only one always cared for her older children.

Children and other adults give the mothers considerably more help with older children. The Juxtlahuaca children spend significantly more time caring for their younger siblings than the children of any other sample ($p < .05$, Table 5.3), while nonparental adults, grandmothers and aunts, spend significantly more time in care of older children than in any sample but the Philippines ($p < 0.2$, Table 5.3).

This transition in caretakers begins, as we have said, at weaning when mothers encourage older children to comfort the irritable weanling, and shift his sleeping place from her bed to that of a sibling. Children who are 3 to 6 years old may be urged to help even young children when they are in trouble, but have no responsibility for their care. The oldest daughters are left in charge of younger children when the mothers leave and frequently look after them when mothers are busy. They may even bathe and dress their younger siblings, and take them along when they go to the stream to wash clothes.

Fathers are somewhat less likely to look after older children than they are to be in charge of infants. Sixty-four per cent of these fathers sometimes take care of older children. Usually this consists of taking care of boys, particularly when they go with their fathers to the fields to work.

Work is not demanded of children until they are considered teachable. The Juxtlahuaca mothers believe that children are incapable of learning anything until they are 2 years old, about the time that they are weaned. Until this age they are "in darkness." At about the age of 2 children enter a stage that is called "this child now knows." Children in this second stage are believed to have "awareness" and be capable of learning through imitation. When the children get their second set of teeth, at the age of 6 or 7, they acquire the ability to reason and become teachable. This period of teachability is maximal between the ages of 6 and 12. When children enter adolescence the probability of changes in their basic character become increasingly small. After the age of 18, character is firmly set and cannot be altered.

The responsibility training of these mothers is based on this conception of their children's character. Older children have more chores to do than younger ones ($p = .05$) and usually do them more frequently

($p < .20$, Table 6.5). They believe that young children should "play when they want to and help when they want to." Children under 6 years of age do a number of small tasks to help around the house but they are not expected to do them regularly. The jobs done by young girls include helping with the dishes, bringing firewood, and helping their mothers or older sisters bring water from the stream. Girls begin to learn the correct postures for carrying water and grinding corn through playful imitation before they are strong enough to actually do these jobs. Young boys start learning to feed and care for animals and may bring their fathers' lunches to them in the fields. Chores are not strongly sex-typed in early childhood and young boys may do tasks that are considered "women's work." Both boys and girls run errands. Sixty-four per cent of the Juxtlahauca mothers report that their children run a percentage of errands that is higher than in any group ($p < .01$, Table 6.3). Younger children tend to run errands more frequently then older ones (Table 6.5).

After children reach the "age of reason" they are expected to assume their share of the family's labor. Work is no longer voluntary and is now more differentiated with respect to sex. Since children often do not attend school regularly, they are available to help around the house. Girls take care of younger siblings, carry water, do some of the shopping, sweep the house, wash dishes and clothes, and care for the family fowl and pigs. About one-half of the girls help cook; no boys do this job ($p = .05$, Table 6.4). Boys bring wood in the nearby hills, split logs for firewood, and stack them in neat piles in the courtyards. They feed and water the burros and goats, a task that is seldom done by girls ($p = .03$, Table 6.4. Boys also help in the fields doing some of the light field work and bringing fodder for the animals back to the houses. None of the mothers report that girls help in fields or gardens ($p < .10$, Table 6.4), however, during harvest and planting the whole family may go to the fields. At these times girls help prepare food and take care of small children. Small animals such as the chickens, turkeys, and pigs that are kept around the homes might be fed by either boys or girls. Feeding animals is taught, however, as a male chore and is not reported by the mothers as a task done by girls.

The chores of girls are usually more time consuming than those of boys. However, if there are no sons in a family, girls are not expected to take on male tasks, the father does the work himself; but in families without daughters, boys do jobs that are normally done by girls and women. Of the mothers in the sample who had infants, it happened that in several instances there were no daughters of the appropriate age to act as caretakers and therefore boys were pressed into that role. This led to the empirical finding that more of the boys in the sample were taking care of infants than were girls. It may be for this reason that the total number of chores reported for boys and girls is approximately the same (Table 6.4). Girls are expected to be more responsible than boys, and an analysis of the observational material reveals that this is true in actual performance. Girls are more responsible about doing their chores, and their play more frequently imitates adult activity than does the play of boys.

The expectations that older children will be more responsible than younger ones and girls will be more responsible than boys is reinforced by the expectations that older children will obey more promptly than younger ones ($p = .008$, Table 8.5) and girls more promptly than boys ($p = .02$, Table 8.4).

Responsibility training is also reinforced by maternal preference that children, particularly girls and older children, play alone near the house. The reason for this preference is the same as for the Gusii mothers, they want to keep their children from dominating other children or fighting with them. As in Nyansongo the effect of this practice is to keep the children close to home and available to help around the house.

Figure 12.1 shows that the Juxtlahuaca mothers are well above the pancultural mean of zero on both aggression training factors. They punish all aggression more than most groups of mothers but they are particularly severe in punishing aggression among peers.

The Juxtlahuaca mothers are significantly higher than any other group on the factor measuring severity of punishment of aggression to peers. They are particularly likely to use physical punishment themselves to discourage physical aggression ($p < .002$, Table 8.3). Their position on the individual scales that load highly on this factor, while tending to extremes, is not significantly different from that of other societies.

The Juxtlahuaca adults are relatively unaggressive so that children have peaceful models with whom to identify. Envy and competitiveness are regarded as minor crimes in this community. Men of prominence make suggestions rather than giving orders to their followers, and group decisions are taken by unanimous consensus rather than simple majority or dictation by authority figures. Men cooperate in working communal lands, and may harvest collectively. Most of the activities of the community involve cooperative rather than individual or competitive activities. Men sometimes quarrel about women, land, or politics but physical aggression is rare. When it occurs the assailant is usually drunk and the reaction of his peers may be to quiet him rather than to retaliate. The prohibitions on overt aggression are buttressed by the belief that anger and hostility can make a person ill and eventually kill him.

Despite their overt friendliness, people sometimes suspect their neighbors of using witchcraft.   There is a tendancy to displace the source of evil to outsiders.   The Spanish-speaking Mexicans from other parts of town are viewed with great suspicion.   It is believed that no one in the Mixtecan barrio is a witch.   If someone wants to use sorcery against any enemy they hire a witch from the Spanish section of Juxtlahuaca or a neighboring town.   Barrio people can cast the "evil eye" on others, particularly children.   To protect children from this danger babies are kept inside the house for forty days after they are born and no one but members of the family are allowed to see them, later they are covered, head to toe, with blankets when they sleep.   Witches may cast the evil eye deliberately, but people who are not witches have no control over this power.   Like the Tarong ancestors, the neighbors who may inadvertently bring harm into the house are believed to be innocent of evil intent.

Despite the fact that mothers prefer to have their children play alone they usually play with their close relatives, cousins and siblings.   Among themselves the children play peacefully.   Like their parents they have trouble when they must enter the Spanish-speaking part of town to go to school.   As they go to school children of these higher-status families insult and sometimes attack them.   Many of the Mixtecan mothers give these aggressive incidents as reasons for not sending children to school.   Intimidated by these more aggressive children, the Mexican children seldom retaliate directly.   They may try to avoid the threat or pass it off as a joke.   These timid children can fight or wrestle as long as the tussle is in fun, but when it becomes serious they retreat.   After they have been in school a few months these children either accept their subordinate position or resort to ignoring or redirecting aggression, and retaliate by indirect aggression, such as lying.

The Mixtecan mothers also disapprove of aggression directed to themselves, but they do not react to this as strongly as they do to quarrels among children.   Seventy-three per cent of these mothers have factor scores above the pancultural mean for this factor; with the mothers of Tarong they form a high-middle group, below the Gusii mothers but above the mothers of the other three samples (Table 7.2).   Their intermediate position seems, in part, to be caused by some inconsistency in their training of this behavior.   Eighty-one per cent of the mothers of this sample retaliate to aggression directed against themselves, but 50 per cent of them are rated high in the extent to which they comfort children when they become angry while being scolded.   Despite the fact that they believe young children to be incapable of reason they are more likely to retaliate to the aggression of young children than to that of older ones ($p = .02$, Table 7.5).

The actual use of harsh physical punishment such as a whipping with a stick or belt is almost entirely limited to the punishment of aggression. Use of physical punishment is rare. For example, even though it was reported by every mother, the field observations of mothers' behavior contained no examples whatsoever. Our assumption is that the control of aggression is learned during early childhood with the result that there is less retaliation for aggression for the older children.

Summary

The Juxtlahuaca mothers have extreme positions on two of the factors of this study, warmth and punishment for peer-directed aggression. Our hypothesis is that both of these characteristics stem from the intimacy of their social ties with the other adults of the community. Like the Rajput mothers of Khalapur, the Mixtecan mothers of Juxtlahuaca work in courtyards with their husbands' brothers' wives. Their children share these courtyards with their paternal cousins. The social connections among adults in Juxtlahuaca are even more intimate than in Khalapur because Juxtlahuaca is an endogamous community. Most mothers are, therefore, related to their sisters-in-law by blood as well as marriage.

Under these circumstances mothers who favor their own children over their cousins may disrupt adult relationships by precipitating quarrels among sisters-in-law. Mothers who take sides with their children when they fight with their cousins are particularly likely to have this effect. Treating all children with some emotional distance and strongly discouraging fights among the children are highly functional socialization practices in this type of community. These Mixtecan mothers are more successful in avoiding quarrels that are their Rajput counterparts. Only one Juxtlahuaca family was disrupted by a fight over children during the course of the field study.

The reaction of these mothers to aggression to themselves is not as severe as their reaction to aggression among children. The Juxtlahuaca mothers, like those of Khalapur, may comfort children who become angry while being scolded. Peace is often more important than an issue in an extended family household and mothers evidently feel that they can tolerate some insubordination within the nuclear family.

The responsibility training of children in Juxtlahuaca is based on the belief that they become capable of learning by imitation at the age of 2 and teachable at the age of 6 or 7. When children are weaned, at about 2 years of age, the mothers become more inconsistent in their expression of warmth than they were previously. They put their weanlings to sleep with their older siblings and encourage older girls to take care of them.

Before the age of 6 or 7 chores are not sex-typed and boys may do "women's work." Until they reach the "age of reason" children's work is voluntary. Children of 6 years and older contribute labor regularly to their families. They are expected to do more chores and obey more promptly than their younger siblings. Work also becomes sex-typed after this age, although boys may still do women's work if they have no sisters old enough to do it. Girls generally are expected to be more responsible than boys and to obey more promptly.

Girls help take care of younger children. The oldest girls are left in charge when mothers leave their homes. More children act as baby-sitters in Juxtlahuaca than in any other sample. Aunts and grandmothers also help take care of children so the Juxtlahuaca mothers have a variety of help with the task of child care.

13 ❖ The Mothers of Tarong, Philippines

Figure 13.1 shows the position of the Tarong mothers on our factor pairs. The zero point on the scales represents the pancultural mean of the factor scores. The figure shows that the Tarong mothers are medium in their expression of warmth and are emotionally stable. They spend relatively little time caring for their children. They are above average in punishment for aggression. On the maternal warmth factor (although they are not different from other groups) the Tarong mothers are rated second and sixth or last in emotional instability. Figure 13.1 shows that the Tarong mothers are higher in warmth than they are in instability ($p < .01$).

There are some predictable suspensions to the warmth of the Tarong mothers. One is their withdrawal from a child during weaning, even this may be delayed until the child is 3 or 4 years old if there is no subsequent pregnancy. The second is the aggressive teasing to which infants and young children are subjected. As soon as babies learn to want an object, women tease them by alternatively offering and withdrawing it, until the children burst into frustrated tears. When this happens all the women present laugh, the object is given to the child and he is assured that they are only playing. Although the instigators of this teasing are usually childless women, mothers usually permit it and join in the ensuing laughter.

This teasing appears to be a device whereby children are taught the concept of "nurturant-hostile familiars" which is gradually developed into "kidding," group ridicule, and the potentiality of ostracism. For older children these methods replace physical punishment, though more slowly within the nuclear household. The child being subjected to this "game" also learns the proper response—to howl loudly with imitative fury, then laugh when the object is restored. The proper adult response to the constant kidding of others is to grin happily throughout; the relationship is clear. The notable fact is that before he is a year old, the

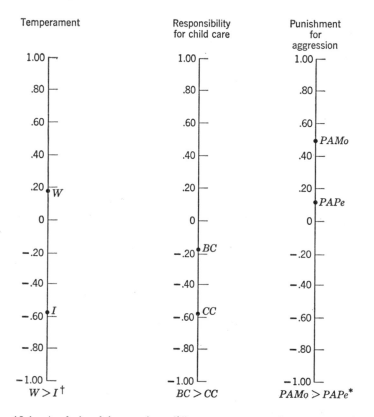

Figure 13.1   Analysis of intrasociety differences on mean factor scores: Tarong. * $p <$ .05, $p <$ .01, W = warmth of mother, I = instability of mother, BC = mother's responsibility for baby care, CC = mother's responsibility for child care, $PAMo$ = punishment for aggression to mother, $PAPe$ = punishment for aggression to peers.

Tarongan child is introduced to the method of social control most prominent in the adult world.

The Philippine and Okinawan mothers are more stable emotionally than any other groups (Table 2.2). Both hostility and warmth are contingent on children's behavior (Table 2.3). Tarong mothers are equally stable with children of all ages and both sexes (Tables 2.4, 2.5). This does not mean that mothers never punish children. They have an intermediate position on their use of physical punishment (Table 2.3). But punishment is delivered with predictable consistency and physical punishment is used only after scoldings have failed. Rewards are generally verbal or edible and are equally consistent. As one mother put it, "Whipping is the helpmate of your mouth, candy in the first hand, a whip in the other." With such a policy the Tarong child is warned and his punishment, when administered, is deserved.

The sociableness of Tarong women makes child care a group project. Tarong women like to feel that "we all (i.e., all women in the sitio) take care of our children." Although this ideal is an exaggeration, no mother has exclusive responsibility for her children. Mothers are expected to stay close to home for the first six months after the birth of a child, and to keep the infant with her whenever possible until it is weaned. But neighbors are on hand when needed and many Tarong women occasionally nurse each other's children, while some few do it regularly. All Tarongan babies are nursed for a day or more after birth by a woman other than their mother; an appropriately symbolic entry into Tarongan group life.[1]

This group care is reflected in the low position of the Tarong mothers on the factors measuring baby and child care. The central scale of Figure 13.1 shows that the Tarong mothers, as a group, are below the pancultural mean on both of these factors and that their means on the two factors do not differ from each other.

This group care is also reflected in the Philippine position on the scales of Factor 4. Although 50 per cent of the Tarong mothers usually take care of infants, 83 per cent of the mothers report that their infants are sometimes cared for by an adult other than the parents (Table 4.3). Eighty-three per cent of the mothers also report that fathers sometimes care for babies. Both these percentages are higher than comparable percentages for any other group and the percentage of Tarong babies that are cared for by nonparental adults is significantly higher than any other group in the study. Fathers usually care for babies for a period when the mothers are recovering from the birth, and may take care of children throughout their childhood when their work permits.

The shift in caretaker at the time of weaning is demonstrated by the fact that the Philippine sample ranks third on the factor measuring infant care (Table 4.2) and sixth on the factor measuring the care of children (Table 5.2); although in neither case does the Tarong sample differ from several others. Whereas 50 per cent of the Tarong mothers usually care for infants (Table 4.2), only 21 per cent usually care for older children (Table 5.2). Even though this latter figure is undoubtedly an underestimate it represents a real shift, since fathers, sib-

---

[1] For details about birth practices see Chapter 5 of *Six Cultures—Studies of Child Rearing.*

lings, and other adults are all more frequently reported as occasional caretakers for older children than for infants (Tables 4.3 and 5.3).

The Tarong sample ranks first in the proportion of time that a non-parental adult takes care of children. The Philippine and Mexican samples are higher on this scale than any others ($p < .02$, Table 5.3). In this connection we should note that these adults are more likely to take care of girls than boys ($p = .05$, Table 5.4). Although grandfathers may take care of older children, grandmothers and aunts are the usual caretakers referred to in this table. These women, particularly grandmothers, like to take a child along on visits to other sitios and barrios to keep them company. Girls are preferred for such occasions since "they behave better than the boys." Girls are also more useful as helpers, and are more often encouraged to stay with a relative. This preference, plus the fact that boys spend more time with their fathers (although this is not obvious from the tabulated data), probably accounts for the reported difference.

Finally the data show that, although 5- and 6-year-old children may be informally in charge of a younger sibling, the mothers do not report that children act as caretakers until they are over 7 ($p = .05$, Table 8.3). Evidently children are not seen as dependable caretakers until after they reach the "age of reason" at 6.

The unusual friendliness of the Tarong women affects most aspects of child rearing. More than most other mothers they tend to rear their children as a group. Even though Tarong mothers are around the house when their children are infants and need not, like the Okinawan mothers, leave home for long periods of time, women sometimes nurse each other's children, a custom seldom found in other groups. When the child must be weaned he is encouraged to adopt a sibling, aunt, or grandmother as partial replacement for the mother. Fathers also help in this transition and take on the duties of housework without losing status, unless there are kin and neighbor women who can easily take on these tasks. The atmosphere throughout is nurturant, easy going, and emotionally stable.

In such a friendly and cooperative community it is obviously essential that people learn responsibility. Tarong men, for example, are obligated to help both relatives and neighbors at any time as part of the Tarongan social ethic. A failure to offer help or extend support is construed as unfriendly, not neighborly, and as a far more serious and disrupting act than petty quarreling. A Tarongan must rally round in time of need, though he is not absolutely required to put a good face on it.

In addition to this generalized readiness to help, a Tarongan man is normally a member of one or more loosely structured cooperative work groups, membership being based on kinship and proximity.[2]   Here work credit is built up against one's own time of need.   These work groups function much as did the American barnraisings, in this case providing manpower for large projects such as house building, leveling additional land, and so on.

Women are not involved with such tasks and there are no women's cooperative work groups of this nature.   But the general obligation to readily offer help is equally important to them and more often relied upon.   Women are dependent upon related or neighboring women for help at all special events such as births, feasts, funerals, and no less importantly, for daily companionship and help caring for their children.

Tarongans' desire for sociability is intense.   They say, "How can a man live if he does not have neighbors to help him?," and refer as much to a need for companionship as to help in its concrete manifestations. To live alone by choice is not only unpleasant and impractical, but indicates a disinterest in relatives and friends that is nearly immoral.

Tarong is one of the three communities in our study where children are expected to do a large variety of chores (Table 6.3).   Responsibility is taught, in part, by assigning chores to children at an early age.   Preschool children help their parents in a variety of tasks.   They may carry water, bring wood from under the house for the stove, unstake the family goats, take them to nearby pasture and bring them home at night, help feed the chickens, pick vegetables, or occasionally even cut rice. Children also take some care of babies at the age of 4 or 5.   A child of this age may watch that his young sibling does not fall off the porch, or he may walk the baby in the yard.   Five-year-old children, both boys and girls, are sent to play in the yard with a toddler at their heels, and are expected to keep the younger child safe and out of mischief.   Although caretaking children of this age are given immediate adult aid in even a minor emergency, they do help keep toddlers out of their mothers' way.   Since these 2 year olds often are recently displaced weanlings, they may be very fussy burdens for their young caretakers.

Before the age of 6, children are not usually expected to do tasks on their own initiative.   Since responsibility entails minimum self-reliance, even for adults, children are discouraged from attempting tasks too difficult for them and are encouraged to seek aid whenever they are in trouble.   Somewhere between the ages of 4, when children begin to

[2] For details about types of work groups and their composition, see Chapter 5 of *Six Cultures—Studies of Child Rearing.*

have sense, and 6 when they are presumed trainable, children should begin to do regular chores without being told. But adults are ambivalent about encouraging self-initiative in children, both because they fear children will waste time and effort by doing jobs ineptly, and because they do not want their children to become so self-reliant that they grow obstinate and uncooperative.

This ambivalence of parents leads to inconsistent reinforcement for self-initiated behavior. On the one hand, children may be punished for doing a job badly, particularly if the failure has destroyed property or made more work for the mother. On the other hand, children are praised highly for successfully completing a task beyond their years. The precociousness of such accomplishments is recognized by referring to the child as an adolescent or a young adult. This kind of "up-aging" is high praise indeed, since the people of Tarong do not attribute any sentimental status to the period of childhood. Both children and adults agree that maturity is the best time of life. The incentives for initiative, both praising and intrinsic reinforcement, seem to outweigh the punishment, because Tarong children like those of Taira, tease their parents to help with new jobs and repeatedly try to take on tasks beyond their years. Gradually children learn to walk the middle ground required by their culture. They try out skills on their own initiative, but ask for help if the undertaking proves too difficult.

The assignment of tasks by sex is not as rigid in Tarong as in some other communities. Fathers are expected to take over their wives' jobs of cooking and child care for 11 to 30 days after the birth of each new baby and when their wives are ill. The men do not complain about these jobs and may even humorously challenge each other as to who can claim the best-kept house. This lack of sex-linked specificity is evident in the jobs assigned to children. Both boys and girls take care of siblings and help cook, and both may carry water, gather wood, feed or water animals, or help in fields or gardens.

The assignment of some tasks depends upon the sex distribution in a family. Boys are often taught to cook and may take on this job if no sister is available. Similarly girls help in the fields of a family short of men. As is true in most societies, both boys and girls run errands. But some jobs are preferentially sex-linked: only one boy cleans house, while six girls do this ($p = .05$), and only two girls, as opposed to six boys, pasture animals ($p = .10$, Table 6.4). These differences in chores occur as a matter of course as children begin to imitate their same-sex parent. While a girl proudly follows her mother to the river to help wash, a boy, with equal pride helps his father bring home the carabao. The girls' chores are more frequent, because women's work is the more varied and because they are more likely to be close to home when mothers need them; but the chores of boys are more arduous and time consuming, so that the work is not unequally divided.

There are two chores that are reportedly assigned to older children; cooking and running errands (Table 6.5). The important factor in chore assignment is really individual maturity. A child evidencing sufficient maturity to do a job well will be encouraged to do it, regardless of chronological age. However, sibling position does modify this picture somewhat. The eldest child finds himself prodded into maturity whereas the youngest is babied well past the normal age.

Two other influences on chore assignment should be mentioned although they are probably less important than those already discussed. First, the economic level of the family is the primary determinant of the amount of time the mother spends working (beyond doing housekeeping tasks). The amount of her free time will, in turn, determine how many tasks she will urge her children to do for her. One child of 9 years from a very poor family essentially took care of the house and younger siblings while his parents were out working.

Second, the number of persons other than the nuclear family who live in a household generally affects children's chores. Of the twenty-four sample children, six lived in households including a grandmother or aunt. Such a woman is likely to take on some household tasks and thus reduce the number of chores done by the children.

This friendliness also affects the pattern of aggression training, which necessarily begins young. The third column of Figure 13.1 shows that the Tarong mothers are relatively high in their punishment of aggression, particularly when it is directed to themselves.

The concern for ingroup aggression is a result of the Tarongan's view of people. These villagers divide their social world into three distances: the "neighbors," including close kinsmen and their spouses who are often also kinsmen, living in the same housing group or sitio; the "familiars," including kinsmen and friends who live in the same barrio, some kinsmen in adjacent barrios where in-laws may reside, and some school acquaintances. Beyond these two groups of friends and relations are the "outsiders," strangers who are automatically viewed with initial suspicion.

The interdependence of the kin group makes the maintenance of intrasitio quarrels virtually impossible. When quarrels develop among members of the same sitio, the quarrel must either be resolved or one of the factions must move their residence. In order to avoid such social dislocation the Tarongans do not support intra-sitio quarrels. When disputes do arise, as is inevitable when people's lives are so intimately interwoven, the participants occasionally voice their complaints in loud and angry quarrels which clear the air, leaving little bitterness. The villagers consider bullying intolerable and frown on premeditated retaliation, even when justified, but they recognize that human frailty leads to occasional bad temper, and consider that spontaneous explosions are safer than suppressed hostility. Nevertheless, all the group's pressures will be brought to bear to settle the dispute.

Occasional long-term grudges may erupt into violence, particularly across sitio or barrio lines. Personal feuds are not unheard of and political disputes or insults may send men home to fetch their knives. Even when this happens, social control does not break down. Men more frequently threaten one another with their knives than strike with them, although killings have occurred. Elder men may threaten younger, hotheaded sons and nephews with withdrawal of economic assistance and social support, unless they settle their disputes. The need for caution in expressions of ill temper is successfully impressed upon boys of 16 years or younger, whose quarrels might result in bloodshed. Parents are not loath to make such threats since the sins of hostile children are blamed on faulty training. There is a strong feeling that within-barrio disputes should be settled within the barrio. Therefore every effort will be made to reach agreement between members of this group without seeking outside legal aid. Threats of social ostracism are usually effective in settling such quarrels.

Outside the barrio are strangers who are greeted with a polite friendliness often concealing distrust. One of the adjacent barrios is believed to be the home of witches who poison those rash enough to venture there without protective magic talismans or accept their food and water. This fear is typical of the tendency of Tarongans to attribute trouble, particularly illness, to evil forces from outside the barrio. Only one woman in the barrio was thought to be a witch, but witches were more numerous in surrounding areas.

Illness is also attributed to spirits. It may be caused either by spirits of the ancestors who, since they were Tarongans, are not evil, but who may unwittingly cause chills and nausea by their friendly greeting to familiars. More commonly, illness is caused by "those who are not human," a variety of spirits who are deliberately malevolent. Like witches, these spirits are avoided if possible and magic is used to counteract the effects of unavoidable contact.

This division of the world into friends and strangers is quickly introduced to children, along with the appropriate responses. As infants they are introduced to friends. Each new infant is greeted with enthusiasm. Neighbors come to admire and pat the child and visit with the mother. The neighbor's children come along and beg to hold and play with the baby. For the first two years at least, the infant is indulged whenever possible by his family and neighbors.

This happy period comes to an end when the mother becomes pregnant once again. Sometime during the pregnancy, early if the child is old enough, later if he is too young, the toddler must be weaned, not only from the mother's breast but from her attention and indulgence. At this point the toddler is introduced to the Wawak, a spirit who kills and eats bad children. This spirit (as well as physical devices like putting pepper or manure on the breasts) is used to discourage children who still want to nurse. The Wawak sometimes materializes in the form of an old woman in a black cloak and mask who stalks the barrio once or twice a year at the request of parents. Extracting promises of good behavior as a condition for protection, the parents hide their frightened children while the Wawak peers into a window, moans, and passes on. This apparition validates parental strictures and is usually effective until 8 or 9.

Another validating device is the parentally encouraged scolding by any fortuitous male who might appear, such as an official, visitor, etc., who is a stranger to the child. These scoldings are quite patterned and all strangers can handle the situation well enough to shame and frighten a child into tears. It also, of course, reinforces his growing understanding of the outside world as possibly hostile.

While outside threats are used to discipline young children, the family group takes over to assist in their transition during weaning. Family members offer sympathy, attention, and special fruits or sweets in an effort to distract the upset weanling from his deprivation. These substitutes are only gradually successful and until the toddler attaches himself to an older sibling, aunt, or grandmother, he is, like the Taira baby, a crying, unhappy child. Eventually the child does widen his horizon to include his siblings and the women of the neighbor's houses, who can act as partial substitutes for the now busy mother. Thus, by the very weaning that brings on temporary bad temper, the child learns to extend his affectional ties to the larger kingroup.

Adult reaction to the aggression of children is similar to their attitudes regarding the aggression of adults. Children are not expected to be stoic in their emotional expression. Fighting among youngsters is expected. But bullying is intolerable and the Tarong mothers rank the lowest on reward for retaliation, although they are not substantially different from the mothers of three other groups (Table 7.3).

There is no cultural justification for children's (and many adults') retaliation. Mothers do not ask who started a fight or why; fighting is wrong and all children involved are equally punished. Children's quarrels, like adult's, are avoided when possible and quickly forgotten when they occur. The ability to forget is in large part due to the lack of a concept of "just" retaliation, at least at the child's level.

Among children from the same sitio aggression most often takes the form of teasing, as it does around adults. This device may range from fun to a powerful threat of social ostracism that quickly brings a deviant into line. Except for the prerogative of young boys to pinch the genitals of little girls who do not keep their skirts in place, this teasing is equally popular with cross-sex and same-sex groups. The play group of the young child includes all the children of his sitio or house cluster within the sitio. Ages range from toddlers through young teenage school children watching over the young ones and cross-sex play is more common than same sex play.

By the time children have reached the age of 8 or 9, there is a preference for close friendships with one or more of the same sex, but this is more noticeable in the sex-divided classrooms and schoolyard than in sitio yards. Though even here, similar chores are more likely to bring same sex children together and differences in reaction to aggression are noticeable; most girls have learned to avoid or ignore the teasing of boys and to respond with teasing only to the attacks of girls, while boys ignore girls' teasing but may fight another boy. Children of both sexes may report unwarranted attacks to an adult.

When the Tarong children enter school their friendships rarely cross sitio lines. By this time they have learned to distrust strangers and the quarrels among school children usually follow the factions already laid down by kinship ties. The occasional child who has no one from his own sitio in school is very lonely and, like an adult without close relatives, tries to attach himself to schoolmates living near his home. The inter-sitio disputes that take place in school often result in quarrels but only occasionally in more overt scuffles. Such disputes are never encouraged by parents.

The cooperativeness of the Tarong children and the primacy of their friendship ties inhibits competition. Children from the same sitio help each other with their homework and may hand in identical homework papers. The children do not strive for high achievement and generally agree that friendships are easier if all marks are about the same in school. These attitudes are encouraged by the parents who prize cooperativeness. They further point to a child too shy to answer by himself in class with a proud "He is ashamed," for boldness in one so young is considered a bad sign. This attitude plus the fear of strangers makes most children mute when asked questions by an outsider. Nevertheless, school contacts eventually produce friendship ties beyond sitio boundaries and extend the child's horizons.

When children reach adolescence they visit neighboring barrios to attend dances and other social gatherings to meet potential marriage partners. Still shy with outsiders, the Tarong adolescent pairs off with one of the same sex so that he or she has an inseparable companion who can act as chaperone, confidant, and crutch. Teen-age boys, who might quarrel with boys from other barrios whom they meet at dances, are warned against the dangers of such outgroup fighting and soon learn to be careful since their opponents may be armed. Cross-sex aggression at this age is very rare, and teasing is more likely to be flirtatious than aggressive.

The Tarong mothers are rated high on the consistency of their obedience training, but with the New England mothers they are significantly lower than any other group in expecting prompt obedience. These rankings are in accord with observations. A Tarong child is thought to be obedient and if he is dependable, he need not be prompt. Mothers often ask a child several times to do something, and if the child eventually complies he is said to have obeyed. Although the mothers usually follow through on their demands, children sometimes avoid requests by visiting a neighbor's house until the mother has forgotten about it, found another child to do it, or done the job herself. If the task has been done without undue disruption the child may not be scolded upon his return. Outright defiance, however, challenges both authority and the nurturant atmosphere of the Tarong home and is promptly punished.

Tarong mothers discourage aggression directed at themselves, just as they discourage peer-directed aggression. While children are being weaned, usually between the ages of 2 and 3, temper tantrums are common and the weanlings may hit, kick, and scream at their mothers. At this time aggression is laughingly tolerated, since adults recognize that this transition is a difficult period for children. Aggression by older children is viewed more seriously.

As a group, the Philippine and Mexican mothers are less strict than the African mothers in punishing mother-directed aggression but stricter than the other three societies (Table 7.2). None of the Philippine mothers reward mother-directed aggression and 82 per cent punish such behavior (Table 7.3). There is a tendency ($p = .10$) for mothers to retaliate more intensely to attacks by older children than to attacks by younger ones (Table 7.4). Most school-age children are sufficiently self-controlled to express their anger only verbally. Similarly, while some arguments between adolescents and adults are considered part of growing up, they seldom erupt into physical violence. One teen-aged boy who threatened his father with a knife was unanimously diagnosed as a victim of spirit control, since it was inconceivable to Tarongans that he could have done this of his own free will.

Summary

The most unusual characteristics of the Tarong mothers are their emotional stability and extent to which others help them with their child care. The hypothesis presented concerning the origins of these two factors assumes that these two characteristics are functionally related; that is, the emotional stability of this group of mothers is due, in part, to the presence of other adults who can help them care for children.

The close mutual dependence of adults on each other is a general characteristic of life in Tarong that affects most social interaction. Children are prepared for this life of mutual interdependence by introduction to sitio sociability and nurturance. Responsibility is also encouraged by an early introduction to chores. All children above the age of 3 have at least one chore to do. Children do these tasks first upon request and later on their own initiative. They are never expected to persist unaided in a task too difficult for them to manage, since self-reliance is not a Tarongan value.

Indeed, too much independence is threatening to this intimate community and children are encouraged to be shy in public. Competitiveness is discouraged and deliberate aggression is viewed with great alarm. Spontaneous outbursts of anger are expected and smoothed over without hard feelings in both children and adults. More serious aggression is prevented by bringing strong group pressure to stop fights, particularly among kinsmen, and blaming strangers or spirits for many troubles. All of these attitudes are impressed on children, who play chiefly with their siblings and sitio-mates and are taught to be afraid of strangers and of spirits. By the time the children enter school these attitudes are so fixed that they make close friends very slowly with children who are not their neighbors or relatives. Aggression in school is more overt than in the sitio and the opposing factions usually follow kinship-residence lines.

Aggression to the mothers is discouraged in much the same way as other ingroup aggression. Spontaneous outbursts of anger are tolerated, particularly in children who are being weaned, but as children grow older they are expected to confine their anger to complaints; physical assaults upon the mother by older children are rare and are severely punished.

Finally the predictable but easy-going policies that mold much of the behavior of the Tarong mothers are most clearly seen in their training of obedience. The mothers report that they usually enforce requests they make to children but do not necessarily expect prompt compliance. If the children finally carry out their tasks, even after several reminders, they are said to have obeyed. In this, as in most Tarongan socialization practices, the resultant learning pattern is directly applicable to the adult world.

14 ❖ The Mothers of Taira, Okinawa

Figure 14.1 shows the positions of the Taira mothers on three pairs of factors. These mothers are, as a group, highest on the warmth factor. They are lower than average on the instability factor. Their means on these two factors are significantly different from each other ($p < .01$); Taira mothers are both warm and stable. Taira mothers are close to the pancultural mean of zero on the child-care and aggression-training factors. They have similar mean factor scores for the baby and older child-care factors and for the factors measuring peer-directed aggression and mother-directed aggression.

The Taira mothers are the warmest in the sample, although not significantly warmer than the Philippine, African, and New England mothers (Table 2.2). They are, moreover, less hostile, in general, than any other group; they use more praise than any other group and they use less physical punishment than any but the United States mothers (Table 2.3). This warmth is most apparent in the treatment of infants. The belief that infants are godlike and must therefore be indulged is accompanied by a belief that the bad habit of crying is formed in the first four months of life. To prevent the formation of this habit mothers, fathers, and grandmothers rush to comfort a crying infant. He is picked up at once, cuddled, nursed, whether he is hungry or not, and if necessary is held for long periods of time until he stops crying. If a mother should delay her attention because she is busy the grandmother, father, or older sibling will insist that she attend to the infant at once.

This extreme indulgence is gradually withdrawn by the mother as she resumes her usual work of gathering firewood in the mountains, a job which absents her from the home for most of the day. When the mother is away the infant is usually carried by its grandmother in the morning and the early afternoon. When the baby's older sibling returns home from school the infant may be transferred to her back so that the grandmother can garden. Mothers who have no help can do minor work in the fields with the burden of their babies on their backs. To do their regular field or mountain work they have to wait until an

222

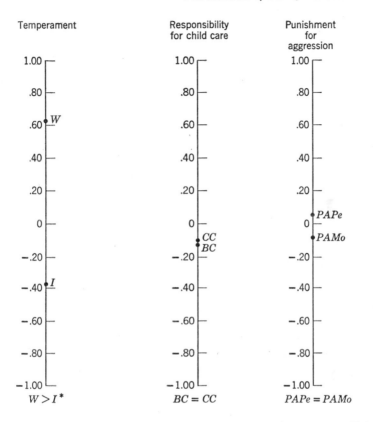

Figure 14.1   Analysis of intrasociety differences on mean factor scores: Taira.
* *p* < .01, *W* = warmth of mother, *I* = instability of mother, *BC* = mother's responsibility for baby care, *CC* = mother's responsibility for child care, *PAMo* = punishment for aggression to mother, *PAPe* = punishment for aggression to peers.

older child, a relative, or a neighbor's child comes home from school to take the baby. In any event the infants are not left alone. Despite this attention infants are upset and cross during this weaning period.

When the process is complete, however, they have enlarged their circle of affection to include more relatives. This constant adult attendance continues until the birth of the next child is a few months away. At this time most mothers abruptly wean their youngsters from both breast and back and, at the same time, greet their crying with anger and impatience instead of the familiar comfort and concern. Praise, which has hitherto been lavished for almost all behavior, gives way somewhat to promises of special food or clothing, promises which are not usually kept. Praise, however, remains as an important reinforcement, as shown by the finding that 83 per cent of the Taira mothers are above the pancultural mean on the amount of praise they give their children (Table 2.3). It is now used differentially, to reward good behavior. As the child approaches the crucial seventh year that marks the end of his divine nature and the beginning of his capacity to be responsible, his bad behavior is increasingly punished with the admonition "naughty child."

The aggressive humor of the Tairan's is another mitigation of their general warmth. Infants are sometimes teased even before they understand its meaning and children are occasionally teased by parents beyond the limits of their good tempers' endurance.

Finally, although the Taira mothers infrequently use physical punishment, it should be mentioned that they have several very severe punishments that, although rarely carried out, are used as threats. The most severe of these is cauterizing a patch of skin with moxa, a burning powder. Children may have their hands or feet tied for several minutes to an hour for going to forbidden places or playing with forbidden objects. Less severe punishments include hitting and pinching. Children, when struck, are usually struck with the hand rather than a switch or stick. Grandmothers particularly may pinch naughty children. All these punishments, however, are relatively rare and the Taira mothers tend to rely most heavily on praise to train their children.

The warmth of the Taira mothers is consistent. The Okinawan and Philippine mothers are significantly more stable emotionally than those of any other group (Table 3.2). Along with the mothers of the Indian sample they comprise the lowest group on both variation of hostility and variation of warmth. But whereas the Indian mothers are consistently cold the Okinawan mothers are consistently warm (Table 3.3). It is noteworthy that, despite the professed belief that children are divinely irresponsible and ought to be indulged, the mothers' warmth is significantly more variable with younger children ($p = .04$) and the same trend in hostility variation is strongly apparent, although it fails to reach statistical significance (Table 3.5). This finding needs to be interpreted against a background of general consistency. By the time the children reach first grade even the warm and patient mothers of Taira may become irritable when their children fail to obey them after they have returned from a tiring day of work. At such times the children, most of whom have learned to judge their parents' moods, are more likely to obey than when the parents are rested and relaxed, but when they do not the busy, tired and harassed mothers may scold and slap their youngsters. The decline of this irritability with older children is probably due to the more responsible behavior of the latter which makes such outbursts un-necessary.

Taira mothers are not unusual in the amount of time they spend with children (see Figure 14.1). The Taira babies are cared for primarily by their mothers during the first three or four months when they must be nursed frequently. Since the mothers' absence from their usual work of cutting firewood for sale seriously diminishes the families' incomes, most babies are soon turned over to a grandmother or to another mother who can also nurse the infant, or some other women too old for heavy work. Over half of the Taira babies are sometimes cared for by other adult relatives, or, for short periods, by their fathers. Babies are sometimes strapped to the backs of older children, who play carrying their charges. However the people of Taira use children for baby-tending less than other groups in the sample although the Maretzkis' ethnography sug-gests that this may be an understatement (Table 4.3).

As the babies get older they are turned over to the care of older sib-lings while the grandmother goes back to her gardening or takes on the care of a new baby. This shift of caretakers becomes evident when one compares the data of Table 4.3 and Table 5.3. Okinawa ranks third in the proportion of time that adults other than the parents care for babies, and sixth in the proportion of time that nonparental adults care for children of 2 years and over. On the other hand, twice as many mothers report that children care for younger children as report that children care for infants.

Unlike other adults fathers are more likely to care for older children than for infants. The amount of time that the mother is in charge of her children decreases only slightly as they get older. However, the closeness of supervision and the amount of attention devoted to the child decrease as he gets older.

As supervision decreases, responsibility increases. The pancultural tendency for older children to be assigned chores more frequently than younger ones is strongest in the Taira sample. Table 6.2 indicates that only two of the twelve children under the age of 6 years had daily chores. Actually five of the remaining ten children had no regular chores. This is in sharp contrast to the older children, eleven of whom have chores to do daily or several times a day while the twelfth does chores several times a week. The probability of this difference is .001, higher than comparable probabilities in any other sample. Older Taira children also have more varied chores than do the younger ones ($p = .04$) but this contrast is comparable in magnitude to that of some other samples (Table 6.2).

The reluctance to assign chores to young children is perhaps related to the Taira belief that children, who are considered to be gifts of the gods, are themselves godlike until the age of 6. This godlike nature, like that of the ancestral spirits, is willful, unpredictable, and untrainable. At about the age of 7, the children outgrow this personality, for reasons which the parents were unable to explain, and become responsible and teachable. This change in status is ritually recognized by a switch from unceremonious burials for children under 7 to adult funerals for children older than 7. It coincides with entry into first grade, a rise in status that is recognized by both children and adults. The assignment of daily chores to virtually all children older than 7 indicates that an emphasis on industriousness is quickly manifested once the children reach the "age of reason," although the Taira mothers, the warmest in our sample, are lenient with their children about temporary lapses of performance.

There is no sex difference in either the number of chores assigned or their frequency, but girls are expected to be more conscientious than boys in the performance of their duties. Most of the chores assigned to children, caring for babies, cooking and housecleaning, folding bedding, bringing water, and caring for the animals, are also done by women but not by the men. Because these activities are women's work, mothers are concerned that their daughters learn to do them well and reliably, while for boys they are only temporary assignments. It is notable, however, that although feeding and watering animals is women's work, only boys were assigned this as a regular chore (Table 6.4). Girls sometimes help feed the pigs.

Pasturing animals, typically a male task, does not occur in Taira. Fodder is cut and brought to the pigs and goats that comprise most of the village livestock. Seven families own horses, and fodder is also brought to them. Children under 10 years of age usually do not help in the fields. Cutting wood in the mountains is too arduous a task for children under 10 as is most of the work for wet rice cultivation. Children may help with the rice harvest, but they are not expected to do so regularly until they are over 10. Younger children sometimes go with their parents to the fields to sow or clean sweet potatoes.

While the field study was being conducted a few families raised silkworms and the children of these families helped pick leaves for them to eat. Sometimes neighbor children would help clean the silkworm cocoons playfully enjoying their silky texture.

It is obvious from the interview quotations presented in Chapter 6 that the Taira mothers say they praise their children for doing their chores well, particularly when they do more than is expected of them.

This policy is more successful than the negative one of the Khalapur Rajput mothers, since the Taira children are often eager to assume new responsibilities, a motivation usually lacking in the Khalapur children. First grade children sometimes want to go to the mountains to help cut wood, although this work is considered too heavy for young children. Children who are too young to carry infants on their backs strut proudly when someone ties a doll or rolled cloth on them, and they are praised for their imitation. Four- and 5-year-old children tease their mothers for the privilege of carrying a newborn sibling. A sturdy kindergartner is allowed to carry a baby for short periods of time, to the envy of his peers. It should be said that as the novelty wears off and the baby grows heavier, older girls, who regularly carry younger siblings, find their burden irksome and may delay their return from school to avoid it. Since obedience training is not strict this strategy is frequently successful. Nevertheless, despite the discouragement of their mothers and the weariness of their elder sisters each new group of youngsters eagerly anticipates their future responsibility.

The Taira villagers are a gentle and sociable group, although there are indications of underlying tensions, particularly between sexes. Quarrels are rare and fights are rarer. Young men may exchange blows when drunk, but such fights do not result in long-term grudges. The villagers abhor violence and consider murder unthinkable. Children are, from birth, encouraged to be friendly. When a baby comes the women who attend the birth sing, "May this baby always laugh and be pleasant." Later children are taught to be friendly and are discouraged from playing alone or with unfriendly children. But the occurrence of aggression does not cause great concern. Figure 14.1 shows that the Taira mothers occupy a middle position on the peer-aggression training factor. Some parents expect a certain amount of aggression from children; as they put it, "To fight and play are children's work." Since they recognize that children's fights are quickly forgotten by the participants, adults try not to interfere unless the children are in danger of injuring each other. Children's fights do sometimes become intense enough to result in hitting, biting, stick and rock throwing. In order to prevent such serious aggression some parents channel fights between boys into formal wrestling matches.

Less overt manifestations of aggression are more common. Gossip is a standard form of social censure among adults. The indirect style of aggressive outlet is illustrated by gossip patterns. The person who is the object of censure is not publically ostracized and his offense is not mentioned in his presence. But violations of mores are discussed among the villagers and relatives or other villagers finally appraise the offender of public sentiment. Children are not included in this type of aggression. Children gossip among themselves about adult affairs but their discussions do not become malicious. Another form of indirect aggression is teasing and acrid humor. Teasing is particularly characteristic of women joking among themselves but it can be directed both at children and adults. Even though it is never overtly offensive it may be upsetting, particularly to children.

There is evidence of cross-sex hostility among both children and adults. Both parents and teachers expect boys to tease and bully girls. When the children are playing in the village the amount of cross-sex teasing is not much greater than the frequency of girl to girl or boy to boy horseplay, and the girls may hold their own, particularly in verbal aggression, but in school and on the way to school and back, boys direct most of their aggression to their female classmates. On these occasions the bullying is more intense and all but the most aggressive girls are cowed by it. Although the teachers try to curb aggression in the classroom, much of the bullying seems to occur with their tacit acceptance and on most school days several girls are reduced to tears by their male tormentors. This same cross-sex aggressiveness may sometimes be observed among adults particularly in mother-son relationships.

In view of the other evidences of cross-sex aggression it is interesting that the Taira mothers are generally moderate in their reactions to aggression from their children (Figure 14.1), and punish boys more severely than girls for being aggressive to them ($p = .05$, Table 7.5). This policy is clearly not in line with the assumption that boys will be more aggressive than girls and may reflect a greater antagonism between mothers and sons than between mothers and daughters. This differential treatment seems to be unusual. The Taira sample is the only one with a significant sex difference in the mothers' retaliation to mother-directed anger. This aggression of mothers to sons is particularly striking against the background of their general warmth.

Summary

The Taira mothers are unusual in their warmth and their stability. We attribute this fortunate combination of characteristics to the fact that these mothers have privacy in their homes, combined with the support of nearby relatives who help them with their children. This community pattern permits Taira mothers to be warm and affectionate when interacting with their children, without fear of inciting the jealousy of other children or their mothers, and to leave their homes and children to work or visit secure in the knowledge that the children are in the capable hands of other warm and stable women. Although these mothers do not spend an unusually small amount of time with their children, they can rely on others to help them with this task when necessary.

This warm and stable atmosphere permits mothers to be relatively tolerant of aggression when it does occur. Aggression, when expressed, is often indirect and takes the form of teasing. Such teasing may shade off into coercive bullying as does some of the teasing that boys direct at girls. This kind of cross-sex aggression has some cultural sanction and is sometimes reflected in the lives of the adults. Consistently aggressive children are, however, ostracized both by parents and by peers and usually learn to be more sociable. The effectiveness of this positive child training is evidenced by the eagerness with which the children seek adult responsibilities. Regular chores are usually not assigned until the children reach the age of 6 or 7. All of the children over 7 have regular tasks around the house. Usually these require daily care. The mothers report that children beg to help with tasks that are beyond their years and girls especially may take on work that would not be required of them. Many older children, particularly girls, relieve adults of caring for the younger children. They may play with babies on their backs or with toddlers at their heels. They were observed to be reliable in keeping their young charges safe from harm. Like adults, they share the task of caring for the young Taira children.

15 ❖ The Rajput Mothers
of Khalapur, India

Figure 15.1 shows the position of the Khalapur mothers on our three pairs of factors. The figure shows that the Khalapur means are relatively low on all of the scales. The highest mean is .20 and four of the six means are negative. Let us first consider the temperament scale.

The Rajput mothers are rated as the least warm group of this international sample. With the Mexican mothers, the Khalapur mothers have significantly lower factor scores on the "maternal warmth" factor than any of the other four societies (Table 2.1). The Khalapur mothers are also ranked lowest on the individual scales of "warmth of mother" and "amount of praise" given the children, although there are not significant differences between this group and the most other samples on these variables (Table 2.2).

This emotional coldness is a consistent personality trait. We have already said that moodiness and emotional outbursts are discouraged in children. The mothers, in turn, rank relatively low in the emotional instability factor. They are the lowest (rank 4) of a middle group of three on the factor scores (Table 3.1), and the highest (rank 4) of a low group of three on the scales of mood variation of hostility and mood variation of warmth (Table 3.2).

Figure 15.1 shows that the Khalapur mothers are very close to the pancultural mean of zero on emotional stability and considerably below it in warmth. Their warmth and stability scores do not, however, differ from each other. This finding is consistent with the values of the Khalapur mothers that favor emotional control.

The lack of emotional expression is one method of communicating to the children that moodiness is not to be tolerated. The Rajput mothers do not emphasize self-reliance and are willing to help their children bathe, dress, etc., even when the children could do these tasks themselves; but they are notably unresponsive to the emotional needs of their children. They frequently scold children for crying, even when they

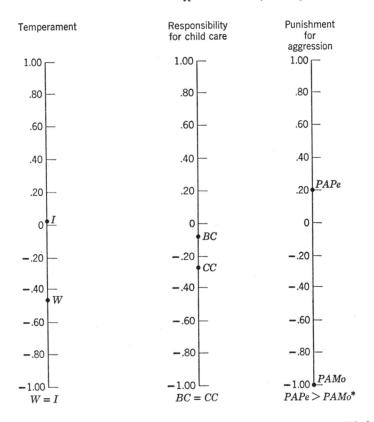

Figure 15.1   Analysis of intrasociety differences on mean factor scores: Khalapur. * $p < .01$, W = warmth of mother, I = instability of mother, BC = mother's responsibility for baby care, CC = mother's responsibility for child care, $PAMo$ = punishment for aggression to mother, $PAPe$ = punishment for aggression to peers.

have been physically hurt. Demands for attention, fussiness, and whining meet with similar impatience. For instance, one of the mother's most frequent complaints about her children is that they cry and whine for food before it is ready. Since these emotional displays are not as threatening as overt aggression, they are not met with consolation and are seldom reinforced.

Training in emotional unresponsiveness begins at birth. Babies are put to sleep on cots and completely covered with thick cotton quilts. Unless they are hungry or fussing they are allowed to stay there undisturbed. With rare exceptions, neither adults nor children play with babies. They are fed and picked up and held when crying, but they are not encouraged to respond. It is interesting to note that most Rajput children are not upset by weaning. Their absence of reaction contrasts sharply with the observations in some other countries. In reporting on the data from the Philippines and Okinawa, the authors note that children are most upset when they are weaned and that this response seems to be caused more by the sudden absence of the mothers' time and close affection than by the withdrawal of the breast. This disruption of affection does not accompany the weaning of the Rajput child, since it was never lavished on him as an infant.

The absence of praise is the result of a deliberate policy, designed to train the compliant personality required in an extended family. The parents believe that if children are praised they will become spoiled because they will think that the parents "love them too much." The concern here seems to be that the child who is "loved too much" will be not only grudging in obedience, which, like minor bickering, is tolerable but will also be openly rebellious and recalcitrant. This policy was emphasized so strongly that, although we almost never heard a woman praise a child, the men complained that women lost control of children because of too much praise.

These Rajput mothers are the only group in the sample whose warmth depends to some extent upon the sex of their children, that is, they are less warm ($p < .001$) and more hostile ($p < .10$) to boys than to girls (Table 2.4). They also tend to use frequent and intense physical punishment with boys rather than girls. This hostility to boys is particularly interesting in view of the fact that these Rajputs, like most Indians, want to have sons rather than daughters. A son must perform certain ceremonies at his father's funeral to insure the safe transition of the soul from one world to the next. If a man dies without a son his spiritual life is endangered. In the lawless village life that prevailed until recently a family's power rested in large part upon the number of fighting men it had. Daughters are disliked because their dowrys are a heavy drain upon the family finances and because daughters must marry into families whose subcaste status is higher than their own. Since the Khalapur Rajputs are themselves from a highly ranked subcaste, the pride of many men is severely wounded by the inferior role they must play when visiting their daughters-in-law. So great was the aversion to girls that these people practiced female infanticide until about the turn of the century. This infanticide was only stopped by vigorous governmental interference and after one government inspector had been murdered by the irate villagers.

What, then, is the explanation for this differential warmth? Unfortunately we did not recognize this tendency while in the village, so the interpretation of it must be inferential. When the Rajput women are asked what sex they wish a child to be, when they are pregnant, they most frequently reply a boy, although a few will say they do not care. When asked, however, whether they *like* boys or girls mothers say that they like girls, or that they have no preference, and very few report preferring boys. Therefore, although desiring sons for their own prestige and that of their husband's family, they do report a preference for daughters in terms of their emotional reaction.

There is some evidence that the women see this preference for sons as a male-imposed value. One woman commented that they wished for sons when pregnant because their husbands said they should. It seems probable that a culturally sanctioned preference for boys requires of women a kind of self-degradation which they resent. Many of the stories told by women concern the unfair treatment of a faithful wife by a misguided or inconsiderate husband. Since a good wife is never hostile to her husband these resentments cannot be expressed directly to the men. It may be that they are expressed in the coldness with which these women treat their sons.

The emotional stability of the Rajput mothers is not contingent upon the sex of the child but is contingent upon the child's age. These mothers seem to be more unstable with older children than with younger ones (Table 3.3). Like the mothers of other places they do not expect much of little children. Evidently they are willing to be patient with children who are too young to know the value of emotional control themselves.

The second scale in Figure 15.1 represents the mothers' participation in child care. Rajput mothers are below the pancultural mean in the amount of time they are in charge of babies and older children. Their responsibility for child care depends relatively little on the children's age since their means on these two factors do not differ from each other. The Rajput mothers rank fourth on the baby-tending factor (Table 4.1) and fifth on the factor concerned with the care of older children (Table 5.1). They are, therefore, somewhat low in the amount of time they spend in child care relative to other groups, despite the fact that they are housebound.

Compared to other societies, adults other than parents also do not spend much time caring for the children, although they live in the same house (Tables 4.2 and 5.2).

Grandmothers and older girls may help mothers with their child care. In some houses a grandmother may spend more time with a young grandchild than the mother, who is busy with cooking and other household chores. In such cases the grandmother may often dress, bathe, and feed the child, although these tasks are usually left to the mother. Aunts sometimes help take care of children, but this is not as frequent. Because the wives always come from another village they are usually strangers to each other when they marry. Sometimes the younger wives of a household get along well enough to assist each other with child care. More frequently, however, they are afraid that quarrels about the children will disrupt household harmony, and avoid this by caring for their own children. Mothers are more likely to submit to the decisions of their mothers-in-law regarding children, so a grandmother is the most usual secondary caretaker. The slight difference between the amount of maternal responsibility for baby and child care reflects the fact that other women are particularly unlikely to care for a baby before it is weaned. Rajput women almost never nurse each other's children, even if the mother dies in childbirth.

Men may be in charge of older boys when they are helping in the fields or playing in the men's quarters, but, except for a few who are quite old and not involved in village politics, they do not usually take care of babies. This is evidenced by the fact that the Indian sample, with the African, is substantially lower than the other societies on the proportion of fathers who take care of babies.

Younger children follow their older siblings and cousins out to play and are informally looked after by them, but older children do not usually care for infants in a formal way (Tables 4.2 and 5.2). Older girls may carry babies when their mother is busy but since daughters are guests in their own homes they are not, if possible, loaded down with chores. There were only two girls in the sample who regularly cared for babies. One was the daughter of a widow. Her mother was, like most Rajput widows, dependent upon her late husband's brother for support. The baby that her daughter cared for was the infant son of this living brother; he was the cousin, not the sibling of his child nurse. The other girl, the daughter of a widower, cared for her infant half-brother, the son of her father's second wife. Both of these cases, while in no way scandalous, represent minor exploitation. There was no mother in the sample who required her daughter to care for children regularly.

Boys are less likely to be asked to care for children than are girls, particularly if they have sisters, but boys may look after younger brothers while they play, work, or go to school.

The reluctance to ask older children to care for younger ones is part of a general lack of emphasis upon responsibility.

There are no significant differences among the societies of our sample in the amount of responsibility assigned to children, but within the limited range of the factor score distribution, the Rajputs of Khalapur rank lowest in responsibility training (Table 6.1). The Rajput children have fewer chores and do them less frequently than the children of any other group. This lack of emphasis upon responsibility training in children is rooted in the social structure and values of the villagers.

The Rajputs are a high-caste group, and a number of menial tasks, which in other societies might be done by children, are done by low-caste servants. These servant families are attached to each Rajput family and owe each other services and payments that are traditionally defined. These reciprocal obligations, considerations of high-caste status, and the definition of some tasks as ritually impure lead Rajput families to pay for certain services even when they themselves are relatively poor. The presence of these servants is one reason why children, particularly young children, do not have many chores (Table 6.2). Three of the chores mentioned in the interview, helping in the fields, pasturing animals, and carrying water, are usually done by servants. Boys may help the men in the fields when not in school and girls carry water when extra water is needed, but they are not regular assignments.

Another reason for the de-emphasis upon responsibility concerns the values of these people. The Rajputs are traditionally a caste of warriors and rulers and the men feel that farming is beneath them and more properly left to servants. Most Rajput farmers have hired low-caste field hands and, if the family is sufficiently wealthy, most of the farming is done by servants. The fathers, therefore, do not instill any love for farming or pride in its accomplishments in their sons.

Girls tend to do chores less frequently than boys, although this trend is not statistically significant with this small sample. There is considerable reluctance to ask a girl to work because a daughter is considered to be a guest in her own home. The bulk of the housework is done by the young daughters-in-law and the Rajput mothers feel that their daughters will have to work so hard in their husband's houses they should not be asked to work in their own homes. Complex tasks which require a period of training are particularly unlikely to be assigned to girls. It is for this reason that none of the Rajput girls help with the cooking (Table 6.3).

Mention should be made of two other tasks, gathering wood and running errands. None of the Rajput children gather wood (Table 6.3). This is because the chief fuel is cow dung cakes which are made by the women. Since virtually all the land is in fields or fruit groves there is very little wood around. Because of the hot sun the few shade trees standing in the fields are too valuable to cut. A little wood is used in cooking but this comes from branches of trees that are stripped off in winter. Since this is a somewhat difficult and dangerous job, it is done by men, not boys. Running errands is the job most frequently assigned to

children.   One-fourth of the Kalapur children run errands (Table 6.3).
Actually, every house has of necessity some children who are errand
runners.   The Rajput women do not leave their courtyards, a custom
adopted from the Moslems.   The Rajput men, when not working in the
fields, spend their time with other men in living quarters that are
separate from the women's courtyards.   The children, therefore are the
only people available for bringing messages to the men or taking lunch
to the fields or shop.   In households where there are no older children
this task may be assigned years before the child is asked to do any other
chore.

The third scale in Figure 15.1 is concerned with aggression training.
The Khalapur mothers have a middle position on the severity with which
they punish children for fighting with their peers.   They are more concerned with aggression directed at peers than at themselves and punish
the former more severely ($p < .01$).   We have suggested in previous
chapters that their concern for peer aggression stems from a desire to
prevent quarrels which would disrupt relations among the women who
must live together in a common courtyard.   Their permissiveness, concerning aggression to themselves, seems to stem from the lack of participation of women and children in the economy.

The Rajput mothers' punishment of aggression to peers is attenuated
by two things, their lack of emphasis upon obedience and the warrior
ideal of the Rajput caste.   These mothers are usually consistent about
their rules against aggression and they do not reward retaliation to peers
(Table 8.2).   Several Khalapur mothers were shocked at the suggestion
that they might encourage aggression in their children.   Generally,
mothers scold all children who are involved in a quarrel without attempting to determine anybody's guilt, unless one child is several years older
than the other, in which case he gets scolded.

However, these mothers are not consistent about obedience training,
although these scales load together on the same factor.   The Indians
rank lowest on consistency of obedience training and, with the United
States mothers, are significantly lower on this variable than the mothers
of any other group (Table 7.2).   This failure to enforce obedience
nullifies to some extent the consistency of the mother's treatment of
aggression.   That is, when mothers act they always punish the children
for fighting, but often they ignore the situation, particularly if no one is
getting hurt or complaining loudly.

In this connection it should be noted that the men's behavior concerning aggression, at least in boys, is different from the women's and is
mitigated by conflicting attitudes about aggression.   On the one hand,
the Rajputs are, as we have said, a warrior caste and still maintain their

military values. Furthermore, village life is not without violence. The village is split into various factions arising from blood feuds that are continued for generations as a point of honor, and may, even now in a more peaceful era, erupt into violence. Also, crop stealing sometimes occurs and the men stand guard on their ripening crops day and night, and may be called on to defend them. Because of these contingencies, many men carry bamboo staffs the ends of which may be weighted with lead bound with wire and studded with nails. Formerly "staff power" was the final arbitrator in male disputes, and, although the law suit is now a more frequent and preferred weapon, an angry man may still engage his opponents in what the villagers call a "conversation of sticks." On the other hand, many of the village men were influenced by the teachings of Ghandi, including his principle of nonviolence. This essentially Brahminical tradition is directly contradictory to many of the ancient Rajput values.

The villagers are, thus, in a period of change during which their attitudes about aggression are shifting. As is usual in such situations, the result has been considerable conflict and confusion. As a result of this conflict the men, though reluctant to encourage aggression in their sons, grudgingly admitted that they sometimes told their sons to fight back if attacked. They admitted more freely that they taught boys to be brave. By this they meant that one should not be intimidated or bullied. A brave man does not necessarily fight, but he does not run.

Our final impression of peer-aggression training among these people was that it is not unlike the situation that prevails in many American families. Although mothers accept the principle that boys must learn to be aggressive when the occasion justifies it, they usually discourage fighting in the interests of peace in the house and the encouragement of more gentlemanly behavior. Men, on the other hand, while agreeing that nonviolence is more desirable than aggression, encourage their sons to "fight for their rights and honor as a sign of manliness."

The reaction of the mothers to aggression to themselves is quite different from their reaction to fights among the children. The Khalapur mothers are significantly more permissive about self-directed aggression than the mothers in any other group (Table 7.1). As we said in Chapter 4 this is because some Khalapur mothers actually console their children if they become angry while being scolded. This is the only situation we encountered where some mothers consistently reward aggression in their children. It is related to the lack of emphasis upon obedience that appears in both the peer-directed aggression and mother-directed aggression factors.

For many of the Rajputs an issue is seldom as important as keeping ingroup peace. This emphasis on "peace at any price" can sometimes be seen in village politics and is even more obvious in disputes within the family. An extended family that shares cramped living quarters and the produce of a farm that is limited in size is fraught with many tensions. Emotional control is therefore valued and outbursts of aggression are generally discouraged. This discouragement is usually successful, although at the price of considerable suppressed hostility. When this hostility becomes overt in anyone, child or adult, people immediately try to calm them down. The justice or injustice of their indignation is a secondary consideration until the crisis of rage has passed. It is evidently this anxiety about rage that leads many mothers to abandon their stand and comfort children even when the child's anger is initiated by the mother's displeasure at some previous offense.

As a result of this somewhat inconsistent policy regarding aggression training, the children engage in a good deal of minor bickering, name calling, snatching, and semiaggressive teasing, but serious fights are few, bullies are uncommon, and temper tantrums are virtually nonexistent. The lax obedience training is also reflected in the behavior of the children who frequently procrastinate and protest their mother's orders. Older boys, as they recognize the low status of women in the family, may refuse to carry out an order. Usually, however, the children do obey but grudgingly and slowly. Men are held in considerably more awe than women and are usually obeyed without question.

Summary

The Khalapur mothers are unusual in their lack of warmth in interaction with their children; this is accompanied in a lesser degree by emotional stability. We believe that this lack of emotional expressiveness is necessitated by the requirements of being confined in courtyards with a group of unrelated women. Under these circumstances jealousies regarding favoritism to children can easily arise. The custom of treating all children, particularly boys, with a certain distance, guards against such accusations, and trains the children, in turn, to control their own emotions.

These Rajput mothers are also unusual in the degree to which they permit children to aggress against them. This tolerance seems to stem from the economic helplessness of the Rajput women and their relatively low status in the community. Desire to avoid emotional outbursts also contributes to this trait. The mothers often comfort children who become angry while being scolded, rather than enforcing discipline.

Khalapur mothers discourage fighting among children, but some fathers admit to training boys to uphold the warrior tradition of the Rajput caste.

Child care is primarily a woman's job. Men may look out for older boys when their sons are helping them but the Rajput men have little responsibility for their children. Mothers are the chief caretakers. Grandmothers sometimes help and aunts or older sisters may assist if no other substitute is present.

Since the Rajputs are a high-caste group, traditionally warriors, the Rajput men have no great love for farming. Boys help in the fields when necessary but are excused from this work in wealthy families. Daughters are considered guests in their own homes and are not asked to work if adults in the family or servants can do their jobs. Responsibility, as measured in the interviews, is not, therefore, a valued trait.

16 ❖ The Gusii Mothers of Nyansongo: Kenya, Africa

Figure 16.1 shows the positions of the mean factor scores of the Nyansongo mothers on three pairs of factors. The first column of Figure 16.1 shows that the mean of these mothers on the maternal instability factor is 1.00 at the extreme end of the scale. The Nyansongo mothers are highly unstable in relation to the other groups of this study. Their position on the maternal-warmth factor, on the other hand, is at the pancultural mean of zero, indicating that they are average in relation to the other groups in their expression of warmth. As might be expected, the Nyansongo mothers are more unstable than warm ($p < .01$). Scale 2 of Figure 16.1 shows that these mothers spend more time caring for older children than for babies ($p < .05$). Scale 3 indicates that they are very punitive when their children are aggressive to them but about average in their reactions to peer-directed aggression. Again, they are more concerned about aggression to themselves than about aggression among children ($p < .01$).

The distinctive pattern of factor scores for the Nyansongo mothers reflects, first, the social position of Gusii women and the authoritarian Gusii structure of role relationships and, second, the social divisiveness and lack of formal schooling characteristic of the Nyansongo community itself.

The Nyansongo mothers are unusual in their emotional instability. All the Gusii mothers have factor scores above the pancultural mean on the emotional instability factor, and the sample is significantly higher on this factor than is any other ($p < .006$, Table 3.2). One hundred per cent of these mothers are rated high in variation of hostility and 88 per cent are rated high in variation of warmth. They are significantly higher than any other sample on both scales ($p < .05$ and $p < .02$, respectively, Table 3.3).

This emotional instability appears to be related to their work burden. They do not want to be bothered by troublesome children and may act

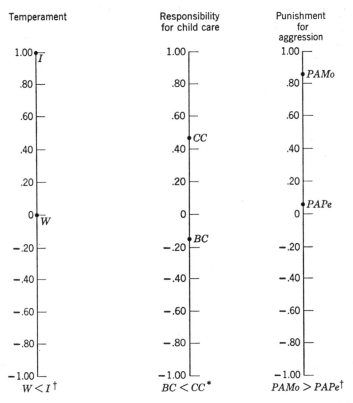

Figure 16.1 Analysis of intrasociety differences on mean factor scores: Nyansongo. * $p < .05$, † $p < .01$, W = warmth of mother, I = instability of mother, BC = mother's responsibility for baby care, CC = mother's responsibility for child care, $PAMo$ = punishment for aggression to mother, $PAPe$ = punishment for aggression to peers.

irritably toward them; however, when they have some leisure time they may be rather permissive, thus their reaction to the child depends more on whether they have time to lavish attention on him than on general principles concerning his conduct. In addition, their moodiness and irritability may fluctuate with variations in fatigue in the daily and annual cycle. Finally, the ambivalence of Gusii women to their husbands and their husbands' kin groups (as expressed in the high level of sex antagonism), and their concern over the interpersonal hostility found in the neighborhood, may also contribute to the emotional instability of Nyansongo mothers.

From the child's point of view, this unpredictability begins when he is weaned. The Gusii mothers feel that the weanling must not compete for her attention with the newborn child. The Nyansongo word for weaning means "to step on," a term which communicates much of adult feeling for this process. Mothers believe that the more severe the weaning the more quickly and smoothly will the transition be achieved. They therefore wean as abruptly as possible, but may relent if the child is persistently upset. Mothers who cannot face their children's unhappiness but who want them to be weaned without delay may send them to live with a grandmother or co-wife. Most mothers are capable of ignoring their children's cries and do not react to them. The child must be weaned by the time the new baby is born, since, as has been said, jealousy of toddlers to their infant siblings is thought to be potentially murderous and is viewed with great alarm.

From the time that the child is weaned mothers have little patience with excessive demands for help or attention. They expect children to bear small hurts stoically and pay no attention to such incidents. If children complain they may be given sympathy but mothers are also likely to say, "Don't cry, it's your own fault." Mothers also expect children to be self-reliant and may cane them for asking help in a task that they can do themselves.

The moderate warmth of the Gusii mothers should be viewed against their instability and authoritarianism. Figure 16.1 shows that these mothers are less warm than unstable ($p < .01$). They fall in the middle of a high group of four societies in the warmth-of-mother factor (Table 22). They are rated as being intermediate in expression of both warmth and hostility. They use a fair amount of praise but rely more heavily on physical punishment to control their children (Table 2.3). The Gusii mothers believe that they must punish children in order to teach respect for their authority. The learning of this respect is believed to be particularly important because it is seen as the basis of respect for all elders. As one mother said to a child who had been talking back to her, "I am not your peer. You must respect me. If you don't respect me, you won't respect any elders."

Gusii mothers use a variety of punishments to enforce respect. Of these caneing is considered to be the most effective punishment for children from 3 to 6 years old, who have not yet acquired sufficient sense to control themselves or understand more subtle punishments. This belief accounts for the finding that 88 per cent of these mothers are rated high on the frequency with which they cane their children. Along with the Mexican and Indian mothers they are substantially higher than the other samples on this scale (Table 2.3).

At about the age of 6 children acquire sense and the ability to control themselves. After this age caneing is used less frequently ($p = .003$, Table 2.4). Mothers punish older children by depriving them of food, locking them out of the house to sleep in the cold, often without clothes or a blanket, giving them hard work as punishment, and threatening them with their fathers' wrath. Exceptionally obedient children may be simply warned or scolded. Some children do not acquire sense when they are 6 years old, but they are thought to be relatively incorrigible after this age and are caned less frequently simply because the mothers feel it would be ineffective. Caneing may still be used as a punishment, however, until children are initiated. After initiation they begin to have adult status and should not be subjected to this "childish" punishment.

The punishments that are used with older children, particularly exclusion from the house and food deprivation, are often ineffective because children simply go next door and stay in the house of their grandmother, or mother's co-wife. Women do not feel that they must back up each other's discipline and will always feed a child who comes to them. Since the mothers are inconsistent in their moods children often avoid punishment by visiting a relative when they have done something wrong. If they wait until their mothers have calmed down after discovering their offense and act contrite on their return the busy mothers may ignore the incident or settle for a warning.

Since the Nyansongo household consists of a woman and her children, with a father who is often absent, these mothers have less help in caring for their children than the mothers of some other samples. Each Gusii married woman manages her own household within a polygynous family. She has a hut to house herself and her children, special fields on which she raises food for herself and them, and the responsibility of running a separate domestic and economic unit. The husband contributes relatively little to the labor force at home, and many husbands are away working on plantations, police posts, and urban areas. She cooperates to some extent with her co-wives and other women, but this cooperation is limited by suspicion and jealousy among co-wives and the general lack of community cohesion. The result is that the married woman is independently responsible for a great deal of agricultural and domestic work, from which she can gain relief only by having her children help her, and her busy routine leaves little time or energy for playful and affectionate interaction with her children. Nyansongo mothers rank lowest on the factor measuring the proportion of time they spend with infants (Table 4.2) and on the mother-care scale (Table 4.3), although they are not significantly different from any sample except the New England one in this respect.

Figure 16.1 shows that these mothers spend more time responsible for older children than for babies ($p < .05$). This result is somewhat misleading since the children are caring for the babies. Children are the only persons whose labor a woman can commandeer, and this is facilitated by the lack of formal education; the Nyansongo children are not diverted from helping their mothers by school.

That children are the chief alternate caretakers is indicated by the fact that this sample is low in the proportion of time other adults or fathers care for infants (Table 4.3). This leaves the older children who are substantially more likely to care for infants in Nyansongo than in any other sample (Table 4.3). Generally the oldest initiated girl is placed in charge of younger children when the mother is away, and her chief job is to care for the infant.

The mothers are themselves in almost exclusive charge of children between the time that they are weaned and the time they are initiated. They live in her house and are fed by her; she is held responsible for their health and their behavior. The Gusii mothers resemble those of New England in that they spend significantly more time in charge of their children than the mothers of any other sample (Table 5.2 and 5.3).

This does not mean that the Nyansongo mothers spend a great deal of time actually interacting with their children. They have domestic and agricultural duties that take up most of their time. Like their New England counterparts, they encourage self-reliance and become impatient with excess dependency. Unlike the New England mothers they utilize the help of older children who do not attend school. Older children are often left with no one to look after them directly, but are kept close to home and within earshot of their mothers. Older children may still be used as caretakers for younger ones who are no longer infants. Nineteen per cent of the Nyansongo children sometimes care for siblings (Table 5.3).

Co-wives help each other care for children when they are on good terms with each other, but when co-wives are not speaking, as is often the case, they avoid each others children and refrain from disciplining them for fear of being accused of witchcraft or sued for injury. The extent to which an uncle punishes a nephew depends on these same considerations.

More distant relatives seldom care for children. Neighbors may scold but seldom beat them for fear they will be sued for injury. They will report deviation to the parents if they feel that this is called for.

Nyansongo fathers do not usually care for children. When a father has several wives who live in separate houses, he necessarily spends less time with the children in each house than fathers in monogamous families. Many Gusii fathers have jobs in cities that take them away from their community for extended periods of time.

The Gusii men are particularly unlikely to care for infants. Along with the Rajput men of the Indian sample they care for babies substantially less than the fathers in any other sample (Table 4.3). They also care for older children less than any other group, but their position on this scale is not so unusual (Table 5.3).

The role of Gusii fathers is that of disciplinarian. Nyansongo children fear their fathers, who do punish them more severely (although less frequently) than their mothers and who are used as bogeymen by the mother. The fear of the father is probably augmented by his aloofness.

A remote figure, the Nyansongo father is viewed as strict, unapproachable, and somewhat menacing. This is antecedent to the elaborate intergenerational avoidances practiced by Gusii adults, which form an integral part of their authoritarian structure of role relations.

The hostile reactions of the Nyansongo mothers to aggression from their children should be in the context of these authoritarian role relationships. In their community life and political system, the Gusii orient themselves in terms of dominance by a leader and submission to him, with command and obedience taking precedence over the development of total group consensus in decision making. The area of which Nyansongo is a part is dominated by an autocratic chief who provides jobs and influence and administers rewards and punishments to people in the community. Nyansongans are somewhat dependent on him economically; they bring their local troubles to him for settlement, and they accept his orders as mandatory. The Gusii are also extremely litigious, resorting to court action in minor disputes and infractions as well as major ones. Persons of higher status by virtue of age, wealth, governmental position, or education are highly respected and can order other persons about for their own advantage. At the family level, the head of the homestead is supposed to be an autocrat vis-à-vis his wives and sons, and his status in the community is enhanced if he does in fact exact a high degree of respect and obedience from them. A homestead head who is wealthy receives the maximum deferences and submission from his poorer neighbors, and an aged man will be listened to by a group of elders even if he is not wealthy or wise. Altogether, this amounts to an authoritarianism in which authority at any level is concentrated in the hands of a few leaders, and others bow to the will of the leader.

The influence of this authoritarianism can be seen in the high position of the Nyansongo mothers on punishment of mother-directed aggression. Those mothers are completely unwilling to tolerate any behavior on the part of a child which might be interpreted as a direct assault on their authority. One-hundred per cent of the Gusii mothers have factor scores above the pancultural mean for this factor and their group is significantly higher than any other sample (Table 7.2). None of the Nyansongo mothers reward their children for defying them, and 94 per cent are high in their retaliation to this kind of attack (Table 7.3). Children are expected to be respectful to adults above all, and there are no circumstances under which aggression toward parents is considered justifiable. Nyansongo mothers may punish infants for flailing them in the face, and the maternal reaction to the aggression of older children is more severe. It is thought that a child who cannot respect his own parents will grow up lacking in the proper respect for elders and political leaders, which is expected of every Gusii adult. This child-training attitude is also reflected in the fact that Nyansongo mothers are the highest of the six cultures on expectation of prompt obedience. The parent-child relationship is seen as a dominance-submission relationship in which the child is to acquire the authoritarianism appropriate for conformity to the adult authority system. To enforce the submission and obedience of Gusii children requires some severe measures. Thus Nyansongans are high on frequency and intensity of physical punishment, which they view as essential in child training.

Nyansongo mothers are less concerned about aggression among children than they are about aggression to adults (Figure 16.1; $p < .01$). Aggression among peers does not threaten the important role relationships in this society.

The intermediate score of the Nyansongans on the peer-directed aggression factor can also be understood in the context of the mother's busy day. Nyansongo mothers disapprove of peer-directed aggression in the abstract, but in fact their work does not permit them the degree of supervision which would be required to prevent and control the fighting of their children. Thus they develop a measure of tolerance for this fighting which they are unable to suppress. Children's fights with cousins or more distant relatives are usually viewed with more alarm than fights among siblings.

Children are kept near home so that they will not get in trouble with the children of families with whom the mother is not friendly. When co-wives are not on good terms with each other children may not even play in adjoining houses. Most children are not so restricted but play chiefly with siblings, half-siblings, and cousins who live nearby. The availability of Gusii children as servants in the home stems from this concern that they will get into trouble if they stray. So great is the litigiousness of this society that the women are concerned lest injury in children's fights involve them in a lawsuit. As a result of this concern and their own aggressiveness, the Gusii mothers tend to fight their children's battles for them. Children soon learn this and cry louder when attacked in the presence of adults than when they are alone. Mothers tell their children not to fight and to avoid attackers.

The mothers who reported rewarding some retaliation told their children to fight back the next time a fight occurred, but not to renew the current one. More commonly, mothers either expect children to report attacks to them, or encourage them to do so. Girls, who seldom initiate a fight, often report aggression. Boys may report it, if they are not guilty, or may simply fight when adults are not around. When this happens the mother "conducts a trial." Like the Orchard Town mothers, Gusii mothers consider the instigator of a fight to be responsible unless rightfully provoked. If the instigator proves to be the mother's own child she canes him. Fights among siblings are settled exclusively by parents. Fights with neighbors children are more complex and serious. If the attacker is a neighbor's child the mother either canes the neighbor's child or complains to his mother, who is then expected to punish her own child. If she fails to do this she puts herself under suspicion. One Gusii mother said that she would go to a neighbor and ask "if they sent that boy to fight my son." The ease with which these mothers get embroiled in their children's fights enhances their anxiety about them. Children are warned not to play with others who are known to be particularly aggressive.

The determination of a child's guilt may depend on factors other than who started the fight. The child's motivation is considered and sometimes really evil motives are attributed to children. If an older child attacks a younger one he may be punished even if he was provoked, since punishment is a prerogative of parents that should not be usurped. Mothers react strongly when an older child, usually the one just weaned, attacks the newborn infant or cries when the mother is holding it. Such behavior is interpreted as murderous jealousy, a death wish that may kill the baby or make him sick. If the intensity of the retaliation is regarded by the mother as too strong for the provocation she will punish both children or perhaps the one who retaliated.

One of the most serious offenses is for a boy to attack a girl who is not his sibling. Such attacks are regarded as sexual in motivation even among young children. Preadolescent boys and girls do indulge in sex play when adults are not around. When girls approach initiation they begin to spurn the advances of their male playmates, who are still several years away from their initiation. The attacks of herd boys on these girls are evidently the result, in part, of this rejection. One of the reasons given by girls for desiring to be initiated was to avoid these attacks, since parents take strong action to stop attacks of uninitiated boys on initiated girls.

Since the Gusii mothers do sometimes tell their sons to fight back, they hold an intermediate position on the peer-aggression factor (Table 8.2). One-half the Gusii mothers are highly consistent in their rules against aggression, this proportion does not differ significantly from that of most samples. Only 6 per cent of these mothers were rated high in reward for retaliation, a proportion that is similar to the mothers of the Indian, Mexican, and Philippine samples (Table 8.3). The effectiveness of this is influenced by intermediate consistency on obedience training. Gusii mothers expect children to obey them promptly but may not always follow through when they do not (Table 8.3). They are unusual in that they expect boys to obey more promptly than girls. Perhaps they are afraid that if their irresponsible boys do not obey promptly they will not obey at all.

Submission and obedience of children are important in Nyansongo because the overworked Nyansongo require their children to work early and hard in the domestic economy. This is clearly seen in infant care and is true in other areas as well.

The use of children in the domestic labor force means that they must stay relatively near home, where the tasks are to be performed under mother's direction. Nyansongo mothers do not want their children to stray too far from their place of work, and this attitude is reinforced by the suspicion and divisiveness in the neighborhood which leads the mothers to view the aimless wandering of her child as potentially dangerous. These mothers believe it is both safer and more facilitating to the work for children to be near. Since the fields are usually near the house, the emphasis on staying at home and staying at work and the absence of formal schooling all lead to high responsibility.

The Gusii rank the highest on the responsibility factor although they are not significantly different from other samples in this respect. As is true in most societies older children have more chores to do than younger ones and tend to do them more often (Table 6.5). When a child is 2 or 3 years old and his "follower" is born, the child begins to run errands in the household and bring food to his father. Later he is sent on longer errands by his parents. So common is this practice that adults do not consider it a chore and may fail to report it (Table 6.4). Before initiation, at about 8 years for girls and 12 years for boys, chores are not strongly sex-typed. There are no significant differences between the number of boys versus girls doing any of the chores listed in Table 6.5.

The only task that children never do is help clean house. This is because houses are seldom cleaned at all. Most of the work is done in the yard outside the house. Refuse is allowed to pile up until the space is needed for some feast or ceremony and then cleaned away. When the house becomes too dirty the mother sweeps it out but this is done too rarely to be a chore for children.

The Gusii sample is ranked first on the percentage of children who help cook, carry water, and work in fields and gardens (Table 6.3). Only children of 7 years and older cook, and all of them do so (Table 6.5). Girls usually begin to learn to cook at about the age of 7 or 8, just before initiation, when they are trying to impress parents with their responsibility. Boys are not required to cook as often and may learn later, but all boys in the sample did some cooking by the age of 10.

Seventy-five per cent of the Gusii children carry water. Along with the children of the Mexican sample, they are significantly higher on this measure than any other group (Table 6.3). Carrying water is a fairly strenuous job because virtually every house in Nyansongo is on a hill and water must be brought from the stream below since there are no wells. Houses vary in how far they are from the stream. The greatest distance may be a quarter of a mile and in places the pathway may be steep. Girls are taught to do this early and begin to follow their older sisters at about the age of 3 carrying small pots of water on their heads. Children are severely punished if they drop and break a pot since these are relatively valuable.

The Gusii are significantly higher than any other sample in the proportion of children who help in fields and gardens. Ninety per cent of the Gusii children do this and the amount of work they do may be considerable. Four-year-old boys sometimes voluntarily work beside their mothers in the fields and hoe a little corn. Some 6-year-old girls spontaneously howed, sowed, weeded, and harvested a field of corn all by themselves. Field work is not expected of children until they are over 7, but by then it is expected of most of them ($p < .005$, Table 6.5). Both boys and girls do the same type of work, hoe, weed, and harvest corn but girls are the more steady workers. The average girl of 8 can do most agricultural chores except break fallow ground and harvest the eleusine crop.

Gusii children may also care for animals (Table 6.3). While 3-year-old girls follow their older sisters to the stream to carry water, boys of the same age follow their older brothers who are going to herd cattle, and by the time boys are 4 years old they are beating cattle on the rump to keep them in line. Pastures are usually downhill from the house, between it and the stream where animals are watered. They are almost always within earshot of the house and usually within sight of it, so that the young herd boys are not far from home. While herding, boys may gather wood for fires. The ownership of cattle may do more than anything else in determining the whereabouts of children and their activities. Children who were free to roam and play find their activities drastically curtailed when the family acquires a herd of bride-wealth cattle. Herd boys are often irresponsible and may desert the cattle. When girls herd cattle they do it much more conscientiously.

When mothers leave the houses the children are placed in the care of the oldest uninitiated girl. If no girl is available a boy is placed in charge. Since girls are initiated at the age of 7 or 8, most child caretakers are younger than this.

Initiation changes expectations and behavior in responsibility, particularly for girls. Uninitiated girls are more responsible than uninitiated boys. Girls are eager for initiation so that they may rise in status with their peers and assume the role of marriageable girls. Mothers discourage their daughters' plea to be initiated in order to be sure that they are sufficiently determined to endure the painful circumcision ceremony. In order to prove their worth girls work very hard before the time of the initiation to prove they are responsible enough to assume their new status.

After initiation this situation changes. The chores of girls now become much less. Since they are now interested in boys they begin to go away from home on trips to the market where they meet their suitors. They are freed from the confining task of caring for the younger siblings, although they may supervise the younger caretaker when they are home. As the girls grow older and become more interested in marriage they become increasingly irresponsible. They remain away from home more than they should for the good of their reputations. Parents fear that they will elope with a poor young man of their choice rather than accept the parents' choice of groom, who may well be an older, richer man who wants a secondary wife. This conflict causes increasing friction between girls and their parents until they are married.

With boys the situation is reversed. Uninitiated boys are irresponsible and troublesome. They are not as eager for initiation as are girls because it does not clearly reduce their work but does terminate the warm dependency they have enjoyed with their mothers. Boys must sometimes be persuaded by their fathers to join their peers at the initiation. Once initiated, however, boys assume their adult roles in the kinship system and their share of adult male work. They are now exempted from doing women's tasks. If they have younger brothers they stop herding cattle and work in the fields. Like the girls they take trips to the markets as they grow older and examine the girls there as prospective mistresses or wives.   In their middle-teens they go to work on European plantations to earn their bride-wealth.   Initiation into adult status makes boys more responsible than they were before.

It should be mentioned that the work of Gusii children and adults is done within the context of a system of hierarchical authority that extends from top to bottom.   The Gusii chief may order anyone in the tribe to do him a trivial favor with full confidence that it will be done.   Powerful men order the less powerful around.   Wealthy men exploit their poor relations.   The Gusii say, "the property of a poor man belongs to the rich."   Men assign the work of their households to their children and wives and are very angry if their orders are not carried out.   Mothers in turn pass work on to their children.   An adult will not fetch an object if he can order a child to do it, even if the child is farther from the object than is the adult.   Mothers constantly give orders to children to help her in small ways.   Older children may pass such orders on to younger ones but must see that they are carried out.   Mothers frequently give orders for things that they could well do themselves and they expect to be obeyed promptly because if they are not it would be easier to do the job themselves.   All the Gusii mothers are above the pancultural mean in expectation of prompt obedience, and as a group they are significantly higher than any other sample on this scale although they may not always follow through when the child does not obey.

Summary

The Gusii mothers of Nyansongo are unusual in their irrascibility, their severity toward insubordination from their children, and their heavy responsibility for the care of older children.   They are also high in their expectations of responsibility in children.

It is our hypothesis that these characteristics are related and determined largely by the contingencies of Gusii social and economic structure. Gusii mothers have more work to do and fewer people to help them with it than the mothers of the other samples.   Besides their duties in child rearing they must raise garden crops and supervise a herd of cattle. Fathers often work away from the community and, when home, divide their time among several wives.   Co-wives are available to help if they are friendly, but frequently suspicion that the co-wife will or has bewitched children makes women refrain from caring for each other's children. Grandmothers and older children share the responsibilities of child care, but since grandmothers in a polygynous society have many daughters-in-law, children are the primary helpers.

The high responsibility demands upon the children stem from grim necessity.   The severity with which the mothers react to any defiance of their authority stems, in turn, from the necessity of insuring that children will obey them and help with the work.   Since fathers are often not around they are not as useful to back up mothers' authority as they are in other cultures.

The irrascibility of these mothers seems to be augmented by the burden of constant supervision of the children in the work force.   Mothers keep their children close to home, so that they will be available for chores and not get into fights with neighbor's children and, having so confined them, are faced with the obligation of supervising their activities.

The burden of such supervision is clear, for instance, with respect to infant care.   Older children chiefly care for infants but mothers must, in turn, supervise the older children.   Since initiated girls do not usually care for babies, these child caretakers are under 8 or 9 years old.   Alternate adult caretakers, with whom a baby may safely be left in the mother's absence, are rare.   In spite of their heavy responsibilities the interaction of these mothers with their children is moderately, if not consistently warm.   In view of their responsibilities the warmth is perhaps more surprising than the instability.

17 ❖ Antecedents of Child Rearing: An Intracultural Test of Some Hypotheses

In the preceding chapters we have described the factors or dimensions along which the major differences between mothers and their reported practices can be described, and we have presented some hypotheses about the social and cultural determiners of why the mothers in our six communities differ from culture to culture on these child-training factors. The reader may find it valuable to place what we have reported so far in the context of Figure 17.1, which is reprinted here from the introduction to *Six Cultures—Studies of Child Rearing.*

Our hypotheses have tried to explain the differences between communities in their child-rearing practices by relating them to differences in the "maintenance systems" of the various communities. When we hypothesize, for example, that child-training practices in aggression training will vary with whether or not the mother makes an independent contribution to the family economy in some manner, then we are tying the variation in child-rearing practices (see Figure 17.1) into the roles the mother plays in the economic maintenance systems of the community. We are suggesting, tentatively, that if mothers in a society are expected to make an economic contribution, then this will lead the mother (in the long or the short run) to build her relations with her children around these activities. She must be more efficient in dealing with them in less time. Therefore, she will tend to be less permissive and will carry home her work role. She will not stand for anger or "back-talk," and will punish aggression in the manner of a job supervisor.

The tie-up between the child-training role of the mother and her economic role may have occurred so long ago in the society that the mothers no longer see the tie-up themselves or, on the other hand, this tie-up may be occurring in a self-conscious manner whenever a mother has a child and must resolve the problem on her own. We do not know

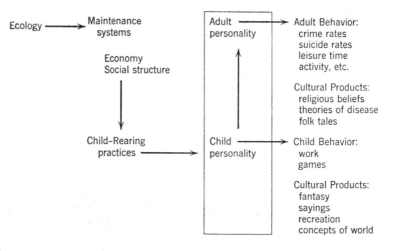

Figure 17-1
From Beatrice B. Whiting (Ed.), *Six Cultures—Studies of Child Rearing,* New York, John Wiley and Sons, 1963, p. 5.

the answer, and we are not hypothesizing on the matter. We are suggesting that there is a causal link, however, recognizing that when the linkage between these two roles has occurred, it may be viewed in one culture as related to the family duties of mothers and children; in another culture as related to the religious rules involving the busy life of mother and child; in yet another it may be done because this is the most sensible and rational way to let a mother deal with her child and also get her jobs done.   In short, the tie-up between the two roles may be, in terms of the present views of the people in the community, indirect or complicated in various ways.   Our assertion is merely that there is a causal tie between the maintenance conditions or the economic expectation the mothers live with and the aggression and obedience training visited on their children. The relationship posited by use may rest upon still other conditions. Further analysis and research will either prove the hypothesis, reject it, or provide some further specification of the conditions for its presence.

Having presented our hypotheses in the context of the data from the six communities which we studied closely, we then turned to a cross-societal study which tried to test the expected relationship between these roles in a large number of communities.   This study added somewhat to our hope that we might be correct in the way we analyzed some of the causes of the different behaviors of the mothers toward their children in our own six communities.

There remains one additional way that, in principle, we can check on our hypothesized relationships between maintenance systems and child-training practices. We can see if *variation around the statistical norms* of the maintenance system in a particular society is correlated with variation in the predicted direction around the statistical norms of that society's child-rearing practices. For example, if our hypothesis that mothers who contribute to the economy are likely to expect more obedience and less aggression from their children is truly a powerful hypothesis, then regardless of the position of the community norm on our pancultural factor dimension, mothers who are high in contribution to the economy, relative to the other mothers in their particular community, should correspondingly place relatively more emphasis on the obedience and parent-directed aggression training of their children.

Let up point out at once that this is an extremely stringent test of the hypothesis, perhaps impossibly stringent in our case. Consider the following list of issues that arise when we shift our hypothesis to be tested to this individual differences level instead of leaving it at the societal level.

1. We give up one of the major virtues of cross-societal studies where, in dealing with behavioral norms, i.e., modal and/or average behavior patterns, we are evading many of the issues that arise from studying deviation within a community. When we look at the mother who lives in a community such as our African one, where the modal or average mother makes a considerable economic contribution, and we look at the mother who makes no such contribution (or a minimal or a maximal one), then we are looking at a deviant. Pandora's box of possibilities appears to open. This mother may not work because she is lazy. If she is lazy in one thing, she may be lazy in another, and either tries to put *all* household duties off on her children, or *none* of them, because of the trouble of following up on the required obedience training. She may be less intelligent than most of the wives. She may have made some particular arrangement whereby she makes no independent economic contribution, but makes up for this by way of entertaining others. Furthermore, the deviant mother may be coerced by community norms to raise her children in the modal pattern, since it is this pattern that the children are expected to enter. We may, therefore, find that a mother who does not work herself still raises her children as if she were working, because this type of child rearing instills the valued virtues of the community, or because she expects her own daughters to work. Similarly, mothers who live in nuclear houses when the modal household is extended may raise her children for future residence in extended family houses.

2. When we move to the individual level to test our hypothesis we often find little or no variance when we go from mother to mother on either

the economic contribution dimension, or on the child-training dimension, or on both.   Even if there is *some* variation as we go from mother to mother on these dimensions, the difference in economic contribution pressures, for example, may not be great enough to make the mother need to put this role together with her child-rearing role.   This points up the fact that in the present state of our knowledge our scales usually reflect merely an *ordering,* but we know little else about them.   In analogy to temperature, we do not know if economic contribution pressures reach a point analogous to 32° Farenheit, such that role-elision must occur, as freezing must occur in water at that temperature.   This is part of the risk of research with unproven tools, as we pointed out in our Introduction.

3. Technically speaking, when we move from the societal level to the individual level, we encounter the increased error in assessment that arises from shifting from a generally more reliable average or mode, to the single score which characterizes an individual.   This decreases the chances of any differences reaching significance either in our predicted direction or otherwise.   The choice of a fair test of our hypotheses is thereby reduced.

4. Basic matters such as the distribution of family types found within a community may vary over time.   We may discover a fairly high proportion of nuclear families in a community and this might lead us to the interpretation that our sample child has always lived in such a structure or that say, in India, one-fourth of all the children or their mothers have always lived in a nuclear home, because we find that one-fourth of them *now* do.   These interpretations may not be safe because the kind of family structure one lives in depends upon the stage in the family cycle that one is in.   Young married couples may live in extended families and their youngest children may be born into such large groupings.   When the grandmother and grandfather die off and the structure changes, differences may arise between the people of the generation of the "young married couples," so they split apart.   Their later children may be born in stem families or in totally nucleated families.   Or, possibly, some later-born children may first see the light of day in a new extended family, where their father is grandfather of other newborns and the head man of a large family establishment.   Polygynous families present a similar problem.   Although most families at any one time are monogamous among the Gusii, most children are partially or totally raised in polygynous families.

5. As we move from cross-cultural to intracultural analyses, the *relative prominence or weight* of a value or practice can enter the picture to make the hypothesis difficult to test.   For example, mothers who are

working may have a tendency, as we hypothesize, to handle her children in the efficient and occasionally harsh manner of a supervisor, but a more powerful and dominant value, such as a general love for close and warm relationships with others may get in the way of such harshness and lead such mothers to train children through reward rather than through punishment. In another case, the working mother may be caught up in a network of family ties and must "keep her place" and not take on "bossy ways" even with her own children. Therefore, when we get close to the individual actors in the community, our hypothesis may be ruled out, not because we are wrong about people's behavior tendencies, but because the behavioral effects of another of our hypotheses may be showing up so powerfully that the first one is masked.

6. Finally, we do not view our hypotheses as refined enough in their present form to take care of the many special solutions to cultural problems that particular members of a society may discover on their own. Not only are some *cultural* alternatives available to the mothers, but our view of "culture" does not preclude continuous individual creativity in coming to terms with such problems as the need for mothers to do economic work in a difficult ecology. Much of our within-group variance may be due to such special solutions and is probably more a function of mothers' personality traits than of cultural pressures.

One of the major technical discoveries of our exploratory research is that interviews with mothers, which are adequate to uncover the communities' mean on a pancultural dimension, may have to be made more extensive and more precise when we wish to pick up all the cultural and individual alternatives available, and thus be able to place the mothers on a more finely graduated dimension of theoretical interest.

All of the problems listed above probably occurred to some degree in the present attempt to see if our hypotheses are upheld when the factor scores of mothers of the six communities are dichotomized as closely as possible around their *own community average*. In some instances more than half of the mothers of one society fall on a single scale point, for example. Further, it is to be expected on the basis of the general lore of this kind of research that when we shift to the small sample of mothers to which we are limited in each community, the unreliability of the placement of a particular mother rises to the point where even negative findings may be masked.

On the other hand, the major portion of the variance of all our factors is variation among mothers in the same community. Although much of this variance may be due to idiosyncratic factors that we have not measured, we would expect some of it to be caused by within-group variation of the type of social structure systems that seem to contribute to differences between our groups. As we shall see, this does appear to be the case.

Maternal Warmth

Our hypothesis regarding the background conditions for a mother to be high in her display of warmth to her child has been a simple one so far and probably requires further specification. Our suggestion has been that mothers who raise their children in the privacy of a nuclear family household are more free to express their own affection, pride, and anger toward their children than are mothers who live in more extensive family arrangements, unless they are so isolated in their privacy that they must control themselves to avoid quarrels among siblings. The nuclear or isolated mothers are more free because they do not face the criticism which arises in the more extended contexts, unless they exercise and teach emotional control by being controlled with their own children.

Probably the most direct test possible of this idea is recorded in Table 17.1, Section *A*, where we have considered only those cases where the sample child lives in some contact with a nearby cousin. It is interesting to note that within each of the four cultural groups where there is some variance on this matter, there is a weak trend for mothers to score low on maternal warmth where her child has several close cousins nearby, than where her child has few such cousins. These trends, though they do not meet significance standards by any test, are consistently in the direction we predict, and may reflect the greater pressure for muting warmth referred to in our hypothesis.

When we turn to Section *B* of Table 17.1, however, where we related the warmth scores to family type, our hypothesis calls for some interpretation, since there is a fairly strong trend in three of the cultural groups for children to receive more warmth in stem households than they do in the nuclear household. First, however, a word about this section of the table. The Gusii group and the Orchard Town group are not included here because there is almost no variance in family type within the communities; technically they are all nuclear families. In the other four communities, however, there is enough variance on family type to do an analysis in which we have focused on the nuclear family as compared to the stem family, since these are the two most prevalent types. The former is a family which includes only the children of our sample child's generation, and his mother and father. The stem family includes one or more grandparents and is often in the grandparents own place of residence. In the Mexican case, we have included one "young lineal"

Table 17.1   Comparison of Maternal Warmth Factor Scores with (A) Number of Cousins Living in Court or Yard, (B) House Type, (C) Number of Adults in House, (D) Number of Siblings in House, and (E) Birth Order

Society	Warmth	A^a Maternal Warmth vs. Number of Cousins in Court or Yard		B^b Maternal Warmth vs. House Type		C^c Maternal Warmth vs. Number of Adults in Household	
		Low	High	Nuclear	Stem	Low	High
Mexico	High	4	3	9	4	7	6
	Low	3	4	7	2	7	2
Philippines	High	6	5	7	4	5	7
	Low	4	4	10	1	8	3
Okinawa	High			5	7	3	9
	Low			6	5	6	6
India	High	3	2	3	2	6	5
	Low	5	5	3	0	7	6
Africa	High	5	2				
	Low	1	3				

Society	Warmth	D^d Maternal Warmth vs. Number of Siblings		E^e Maternal Warmth vs. Birth Order			
		Low	High	Only	Youngest	Oldest	Middle
United States	High	5	6	2	6	3	2
	Low	5	8	0	4	3	4
Mexico	High	2	7	0	2	5	6
	Low	4	9	0	1	5	2
Philippines	High	6	5	2	2	3	5
	Low	8	4	0	1	4	6
Okinawa	High	10	2	0	2	1	9
	Low	6	6	0	0	6	6
India	High	7	6	2	3	2	4
	Low	5	6	1	5	4	3
Africa	High	5	0	1	3	2	5
	Low	4	7	0	0	3	2

[a] Summary z for this section not significant.
[b] Summary z for this section = 1.63; p = .05, one tail test.
[c] Summary z for this section = 1.84; $p < .05$, one tail test.
[d] Summary z for this section = 1.71; $p < .05$, one tail test.   These means refer to siblings of the sample child.   Add one to each mean to obtain average total children in household.
[e] Summary z for this section = 2.28; $p < .05$.

type family, which is a household which includes the people usually found in a stem household, plus a married sibling of our sample child.   In India, of course, there was a great range of family types in the sample studied, but most of these were left out when we focused on the two types which were most common in Okinawa, the Philippine barrio group, and the Mexican group.

This general trend (which has an overall significance at the .05 level) [1] for more warmth in the stem household can be quickly reinterpreted, however, by looking at Section *C* of Table 17.1, where maternal warmth is related to the number of adults living in the house.   The main difference between a nuclear and a stem household is that there are more adults within the household in the latter, and the overall statistically significant trend in Section *C* is consistent with that of Section *B,* in that there is more warmth for the child if he lives in a house with a greater number of adults.   It should be noted, however, that the general trend is not present in the Mexican group in Section *B* of the Table (though it *is* present there in Section *C*), and it is not present in the Indian group in Section *C* (though it *is* present there in Section *B* for this group).

These results lead us to conclude that the presence of grandparents in a house, particularly a grandmother, reduces the isolation of mothers in nuclear families, provides an alternate caretaker, and therefore allows the mother to express more warmth to the children than when she is their sole custodian.   But, as we suspected, the presence of sisters-in-law or co-wives, often unrelated to the mother and with children of their own to care for, provides a fertile field for bickering and leads to a muting of affects to avoid such strife.   In such houses grandmothers must also be wary of showing favoritism which might incite jealousies among their daughters-in-law.   Such extended houses appear in Mexico and India, and the relationships among warmth and household structure appear to be unclear for these two groups.   This may well be an example of a tendency for the members of a deviant or non-ideal family to behave as if they were living under the modal or ideal living conditions for their group.

The unpredicted finding of our within-group analysis that children receive more warmth from their mothers when there are many rather than few adults in the house.   It is well to note that this trend does not show up in the Indian sample, where the space-to-person ratio was the smallest.   Again, this may indicate a curvilinear relationship such that a few additional adults are helpful and tend to produce conditions favorable

---

[1] Note: In the test used here and elsewhere in this chapter, chi squares for each culture were transformed to z; the average z was multiplied by the square root of n (where n is number of cultures) and this "summated z" was evaluated in a normal distribution table.   In averaging, reversed z's were subtracted.

to warmth, but more than this number produce tense conditions that are unfavorable to such emotional expressiveness. Although this interpretation may seem complex, these data as they stand suggest that a linear interpretation would be even more complex, for we are faced with the intriguing contradiction that the presence of an excess of cousins reduces maternal warmth, whereas an excess of adults increases it. Since adults produce children, the number of cousins present will ordinarily be large when many adult relatives are also present. Assessing maternal warmth then is a matter of considering the adult-to-child ratio in every household.

For the present, it seems simpler to assume that the presence of a grandmother, who usually has no young children of her own, relieves the childcare chores of mothers, so that they can be warmer with their children, even when they have several children. The addition of a new sister-in-law may be a further help, at least until she herself has children. Beyond this, additional persons probably begin to produce conditions that call for attenuated emotionality, particularly if they must share cramped quarters.

Section *D* of Table 17.1 supports our suggestion that mothers may mute their affectional expression to avoid jealousies among their own children, as well as among cousins. In Section *D* we present the relationships between maternal warmth scores and the number of siblings of the sample child. The trend in four of the communities (United States, Okinawa, India, and Africa) is for a child to receive less warmth if he has a large number of siblings for the society, than if his number of siblings is low for the society (combined $p < .05$). There is no such trend at all in Mexico and it is reversed in the Philippine group. But if the general trend does hold, it may betoken the same human tendency assumed in our original hypothesis, i.e., the larger number of siblings tends to mute the mother's warmth in a manner analogous to the way the larger number of cousins does. The mother must avoid the problems that can arise from any show of favoritism or special treatment in front of the host of little witnesses within her immediate family or outside of this close kin group.

The mother's world is even more complicated, as is demonstrated in Section *E* of Table 17.1, where it is evident that mothers vary warmth according to the order of the child in her own family. In this section we have categorized each child as to whether he (or she) is an only child, a youngest child, an oldest child, or some middle child. Unfortunately, such family positions are not independent of the family size, or are our samples large enough to do a meaningful analysis which can *control* on family size. An only child is obviously in a small family (as far as siblings is concerned, at least); a youngest or an oldest child must be in at least a two-child family, and the family may in fact have any size; a middle child must be in at least a three-child family, but here again, the family may be of any size. However, internal logic of the relationships in Section *E* is such that it may be that the family size effect (of muting warmth) does not gainsay what we find here.

There are three trends that we should point out in Section *E*. First, note how *only* children tend to receive a high degree of warmth, since in only one of the eight cases does the child receive less than the average for his cultural group, if he is an only child. This, of course, represents the extreme of the tendency for warmth to be high when the number of children is low. Second, note how the *youngest* child is receiving significantly more warmth than the *oldest* child is receiving. This second trend is present in five of the six cultural groups. Finally, in four of the cultural groups there is a trend for the oldest child to receive less warmth from his mother than even the middle children. Certainly, viewing the oldest child in relation to *all* the other categories, there is a rather strong and overall significant tendency for him to receive less warmth than the other children.

Summarizing our trends in these data from the point of view of the child, we find that he will receive more warmth if he is in a household with more adults; if he has few cousins living nearby or in the common courtyard; if he has few siblings, rather than many, and if he is an only, a youngest, or some birth order other than that of "oldest" child in the family. If these relationships are seen from the point of view of the mother, she will either have less warmth to give or will feel constrained to give less if she has many children, is dealing with the eldest of her brood, has few adults in the house, or tends to deal with her child in the context of a large number of nieces and nephews.

Maternal Instability

Our hypothesis concerning the antecedent conditions for high emotional instability in mothers centers around the stress of heavy responsibility for child care with relatively little periodic relief. Since, within a family, such relief is probably affected most by the number of other adult caretakers and the number of children who require care, we have related our scores on maternal instability to both of these variables in Table 17.2.[2]

Section *A* of Table 17.2 shows the relationships between maternal

[2] We also related the maternal instability factor scores to the mothers reports of the amount of time they spend with children. The results of this analysis are usually in the predicted direction, but the variance on the amount of time that mothers' report spending with infants and children is often low. This resulted in a number of uneven divisions of the cases and the results are not presented here.

Table 17.2 *Comparison of Maternal-Instability Factor Scores with (A) Household Type, (B) Number of Siblings, and (C) Number of Male Adults in Household*

Society	Instability	A^a Maternal Instability vs. Household Type		B^b Maternal Instability vs. Number of Siblings	
		Nuclear	Stem	Low	High
United States	High			2	9*
	Low			8	5
Mexico	High	9	3	7	5
	Low	7	3	8	2
Philippines	High	10	1	4	8
	Low	7	4	5	6
Okinawa	High	4	7	9	2
	Low	7	5	7	6
India	High	5	0*	3	8*
	Low	1	2	9	4
Africa	High			2	5
	Low			9	4

Society	Instability	C^c Maternal Instability vs. Number of Male Adults in Household	
		Low	High
Mexico	High	9	3
	Low	7	3
Philippines	High	10	2
	Low	7	4
Okinawa	High	10	1
	Low	7	6
India	High	6	5
	Low	4	9

[a] Summary z for this section not significant.
[b] Summary z for this section = 2.62; $p < .01$, one tail test.
[c] Summary z for this section = 3.28; $p < .01$, two tail test.
* Significant at the .05 level.

instability and whether mothers are in nuclear or stem families. As expected, mothers tend to be more stable emotionally when they live in stem families. This trend is present in three of the four societies with some variation in family structure and is significant for the Indian mothers, who are confined by custom to their courtyards, and who are therefore particularly isolated if they have no older woman who can leave the courtyard when necessary. The one exception to this trend is in Okinawa. The mothers are generally stable, helpful women often live nearby, and older children help with much of the child care. The association between maternal instability and the total number of women in the house is even less impressive and these data are not included in the table.

A stronger determinant of maternal instability appears in Section *B*. Mothers are more unstable when they must deal with a large number of children than when they have small families. This trend is significant within the Indian, African, and United States groups. It is directional in the Mexican and Philippine communities. The trend has a strong statistical significance overall. Again, the reversal is Okinawa, where there is a fairly strong tendency for a mother to be more stable in her emotions if she has a *larger* number of children, who in her particular case help to pick up the load of responsibility and care for the younger children. We wonder if this finding is related to the restraints on warmth which were discussed before for mothers with many offspring. If mothers are called upon to display less warmth as their families increase and, apparently, to display it differentially to children of different ages, the strain of differentially controlling warmth might be a source of emotional instability.

We find then, that the number of children needing to be tended increases instability, but the presence of other women does not necessarily decrease it.

Section *C* of Table 17.2 shows an unexpected influence on maternal instability. Mothers tend to be more unstable when the only man living in the household is their husband, than they are when other men are present! This trend is consistent in the Indian, Mexican, Philippine, and Okinawan samples. The husband appears to have the same effect upon women's instability as does an additional child. Barry, Bacon, and Child (1957) argue that adults must be prepared to assume the work roles of the opposite sex in nuclear families, but do not have this role requirement in extended families. It is probably true that women who have only their husbands in the house must sometimes take on the husbands' duties as well as their own, whereas women living in extended families can count on other family men to take over for their husbands if necessary.

Maternal Responsibility for Infant and Child Care

We have hypothesized that the amount of time mothers spend with infants and older children is a simple, inverse function of the presence of available alternate caretakers. For our within-group analysis we have tested this hypothesis by comparing the amount of time that mothers report caring for their children when they were babies with the number of adult females, in addition to the mother, living in the house and the number of older siblings of the child.

This within-group test of the child-care hypothesis is hampered by a lack of variance in some communities, notably the United States and African samples, where mothers usually had little or no help in caring for their children. In the four communities where this relationship can be tested (Mexico, the Philippines, Okinawa, and India), mothers spend less time caring for infants when two or more women share their house (see Table 17.3, Section *B*). This relationship is significant at the .02 level, when the four communities are combined. As would be expected, the same relationship exists between low maternal and stem versus nuclear houses, but the relationship is not as strong and does not attain significance (Table 17.3, Section *A*).

Section *C* of this table shows a fairly strong trend in four communities for mothers to spend less time with infants if there are older siblings, than if she has only one child. There are reverse trends, however, in the Philippines and Okinawa.

Table 17.4 presents these same three relationships in terms of the amount of time that mothers care for older children. In this case it is the presence of stem, as opposed to nuclear, houses that is most strongly associated with low maternal care. The presence of women in addition to a grandmother in the house, or the presence of older siblings, has no strong effect upon the amount of time that mothers care for older children, although the influence is in the predicted direction. The relation of the mother's score on child care to the presence or absence of older siblings is recorded in Section *C* of Table 17.4. The trend in four of the communities (United States, Mexico, Okinawa, and Africa) is for older sibs to apparently ease the mother's child-care load, but there is no trend in India and there is a bit of a reversal in the Philippines group. The problem in this analysis is that we have no check on how *much* older the older sibling is. A 4 year old may be little help in the care of a 3 year old.

These data support our general hypothesis. We will need more detailed data on caretakers to test these ideas more definitively. For instance, we have not been able to assess systematically in this analysis the role of neighbors or maternal relatives in helping with children.

Table 17.3   Comparison of Proportion-of-Time-that-Mother-Cares-for-Baby Factor Scores with (A) Household Type, (B) Number of Women in House, and (C) Presence of Older Siblings of Baby

Society	Maternal Care	A^a Maternal Care of Babies vs. Household Type		B^b Maternal Care of Babies vs. Number of Women in House*	
		Nuclear	Stem	One	Two or More
Mexico	High	8	1	9	0
	Low	8	5	8	5
Philippines	High	8	2	7	3
	Low	9	4	8	5
Okinawa	High	8	5	7	6
	Low	3	7	3	8
India	High	3	2	5	6
	Low	3	0	3	10

Society	Maternal Care	C^c Maternal Care of Babies vs. Presence of Older Siblings	
		No	Yes
United States	High	4	5
	Low	3	12
Mexico	High	6	3
	Low	4	9
Philippines	High	4	7
	Low	5	7
Okinawa	High	3	10
	Low	4	7
India	High	5	6
	Low	4	9
Africa	High	3	3
	Low	3	12

[a] Summary z for this section; not significant.

[b] Summary z for this section = 2.38; $p < .02$.

[c] Summary z for this section = 1.57; $p = .058$, one tail test.

* This number represents women in addition to the mother.

Table 17.4 Comparison of Proportion-of-Time-that-Mother-Cares-for-Noninfant-Children Factor Scores with (A) Household Type, (B) Number of Women in the House, and (C) Number of Older Siblings of Child

Society	Maternal Care	A^a Maternal Care of Children vs. Household Type		B^b Maternal Care of Children vs. Number of Women in House*	
		Nuclear	Stem†	One	Two or More
Mexico	High	8	1	9	3
	Low	8	5	8	2
Philippines	High	8	2	7	4
	Low	9	4	7	5
Okinawa	High	8	5	6	6
	Low	3	7	4	8
India	High	3	2	7	3
	Low	3	0	7	7

C^c
Maternal Care of Children vs. Presence of Older Siblings

Society	Maternal Care	No	Yes
United States	High	4	7
	Low	3	10
Mexico	High	5	6
	Low	3	6
Philippines	High	4	7
	Low	5	7
Okinawa	High	5	7
	Low	2	10
India	High	3	7
	Low	5	9
Africa	High	4	5
	Low	2	5

[a] Summary z for this section = 1.76; $p < .04$, one tail test.
[b] Summary z for this section; not significant.
[c] Summary z for this section = 1.50; $p = .07$, one tail test.
* This number represents women in addition to the mother.
† All other types left out for comparability.

In Okinawan we find that five mothers, whose own mothers live away or are dead, score high on infant and child care, while three out of four mothers who live near their own mothers score low on this variable. We also lack sufficiently detailed information about the extent to which women living in the house actually do help with each other's children. A grandmother living in the house is a potential helpmate, but if she is too old and feeble to be a help, or if she refuses to be bothered, she may well be an additional burden, rather than an aid. We do not have much data on such considerations.

Responsibility Training

Our major hypothesis regarding the conditions for the existence of strong responsibility pressures suggests that mothers who must make independent contributions to the family income will enlist the services of children to help them with their work. This enlistment leads to high frequency and number of chores.

For various reasons we can test this hypothesis in only two of the cultural groups, Orchard Town, New England, and Tarong, Philippines (see Table 17.5, Section *A*). There was no intracultural variability in the Gusii group or in the Indian group, since *all* the Gusii mothers except one (a chronic invalid), and *none* of the Rajput mothers, contributed to the family income. No information is presently avaliable concerning the economic contributions of individual mothers in the Mexican and Okinawan communities.

The trends for the United States and Philippine samples are consistently in favor of the hypothesis, though the relationships are not significant statistically. In both communities, mothers who make some contribution to the family finances have higher factor scores on responsibility training than mothers who do not make such a contribution.

A second obvious basis for pressuring a child into doing chores arises when the child has a number of younger siblings. Given this condition, parents will tend to place more varied and frequent chores, including the care of the younger siblings, on the shoulders of the sample child. Table 17.5, Section *B*, shows that this tendency is significant in our data for the United States, Okinawa, and India and directional in the Philippines. There is no trend in the African group and a weak reversal in Mexico. The overall trend is statistically significant ($p < .02$). This finding is consistent with the (nonsignificant) trend toward less responsibility pressure where there is a relatively high number of older siblings in the child's family (see Table 17.5, Section *C*). As we would expect from these opposing trends, there is no clear relationship between

Table 17.5 Comparison of Responsibility-Training Factor Scores with (A) Mother's Contribution to Family Finances, (B) Number of Younger Siblings, (C) Number of Older Siblings, (D) Total Number of Siblings, and (E) Birth Order

Society	Responsibility Training	A^a Responsibility Training vs. Mother's Contribution to Family Finances		B^b Responsibility Training vs. Number of Younger Siblings	
		No	Yes	Low	High
United States	High	8	4	5	7
	Low	7	5	5	7
Mexico	High	4	6	7	3
	Low	6	6	8	4
Philippines	High	6	5	4	8
	Low	3	9	5	6
Okinawa	High	10	4	9	5
	Low	5	5	7	3
India	High	5	3	3	5
	Low	8	8	9	7
Africa	High	4	4	4	4
	Low	5	3	5	3

Society	Responsibility Training	C^c Responsibility Training vs. Number of Older Siblings		D^d Responsibility Training vs. Total Number of Siblings	
		Low	High	Low	High
United States	High	6	6	4	8*
	Low	8	4	9	3
Mexico	High			7	3
	Low			7	5
Philippines	High	3	6	7	5
	Low	8	6	7	3
Okinawa	High			4	10*
	Low			8	2
India	High			3	5*
	Low			14	2
Africa	High			4	4
	Low			4	4

Table 17.5 (Continued)   Comparison of Responsibility-Training Factor Scores with (A) Mother's Contribution to Family Finances, (B) Number of Younger Siblings, (C) Number of Older Siblings, (D) Total Number of Siblings, and (E) Birth Order

		E^e Responsibility Training vs. Birth Order			
Society	Responsibility Training	Only	Youngest	Oldest	Other
United States	High	1	3	4	4
	Low	1	8	1	2
Mexico	High	0	2	4	4
	Low	0	1	6	5
Philippines	High	1	1	5	5
	Low	1	3	2	5
Okinawa	High	0	1	5	8
	Low	0	1	2	7
India	High	0	2	3	3
	Low	3	6	3	4
Africa	High	0	1	3	4
	Low	1	2	2	3

[a] Summary z for this section; not significant.
[b] Summary z for this section $= 2.65$; $p < .02$, two tail test.
[c] Summary z for this section; not significant.
[d] Summary z for this section; not significant.
[e] Summary z for all cultures on youngest vs. oldest child $= 1.98$; $p = < .05$, two tail test.
* Significant at .05 level.

responsibility training and the total number of siblings of the child (Table 17.5, Section *D*).

These relationships are probably displayed most clearly in Section *E* of Table 17.5, where responsibility factor scores are related to the birth order positions in the family. The patterns in this table are almost a mirror image of those in Section *E* of Table 17.1, where maternal warmth scores were related to birth order. There is a clear tendency in all of the communities, except the Mexican one, for the oldest child to receive high scores in responsibility training, as compared to the youngest child. This overall trend is significant statistically ($p < .05$). The only child still gets preferred treatment in that six out of eight only children have low scores on responsibility training. The main difference in pattern compared to the maternal warmth table rests with the middle category children, who receive no preferential treatment on responsibility training, although they do tend to receive more maternal warmth.

In summary then, a child receives strong pressures toward responsibility if he is an oldest child; if he has a large number of younger siblings for his culture, or if his mother is making a contribution toward the family economy. From the point of view of the mother, she appears to rationally respond to the pressures put upon her by using the best assistance available to her in doling out responsibility assignments.

Aggression Training: Mother-Directed Aggression

When analyzing between-culture differences in severity of mother-directed aggression, we noted that the African mothers are unusually high on this factor, while the Indian mothers are unusually low. Our hypothesis explaining their between-group differences suggests that mothers

Table 17.6 Comparison of Mother-Directed-Aggression Training Factor Scores with (A) Mother's Contribution to Family Finances, (B) Frequency of Children's Chores, (C) Household Type, (D) Total Number of Adults in House, (E) Total Number of Siblings, (F) Total Number of Males, and (G) Total Number of Females

| | | A^a Mother-Directed Aggression Training vs. Mothers' Contribution to Family Finances | | B^b Mother-Directed Aggression Training vs. Frequency of Chores | | |
Society	Mother-Directed Aggression Training	No	Yes	Low	Middle	High[1]
United States	High	5	5	1	8	3
	Low	9	5	5	4	3
Mexico	High			6		5
	Low			8		3
Philippines	High	3	3	6		8
	Low	11	6	6		3
Okinawa	High			7		6
	Low			4		7
India	High			3	3	4
	Low			6	2	6
Africa	High			2		5
	Low			5		4

Table 17.6 (Continued) Comparison of Mother-Directed-Aggression Training Factor Scores with (A) Mothers' Contribution to Family Finances, (B) Frequency of Children's Chores, (C) Household Type, (D) Total Number of Adults in House, (E) Total Number of Siblings, (F) Total Number of Adult Males, and (G) Total Number of Adult Females

Society	Mother-Directed Aggression Training	C[c] Mother-Directed Aggression Training vs. Household Type		D[d] Mother-Directed Aggression Training vs. Total Number of Adults in House	
		Nuclear	Stem	Low	High
United States	High				
	Low				
Mexico	High	6	5	5	6
	Low	10	1	9	2
Philippines	High	9	4	8	6
	Low	8	1	5	4
Okinawa	High	3	9*	3	10
	Low	8	3	6	5
India	High	2	1	4	7*
	Low	4	1	10	3
Africa	High				
	Low				

Society	Mother-Directed Aggression Training	E[e] Mother-Directed Aggression Training vs. Total Number of Siblings	
		Low	High
United States	High	5	7
	Low	5	7
Mexico	High	9	2
	Low	6	5
Philippines	High	7	7
	Low	7	2
Okinawa	High	10	3
	Low	6	5
India	High	8	3*
	Low	4	9
Africa	High	4	3
	Low	5	4

Table 17.6 (Continued) Comparison of Mother-Directed-Aggression Training Factor Scores with (A) Mothers' Contribution to Family Finances, (B) Frequency of Children's Chores, (C) Household Type, (D) Total Number of Adults in House, (E) Total Number of Siblings, (F) Total Number of Adult Males, and (G) Total Number of Adult Females

Society	Mother-Directed Aggression Training	F[f] Mother-Directed Aggression Training vs. Total Number of Adult Males		G[g] Mother-Directed Aggression Training vs. Total Number of Adult Females	
		Low†	High	Low‡	High
Mexico	High	7	4	6	5
	Low	9	2	11	0
Philippines	High	10	4	9	5
	Low	7	2	6	3
Okinawa	High	8	5	4	9
	Low	8	2	6	5
India	High	4	7	5	6
	Low	10	3	9	4

[a] Mother-directed aggression is measured by scale 18, not factor scores for this comparison.

[b] Summary z for this section; not significant.

[c] Summary z for this section = 2.86; $p < .01$.

[d] Summary z for this section = 2.64; $p < .01$.

[e] Summary z for this section = 1.35; not significant.

[f] Summary z for this section = 2.46; $p < .05$, two tail test.

[g] Summary z for this section = 5.24; $p < .01$, two tail test.

* Significant at .05 level.

† All but India break between one and two males, India breaks between two and three.

‡ All but India break between one and two females, India breaks between two and three.

[1] Due to particularly poor distributions, it was necessary to break the New England and the Indian samples into closest thirds on the chores variable. Our trend interpretation rests upon the upper and lower thirds in these two societies, or as near to this as possible.

with heavy work loads, such as the Gusii mothers, will bring their children into the work pattern as assistants. Such mothers then take on the role of work supervisor and in this capacity must insure responsibility by punishing defiance by their child helpers.

A within-group test of part of this hypothesis appears in Sections *A* and *B* of Table 17.6. Section *A* shows that both United States and Philippine mothers who do not work tend to be less punitive about aggression to themselves than mothers who do work. Section *B* of this table shows that, in five of our six groups, mothers tend to be more punitive about aggression to themselves when the children do chores frequently. The only exception is Okinawa, where requirements for chores tend to be generally low and where the mothers are strikingly prone to use praise and warmth as the techniques for handling their children. Because of the particularly difficult distributions on the frequency-of-chore scale, we have not attempted a statistical evaluation of this trend. Both types of results support our hypothesis.

Sections *C*, *D*, and *E* of Table 17.6 show some correlates of mother-directed-aggression training. One strong and consistent trend appears in Section *C*. It shows that mothers in stem families punish aggression to themselves more severely than do mothers in nuclear family households. The overall probability of this relationship is less than .01. This association may be interpreted by noting the tendency portrayed in Section *D* for mothers to be more punitive about this kind of aggression when the number of adults living in the house is relatively high. As may be seen from Sections *F* and *G*, punishment for aggression to mothers is related both to the number of women and to the number of men in a household. Although this trend is less consistent because of a reversal in the Philippine sample, it also has a combined probability of .01. A child who is permitted to defy his mother's authority in such households may also defy the elder family members, or set a bad example for his cousins. We had predicted that peer-to-peer aggression would be strongly punished in extended family households. It is not surprising to find this practice extending to aggression to authority as well.

Section *E* has been included in this table to show that punitiveness for mother-directed agression is not strongly related to the presence of siblings in the household. Whereas there are strong trends in Mexico, Okinawa, and India (significant in India) for punishment of this behavior to decrease, as does warmth, with an increase of siblings, this trend is either absent or reversed in other groups and fails to reach overall significance.

In summary, children are strongly punished for insubordination to their mothers when the mothers work or live in households with members of other nuclear families, or when the children are expected to do chores frequently.   All these results are consistent with our hypothesis.

Aggression Training: Peer-Directed Aggression

Our hypothesis about the antecedents of punishment for peer-directed aggression suggests that this behavior will be severely punished in families who share living quarters with relatives with whom they must maintain close-knit ties of friendship.

Section *A* of Table 17.7 supports our contention that the aspect of shared living space and not merely close relationships may be crucial in determining this relationship.   This table presents the relationship between punishment for peer-directed aggression and the number of female relatives (and presumably their children) living nearby, but necessarily in the same house.   There is a tendency for children in the United States, Philippine, and Okinawan samples to be more strongly punished for fighting with their peers when such relatives live nearby.   This trend does attain significance in Okinawa.   However, this relationship is absent or reversed in the Mexican, Indian, and African samples. The overall relationship is, of course, not significant.

Sections *B* and *C* of Table 17.7 show that we are generally correct in our assumption that children will be punished more harshly for fighting when other adults live in the same house, although the relationship is not as strong as it is for mother-directed aggression training.   In three of the four communities where such a test is possible, children of stem families tend to be punished for fighting more severely than do children of nuclear family households.   The trend does not appear in the Philippine sample, but its overall significance is less than .05.   The same relationship is seen between punishment for peer-directed aggression and the total number of adults in the house, but it is also not significant.

Sections *D* and *E* of Table 17.7 show that it is the number of women and not the number of men present in the house that influences the punishment of peer-directed aggression.   The enumeration of men in the total number of adults (Section *C*) this obscures the relationship between variable and the presence of adult women.   Since it is the women who must live with each other and the children, work in close association, and avoid becoming involved in the children's quarrels, it is not surprising that it is the presence of additional women in the house that affects punishment for children's fighting.

Extended family living is not the only condition under which people must maintain close ties of friendship, despite prolonged close contact. A large nuclear family sharing a small house faces much the same kind

Table 17.7   Comparison of Peer-Directed-Aggression-Training Factor Scores with (A) Number of Adult Female Relatives Living Nearby, (B) Household Type, (C) Number of Adults in Household, (D) Number of Female Adults in Household, (E) Number of Male Adults in Household, (F) Total Number of Siblings, and (G) Birth Order

Society	Peer-Directed Aggression Training	A^a Peer-Directed Aggression Training vs. Number of Adult Female Relatives Living Nearby		B^b Peer-Directed Aggression Training vs. Household Type	
		Low	High	Nuclear	Stem
United States	High	5	7		
	Low	7	5		
Mexico	High	6	4	5	5*
	Low	7	5	11	1
Philippines	High	5	8	9	3
	Low	5	5	8	2
Okinawa	High	4	9*	5	8
	Low	8	3	6	5
India	High	9	3	3	2
	Low	6	6	3	0
Africa	High	5	5		
	Low	2	4		

Society	Peer-Directed Aggression Training	C^c Peer-Directed Aggression Training vs. Number of Adults in Household		D^d Peer-Directed Aggression Training vs. Number of Female Adults in Household	
		Low	High	Low	High
Mexico	High	5	5	6	4
	Low	9	3	11	1
Philippines	High	7	6	8	5
	Low	6	4	7	3
Okinawa	High	3	10	4	9
	Low	6	5	6	5
India	High	7	5	6	6
	Low	3	9	3	9

Table 17.7 (Continued)   Comparison of Peer-Directed-Aggression-Training Factor Scores with (A) Number of Adult Female Relatives Living Nearby, (B) Household Type, (C) Number of Adults in Household, (D) Number of Female Adults in Household, (E) Number of Male Adults in Household, (F) Total Number of Siblings, and (G) Birth Order

Society	Peer-Directed Aggression Training	E[e] Peer-Directed Aggression Training vs. Number of Male Adults in Household	
		Low	High
Mexico	High	6	4
	Low	10	2
Philippines	High	10	3
	Low	7	3
Okinawa	High	9	4
	Low	8	3
India	High	6	6
	Low	4	8

Society	Peer-Directed Aggression Training	F[f] Peer-Directed Aggression Training vs. Number of Siblings		G[g] Peer-Directed Aggression Training vs. Birth Order			
		Low	High	Only	Youngest	Oldest	Other
United States	High	4	8	1	3	4	4
	Low	6	6	1	8	1	2
Mexico	High	7	3	0	2	4	4
	Low	8	4	0	1	6	5
Philippines	High	7	6	2	2	3	6
	Low	6	3	0	1	4	5
Okinawa	High	5	8*	0	2	2	9
	Low	11	0	0	0	5	6
India	High	3	9*	1	3	3	5
	Low	9	3	2	4	4	2
Africa	High	5	5	1	2	3	4
	Low	4	2	0	1	2	3

[a] Summary z for this section; not significant.
[b] Summary z for this section = 1.80; $p < .05$, one tail test.
[c] Summary z for this section; not significant.
[d] Summary z for this section = 1.50; $p = .06$, one tail test.
[e] Summary z for this section: not significant.
[f] Summary z for this section = 3.08; $p < .01$, two tail test.
[g] Summary z for this section; not significant.
* Significant at .05 level.

of problem.   We could not test this aspect of our hypothesis in the HRAF analysis, but in Section *F* of Table 17.7 we examine this relationship in terms of within-group variation.   The results leave little doubt that children with many siblings are punished for fighting more severely than are children with few siblings.   This tendency is present in all of the samples except Mexico, where no trend appears.   The relationship between severe punishment for fighting and large numbers of siblings is significant in the Okinawan and Indian samples ($p < .05$), and the probability of the *z* for this relationship is less than .01.   This is the strongest within-group relationship to emerge from our analysis.

We have included Section *G* in Table 17.7 to show that there is no general pancultural relationship between peer-aggression punishment and birth order.   There is one interesting significant relationship within the table for the New England group, where the youngest child, compared to all other children, is treated less punitively for peer-directed aggression. There is also a relationship within the Okinawan sample which is almost significant for the oldest child, relative to all others, to be treated permissively in this regard.   Perhaps this latter case displays the effects of the high warmth that the older Okinawan children have received for so long, making them mature and adultlike in their peer relationships.   But such questions must await a later book.

Peer aggression punitiveness, in summary, seems to occur as a result of the problems that arise in a family with many siblings in one house and is relatively unaffected by the presence of relatives in the nearby community.   It is interesting to note that, whereas the factor scores for mother-directed aggression are sensitive to the presence of additional adults, but unaffected by the number of children present, the factor scores for peer-directed aggression are sensitive to the number of both adults and children in the house.

Summary

The results of our analysis of individual differences reveals that family composition has some fairly strong effects on mother-child relationships. The number of additional adults appears to be an important influence on some of our factors; others are affected chiefly by the number of children in the family, and still others by the presence of both adults and children.

We find, for instance, that additional women in a household seem to relieve mothers of the burden of excessive child care.   Perhaps for this reason, mothers express their warmth more freely and are more emotionally stable if they live in stem families, although we suspect that multiple family living may reverse this effect. Some support for this suspicion is supplied by the tentative nature of this relationship in the Mexican and Indian samples and by the finding that additional adults in the house, while still associated with high maternal warmth, also produce conditions under which children are severely punished for aggression to mothers or to other children. Older siblings also help in caring for infants and younger children, as is evidenced by the high responsibility training for children who have several younger siblings. Children, however, do not have the soothing effect on mothers' personality that is produced by the aid of other women. We infer this from the findings that mothers with several children are more emotionally unstable than are mothers with fewer offspring and mothers are sparing in the warmth they give their children when several siblings or cousins share the house.

Finally, birth order affects the way in which children may be treated by their mothers. Oldest children receive little warmth, but are assigned frequent chores, while youngest children receive more warmth for less work. The last child, who is always the baby of the family, seems to have some pancultural generality, as does the "spoiled" only child who receives much the same treatment as the youngest.

The combined importance, in one way or another, of the number, age, and status of the people in the household in determining how mothers treat their children is impressive. Our analysis of extra-family influences such as the presence of relatives in the neighborhood, or the mothers' work roles, is far from complete, but for the present these considerations seem to have much less influence on our factor scores than does household composition. Assuming that the mothers' answers do reflect reality and that our ratings accurately reflect these answers, it appears that our mothers were responding to immediate and massive pressures from within their households in answering our questions.

As for our hypotheses, they fared better than we expected in the light of the many difficulties which we enumerated at the beginning of this chapter. Ideally, our data would show significant effects in every culture, but the conditions of analysis are far too crude for that. The significance of many of the combined within-group trends is as much as could be hoped for from these measurements. The unidirectionality of these combined data indicate that mothers in widely different cultures react in the same fashion to comparable pressures from their families.

These discoveries of the uniformity of the effects of household structure across diverse societies add a new and powerful dimension to cross-cultural research. A more careful analysis of these social structure factors, which vary to some extent in all societies, should enable future investigators to relate the data on individual families to the cultural norms of the communities in which these families live, and to place these findings in cross-cultural perspective.   One of the major contributions of this book may be a clearer specification of important influences on child training that are amenable to analysis both across societies and within societies.   Our data lead us to expect that at least some of these influences show promise of comparable relationships for these two realms of investigation.   If this proves to be the case, we should be able soon to make significant advances in unifying previously diverse lines of investigation in social science research.

18 ❖ Conclusions

Introduction

We have now reached the end of our investigations and we have come to the place where we can summarize our findings, place them in the context of the total project, and discuss their implications.

The field guide used by all our field teams (Whiting et al., 1954) as the basic outline for our research defined nine variables. These were succorance, achievement, self-reliance, obedience, nurturance, responsibility, sociability, dominance, and aggression. For the mother interview, these variables were defined in terms of the antecedent conditions for the training of these behaviors in the children. These variables do not, of course, represent all possible dimensions. Furthermore, the data included in the factor analysis do not include all the information in the mother interviews. Questions had to be excluded because they were not asked in some of our societies; because the answers of the mothers showed little or no variance in some societies, or because the coding of them was unreliable. Therefore the dimensions described in this study are not an exhaustive list of the important considerations in mother-child relationships. They should be viewed, rather, as a set of meaningful and, hopefully, useful pancultural dimensions which help to simplify the task of grasping some of the variability that occurs from community to community in different societies and among mothers of the same communities.

The first test of the usefulness of these dimensions will come when they are correlated with variables of children's behavior that are now being coded at Harvard. The six culture study was designed primarily to determine what maternal child-training practices influence children's behavior and to specify, if possible, the nature of these influences. If the mothers' position on our child-training variables can predict some aspects of her children's behavior, then they will be useful tools of science. At present we can only speculate on the possible influences of our factors upon children's behavior, since the actual analysis has not yet been done.

The factors that emerge from our analysis are not altogether the same nine variables that went into the interview. This is not necessarily bad, since the factor analysis would have added nothing to our understanding if the factors that emerged were identical to the original dimensions. The factor of responsibility training and the two aggression-training factors are the ones most similar to the original variables. These should influence children's behavior in their respective realms. Maternal warmth is probably an important antecedent in the development of nurturance and succorance in children. Maternal irritability may well influence sociability in children. The amount of time that mothers spend with children should be relevant to self-reliance, responsibility, and achievement training.

So much for speculations on the future of our factors; let us turn to a summary of what we know about them now. We will do this by describing the conditions of the communities which hold extreme positions on each of the factors relative to communities in other cultures, and the conditions of the mothers within each of our societies who have extreme positions on the factors relative to others in their own communities. We will interpret both sets of data in terms of our hypotheses, and evaluate our confidence in our interpretations in the light of the degree to which the tests of these hypotheses presented in Chapter 9 confirm or refute them.

Maternal Warmth

The maternal warmth factor is defined by four scales: general warmth of mother, general hostility of mother, amount of praise used by mother, and amount of punishment used by mother.

The two societies where mothers are least warm are Mexico and India. Both are characterized by courtyard or semicourtyard living. The African and Philippine societies, where mothers live in separate houses surrounding a partially enclosed yard, are intermediate in warmth. The Okinawan mothers, who have still more privacy, are the warmest sample in the study. The New England mothers, who have the most privacy of all, so much that they are overburdened with almost exclusive responsibility for child care, rank fourth in their warmth. This distribution led us to speculate that the degree of warmth expressed by mothers is related to the privacy of living arrangements. The direction of this relationship may be curvilinear. Mothers in close and crowded quarters may control their emotional expressiveness to avoid quarrels between their children and their cousins, and between themselves and their sisters-in-law. Mothers who are really isolated from their relatives and substitute caretakers may control expressiveness in somewhat the same way to avoid further wear and tear on their own frayed nerves and fights among siblings for their own praise and affection.

In its most subtle form then, this hypothesis predicts a curvilinear relationship between privacy and maternal warmth with mothers who have intermediate privacy being the most warm and mothers in crowded living quarters being the lowest of the two low extremes. Unfortunately the data presently available to us do not permit the testing of this curvilinear relationship. By using material from the HRAF files, we were able to investigate the position of societies on the variables of the maternal warmth factor as a function of living in predominantly single family or multiple family dwellings. The results of this analysis show that mothers who live in multiple family houses are less warm, less hostile, and use less praise and less physical punishment than do mothers who live in single family dwellings. None of these relationships are significant, and they are not entirely in accord with the results of the six-culture study, since mothers who are high on the Maternal Warmth Factor are *low* on hostility and do *not* make extensive use of physical punishment. The HRAF results on these four variables do tend to confirm the general hypothesis that mothers without privacy are controlled in their emotions. An additional finding, from the HRAF analysis, further complicates our findings. Mothers in multiple family dwellings are more permissive than are mothers in single family houses, although the difference is not significant. Whereas permissiveness might be viewed as part of a syndrome of controlled emotionality on the part of mothers, it hardly seems designed to reinforce this attribute in children. This result reminds us of the most confined group of mothers, those of the Indian sample, who tried to avoid outbursts from their children, but who frequently gave in to maintain peace, when children angrily defied them.

The within-community analysis of maternal warmth lends support for our contention that the relationship between warmth and the presence of others may be curvilinear. Here we find that children are treated more warmly when a grandmother is present than they are when mothers have no other adult women in the house. But this trend does not exist in Mexico and India, where larger extended families are in evidence. Furthermore, we find that the presence of large numbers of cousins and the presence of large numbers of siblings reduce maternal warmth. The one is an inevitable by-product of extended family living and the other a particularly tiring burden for the mothers of isolated nuclear houses. As we had expected then, mothers who must cope more than others, either with their own children or their children's cousins, are muted in their warmth, while mothers who have the help of a grandmother are free in their expressions of affection. The birth order of the children also affects maternal warmth with the oldest child receiving less maternal warmth, at least after he has siblings, and the youngest child receiving the most warmth. As would be expected from the data on number of siblings, an only child receives more warmth than the child with siblings.

Maternal Instability

This factor is defined by only two scales: mood variation of hostility and mood variation of warmth. The Gusii mothers of Africa are the most unstable group, with the New England mothers ranking second. The mothers in the Philippines and Okinawa are the most stable of our study. It is our hypothesis that mothers become emotionally unstable when they are forced to spend long periods of time without help in caring for their children, and that this instability will be further augmented if mothers have extensive economic or domestic chores, in addition to prolonged responsibility for children. This hypothesis was definitely not confirmed by the HRAF analysis. The time that mothers spend caring for infants and older is unrelated to the variation of their warmth or their hostility.

The hypothesis is supported, however, by the within-group analysis which shows that mothers are more stable when they live in stem families and have the assistance of grandparents. Also, they are more stable when they have relatively small numbers of children to cope with. The relationship between maternal instability and number of children is considerably stronger than the relationship between maternal instability and household composition. Inability to control for nuclear family size in the HRAF analysis may be responsible for the absence of relationship between maternal child-care responsibilities and instability in the HRAF analysis.

Proportion of Time that Mothers Care for Children

Two child-care factors emerged from our analysis: one measuring responsibility for baby care and the other measuring the degree of responsibility for the care of older children. The baby care factor is defined by two scales: the proportion of time that the mother cares for the baby and the proportion of time that other adults (not the fathers) care for the baby. The child care factor is also defined by two scales, both of which measure the proportion of care-taking (of older children) done by the mother.

The New England mothers spend more time caring for both babies and older children than any other group of mothers in our study. The

African mothers are also very high in the amount of time that they spend caring for older children. Furthermore, the low position of these Gusii mothers on the baby care factor is misleading since, for the most part, it is only their own older children who help them care for babies.

We hypothesized that the amount of time that mothers are responsible for children varies inversely with the availability of alternative caretakers. This hypothesis receives strong support from the HRAF analysis. Within an age group, the amount of time that mothers spend caring for either babies or older children is negatively correlated with the amount of time spent by others, with the exception of a positive correlation between the time that mothers and fathers care for older children. This appears to represent parent-centered versus relative-centered socialization. The amount of time that mothers spend caring for either infants or older children is relatively unaffected by the time that others care for children of the older or younger age group. This supports our finding two independent factors of child care: one for babies and one for older children.

The within-group analysis of this hypothesis also shows that mothers spend less time with babies and older children when other women share the house and when the children have older siblings to help care for them. These relationships are particularly strong for infant care. All things considered, this hypothesis is the one that is more strongly confirmed than any other.

Responsibility Training

This factor is defined by three scales: frequency of chores, number of chores, and age of child. As might be expected, older children have more chores and do them more frequently. This factor is the only one of our analysis that is substantially affected by the age of the children and it is also the only factor with no significant between-society differences.

Since there are no significant differences between the communities of our study on the degree to which they emphasize responsibility, we have no clear basis for suggesting cultural conditions that might lead to high or low responsibility training. It would seem from our data that responsibility is related to age in much the same way in most or all societies. However, if we consider the rank order of the groups of mothers, regardless of the degree of difference between them, we note that this ordering bears some relationship to the importance of the mothers' economic duties. Furthermore, on several of the scales measuring degree of children's responsibility for particular kinds of chores, there is a fairly consistent between-group break, with the Mexican, Philippine, and African children having more responsibility than the children in New England, Okinawa, and the Philippines. The African mothers, who must often work without help from their husbands, contribute more labor to agricultural activities than the mothers in any other group. The Mexican mothers often go to market and the mothers in the Philippines may do this, although usually not until they are relatively old. New England mothers sometimes work and Okinawan mothers often help to gather firewood, which is sold in family units. The mothers in the Indian sample are prevented by purdah restrictions from doing any work outside their homes.

On the basis of these considerations, we suggested that responsibility training might be higher in those societies where the mothers make independent contributions to their families' income. Such mothers, we argue, will be more likely to enlist the help of children to help them with their more extensive duties. Unfortunately the material available in the HRAF files was not sufficiently detailed to enable us to measure variation in the amount that women contribute to the economy. We could obtain no direct measure of the extent to which the women make a direct financial contribution to the economy, nor to the extent to which the mothers have to exert supervisory control over their children in this regard. It was necessary to settle for a scale which reflects the woman's differential participation in subsistence activities. There is little overall relationship between this measure of women's importance in subsistence activities and degree of responsibility training for children, although there is some trend in the predicted direction for girls.

Since almost all of the variance of this factor is due to within-group variation and there are no significant differences among groups, it is not surprising that the between-group HRAF analysis fails to reveal strong cross-cultural differences. In the light of the factor data, one would expect this hypothesis, if valid, to fare better on the within-group analysis than the between-group analysis, and so it does.

The analysis of individual differences among mothers reveals that in the United States and the Philippines, where the test could be made, mothers do assign more frequent chores when they contribute to the families' finances. Furthermore, we find that mothers emphasize responsibility with oldest children and with children who have many younger siblings.

Aggression Training: Mother-Directed Aggression

This factor is defined by two scales: the degree to which the mother is nonpunitive when the child becomes angry with her, and the degree to which the mother is aggressive when the child is angry with her.

The Gusii mothers put the most pressure on children to obey and respect adults. They consider any defiance of themselves as an attack against all authority and they punish it severely. On the low end of this factor, the Indian mothers of Khalapur do little to avert their children's aggression and may even console an angry child. The Philippine and Mexican mothers, less punitive than those of Africa, rank second and third on this factor, while the Okinawan and New England mothers, who are less punitive than the Mexican and Philippine group but more punitive than the Indian mothers, rank fourth and fifth. This rank order is similar to the one on the responsibility factor, which leads us to suspect that the antecedents may be similar. Mothers who have extensive duties other than child training, particularly those producing some degree of economic independence, may be more severe in punishing insubordination from their children than mothers who lack this type of power and status.

To test this hypothesis, we used the same scale of women's participation in the economy that was used to relate to the responsibility training data. Despite the fact that this scale is only a rough approximation of the measure that we really want, there is a strong trend in the cross-cultural data which suggests that mothers who make a heavy contribution to the subsistence of the family are less permissive than are mothers who make less of a contribution. The social psychological dynamics that intervene here between a mother coping with making a contribution and her obedience demands or parent-directed aggression control are not yet clear. We learned from the cross-cultural test of responsibility training that it is not generally related to the chores required of the children. It may be that mothers who achieve high status through their economic contributions punish defiance in order to emphasize and enforce their status. The lack of relationship between maternal instability and extensiveness of child-care duties does not support the interpretation that mothers who are overworked are simply more impatient with their children, although this may be the case for mothers with excessive responsibilities, as the ones in our Gusii sample.

The within-group analysis also supports our hypothesis. Mothers in the United States and Philippines do tend to be more punitive about aggression to themselves when they earn some money of their own, and mothers in all communities, except Okinawa, tend to punish insubordination more severely when their children do chores relatively frequently.

We also find that punishment for defiance of maternal authority tends to be increased as the number of persons who live in the house increases, probably because of fear that such disobedience will spread to other family members.

Aggression Training: Peer-Directed Aggression

The final factor of our study is defined by three scales: consistency of rules against aggression, reward for retaliation to peers, and consistency of mother's follow-through on nonroutine obedience demands.

In our Mexican village, mothers put great pressure on their children to prevent fights with other children. In New England, on the other hand, children may be rewarded for moderate and just peer-to-peer aggression. All other groups are virtually identical in their treatment of this behavior. Why do we find this ordering? We suggest that it is related to the degree to which families must live in close and constant contact with their relatives. Mexican mothers live in courtyards with their husband's relatives, who may also be their own blood relatives, and the children play with siblings and cousins. The Indian community in Juxtlahuaca is a low-status community and its inhabitants cannot vent their aggression against their more powerful Mexican neighbors. Family ties are important to everyone concerned, and cannot be allowed to be disrupted by the quarrels of children. In Orchard Town, homes are private, relatives seldom live nearby, and it is possible to sever social relationships with neighbors, if this becomes necessary. These living pattern differences are reflected in the attitudes of the mothers of these groups concerning their children's aggression. The Mexican mothers keep their children in the courtyard and sometimes do not send them to school because of an intense concern that the children may quarrel with children outside of the family. The Orchard Town mothers encourage their children to play with neighbor children and settle their own disputes. They attempt to remain uninvolved in their children's fights.

The mothers of Khalapur are more casual about punishment for peer-to-peer aggression than would be expected from this hypothesis, although all the mothers disapproved of it. We think that their position as a high-status, powerful group with warrior tradition may well lower their aggression punishment. Since the Rajputs are exogamous, the Khalapur mothers were usually not with their own relatives and their emotional ties with their husbands' village were less strong than their ties with their own home. Finally, in-group aggression is a serious, unsolved problem for this social group.

We have some cross-cultural confirmation for this hypothesis in a study done by Whiting (1959) in which he finds that nuclear family cultures are least punitive of peer-to-peer aggression, while extended family cultures are the most punitive. Our within-culture analysis strongly supports this hypothesis. In three of the four communities, where stem families are present, children in such families tend to be punished for fighting more severely than children of nuclear family households. Furthermore, children with several siblings are punished for fighting more severely in five of our six communities than are only children, or children with relatively few siblings.

More research is needed to pinpoint the psychological dynamics of this type of training. What kinds of persons must be present in the environment to inhibit peer-aggression training? Must they be relatives or would the presence of high-status neighbors have the same effect? Are children who grow up living near the father's boss, i.e., a higher-status family, or a local church and minister's family more chastened for their peer aggression than those who do not? Most of the variance of this factor is due to individual differences among the mothers. Considerations such as the above, either in the present living conditions of the children or in those of the parents that shaped their personalities, may be responsible for some of this variance.

Summary

What may be said about the status of our hypotheses in the light of all the data we can presently amass? Two of them, the contention that mothers spend less time with children when other women are available to help, and the contention that children are severely punished for fighting with each other when many people must share cramped living quarters and still maintain their friendships, receive fairly strong support from both our cross-cultural analysis using the HRAF file material and the within-group analysis of differences among the mothers of our six cultures.

Our two hypotheses concerning the determinants of two aspects of maternal personality, warmth, and instability, receive little support from the HRAF analysis but some confirmation from our individual differences analysis. These two factors reflect personality variables of some subtlety. Warmth and emotional instability are difficult to measure in a study of individuals designed specifically for that purpose. It does not surprise us that the ethnological material contained in the accounts of the HRAF files does not support our interpretations of these traits, since the material can at best reflect highly imperfect estimates of the personalities of mothers. The fact that we do find in our within-group analysis that maternal warmth varies with the presence of other people in the household, and that maternal instability does decrease when the burden of child care is eased either by the presence of additional caretakers or a small number of children, leads us to conclude that these two hypotheses are at least worthy of further investigation.

Our hypotheses that rigorous responsibility training and severe punishment for mother-directed aggression occur when mothers make financial contributions of their own to the family finances remained essentially untested.   In the absence of accurate data on the amount of capital contributed by women to the family, either in the HRAF files or in the field notes of our own co-authors, we have been able to assess these hypotheses only by tangential evidence.   We do find a tendency in the HRAF analysis for mothers in societies where women's work is important to the economy to be less permissive than mothers in societies where women do not have this demanding role.   We also find that our meager individual differences data, bearing on these two hypotheses, are in the predicted direction and at least do not contradict them.   A further test of these hypotheses must await more accurate and detailed data.

Our New Perspectives on Studies of Child Training

This book represents over ten years of effort.   It is part of the still incomplete study originally conceived and directed by John Whiting, Irvin Child, and William Lambert.   The first report of the findings of this study is embodied in *Six Cultures—Studies of Child Rearing* edited by Beatrice Whiting.   The last report on the effects of socialization upon children's behavior is still to come.   The present volume, *Mothers of Six Cultures,* has been seven years in preparation.   After close association with our data for so long a time we have reached conclusions about the limitations of our study, and most other studies of child training that have appeared to date, that have serious and far-reaching implications for this field of research.

This study differs from most studies of child rearing in that we have viewed child-rearing practices as the end result to be explained and have looked for their antecedents, whereas most other studies have begun with the child-training practices and looked at their effect upon the child. That analysis of the six culture data is yet to come.   We can now make some suggestions for that analysis and for future studies by other authors in the light of our present data.   We think that our findings about the antecedents of child-training practices have some bearing on the way in which these practices impinge on children.   Most studies in this area have approached socializing practices as if the parents of the investigations were operating in terms of blueprints and curriculums that are guided largely by either cognitively-monitored theories about what is good and bad for the long range development of children, or, at the other extreme, molded by the parents' own unconscious motives and anxieties, which translate themselves into behavior and, in turn, mold the children's psyches without the parents' knowledge or control.

It now appears that the pressures impinging upon the growing child are much more in the nature of by-products of the horde of apparently irrelevant considerations that impinge upon the parents. These considerations of household composition, size of family, work load, etc., determine the time and energy that mothers have available to care for children. They determine the range and content of mother-child relations and the context in which these relations must take place. The coerciveness of these forces becomes apparent in the broad spectrum of cross-cultural comparison. The mother of Orchard Town, alone in her own house and surrounded by neighbors with whom she has no kinship ties; the mother of Khalapur, confined by custom to her courtyard shared by other confined women with whom she has no ties of blood; the mother of Tarong, secure in the village in which she was raised among blood and affinal kinsmen; and the mother of Gusii, supporting her family without her husband's aid and sharing her yard with co-wives whom she may suspect of bewitching her and her children, all face very different worlds. Each must solve the problems of these worlds and pass on to her children, both the problems and their solutions. We think that the message that each passes to her children is more a function of the problems than of a theory of child rearing.

All this seems very obvious once it has been said, but obvious as it may be, these forces have been ignored in many studies. A search of the literature for reference material reveals little that pertains to the influence of family size, household composition, or birth order or treatment of the child. These are the variables that we find so coercive in our analysis. Further, we contend that not only have important variables been neglected, but also the causal factors behind child-training practices have been misinterpreted. The contrast between the view that we are taking and the usual approach to this topic may become clearer if we take it one step further. We have said that psychologists, in past studies, have viewed socialization as if parents were raising children in terms of overarching theories of child rearing, or their own repressed desires. Starting from this assumption, they have then supposed that child-training practices were based upon parental beliefs and values. Beatrice Whiting (1959) suggests that child-training practices are based rather upon "certain conditions in the natural and social environment" that make them necessary for survival. She then goes on to argue that these child-training practices, arising from necessities that do not pertain to children, are rationalized and justified by a structure of beliefs and values designed

to support them.   This interpretation holds that the beliefs do not produce the practices, rather the practices precede and necessitate the beliefs.
We agree with Mrs. Whiting's point of view.   The Rajput mother's
contention that the fate of her child is written on his forehead reflects her
inability to mold her child's fate in a society based on caste.   The belief of
the Orchard Town mother that her children should play out in the
fresh air and then retire early and get plenty of sleep, supports her need
for some relief from constant child care.

In this book we have described and analyzed some of the diversity of
problems faced by mothers in our far-flung communities.   We have
attempted to interpret and explain the ordering of this diversity in the
light of the natural and social conditions faced by the mothers of our
study.   This analysis is by its very nature imprecise compared to laboratory studies, but in essence it deals with matters not amenable to laboratory study.   Experimenters may be interested in how people learn to become responsible, warm, or emotionally unstable, but they have not begun
to manipulate under experimental observation or control the complexity
of behavior displayed by our mothers.   It may be that they never will.
In any case, our data and analysis, limited though they may be, have, we
believe, cast enough light upon some of the problems of child rearing so
that we see more clearly the direction of future research.   Our message
and advice to those who follow us is that studies of child-training practices should not be conducted without a careful description and analysis
of the environment that forms the context of these studies.   This analysis
should include a census of the number of children in the family and
their ordinal position; a careful study of the mother's total role requirements for her family and community; a description of the father's role as
husband, child caretaker, and model bread-winner and determiner of
family status; some designation of the position of the family in the community and its relationships with neighbors and relatives; an account of
the influence of nonparental caretakers on the child and the amount of
time that the child spends with them; an estimate of variation in child-
training techniques brought about by the use of various caretakers with
varied requirements, and a measurement of the living space available to
the family and a description of the way that it is utilized.

Obviously, this outline of research requirements represents a goal that
we ourselves have not begun to reach in the study presented here.   We
offer it as a guide for future studies, knowing that if future researchers
use this guide they will, in turn, discover further problems and com-
plexities which await investigation.   Our suggestions will then become
obsolete, but for the present we believe they combine some of the virtues
of the detailed field investigation that are the hallmark of anthropology,

and the analytical precision developed in psychology, and will benefit both disciplines. Our message to psychologists from anthropology is not to ignore the cultural context of individual behavior. Our message to anthropologists from psychology is not to ignore the precise measurement of individuals that specifies variation of behavior among people who share a common culture. We can only hope that some of our colleagues in both disciplines will agree with us and take our advice, for we are curious to know the answers to some questions raised in our investigation.

References

Baldwin, A. L., Kalhorn, Joan, and Breese, F. H.   The appraisal of parent behavior.   *Psychol. Monogr.*, 1949, **63**, No. 4.

Barry, H., Bacon, Margaret K., and Child, I. L.   A cross cultural study of some sex differences in socialization.   *J. abnorm. soc. Psychol.*, 1957, **55**, 327–332.

Becker, W. C., Peterson, D. R., Luria, Zella, Showmaker, D. J., and Helmer, L. A.   Relations of factors derived from parent-interview ratings to behavior problems of five-year-olds.   *Child Develpm.*, 1962, **33**, 509–533.

Becker, W. C., and Krug, R. S.   A circumplex model of social behavior in children. *Child Developm.*, 1964, **35**, 371–396.

Brown, Judith K.   A cross-cultural study of female initiation rites.   *Amer. Anthropologist,* 1963, **65**, 837–853.

Edwards, A. L.   *Experimental design in psychological research.*   New York: Rinehart and Co., Inc., 1950.   Pp. 126–127.

Finney, D. J.   The Fisher-Yates Test of Significance in 2 × 2 contingency tables. *Biometrika,* 1948, **35**, Parts I and II.

Harman, H. H.   *Modern factor analysis.*   Chicago: University of Chicago Press, 1960.   Ch. 16.

Heath, D. B.   Sexual division of labor and cross-cultural research.   *Soc. Forces,* 1958–59, **37**, 77–79.

Lambert, W. W.   Interpersonal behavior.   In P. H. Mussen (Ed.), *Handbook of research methods in child development.* New York: John Wiley and Sons, 1960.   Pp. 854–917.

Latscha, R.   Tests of significance in a 2 × 2 contingency table: Extension of Finney's Table. *Biometrika,* 1953, **40**, Parts I and II.

LeVine, R. A.   Gusii sex offenses: A study in social control.   *Amer. Anthropologist,* 1959, **61**, 965–990.

LeVine, R. A.   The internalization of political values in stateless societies. *Human Organism,* 1960, **19**, 51–58.

LeVine, R. A.   Witchcraft and co-wife proximity in Southwestern Kenya. *Ethnology,* 1962, **1**, 39–45.

Lindquist, E. F.   *Design analysis of experiments in psychology and education.* Boston: Houghton Mifflin and Co., 1953.   Pp. 78–81.

Milton, G. A.   A factor analytic study of child-rearing behaviors.   *Child Develpm.,* 1958, **29**, 381–392.

Murdock, G. (Ed.) *Ethnology: An international journal of cultural and social anthropology,* Ethnographic Atlas, 1962–63, Vols. 1 and 2.

Murdock, J. P., and Whiting, J. W. M.   Cultural determination of parental attitudes: The relationship between the social structure, particularly family structure and parental behavior. In M. J. E. Senn (Ed.), *Problems of infancy and childhood*. Caldwell, N. J.: Josiah Macy, Jr. Foundation, 1951.

Schaefer, E. S., and Bell, R. Q. Patterns of attitudes toward child rearing and the family. *J. abnorm. soc. Psychol.*, 1957, 54, 391–395.

Schaefer, E. S., and Bell, R. Q. Development of a parental research instrument. *Child Develpm.*, 1958, 29, 339–361.

Schaefer, E. S. A circumplex model for maternal behavior. *J. abnorm. soc. Psychol.*, 1959, 59, 226–235.

Sears, R. R., Maccoby, Eleanor E., and Levin. H. *Patterns of child rearing.* Evanston, Illinois: Row, Peterson and Co., 1957.

Sewell, W. H., Mussen, P. H., and Harris, C. W. Relationships among child-training practices. *Amer. Sociol. Rev.*, 1955, 20, 137–148.

Siegel, S. *Nonparametric statistics for the behavioral sciences.* New York: McGraw-Hill Book Co., 1956. Pp. 116–127.

Takala, M., and Takala, Annika. *Child-rearing practices and attitudes as measured by different techniques.* Jyvaskyla, Finland: Centre for Educational Research, 1960.

Thurstone, L. L. *Multiple-factor analysis.* Chicago: University of Chicago Press, 1947.

Whiting, Beatrice. Some effects of beliefs about the nature of the child on parental practice. Paper read at American Anthropological Association, 1959.

Whiting, Beatrice (Ed.) *Six cultures—Studies of child rearing.* New York: John Wiley and Sons, 1963.

Whiting, J. W. M., Child, I. L., Lambert, W. W., Fischer, Ann M., Fischer, J. L., Nydegger, Corinne, Nydegger, W., Maretzki, Hatsumi, Maretzki, T., Minturn, Leigh, Romney, K., and Romney, Romaine. *Field guide for a study of socialization in five cultures.* Cambridge, Massachusetts: Laboratory of Human Development, 1955.

Whiting, J. W. M. Cultural and sociological influences on development. In *Growth and development of the child in his setting.* Maryland: Maryland Child Growth and Development Institute, 1959.

Whiting, J. W. M., and Whiting, Beatrice B. Contributions of anthropology to the methods of studying child rearing. In P. Mussen (Ed.), *Handbook of research methods in child development.* New York: John Wiley and Sons, 1960. Pp. 918–944.

Whiting, J. W. M. Specialization process and personality. In F. L. K. Hsu (Ed.), *Psychological anthropology: Approaches to culture and personality.* Homewood, Illinois: Dorsey Press, 1961. Pp. 355–380.

Zuckerman, M., Ribback, B. B., Monashkin, L., and Norton, J. A., Jr. Normative data and factor analysis on the parental attitude research instrument. *J. consult. Psychol.*, 1958, 22, 165–171.

SECTION THREE

❖ ❖ ❖ ❖ ❖ ❖

Appendixes

I ❖ Oblique Rotation of Factors

In addition to the orthogonal rotation the centroid factors were rotated obliquely using the Oblimax rotation program. The pattern loadings of the reference vectors were then plotted for each pair of factors, and these plots were reproduced on film strips. The placement of the factors, in relation to each other, was then corrected visually from the projected films.[1] The final corrected matrix is presented in Table 1. The results of the Oblimax rotation are similar to those of the orthogonal Varimax rotation. With one exception the factors which emerge are basically the same as the Varimax factors. Table 2 shows the correlations among the Oblimax factors. In general these correlations are low. The highest correlation in Table 2 is the —.37 correlation between Factors 2 and 6. These two factors represent aspects of the second Varimax factor and could be condensed into one factor in the Oblimax analysis. In order to make the interpretation of factors comparable to the interpretation of the Varimax factors, the cut-off point of a .40 loading was used for factor definition.

Factor 1: Aggression Training, Peer-Directed Aggression. This factor is similar to the third Varimax factor but is reversed in direction. It is defined by three scales.

> Consistency of aggression rules (scale 12, —.74)
> Reward for retaliation to peers (scale 17, +.79)
> Degree to which mother expects immediate obedience (scale 26, —.42)

In the Varimax Factor 3, scale 26 has a loading of only .37, just below the cut-off point, while scale 14, consistency of mother's follow-through on nonroutine demands for obedience, has a loading of +.49. On the Oblimax factor scale 14 has a loading of —.34. On both Varimax Factor 3 and Oblimax Factor 1 the two aggression-training scales have

---

[1] The authors are indebted to Professor Ledyard Tucker for his visual correction of the Oblimax rotation.

Table 1   Oblimax Rotation: Primary Factor Pattern

Factor Number

Scale Number	1	2	3	4	5	6	7	8	9	10
1	+.01	+.30	+.18	+.18	−.11	+.17	+.19	+.16	−.18	−.05
2	+.12	+.06	−.02	−.03	+.48	−.19	+.07	+.07	−.02	+.08
3	+.01	+.64	−.26	−.02	+.00	−.17	−.12	−.06	−.02	+.01
4	+.00	+.00	−.02	−.05	+.06	−.01	−.06	+.04	+.70	−.02
5	+.12	+.00	+.67	−.18	+.26	−.13	+.07	−.16	−.07	+.01
6	−.05	+.09	+.11	−.04	−.01	−.06	+.90	+.08	+.08	+.03
7	+.27	+.19	−.54	+.00	+.11	+.23	+.18	−.03	+.00	+.29
8	+.09	−.05	−.08	+.00	+.02	+.01	+.85	−.06	−.07	+.05
9	−.06	+.03	+.00	+.01	+.03	+.04	+.07	−.07	+.06	+.69
10	−.06	+.15	−.04	−.17	+.02	−.05	−.24	+.16	−.09	+.36
11	−.18	+.02	+.07	−.24	+.36	+.25	−.10	−.03	+.22	−.02
12	−.74	+.08	−.03	−.13	−.02	−.10	+.00	+.02	+.10	+.08
13	+.02	+.05	+.53	−.40	+.08	−.04	+.00	−.06	+.02	+.17
14	−.34	−.03	+.09	+.27	+.30	+.35	−.13	−.22	+.05	+.05
15	+.00	−.07	−.35	+.21	+.06	+.24	+.05	−.01	−.06	+.51
16	−.08	−.38	+.00	+.00	+.11	+.04	−.14	+.07	−.16	+.24
17	+.79	+.08	+.03	+.02	+.06	−.02	−.10	−.01	+.10	−.01
18	+.01	−.09	−.01	−.01	−.02	+.65	+.01	+.04	−.01	+.08
19	+.03	+.00	+.03	+.10	−.13	+.04	+.05	+.02	+.62	+.09
20	+.09	+.05	−.10	+.61	+.00	−.05	−.18	−.03	+.05	−.02
21	−.02	+.19	+.04	−.41	+.15	+.23	−.11	+.00	−.01	+.01
22	−.11	−.01	−.12	−.09	+.05	+.12	+.02	−.02	−.12	−.35
23	+.07	+.00	+.06	+.26	+.31	+.23	−.07	+.18	−.09	−.09
24	−.01	+.03	+.05	+.20	−.05	+.05	+.00	+.69	+.06	+.13
25	−.06	−.02	−.13	−.25	+.12	−.05	−.05	+.69	−.01	−.17
26	−.42	−.10	−.10	+.20	+.16	+.11	−.02	−.20	+.05	−.19
27	+.09	+.07	+.06	−.18	+.34	−.14	+.00	+.04	−.07	+.06
28	−.12	+.47	−.03	+.08	+.22	+.14	+.00	+.44	−.02	−.23

the highest loadings.   Since all four scales appear with high loadings in both factors and no other scales have substantial loadings in either, it seems safe to say that they are essentially the same.

Factor 2: Aggression Training, Parent-Directed Aggression.   This factor is defined by one of the scales that define Varimax Factor 6.   Again the direction of the factor is reversed.

> Degree to which mother is positive or nonpunishing when child becomes angry while being scolded (scale 3, +.64)

The second scale defining factor two does not have a high loading on Varimax Factor 6.

> Age of child (scale 28, +.47)

Scales 14, consistency of mother's follow-through on nonroutine demands for obedience, 15, frequency and intensity of physical punishment, and 16, degree to which privileges and gifts are contingent upon child's behavior, all have loadings in the thirties on Varimax Factor 6. Scales 14 and 15 have substantially zero loadings on Oblimax Factor 2, but scale 16, contingency of gifts and privileges, has a loading of —.38 on the Oblimax factor as compared with a loading of +.39 on the Varimax factor.

Scale 18, degree to which mother is aggressive when her child is angry or aggressive, is one of the two defining scales on Varimax Factor 6 with a loading of +.64, but has a loading of only —.09 on the second Oblimax factor. Scale 18 appears as the defining scale with a loading of +.65 in the sixth Oblimax factor. Furthermore, scale 14, consistency of mother's follow-through on nonroutine demands, has a loading of +.35 on Oblimax factor six. Scale 15, frequency and intensity of physical punishment, has a loading of +.24 on the sixth Oblimax factor, but several other scales also have loadings in the middle twenties.

Since the Oblimax Factor 6 is defined by only one high loading it could be reflected and rotated to coincide with Factor 2 without substantially changing any other factor. (These two factors presently have a —.37 correlation with each other. If Factor 6 were reflected this correlation would, of course, be positive.) If this were done the two factors would be defined by the two scales which define the sixth Varimax factor (scales 3 and 18) and two of the three scales with medium loadings on Varimax factor six (scales 14 and 16) would also have medium loadings on the Oblimax factor. The only important difference from the comparable Varimax factor would then be that the Oblimax factor has a high loading on the age of the child, which indicated that mothers are less punitive about aggression toward themselves with older children than with young children.

Factor 3: Warmth of Mother. This factor is defined by three of the four scales that define the second Varimax factor.

General warmth of mother (scale 5, +.67)
General hostility of mother (scale 7, —.54)
Amount of praise (scale 13, +.53)

The fourth defining scale for the Varimax warmth-of-father factor, scale 15, frequency and intensity of physical punishment, has a loading of only —.35 on the Oblimax factor. This loading falls into the intermediate range and is the only scale, other than the three defining scales with a loading of greater than .30 on the third Oblimax factor. The factor seems to be substantially comparable to the Varimax factor.

Factor 4: Proportion of Time that Mother Cared for Baby. Factor 4 is similar to the fourth Varimax factor. It is defined by three scales.

Amount of time that mother cared for baby (scale 20, +.61)

Amount of praise (scale 13, —.40)

Amount of time that an adult other than the mother cared for baby (scale 21, —.40)

On the fourth Varimax factor, scales 20 and 21 have loadings of —.72 and —.46, respectively. Scale 13, amount of praise, has a loading of only —.31 on the Varimax factor. It was suggested on the basis of the Varimax analysis that mothers who spend a high proportion of their time in charge of their babies are less likely to praise them when they become older. The Oblimax analysis provides further confirmation of this relationship.

Factor 5: Peer-Aggression Permissiveness. This factor is defined by the same scale that defines the ninth Varimax factor.

Degree to which mother is positive when child fights with other children (scale 2, +.48)

In the discussion of the corresponding Varimax factor we raised the possibility that this factor may represent some sort of artifact, since scale 2 ought to be positively related to scale 17, reward for retaliation to peers, that defines Oblimax Factor 1 and Varimax Factor 3. This possibility is still present with the Oblimax rotation. On both the Varimax and Oblimax factors scale 27 has a loading in the thirties indicating that mothers with high scores on this factor tend to allow their girls to be more aggressive than boys. On the Varimax factor, scale 5, warmth-of-mother has a loading of +.32. On the Oblimax factor this loading drops to +.26. Three other scales have loadings above .30 on Factor 5. Two of these, consistency of mother's follow through on nonroutine demands for obedience (scale 14, +.30), and age at which child begins to play away from the house (scale 23, +.31), have very low loadings on the ninth Varimax factor. The third, "amount of communication of rules" (scale 11, +.36), however, has a loading of +.28 on the Varimax factor. This loading indicates that mothers who are permissive, as measured by this factor, have clear rules about aggressive behavior, and are not simply permissive because of a confused and inarticulated attitude on the subject. Since the loadings on this factor are relatively low, and somewhat confusing, particularly in relation to another clearer peer-aggression training factor, it should not be taken too seriously. It is possible, however, that the factor represents a psychological dimension for a group of mothers who encourage aggression in girls more than in boys.

Factor 6: Aggression Training, Parent-Directed Aggression. See the discussion of Factor 2, last paragraph.

Factor 7: Emotional Instability of Mother. This factor is defined by the same two scales that define the seventh Varimax factor.

Mood variation of hostility (scale 8, +.85)
Mood variation of warmth (scale 6, +.90)

These are the only two scales with loadings of .30 or greater on the factor. Scale 7, general hostility of mother, which has a loading of +.34 on the Varimax factor has a loading of only +.18 on the Oblimax factor. Nevertheless, in view of the similar loadings on the two defining scales, we can consider the two factors to be comparable.

Factor 8: Responsibility Training. This factor is similar to the first Varimax factor. It is defined by three scales.

Age of child (scale 28, +.44)
Total frequency of chores (scale 24, +.69)
Total number of chores (scale 25, +.69)

These are the only scales with loadings above .30 on the factor. This was also true for the first Varimax factor.

Factor 9: Proportion of Time that Mother Cares for Child. This factor is comparable to Varimax Factor 5. It is defined by two scales:

Proportion of caretaking done by mother (scale 4, +.70)
Amount of time mother cares for child (scale 19, +.62)

These are the only two scales with loadings of greater than .30 on either Varimax Factor 5 or Oblimax Factor 9.

Factor 10: Discipline versus Laissez Faire. This factor is similar to the reflection of the eighth Varimax factor but much easier to interpret. It is defined by two scales.

Degree that mother's warmth is contingent upon child's actions (scale 9, +.69)
Frequency and intensity of physical punishment (scale 15, +.51)

On the eighth Varimax factor scale 9 has a loading of —.50. However scale 15 has a loading of only —.29. On the Varimax factor the second defining scale was scale 22, age at which the child begins to play away from the house, with a loading of +.53. On the Oblimax factor this loading drops to —.35. Scale 24, total frequency of chores, which has a loading of —.22 on the Varimax factor, has a loading of only +.13 on the Oblimax factor. On the other hand, scale 10, degree that mother's hostility is contingent upon child's actions, is moderately important for both factors. It has a loading of —.29 on the Varimax factor and a loading of +.36 on the Oblimax factor.

The Oblimax factor distinguishes mothers in a dimension of contingency of warmth and use of physical punishment.   When a mother's warmth is contingent upon her child's behavior her hostility also tends to be contingent upon the child's behavior.   The factor is somewhat puzzling because mothers who use physical punishment also tend to vary their warmth in the light of children's behavior.   Insofar as the contingency of warmth scale is measuring "love-oriented" discipline, this finding is contrary to the findings of Sears, Maccoby, and Levin (1954) who report that the American mothers who rely on physical punishment to discipline their children tend not to use love-oriented discipline.   As scale 16, contingency of privileges and gifts, also has a positive loading $(+.28)$ on this factor, it would seem that the factor is distinguishing between mothers who discipline frequently and those who tend not to use any discipline.

Correlations among Oblimax Factors

The results of the Oblimax rotation are, with minor exceptions, comparable to the results of the Varimax rotation.   This comparability indicates that we are justified in considering the factors as being relatively independent of each other.   Nevertheless, Table 2 contains a number of correlations which, although low, are significant.   A correlation of .22 or greater is significant at the 1 per cent level, and a correlation of .28 or greater is significant at the .1 per cent level for 133 cases.   Since there are 45 correlations in Table 2 we would expect from zero to one correla-

Table 2   Oblimax Rotation: Primary Factor Correlations

Factor Number

Factor Number	1	2	3	4	5	6	7	8	9	10
1	1.00									
2	−.04	1.00								
3	.02	.05	1.00							
4	.14	.06	.09	1.00						
5	−.02	−.20	.08	.17	1.00					
6	−.09	−.37	.01	−.08	.10	1.00				
7	.17	−.06	−.11	.16	.18	.29	1.00			
8	−.07	−.27	.08	.14	.16	.27	−.06	1.00		
9	.30	.02	.12	.23	.18	.04	.33	.01	1.00	
10	−.29	−.25	−.11	−.08	.11	.29	.19	−.03	−.17	1.00

tion to be significant at the 1 per cent level of chance alone. There are nine correlations greater than .22 in the table, indicating that there are more correlations between factors than would be expected by chance.

Factor 1, training of peer-directed aggression, has a correlation of +.30 with Factor 9, proportion of caretaking done by mother, and a correlation of —.29 with Factor 10, discipline versus laissez faire. These correlations indicate that mothers who reward their children for retaliation tend to be generally lax about discipline and tend to spend a high proportion of their time in charge of their children. Factors 9 and 10 have a correlation of —.17 with each other which is significant at the 5 per cent level.

Factor 2, training of parent-directed aggression, is correlated with three other factors. We have already mentioned the correlation of —.37 between Factors 2 and 6 and suggested that they represent the same factor. Factor 2 also has a correlation of —.27 with Factor 8, responsibility training, and one of —.25 with Factor 10, discipline versus laissez faire. These correlations indicate that mothers who are permissive about aggression directed to themselves do not encourage responsibility and are generally lax about discipline. Consistent with this interpretation is the fact that Factor 6 has a correlation of +.27 with Factor 8 and a correlation of +.29 with Factor 10. Factor 6 also has a correlation of +.29 with Factor 7, emotional instability of mother. Factor 2 is *not* correlated with Factor 7. Finally, both Factor 2 and Factor 7 have correlations that are significant at the 5 per cent level with Factor 5, training of peer-directed aggression. These correlations indicate that mothers who punish peer-directed aggression tend not to punish parent-directed aggression and vice versa.

Factor 4, proportion of time that mother cares for baby, is correlated with Factor 9, proportion of time that mother cares for child. The correlation is —.23, just beyond the 5 per cent level of significance. This correlation indicates that mothers who spend a high proportion of their time caring for babies tend to be the same mothers who spend a high proportion of their time caring for the children when they get older.

Finally, Factors 7 and 9 have a correlation of +.33 with each other, indicating that mothers who spend a high proportion of time caring for children are more unstable in their emotional reactions to their children than are mothers who do not have such exclusive responsibility for their care. Factor 4, the proportion of time that mothers care for babies, has a correlation of +.16 with Factor 7, emotional instability. Since a correlation of .17 or greater is significant at the 5 per cent level it seems safe to conclude that excessive responsibility for child care is associated in our sample with unpredictable variations in the mother's moods.

II ❖ Quotations from Interviews with Mothers

The Mother Interview: Standard English Version

1. First we want to ask you about who takes care of P. Who does this mostly now?
   a. How about when P was a baby?
   b. What about your husband? Now? When P was a baby?
2. What do you do when P asks for help or reassurance?
   a. How about when he falls down or gets a little scratch?
   b. How about when he asks you to fix something or do something?
   c. How about when he can really do it himself?
   d. How about when you are busy doing something else?
3. Now think back to when P was a baby. What did you do when he cried? Example: All babies cry, of course. What did you usually do when P cried when he was very little?
   a. How quickly would you try to tend to him?
   b. How about when you were busy?
   c. How about at night?
   d. How did other members of the household feel about his crying?
   e. How much did you try to keep him from crying, by doing things for him ahead of time?
4. Do you feel that children should express their feelings or keep them to themselves?
   a. What have you done about this with P?
   b. How about laughing?
   c. Getting excited?
   d. Showing anger?
   e. Crying?
5. When did you feel that P was old enough for you to start training him to take care of himself? (If M answers, "He began feeding himself at 2½," ask: "Had you tried to get him to before that?")
   a. How about feeding himself?

  b. How about dressing himself?

  c. How about playing away from the house?

  d. Did you try to teach him to do these things or did he just learn by himself?

6. Tell me about the last time he learned to do something by himself.

  a. What did you do about it?

7. What chores do you expect P to do? How often does he have to do this—is it regularly?

  a. How did you get him to do them?

  b. What happens if P fails to do them?

8. Do you expect P to obey immediately when you ask him to do something, or do you give him a little leeway?

  a. What if he dawdles or delays?

  b. How about following through? Do you always do this or do you sometimes let it go?

9. How satisfied do you feel about how well P does things? (Specify?)

  a. What do you do when he does something well?

  b. Do you care more about his getting them done or doing them especially well?

  c. What do you do if he is careless?

  d. How about when he does poorly?

10. How do you feel about friends for your children?

  a. Do you wish that P would play alone more or with the group more?

  b. What do you do about it?

  c. Is there anyone you'd rather your child didn't play with? Anyone you would rather have him play with?

11. Do you think P should help younger children when they are in difficulty or do you think he should mind his own business?

  a. Could you give an example of what you've done when this came up?

12. Do you like to see children take leadership or do you feel that this tends to make them bossy?

  a. What do you do about this with P?

13. What do you do when P tries to get his own way with you?

  a. How about when he does this with other children?

14. How about when P is playing with one of the other children in the neighborhood and there is a quarrel or fight—how do you handle this?

  a. Do you ever feel that P is too touchy?

  b. Do you ever encourage P to fight back?

15. Sometimes children get angry at their parents when they are being criticized or scolded. How do you handle this with P?

      a. Could you give an example of this?

      b. What if he should kick you or strike you?

16. Some parents have trouble keeping their child from being mean to smaller children and bullying them. How have you managed this?

      a. How about teasing?

17. Could you tell me who in the household has the main charge of P to see that he behaves? Who usually disciplines P when he is naughty? When several are present?

      a. (If husband) Do you ever?; (if wife) Does your husband ever?

      b. How about P's older sibling (if he had one) ?

      c. How about others in the household (nurse, baby-sitters, grand-parents, aunts, uncles, etc.) ?

18. If Y (the person who usually punishes P) is not there, who usually takes over?

      a. Is Y mentioned when someone else punishes P?

19. When P is naughty, how is he usually punished?

      a. How about spanking?

      b. How about not letting him have something he wants?

      c. How about making fun of him?

      d. How about not speaking to him?

      e. How about sending him to his room?

      f. How about warning him about the bogey man?

      g. How about threatening to send him away?

      h. How about referring to God?

20. What methods do you (if she disciplines) use most frequently?

      a. How about your husband (if he disciplines) ?

      b. How about others in the household (if they discipline) ?

21. Do you do anything special when P is good?

      a. What about special gifts?

      b. Privileges?

      c. Allowances?

      d. Praise?

Chapter Two: Maternal Warmth

Okinawa. The Taira mothers are warmer than the mothers of other societies. The mother of 8-year-old Matsue is typical of the Taira group.

> Most of the time we just talk to Matsue when she is naughty telling her why she is being scolded and talked to . . . try to point out why and what not to do. She listens well and so is almost never spanked. When we talk to her she usually apologizes and promises to not do it

again. If she gets stubborn and does not listen after we have told her three or four times we would spank her, but as I said she almost never is spanked because she listens so well.

We all talk and scold first; then if we have done this three or four times and she does not listen, we threaten to spank her and do.

When she has been good I praise her and might give her money to buy candy . . . or sometimes I buy 10 yen worth of sugar and we all have a bit together.

Oh, I am very happy when she does things well and I praise her.

Philippines. The Tarong mothers are also warm. This mother of 3-year-old Benita resents her sister-in-law's discipline, and sometimes conflicts with her husband when she herself is harsh with Benita.

When she is afraid she comes and cuddles and I take care of her . . . . I usually punish her. If I slap her in front of her father, sometimes he reprimands me. I sometimes resent the way my sister-in-law punishes her. She teases Benita until Benita calls her a frog; then my sister-in-law whips her, when it was her own fault all the time. . . . If I hit her it leaves a red mark on my hand, so I usually just threaten to hit her. . . . I don't make fun of her. How could I continue to teach her if I made fun of her? When she is good I may give her a dress, marbles, or toys sometimes. I don't give her privileges because that can become habitual and she will long for it. I do not praise her.

Africa. The Nyansongo mothers rely heavily on caneing as a disciplinary measure, particularly with younger children. The mother of 3-year-old Joseph is fairly typical of this group.

A. When Joseph was a baby and cried at night, I gave him the breast. If he did not stop I let him cry, even all night. I began weaning Joseph when I became pregnant again. He was about 15-months-old. When he wanted to nurse I used to slap him and I slept with my dress on at night.

Q. What did you do when he defecated in the house, after he was old enough to go to the bush?

A. I caned him.

Q. How do you usually punish Joseph now?

A. I use only caneing. I do not see why I should refuse food because he is too little. If it is just a tiny thing, then I rebuke him.

United States. The mother of 4-year-old Tommy shows considerable concern when her son gets hurt and cries. This kind of comment was one basis for the warmth ratings.

Q. How about when Tommy falls down and gets a little scratch?

A. Well lots of times he falls down and gets a little scratch. He doesn't say anything and I don't even know about it, but if he cries I love him and make it all better. If he cries I come a'running. And if it's bad we fix it—make a bunny with Mercurochrome or something like that so it won't hurt so bad. Sometimes a kiss will fix it.

Q. Can you think of what you say?

A. You should be here sometimes when it happens and we'd see. I say, "Mommy will kiss it and make it all better." Sometimes I say, "We'll put Mercurochrome on it and it's going to hurt, but things have to hurt a little bit to get better." He hasn't had too many hurts; usually its something that just a kiss makes a little better.

Q. What's your reaction when he gets hurt?

A. I get scared and worried. I get frightened until I know its all right. Tommy's not the crying type, if he cries I know he's hurt of somebody's been mean to him.

Q. How do you feel when somebody's been mean to him?

A. I get awful mad at that somebody, I know that.

Q. Now think back to when Tommy was a baby. What did you do when he cried? How quickly would you try to tend to him?

A. Oh I'd just let him cry for a couple of minutes and then I'd go into him. It depended on the sound of the cry. Some cries you'd go in to immediately.

Q. How about when you were busy?

A. I'd go to him. I'm sure I would. I mean I was never too busy not to.

Q. How about at night?

A. I always went to him right away when he cried at night because he very rarely cried at night.

Q. How do you feel that children should express their feelings or keep them to themselves?

A. I feel worried if he cries because I figure there's something wrong. Like at night sometimes he cried if I won't read to him—like they'll have an argument about which book I'm going to read and Tommy will cry if he doesn't get his book read, and I'll read this book too. To tell you the truth it upsets me if he cries. I read to him from his book. I don't like to hear him cry and I'll do lots of things to keep him from crying. I just feel he's crying and there's something wrong. I think at different ages you feel differently about it.

Jeanne's mother has a low score on maternal warmth. The following excerpt clearly indicates her impatience with her daughter.

. . . She is at that dawdling age, it drives me wild . . . . I don't care if they don't mind me if they mind other people. I can't stand a fresh kid . . . . I don't like Jeanne to play with Molly. She says "Them things" . . . . Molly is a terrible cynic. . . . Jeanne mimics her. Molly's mother is very insecure. She can really cause trouble if she wants to. . . . I don't like to have my boy play with Bill. They just never play right. They never do anything that isn't doing damage to somebody. . . . I haven't much patience, I'm firmly convinced I shouldn't have had any children anyway.

Mexico. The Juxtlahuaca mothers are more controlled in their emotions than the mothers of most other samples. Mayolo's mother is typical of her group. Mayolo is 5 years old.

Q. What do you do to Mayolo when he begins to cry without any apparent reason or motive?

A. I get angry with him because there is no reason for him to cry. I hit him.

Q. After you have done this, does Mayolo continue crying?

A. I comfort him. I walk him about and I speak nicely to him, so that he will stop, since I hit him.

Q. When Mayolo falls down and starts to cry, what do you do?

A. I would embrace him and speak to him with affection.

Q. What do you do to Mayolo if he does not do things better than other children?

A. I get angry with him and I hit him with my hand.

Q. At times when it is necessary to punish Mayolo, how do you punish him? In what form is this carried out?

A. By scolding him, I tell him not to do it anymore, and that's not good, that it's not suitable to act that way. Sometimes I hit him with my hand, I frighten him but I do not also hit him. I tell him that the cat is going to take him away or that some old man will come by and frighten him, or sometimes I make fun of the child, and yes, at times, I deny him something that he wants to have, or I refuse to talk to him; sometimes also to punish him I don't speak to him, and I show him no approval.

Q. When you are punishing Mayolo, do you tell him that his father would not like him to do this and that you are doing this punishing because his father is not here to do it or to scold him?

A. Yes.

Q. What type of punishment do you use most frequently?

A. Frightening him or telling him in order to frighten him that I'm going to hit him or perhaps I only punish or scold him. If he behaves himself very badly, then I'll hit him.

Q. Who is it that most often punishes Mayolo, you or others?

A. I.

Q. Then if you're not there to punish Mayolo, someone else may punish him, is that not so?

A. Only his father.

Q. When you are not at home to punish Mayolo, who is it that most often does punish him?

A. His father.

Q. We have now spoken of how you punish Mayolo when he misbehaves himself? What do you do to Mayolo or for Mayolo when he does everything as you have asked for, or as you would wish, that is, when he behaves himself, what do you do?

A. I embrace him, I tell him that that's the way to do it. I give him a few pennies, sometimes I give him more than five. Also some food because they love to have something to eat. Sometimes I give him a gift, some fruit, or some little things to play with, sometimes I see that he is behaving well and I leave him just like that, just as he is.

India. The Khalapur mothers are the only ones who exhibit a consistent difference on this factor in the behavior towards boys versus girls. They are more hostile and less warm in their treatment of boys than in their treatment of girls. The most hostile of all is the mother of 5-year-old Mahender.

Q. When Mahender was a baby and crying at night, how quickly would you try to tend to him.

A. It is not in my hands. If a person is bent on crying he will go on crying. When he is crying I pick him up and nurse him and if he is hungry, I give him something to eat.

Q. Do you feel that children should express their feelings? How about laughing?

A. When the child is laughing useless with no reason, I have to scold him.

Q. Tell me about the last time he learned to do something by himself.

A. He has not learned anything; he is mad. He does not know anything . . . Those children who are clever, they do work but he is mad.

Q. What do you do when Mahender does not obey immediately?

A. I beat him. I have no patience. I beat him with a stick. . . . Mahender is a shameless boy. I have to tell him a thing four times and then he does it. Other children do it when you ask them once and you feel so happy.

Q. What do you do when he tries to get his own way with you?

A. I beat him.

Q. How about when he tries to get his own way with other children?

A. Then I have to beat and scold.

Q. What do you do when he fights with other children?

A. I beat, I scold, and stop him from going on the wrong way.

Q. Sometimes children get angry with their parents when they are being scolded. How do you handle this?

A. Still he is not old enough to be angry like this but when he is angry with one of us he goes to the others.

Q. What do you do?

A. I love him and make him sit near me, what else?

Q. What if he should kick or beat you?

A. If he beats he will get a beating in return. . . . All of these questions mean that when the child is wrong we beat and scold him and when he is not wrong we do not beat him. There are some mothers that even when their child is wrong, they do not say anything. You can ask anyone, I am not one of these. If he does anything wrong I want to cut his head off. I am very strict with him. Some children are so good that they always obey but he is mad. So what should I do with him?

Q. What punishment do you use most frequently?

A. Beating is foremost, you cannot shut him in his room all the time.

Q. Do you beat him with a stick or with your hand?

A. With the first thing that comes to my hand . . . with the fire tongs or a spoon.

Q. When he is good, do you praise him?

A. When he does something good we have to praise.

Q. What do you say?

A. I do not say anything to him or pamper him too much.

Q. You do not praise?

A. No.

At this point a sister-in-law comments that the only praise Mahender's mother gives him is "I will put you in the fire," or "May a snake bite you."

The contrast between the treatment of boys and girls may be seen when we compare the answers given by Mahender's mother with those given by the mother of a 5-year-old girl, Reeshmii.

Q. Sometimes children get angry with their parents when they are being criticized or scolded. How do you handle this with Reeshmii?

A. What to do? I console her and make her sit near me. When her father gets angry with her I feel very bad. If someone scolds her and she cries, I say "What do you want? Do you want food?"

Q. When she is naughty, how is she usually punished?
A. I set it right by scolding and saying "Don't fight, don't do anything."
   I don't slap her, I just frighten her. She gets frightened very soon
   and starts crying.
Q. You just threaten to slap her?
A. Yes, she starts crying very soon.
Q. Do you praise her, when she is good?
A. I praise . . . I say "You look very nice like this." I love her very
   much then.

The greater reliance on physical punishment by Mahender's mother is
determined in part by the fact that he is not easily frightened, while
Reeshmii may dissolve into tears at the mere threat of a slap.

Chapter Three: Maternal Instability

Since the mood variation ratings were based on the entire interview,
comments of the mothers in response to any question might be used as
a basis for these ratings. Certain questions, however, were particularly
likely to reveal the impatience or understanding of the mother in dealing with her child. These were questions concerned with the child's
requests for help from the mother, the mother's reaction to disobedience
of the child, and the mother's reaction to mother-directed aggression.
Questions on these topics appear frequently in the following excerpts
from the interview.

Africa. The African mothers are, as a group, high in emotional instability. The mother of Teresa, a 6-year-old girl, is particularly inconsistent in her discipline. The responses of Teresa's mother reflect both
hostility and vacillation. At one point she contradicts a previous answer.

Q. What do you do when Teresa asks for food?
A. If I have no food ready I tell her to wait. If it is ready I give it to
   her.
Q. What do you do when she asks you to do something that she can
   really do herself, like getting dressed?
A. I cane her and if she does not want to get dressed I throw her clothes
   out the door and say, "If you don't want to dress, go out with your
   dress and stay there with it." If a mother dresses a child that age
   she would become a very stupid child. It is a bad thing.
Q. What do you do when she asks for help and you are busy doing something else?
A. There is not much she could ask except for food, then I would cook.

Q. You just said that you would not cook.

A. I would if she had missed her meal. Otherwise I would tell her to wait. . . .

Q. What do you do if Teresa refuses to do her work or does it badly?

A. I rebuke her the first time and then see if she will improve. If not, I cane her.

Q. What do you do when she does not obey her older brothers and sisters?

A. I cane her for anything when she does not obey, but sometimes I leave her because you can tell a child who will understand punishment and improve and one who won't.

Q. What if Teresa, when rebuked or refused food, were to strike you?

A. If she were near, I would cane her very badly and refuse food, but if she ran away I would wait until evening and do the same thing.

United States. As a group, the Orchard Town mothers rank second in emotional instability. As individuals, their scores vary almost as much as the scores for the entire sample. Danny's mother has a score on Factor 7 that is close to the Orchard Town mean of .10. Danny is 4 years old.

Q. What do you do when Danny asks for help or reassurance? How about when he can really do it for himself?

A. I usually tell him to do it himself, if I think he can do it. If I'm in a hurry I do it for him, if I'm not in a hurry I just let him take his time and do it himself; like buttoning his clothes, tying his shoes and things like that. I know he can do it but. . . .

Q. How about when you are busy doing something else?

A. Well, if I'm doing the dishes and he asks me to do something I usually finish first. But if he's on the john I go immediately. But if he wants me to change the channel on the TV I wait until I'm finished. I don't make him wait too long, but I just don't drop everything.

Q. What if he dawdles or delays?

A. Well, it depends on if I'm busy. If I'm busy I don't pay too much attention to see that he does something but if I'm just there for that one reason I have him do it right away.

Q. What do you say to get him to do it?

A. Oh I tell him to do it right now. While I'm standing there.

Q. Do anything else?

A. No . . . I don't. If I'm in a hurry, I do it myself.

Q. How about following through? Do you always do this or do you sometimes let it go?

A. I sometimes let it go . . . in fact more often than I should really.
Q. How do you feel about this?
A. Well, I think that I could be a little bit stricter about it. At least Fritz thinks I could.

Mexico. The Juxtlahuaca mothers also vary considerably from one another in their instability scores. Judi's mother has a score that approximates the mean for the group.

Q. When Judi asks your help for something. What do you do?
A. Sometimes I scold her so that she will do it alone.
Q. When Judi falls down and starts to cry, what do you do?
A. I put my arms around her to make her happy.
Q. What if you are busy?
A. I let her cry for a little while.
Q. How do you usually punish Judi?
A. Sometimes I tell her that she is is rude and disobedient and that she should not be that way. I hit her with my hand . . . sometimes I hit her with a rope, because I have a very bad temper.

India. The warmth of Khalapur mothers tends to be more variable with older children than with younger children. This difference is illustrated in the differential responses of the mothers of two boys, 10-year-old Dhyaan and 4-year-old Kheer. Dhyaan's mother is fairly severe with him, but she also often ignores his behavior, sometimes for no apparent reason.

Q. When you ask Dhyaan to do something, do you always follow through?
A. Sometimes I let it go. If he does not want to do the work, let him not do it.
Q. What do you do if he is careless?
A. Then I get angry and ask him to do it. When he does not pay attention I get angry, and sometimes I ask him politely.
Q. What do you do when Dhyaan is playing in the neighborhood and there is a quarrel or a fight?
A. Sometimes I take him out of that group and scold and beat him, and sometimes I ask him politely. I say that he should not fight with the children or we will fight with the parents.

Kheer's mother seems sensitive to the moods of a young child and the inconsistency of her discipline is based on Kheer's feelings rather than her own. Her reasons for not always following through on discipline are similar to those of Dhyaan's mother.

Q. When you ask Kheer to do something, do you always follow through?

A. I say "If he does not want to do it, let him not do it."   He is a child and sometimes he feels like doing it and sometimes he does not feel like doing it.

Q. Do you think Kheer should help younger children when they are in difficulty?

A. Children are not intelligent.   It depends upon their mood.   Sometimes they will help him and sometimes they will beat him back.

Q. What do you do if he gets angry while being criticised or scolded?

A. If he is angry, let him stay angry, and after some time he will be all right.

Q. When he is naughty do you not let him have something he wants?

A. Why should we refuse?   If we refuse, then can we take care of the children?   With children you have to love them and be very affectionate and give them whatever they want.

Okinawa.   The Okinawan and Philippine mothers are, on the whole, more stable emotionally than the mothers of the other societies.   The mother of 5-year-old Matsue is typical of the Okinawan mothers.   Her score on Factor 7 is close to the mean of the Okinawan sample.   Matsue seems to be the emotionally unstable member of this dyad and her mother takes pains not to upset her.

Q. Do you think that children should express their feelings or keep them to themselves?

A. I just let her express her feelings whatever they may be.   Matsue has a horrible temper.   She throws things at me when I scold her, and when she is angry with her sister for reprimanding her she quickly picks up things and throws.   I just let her go and I think she will be all right when she starts school.

Q. What do you do when she does poorly?

A. I praise her when she does something well but don't scold her when she doesn't do well.   I just talk to her, telling her to do better.   I might ask her to do it over but I don't scold.

Q. What do you do when she gets angry while you are scolding her?

A. Because she is such a shameless, impudent child who loses her temper so easily, I just let her go.   If I am scolding her and she starts a tantrum, I just ignore her.   It is of no use to do anything, she will grow out of it.

Q. What do you do if she bullies younger children?

A. Matsue does not bully little children.   I have not seen or heard that she has.   If she does all I can do is tell her not to because it is a bad thing to do. She is so hard to handle, I have to be careful how I say it, otherwise she will have a tantrum.

The Okinawan mothers tend to be less variable in their expression of warmth and hostility with children over 7, than they are with children under this age. Masao is 8 years old and his mother has a low score on Factor 7. Although the mother says she is short-tempered, her answers indicate that her hostility, as well as her warmth, is usually geared to Masao's behavior.

Q. What do you do when Masao asks for help?
A. Well I think it is a parent's responsibility to look after and help his child whenever he needs it. When he is sad and discouraged I console him by talking with him and trying to find out what the matter is.
Q. What do you do when he does not do his chores?
A. Masao has one regular job and that is to take care of the chickens. He is supposed to feed them every day. I tell him that it is his responsibility and that if he forgets the chickens won't lay and he won't get an egg to eat. . . . If he does not do it I scold him and say, "The chickens are hungry because you do not feed them. If you do not feed them, I will not feed you either.
Q. What do you do when he does something poorly?
A. When he does poorly I scold him and tell him that he should do better, *but it is well to remember that children should not only be scolded when they are wrong but praised when they have done well.* You cannot bring up children only by scolding them.
Q. Do you expect him to obey at once when you ask him to do something?
A. His father is very particular about these things and expects things to be done immediately after requests are made. . . . Both he and I are very short-tempered, impatient people. We do our work hurriedly and expect our children to do the same.
Q. Do you think he should help younger children?
A. I would praise him for helping. You must praise children for doing something good.
Q. What if he tries to get his own way with other children?
A. Sometimes I let him have his way with me, if it is something I think is not harmful or bad. Otherwise I talk to him and point out reasons to talk him out of it. If he tries to do this with other children, I scold him and tell him not to.

Philippines. The Tarong mothers are the most stable group in the sample. The answers of 3-year-old Rodolfo's mother are fairly typical.

Q. What do you do when Rodolfo asks for help?

A. I hurry to help him, especially if he is afraid, because too much fear and the child may be soulless.

Q. What do you do when he asks you to fix something?

A. I help him if I have enough time, but if I am busy I scold him to forestall nagging. I say, "Do it yourself" in a scornful voice. If I am busy I may say "You go and have your aunt do it," in a loud voice.

Q. Do you think that children should express their anger?

A. If I had my way, no, but they do it anyway.

Q. What do you do when they get angry?

A. I both scold and coax them.

Chapter Four: Mothers' Responsibility for Baby Care

United States. The Orchard Town mothers have less help in caring for their babies than the mothers in any other sample. Dorothy's mother is typical of the mothers in their New England community.

Q. Who took care of Dorothy when she was a baby?

A. I did.

Q. Did your husband help?

A. Well, it is a standing joke about that. When I had the first one, with human beings you feel you can't replace them, so I was terrified of a baby and he really didn't do anything. When I was ready to go to the hospital with Dorothy, I said "Gee, Honey, you know you're going to have to help me more with this one." Then she was breast-fed after I told him he would have to take the two o'clock feeding. But he really has helped me, he always has. I don't think I've asked too much of him but he has volunteered. . . . I was in the hospital only three or four days, so he really took over and did all the housework those four days. Then I've been on my feet ever since. I never had any help with any of them. I got right up the day I came home from the hospital and started in.

Q. Would he feed her or change her pants?

A. Oh, definitely, if it was necessary. I don't ever remember if he did but I feel sure he probably did if he ever had to.

Okinawa. In Taira adults work in the mountains several miles from their homes. Often the babies are left with grandmothers while the mothers go to work. Kiyoshi's grandmother is still strong enough to work in the fields herself, so he was cared for by his mother.

I care for him now and when he was a baby. My husband did not look after him when he was a baby, and not even now. After all, I think it is mostly a woman's job to look after children, males don't.

Toshio was cared for by his grandmother, and lived in her house until he was 4 years old.

When he was a baby my mother took care of him . . . and he was brought here when he was 4. I used to go to the mountains and return at lunch and go out again until dinner. He was fed breast milk only during these times. When he was only 2 months old I started to go to the mountains. My mother never used to tell me about him, I was so busy.

Hisako's mother has a factor score very close to the sample mean of —.12. She cared for her baby but had help from a grandmother.

When Hisako was 3 months old I started to work in the fields and mountains. Grandmother took care of her during the day and I took care of her when I returned to the house. She was nursed morning, noon, and in the evening, when I returned.

Philippines. The Tarong mothers frequently enlist the aid of neighbors to help look after babies and young children. Neighbor women may even act as wet nurses when the mother is busy. Most Tarong fathers also act as occasional baby-sitters. Maria's mother spent more time in charge of her baby daughter than any other mother in the Tarong sample, but even she had some help.

I took care of her. My husband seldom did. He was working at construction and had so little time. The mother of Benita helped care for her. Grandmother helped with the other children.

Adriano's mother spent an average amount of time in baby-tending, for a Tarong mother. Since Adriano is only 3 she is still being nursed.

I mostly took care of Adriano when he was a baby. My husband did about half as much as I did. Three of my neighbors also took care of him a good deal. When I go to wash every day anyone will come and feed him if he cries.

India. Among the Khalapur Rajputs, mothers of young children are forbidden to leave the courtyard of their husband's house. Therefore, they are usually near their babies and seldom leave them exclusively in the care of anyone else. Fathers are particularly unlikely to care for babies. As one mother puts it:

When they are small children the fathers won't even hold them. When they are this old (She holds her hand about 2½ feet from the ground). He may go and sit with them and maybe give a piece of bread or two. Otherwise they do not even sit with them.

Sometimes babies are cared for by a favorite grandmother or older sister or cousin. When the sisters-in-law are on good terms with each other, they may informally share some of the burdens of baby-tending. For instance, the mother of Sumeetra says, "Everybody used to look after her. Her father also used to keep her." "Everybody" refers to the sisters-in-law who are the other women of the household.

When a woman is not on good terms with her sisters-in-law she has to care for her children herself. Such is the case with Mahender's mother, who has the highest score on Factor 4 of any mother in Khalapur sample. Her answer is brief, to the point, and indicative of her irascible disposition.

A. I took care of him. Who else would take care of him?
Q. Did your husband help?
A. What will the father do? Bathing, eating, and sleeping the mother will do.

Mexico. In Juxtlahuaca, mothers are more likely to be the primary caretakers of baby girls, while boys are more frequently placed in the care of older children. Consistent with this trend, the Juxtlahuaca mother with the highest score on Factor 4 is the stepmother of a girl, Antonia, while the mother of a boy, Abel, has the lowest score because she left her baby son to be cared for by his oldest sister. Antonia's stepmother has this to say about baby care.

Q. Who took care of Antonia when she was a baby?
A. No one, only I.
Q. Did no one else take care of her before she was able to walk?
A. No one.
Q. When you left the house, who remained to care for her?
A. I carried her.
Q. Did your husband help care for her?
A. Sometimes when he was with her but there are times when he is not. At night he only comes to be with her for a little while and then when it is time to go to work, early in the morning, he goes again.

Abel's mother answers in the following manner.

His sister, the one who died, took care of him, and also I. His sister, poor child, took care of him. She was 11 years of age when she died. When she died I had him. I carried him. I took him to the market because there was no one else with whom he could stay.   I carried him because I was nursing.   If I went to get firewood or to the next town, I carried him with me.   His aunt who is in Mexico and Aurelia took care of him and took turns doing so.   But I mostly took him because I am the mother and I am the one who suffered with him. When he was little his father spent about half a day with him because when the boy was little the father had very little work.

Judith's mother spent an average amount of time in charge of her baby (for a Juxtlahuaca mother).

Q. When Judith was young, who took care of her?
A. Just I.   She was reared alone in the cradle.
Q. Did anyone help?
A. Her grandmother or her aunts.
Q. When you left the house, who remained to take care of her?
A. I left her for a little while sleeping alone or playing if it was daylight.   Sometimes I carried her about.
Q. Did your husband care for her?
A. Only in the morning or at night, because he works in the fields.

Africa.   The Nyansongo mothers spend less time in charge of babies than any other group, but more time in charge of older children than any other group except the New England mothers.   This discrepancy is due to the fact that babies are usually left with older children while the mothers work in the fields.   However, this practice is not usual as evidenced by the fact that Nyansongo babies are less likely to be left in the care of adults other than their parents than the children of any other group.   The baby boy Ogoi was cared for in a manner fairly typical of the Nyansongo mothers.

Nyaboke, his sister, who was then 12 years old, is the one who took care of Ogoi.   She took care of him until he began walking.   Sometimes my co-wife took care of him but not as much as I.

With a first child the mother may have to care for the baby herself.

I took care of Rebecca, since there was no child nurse.   When I went to the fields I carried her on my back everywhere.   After she could walk I would go slowly.   I had no sister-in-law to help, besides my mother-in-law said that I should care for the first child myself.

Chapter Five: Mothers' Responsibility for Child Care

United States.   The mothers of Orchard Town spend more time in charge of their children than any other group in the study.   Dorothy's mother is typical in the proportion of time that she spends caring for her daughter, both when she was a baby and now that she is 4 years old.

> I take care of them. My oldest will be 8 years old in July and I have never been away from these children for a full day—never overnight. One day we went to another town to go to church and we left the oldest with my mother-in-law and the other time I think we went to Boston for the day. I was thinking it was about time I had another day off.

Q. What do you have to do for her now?
A. Very little. I supervise her bath but she takes her own. She brushes her own teeth. She would skip out every morning without touching her hair if I would let her. She selects what she will wear within reason.
Q. How about your husband?
A. Well, he's wonderful with children, just wonderful. I don't think I asked him to look after children one-umteenth as much as a lot of women do. I never take off on a Saturday and say "You take over." I would say that he puts the children to bed at night. He makes sure their teeth are brushed and if they need a bath he supervises. . . . When he is home Saturday, if he goes to the store and the kids are around, he will always take them with him. But I don't think he actually has complete charge of the children very often.

Africa. The Gusii mothers, like those of Orchard Town, spend a great deal of time in charge of older children. The African mothers differ from those of New England in that they spend little time caring for infants. But once the children are able to walk easily the mother is the primary caretaker. Ogoi was cared for by his sister until he was walking. Now that he is 4 years old his mother spends a normal amount of time with him, for a Nyansongo mother.

> I have been in charge since his sister left him. He does not stay with my mother because she is so far away and he is too small to go by himself. The father sometimes takes care of him when he is here.

Aloyosa has the highest score on Factor 5 of any of the Gusii mothers. Since her husband is not with her, she has complete charge of her 6-year-old son. "I am in charge of taking care of him. My husband lives far away and most of the time he is not here. My mother-in-law is dead."

Mexico. The mother of 8-year-old Franco has a factor score that is virtually the same as the total group mean for Factor 5. Judging from her answer, she spends relatively little time with Franco.

Q. Who takes care of Franco during the day?
A. There is no one because the boy goes to his work and he is alone with his soul.   He is the oldest and he takes care of his brothers.
Q. When you are working, who takes care of him?
A. He is alone or with his aunts.   He goes to work with his father, to cut alfalfa.

Okinawa.   In Taira, 5-year-old Toshio, who was cared for by his grandmother until he was 4 years old, is now primarily under the care of his mother.   She is aided by her husband even though he is Toshio's step-father.

> I care for Toshio mostly as my husband is out during the day working. My husband now looks after Toshio like his own child.   Every night when he returns he listens patiently to the boy who tells him all about his day's activities.   He never punishes the child, although he scolds him, so Toshio loves him more than he does me.

The mother of 9-year-old Suko, on the other hand, spends relatively little time caring for him.

> Suko's older sister looks after him mostly now.   I go out to sell fish and work in the fields and she keeps an eye on him after they both return from school.   My husband still looks after him when I am busy and cannot tend to his needs.

India.   The Khalapur mothers spend relatively little of their time caring for their children, despite the fact that other caretakers are also relatively unimportant.   Khalapur children spend a good bit of their time "on their own," although they are seldom far from some adult who is a relative.

Aided by her mother-in-law and, to a lesser extent her sister-in-law, Kamla's mother has an average amount of responsibility for her 10-year-old daughter, despite the fact that she is a widow.   "I and the others in the house give her food and water and see that she is looked after."

Ruupchander's mother considers that her 10-year-old son, who works in the fields with his father, is old enough to look after himself.   She therefore has the lowest score in the Khalapur sample on Factor 5.

A. Nobody cares for him.
Q. Does your husband look after him?
A. Yes.

Philippines.   The Tarong mothers spend relatively less time in charge of their children than the mothers in any other group.   Maria's mother, who spent more time in charge of Lucretia than any other Tarong mother when she was a baby, spends an average amount of time in child care, now that her daughter is 3 years old. Like many Tarong girls Maria is often in the care of an adult other than her parents.

Q. Who does most of the taking care of Maria?
A. Aunt Juliana at Felipa's. She still has clothes there. My husband seldom cares for her. During the day she plays mostly by herself. She often naps at her aunt's.

Tarong mothers tend to leave older children under the care of adolescents. Maria's mother leaves 9-year-old Maria to be cared for by two older sisters, Anita, age 16, and Loreto, age 18. "Anita usually takes care of her now. My husband also helps. Loreto also looks after her a good deal."

Chapter Six: Responsibility Training

Okinawa. Cleaning house and caring for younger siblings are the most usual chores in the Okinawan sample. Both tasks may be done by boys and girls, although girls are more likely to clean house.

When taking care of younger brothers and sisters, the boys are chiefly required to "keep an eye on" a youngster or take a small brother along to play. This job may start as young as 4 or 5 years. Girls may have to carry babies on their backs while they play; sometimes the girls object to this, particularly if the baby is heavy. One mother of an 8-year-old girl says, ". . . It was all right when the baby was still little and did not weigh much but now I guess the baby is heavy and she does not like it too much."

Helping around the house is also a job in which training starts early. The mother of a 3-year-old girl, Sadako, says,

She does take the filled rice bowls and set them on the table at dinner time. She does this whenever she feels like it, it is not a regular job. Everyone praises her whenever she does it and she feels very pleased about it.

From such gentle beginnings the Taira girl gradually takes on larger tasks. Although some mothers of older girls say that their daughters are sometimes negligent of their duties, most seem to be consistently responsible and several reportedly do their work with initiative and enthusiasm that sometimes surprises and amuses their mothers. One mother has this to say about the efforts of her 5-year-old daughter to clean the floor.

Since the 18th of last month she started to mop the floors. It is not a regular job . . . she just does it when she wants to and feels like it. It was sure funny, one day I noticed that some rags were neatly sewn together so that it was a thick padlike rag. With this A. was mopping the floors. I asked her who did this sewing and she said she did. The other mopping rag was not good anymore so she had carefully stitched some new ones together and was busily mopping. I praised her in spite of the fact that it was not good sewing. . . . I wanted to laugh but I thought if I laughed she would be embarrassed and turn against me, so I praised her and told her what a great help she was. I don't expect her to do anything as a job yet.

Another mother of a 10-year-old, Matsue, reports the following.

Her regular chore is to pick up the bedding in the house every morning. She takes this job very seriously and will be the first one up. She has to walk a long way to school and she shoves everyone out of bed to put all the bedding away. . . . She will just rush here and there chasing everyone out of bed until she finishes her work.

Recently she has started to take her own washing down to the river, launder it, bring it home to starch and even iron it. Everyone is talking about it because she picks up not only her clothes but her grandmother's. I don't know what got into her but she will starch and iron her clothes so diligently. I suppose she sees her older sister doing it and she wants to have her clothes nicely done like her, I don't know. But then she does so many things like this without being told that I should not be too surprised. On Sundays when she is not doing baby sitting for the M. family she will take all the sooty pots and pans down to the river and scrub them . . . no one told her but she does it regularly. Why, at 10 years she even started to cook rice and make soup.

The boys are not conscientious or eager about their work, but they also have their chores. Five boys feed and care for animals. Of these, one cares for the family pig, three for chickens, and one for chickens and a horse.

The following is the report of the mother of the 10-year-old Kazuko who cares for the horse.

He has to feed the chickens, get grass for the horse, and clean the lamps every day. We have made him understand that these are his own responsibility . . . sometimes he is so busy playing that I have to call him home to do them. . . . I tell him at these times, "Would you let others do your own job? One should do his work before going out to play." He will then apologize and do the chores.

Philippines. The children of Tarong are fairly busy relative to the children in other communities. There is no type of chore that is not done by some child in the Philippine sample, and this sample is ranked first or second in the number of children who care for siblings, gather wood, pasture animals, and run errands.

Small boys may begin to learn responsibility by running errands. A mother of a 3-year-old son says, "The only help he can do yet is to bring matches to us when asked."

Boys may start taking care of animals at a fairly early age. One 4-year-old boy started grazing the family carabao, but stopped when the animal gored and frightened him. Older boys may take care of a variety of animals, carabao, cows, goats, pigs, and chickens are all mentioned as charges of Tarong boys. One versatile 7-year-old does the following chores.

> His duties are grazing the carabao, bringing water, cutting and burning firewood, sometimes feeding the pig. He can also cook rice and take care of the baby. He generally does his chores every day, if it does not interfere with school.

Girls also may begin their chores when quite young. The people of Tarong live in houses that are built above the ground on stilts. One 3-year-old girl is entrusted with the job of keeping her baby brother from falling off the porch.

> When we are cooking or busy in any way, she looks after the baby. She often does this now that her older brother is in school. We tell her "You play around where he is and when he goes near the stairs, you pull his shirt so he won't fall."

Older girls, like the boys, do a variety of tasks. A 7-year-old girl, Benigna, has the following chores.

> She must tether the goats, bring the chickens to roost, fix a place for the pig, take them back after being tied up, husk flour and look after the baby. She does these things every day.

A 9-year-old girl carries water, brings firewood and gathers vegetables for her family, and a 10-year-old carries the baby, washes the baby's clothes, mends clothes, husks flour and, last, but probably not least, rolls cigars for her father.

India.   In contrast to the Philippine sample, Khalapur is not ranked 1 or 2 on the percentage of children performing any chore.   However, the Khalapur children have a variety of tasks, baby tending, housecleaning, running errands, and watering the animals being the most frequently mentioned.

Since the mothers of the Khalapur sample are unable to leave the house because of purdah restrictions, running errands is a job that must be done by children and is often given even to young children.   One 3-year-old boy shops for his mother three or four times a day.   Boys also help care for the cows, bullocks, and water buffalo.   The mother of a 10-year-old boy says, "He takes the cattle to drink once a day during his recess hour when he comes home from school."

Another mother with an 8-year-old son, Jaipaal, enumerates his tasks.

> He gives water to the cattle, brings grass from the fields and goes to school.   On Sunday he goes with the others and gets green grass for the cattle and gives them water and fodder.   He takes two bullocks to the well and the rest to the pond.   In winter he takes the cattle to drink once a day and in summer twice a day.

Girls learn to help around the house and, again because of the seclusion of women, to bring water from the well if the family runs through the supply that is brought daily by low-caste women.   Since the Khalapur girl is considered a guest in her own home, such training is casual and slow.   Thus the mother of a 5-year-old girl says,

> She has learned recently to clean the plates.   She tried to sweep but she is a child and cannot do it tidily. . . . If I tell her to wash the dishes daily she will wash them.   But we do not want her to.

If a child's mother is a widow, she and her children may be somewhat exploited by other members of the family and then work may be unusually extensive.   Such is the case with this 10-year-old girl Kamlaa.

> She carries the baby, brings water from the well, sweeps the floor, cleans the hearth, takes food to her uncle in the fields, and sometimes makes a few breads.   [The local bread is round and unleavened, like a tortilla, but is made from wheat.] *Of her own wish she never does it.* . . . She sweeps the floor, cleans the hearth, and washes dishes twice a day.   If the water is finished she will bring it as much as four times from the well.   If there is water she does not go.

United States.   Because of the greater technological advancement of the families in the United States sample, the children of Orchard Town are exempt from several chores that must be performed in most of the other societies. None of the Orchard Town children carry water, gather wood, or take animals to pasture. Only two children take care of younger siblings, help cook, or feed and water animals. The United States sample is most similar to the others in this study in the proportion of children who run errands. The only chore that Orchard Town children do more often than other children is help clean house. This, as it has been pointed out, consists largely of cleaning up their own rooms.

The emphasis upon picking up toys is illustrated by this mother of 4-year-old Danny who says,

> I expect him to pick up his room and to pick up the cellar where he plays. That's all. We threaten to go down there and throw everything away if they don't pick it up. My husband goes down there at night and he starts piling everything in a box . . . and you never saw kids get anything picked up so fast in your life.

The mother of 4-year-old Ann expects more from her child than simply picking up toys.

> [She must] make her bed, brush her own teeth, take her own bath. I check afterwards but she is supposed to take her own bath, dress and undress herself, and pick up her toys. I don't expect her to stay at it as long as her (older) sisters but she is supposed to help. She helps set the table and that is about it. . . . She makes her own bed every day, dresses herself every day. Setting the table is frequent. Picking up her toys is supposed to be daily. . . . She's told she can't play until she is finished.

The rather lengthy answer of the next mother is quoted fully because it is a good example of the clarity of the rules that support the expectations of many American mothers, in contrast with the more diffuse expectations of mothers in some other societies.

> She's to keep her room straightened out and her room includes her sisters' room too. [There are two younger sisters.] She does all the evening dishes and all the Saturday dishes one week, and she is to keep the front room and dining room picked up and dusted for the second week. Other than that, if there's any other additional work, it's by request or demand, whichever the situation warrants. Like, if there is no one for Elanor [the youngest sister, age 3 years] to play with I tell her to take care of Elanor today. Occasionally I'll ask her to make cake or biscuits or something like that. She can cook quite well.

She has a rather strenuous day. She comes home and practices. She has a paper route. Then she has the room and the dishes to do after supper. She does not have a great deal of time to play, so I don't like to ask her to take care of Elanor except on occasions when I have to. She does not feel that she is browbeaten when it comes to taking care of the little ones. She mentions the Millgrims, who have to baby-sit maybe twice a week while she does not get it except every other month. . . .

Q. Does she do these things regularly?
A. The dishes and housework, yes.
Q. Are there any exceptions?
A. Birthday's and if she goes out on days when she has to do the dishes. If she goes to someone else's home from school she doesn't have to pick up the front room. If she has company for supper, she must help with the dishes. If she had company she must clear off the table for her brother because it is additional work and it's not his company.

In this United States sample, boys are not required to do chores as frequently as girls. The following is fairly typical of the kinds of work that may be expected from an older boy. The boy who is the subject in this quotation is 9 years old and it is obvious that his work is not as extensive as that of the 9-year-old girl just described.

He is supposed to make his bed every morning and keep his room picked up. These two are regular ones. He mows the lawn once in a while, burns the rubbish, shovels snow in the winter time. This last winter he has been emptying ashes at my mother's house and that has been more or less a regular job.

Mexico. The children of Juxtlahuaca are rated high on a number of chores, carrying water, feeding and watering animals, helping in the fields, running errands, and helping with cooking. As in some other societies, training begins gradually. The mother of a 5-year-old says, "Sometimes when I come home I ask her to give me a plate or to put a plate away. When I go out to get water she takes her little pail along too. Little by little she is learning."

Another mother of a 4-year-old expects more from her daughter. She fetches water, sweeps the house and also runs errands.

Older girls are expected to do more. Rosa, a 7-year-old, has a number of chores. "She brings the water, sweeps the house, watches the baby, gives corn to the pigs and chickens."

The pattern of increasing responsibility for boys is much the same. One 4-year-old son must do the following tasks. "He should go to school on time and do whatever little errand might offer itself. Also he should take care of his little brother and take care of the feed for the animals around the house."

Although the one girl mentioned above does feed chickens, feeding and watering animals is usually a boy's task. The Juxtlahuaca boys care for a variety of animals, fowl, burros, pigs, and cattle. For instance, one 8-year-old boy has the following tasks to do. "His daily work is to cut alfalfa, feed the animals, chickens, turkeys or pigs. Then he is free to come in and eat."

One enterprising youngster, age 8, even owns his own burros.

Mostly Roberto takes care of his burros. He goes on errands for me and keeps the weeds cut down. He has himself four burros. He wasn't crazy. His uncle had an old female burro that he was going to kill because she was ill and was no good any more for carrying things. The uncle said to my boy, "Do you want that burro?" He didn't think the boy would say anything but he said "Yes, I do." After a short time the burro had a little son and then a little daughter and now there are four of them altogether and my boy takes care of them. He says, "You see, mother, now I have 400 pesos all for myself. Someday I'll be able to sell by burros and then, after that, I'll get some more."

Africa. In Nyansongo the circumcision ceremony marks a sudden shift in status from child to young adult. Accompanying this status shift is a shift in the type of work expected of the child.

The first chore for all children is usually bringing water from the river. This task begins when the child is 4 or 5 years old. Thus, the mother of a 4-year-old girl says, "She is unfit to help yet. She can only be sent with a little pan to help her sister get water from the river."

A 5-year-old girl has more to do. "She brings fire from other houses, water from the river in a pan, takes care of the baby and I send her to other houses for vegetables." Baby-tending is usually the job of un-circumcised girls.

After a girl is circumcised she graduates to the "women's work" of gardening, grinding corn, and cooking, which the girls find less confining. One 8-year-old circumcised girl does the following.

Her duties are collecting firewood and digging in soft land but not fresh unbroken land. I want her to work in the woman's cooperative work group as much as she can. She grinds but she can only do enough for us two. I only require her to bring the cow from the river and back, and go for water. She took the cow and brought water before she was circumcised. She started to do that when she was 3. Digging she has just started when she was circumcised.

Watering cattle may also be done by young boys. The mother of a 4-year-old son says, "After all he is too little to help me, but I expect him to bring water from the river and herd cattle."

However another mother with a 5-year-old son considers him too young to go to the river, tending the baby is his job.

Later chores are more extensive. The mother of an unusually conscientious child expects the following.

I expected him to bring water and make fire for me when he was 3 to 6 years old. Now I especially have him garden and clear the bush. This work I expect of him before he is circumcised. He grinds better than others, cooks food very well, collects firewood and brings water. He does this every day, he doesn't miss.

Chapter Seven: Aggression Training; Mother-Directed Aggression

Africa. All the African mothers have factor scores above the pancultural mean for Factor 6. Even a mother with a relatively low score for the society is punitive when faced with self-directed aggression.

Q. Sometimes children become angry with their parents when rebuked. What do you do when this happens?
A. I refuse her food for that. I tell her "You're my child. Do you know where you came from? Do you realize the difficulties in raising you?" I can refuse her food for five days until she realizes.
Q. What if she should strike you?
A. It is amazing for a child to do that when so small [8 years old]. I'd lock her in the house and beat her badly.

The mother of 5-year-old Joseph is more typical of the Nyansongo mothers.

I can only cane him if I find him becoming angry and hitting me. If he is near I would get hold of him and cane him, but if he runs away I would refuse him food for a couple of days more and he will learn himself what he has done wrong.

The mother of 8-year-old Myatiti is, in principle, particularly punitive, even by Nyansongo standards.

If she abused me I would cane her a great deal, saying, "I am one of the parents. I don't see why you should abuse me. If you are very disgusted you can go somewhere. Go cry."

Q. Has this happened?
A. No, because Myatiti knows that she can't abuse her mother or she would be chased out. If she struck me I would beat her and take away her dress. If I was not able to catch her I would just keep refusing her food.

Philippines. The responses of 8-year-old Enrique's mother to these questions are typical of the women of Tarong:

I tell him "That's not what you should do." It happens when I'm sending them to do anything and they do not want to; especially if I keep prodding them. He has never hit me; if he did, I would swat him.

The mother of 8-year-old Elena is more punitive on this issue.

I hurry to whip her if she becomes angry with me. Sometimes when I feed the pigs I ask Elena to drive the chickens and dogs away. Elena would rather play, so I often have to scold her. She seldom gets a whipping, a threat is usually enough. She has never hit me but if she did I would break her like firewood.

Mexico. The question given to the Juxtlahuaca mothers concerning mother-directed aggression differed somewhat from the standard version. These mothers were asked "How does your child behave when you scold him? That is, does he cry or scream or does he say nothing? Does he not speak to you? Does he behave worse than before? What do you do if he behaves this way? What if he then continues that behavior?"

The response of 4-year-old Cortina's mother is fairly typical.

Q. How does Cortina behave when you scold her? That is, does she cry or scream or does she say nothing? Does she not speak to you? Does she behave worse than before?
A. She starts to cry. Sometimes she asks me why am I scolding her since she has done nothing. She cries and then she's quiet and I tell her that "the next time when I tell you to do something do it right away so that I don't have to scold you."
Q. What do you do then if Cortina behaves thus? What if she then continues that behavior?
A. I content her if she's crying. I tell her not to cry, I get her a banana.

Jubenal's mother, who is unusually permissive about mother-directed aggression, comforts her 8-year-old son when he is angry with her. This is consistent with the Juxtlahuaca tendency to be more permissive about mother-directed aggression with older children, at least where the child's anger is restrained.

> He gets angry but he does not answer badly. He doesn't cry, he doesn't say anything to me, he is just quiet and stubborn. He goes outside alone to play or sits down but he doesn't say anything. I make him feel better. "Yes, that's the way, my boy," I tell him. I make him content.

Okinawa. The Okinawan mothers are generally relatively permissive about aggression directed to themselves. They are more likely to punish such aggression in boys than in girls. This contrast is well illustrated by the mothers of the boy Yoshio and the girl Matsue.

> If Yoshio should talk back when he is being scolded, I will talk to him and tell him that I am scolding him because he was naughty and he should not get angry and talk back to me. If he strikes or hits me, I hit his hand or his feet, whatever he strikes me with, and tell him he should not do it.

> Because Matsue is such a shameless, impudent child who loses her temper so easily I just let her go. If I am scolding her and she starts a tantrum, I just ignore her. It is no use to try to do anything; she will grow out of it.

United States. Like the Okinawan mothers, the Orchard Town mothers tend to be permissive about aggression. Nelson's mother thinks that it is best to ignore the anger of her 10-year-old son:

> Yes, he gets mad, like if I scold him for not picking up his things. He always starts to say that it is his sister's fault. Oh, I used to argue quite a bit with him, but I don't think it pays. Lately I have just been sort or ignoring it, telling him what I thought and then walking away and letting him sputter. When you come right down to it, ignoring a lot of things is the best way out of it, up to a point.

> Q. Can you give an example of when he has gotten angry with you?
> A. Yes, it was to do with picking up his room. I was telling him to pick up something and he just got launched on that and I started on him to do something else, and he got mad. He said, "How can I do both things at once?" He was right because I was forcing things on him too fast. Maybe after I have blown off, I cool off and he gets things done and everything is all right again."

Q. What do you do if he hits you?
A. I don't think he ever has. I don't think even when he was little he
   ever did.
Q. How do you think you would react to that?
A. It would probably make me mad and I don't know what I would do.
   I would probably slap him back and tell him not to do it again.

Louisa's mother is more punitive when aggression does occur, but she
tries to prevent it.

> I just will not allow back talk. There have been times when she's
> been very angry with me and wanted to, and from the very time that
> they were disciplined they have understood that I won't allow any
> shouting and saying they won't do it. When they do they get punished
> for it. When Louisa was younger, I used to spank her. That was
> about the main punishment that she got until I realized that that is
> not the way to punish her. I really have not had enough of that to
> know what I would do but I just won't tolerate it. They never have
> done it and when they get older they realize and they just know
> enough not to do it. I hope I haven't frightened them about it. *I
> try not to make such a strong issue so they won't fight back at me—to
> avoid* anything like defiance. If she hit me I think I really would
> spank her then, whether I customarily punish that way or not, because
> it would be the only way they would recognize that they wouldn't be
> allowed to do anything like that.

India.   The Khalapur mothers are generally less punitive about mother-
directed aggression than the mothers in any other sample. However,
these mothers also differ among themselves more than the mothers in
any other sample. This is because a number of the Khalapur mothers
actually console their children when the children become angry with them,
while others scold them, thus producing an unusually high variation.
The mothers of 5-year-old Reeshmii and 10-year-old Jaipaal are typical
of those mothers who believe in quieting children's anger with consolation. Reeshmii's mother says,

> What to do? [when Reeshmii is angry with her] I'll console her and
> make her sit near me. When her father gets angry with her I feel
> very bad. If someone scolds her and she cries, I say "What do you
> want? Do you want food?"

Sumeetra's mother has a factor score of −1.11, virtually the same as
the mean of the Khalapur sample on Factor 6. She consoles minor
aggression but would punish physical violence. Her answer implies that
the latter rarely, if ever, occurs.

Q. What do you do when Sumeetra gets angry with you?

A. I console her and take her in my lap. I say "What is wrong with you? Why are you angry?"

Q. What if she should kick or strike you?

A. A child? Oh no! If the child hits me I will hit her back.

Chapter Eight: Aggression Training, Peer-Directed Aggression

Mexico. As a group, the Mexican mothers are stricter about peer-directed aggression and obedience than the mothers of other societies. The mother of 8-year-old Hidelberto is particularly strict.

Q. What do you wish Hidelberto to do if another child looks for an argument with him?

A. I tell him he should not act superior to other people. I tell him that it is better to come home so as to avoid difficulties. I tell him that he should not go out to hit anybody or to get hit.

Q. What do you do if he does as you want him to do?

A. I tell him that that is good, that a child should not fight, that if he does as I tell him, I won't scold him.

Q. If he does not do as you wish, what do you do?

A. I hit him with a whip on the body and I tell him that he shouldn't do that again.

Q. If he looks for an argument with other children, what do you do?

A. Well, haven't I told you, I have to punish him and tell him not to fight.

Q. What do you do to him if he teases other children?

A. I lock him up in a dark room and then he won't do it again. If I do close him up in a room, it's only at daytime, not at night.

Q. When you tell Hidelberto to do something, does he do it right away, or does he delay?

A. Sometimes when he wants to work he does it right away and when he feels more like playing he delays, whether it's for the game or just because he is lazy.

Q. What do you do if he delays?

A. I scold him.

Q. What do you do if he does it right away?

A. I say to him "You would be very happy if you obey your mother, and I will love you that way, if you are obedient!"

Q. Do you always do this?

A. Yes, of course, yes.

Okinawa. The mother of 5-year-old Kaoru is lenient with her son about obedience. Her reactions to Kaoru's fights with other children depend upon the circumstances of the quarrel, and therefore she has a low score on Factor 3.

Q. What do you do when Kaoru is playing with other children and there is a fight?

A. I don't like to interfere with children's play of fights. One day I was bringing water and Kaoru was fighting with Akira. He was not really fighting seriously, just laughing and hitting Akira, but Akira became angry and began really hitting Kaoru. Even then Kaoru laughed and kept on. I almost thought I should tell Kaoru to stop because Akira was angry, but I went home with the water instead. Of course when he comes home crying after a fight, I tell him to go out and fight back and win the fight. If Kaoru is at fault and I see it I would stop the fight, but otherwise I just let it go. The only time I interfere is when Kembo is involved because he really hurts the children physically. Kaoru is short-tempered and always gets it from Kembo.

Q. Do you expect Kaoru to obey immediately when you tell him to do something, or do you give him a little leeway?

A. If I tell him to do something and he feels like doing it he will, if he doesn't, he won't. I just let him go because if I try to force him he will run away anyway. He will laugh and run off like a streak if he does not want to do it.

Matsue's mother, on the other hand, is strict about both obedience and fighting with other children. Matsue is 10 years old.

Q. What do you do when Matsue tries to get her own way with other children?

A. I call her in and tell her that she is not to do that.

Q. What do you do when she is playing with other children and there is a fight?

A. Usually I would scold my own child and say that she was bad to fight, but I would rather gather all the children who are fighting and let each one tell what happened, and then sort of talk to them saying, "Because you did such and such this happened. Now if you did not do this there would be no fight. It is better not to fight."

Q. Do you ever tell her to fight back?

A. I don't encourage her to fight back. I tell her not to fight at all. Every night after dinner we discuss things and if any of the children have fought that day, they get a talking to, not scolded but asked if they cannot mend their ways.

Q. Do you expect Matsue to obey immediately when you tell her to do something?

A. I expect Matsue to do whatever I ask her to do immediately. Sometimes she may be doing something else and she will say "Wait." I wait a bit and then ask her again and if she does not do it I will ask the third time and say that I cannot wait any longer. Then she will apologize and do it in a hurry. I don't let her go without doing it if I ask her to do something, because if I do it may form a bad habit.

India. The Khalapur mothers usually discourage aggression. They are more variable in their reactions to disobedience.

The mother of 8-year-old Angurii is relatively strict about fights with other children and about obedience.

Q. What do you do when Angurii gets in a fight?
A. Then I beat her and bring her home. Once we found Angurii and Kamlaa fighting. They had hold of each other's cheeks and were pinching. We sent Kamlaa home and brought Angurii home. Kamlaa came back with her grandmother. Her grandmother was angry. We said that it was the fault of both of them and she could beat Angurii if she liked. Then it was all right and they went away.
Q. Do you ever tell her to fight back?
A. No, we don't want the children to fight.
Q. Do you want her to obey at once when you tell her to do something?
A. Yes.
Q. Do you scold her when she ignores her work or runs away?
A. Yes.

Kheer's mother is typical of the Khalapur mothers, her factor score is close to the mean of the sample. Kheer is only 4, so his mother considers him too young to always obey orders.

Q. What do you do when Kheer is in a fight?
A. I scold whoever is a fault.
Q. Do you ever tell him to fight back?
A. Do you ever say this? Do you ever give this bad advice to children, that you go and fight outside?
Q. Do you expect him to obey at once when you tell him to do something?
A. He is a child and sometimes he starts playing or sometimes he does it at once. They do it at once but when they start playing then they do not do it.
Q. Do you always follow through on requests?
A. I say "If he does not want to do it, let him not do it." He is a child and sometimes he feels like doing it and sometimes he does not feel like doing it.

Africa. The mother of 10-year-old Matandura is typical of the Nyansongo sample.

A. If it's all my children, I tell them not to fight.   If it is an outside boy, I'd also tell them not to fight.   If mother of other boys hears that Matandura fought him and I was here and did nothing, she'll think I told Matandura to do so . . . I don't encourage him to fight back. I ask him and other boy who was wrong.   And if I find other boy was wrong, I tell him not to do that again.

Q. What if another child abuses him verbally?

A. I tell Matandura that's nonsense, you leave it and sometimes I say maybe you're the bad one who began it, and he says no I didn't.   If other boy is bigger I tell other boy not to.

Philippines. Ernesto's mother is typical of the Tarong mothers, with respect to her aggression training.   Ernesto is 5 years old.

Q. What do you do if Ernesto is playing with other children and there is a quarrel or fight?

A. If they are quarreling with him, I scold those who are quarreling. I tell them, "There is no outsider among you.   You should get along together."

Q. Do you ever encourage him to fight back?

A. No.   I might say things to adults who were around during a quarrel and did nothing.

Q. Do you expect Ernesto to obey immediately when you ask him to do something?

A. There are times when I want things done right away and I whip him if he delays.   Other times I may not care and, if he feels playful, he takes a while.

Q. Do you always make sure that he has done what you wanted him to do?

A. No.   When he doesn't want to do it, sometimes he just goes away, and I just let him.

The Tarong mothers expect older children to obey more promptly than younger ones.   The contrast in responses between Ernesto's mother and the mother of 8-year-old Prudencio.

Q. Do you expect Prudencio to obey immediately when you ask him to do something, or do you give him a little allowance?

A. Allowance is sometimes given, sometimes not.   He should pasture the animals without delay.   Water carrying may be delayed.   I sometimes do it myself.

Q. What do you do when he delays?
A. I whip him.
Q. Do you always make sure he has done what he was told to do?
A. I generally make sure.

United States. The Orchard Town mothers have, as a group, lower scores on Factor 3 than the mothers in any other community. Their encouragement of retaliation is particularly striking in contrast to the other mothers. This group of mothers is also unusual in that they are more likely to encourage aggression in younger children than in older ones. Evidently the success of their aggression training with young children makes encouragement of aggression among older children unnecessary. The responses of the mother of a 9-year-old boy illustrate this point.

Q. How about when Mike is playing with one of the other children in the neighborhood and there is a quarrel or fight—how do you handle this?
A. Well I'm never around when they're fighting. That would be more for younger. Now when they're fighting they're off.
Q. Well would you do anything when he was younger?
A. Oh, if he was the one that started it I would bring him in the house. Of course when he was little there were a whole lot of boys and they ranged from 10 down and he had no older brother to protect him, and he really at that time had to learn to stand up for himself. I really think because before that he was quite a sissyish child. He really had to get up and fight and there wasn't too much I could do about it—it was either a point of keeping him in the house or letting him be out and take it, and he was out and took it.
Q. Do you ever feel that Mike is too touchy?
A. No. The only time he's touchy is if he's coming down with something. That's how I know he's sick. He's not the whiny type or anything.
Q. Do you ever encourage Mike to fight back?
A. I don't have to encourage him.
Q. Well did you when he was little?
A. Yes I did because there wasn't much I could do about it. You couldn't go to the parents and tell them. Now like if he picked on a younger boy up here and the mother came to me, I would see to it that he didn't touch that boy again and he wouldn't, but they didn't care. I couldn't keep him in the house all the time and so he had to learn.

The tendency of the Orchard Town mothers to let children settle their own disputes is common. The mother of 4-year-old Barbara expresses the same opinions.

Q. How about when Barbara is playing with one of the other children in the neighborhood and there is a quarrel or fight—how do you handle this?

A. Oh I guess it sort of depends what the quarrel is. I usually try to find out what it's about and I usually try to divert them, frankly. I'll suggest that they come in and get something to eat. You can never find out whose at fault, but if it's very unfair I try to settle it, but if it's just a general quarrel—usually I like them to try to settle their own trouble. I don't like tattletales. I usually tell them to go settle their own unless it's too bad.

The mother of 10-year-old Gloria expresses similar attitudes about retaliation although, like the mothers of older boys, she is more hesitant about encouraging retaliation.

Oh, unless somebody's getting hurt pretty badly I'm inclined to let them fight it out. I don't interfere unless somebody's really the underdog. They have to do a certain amount of fighting and quarreling in order to balance the situation. I'm inclined to stop quarrels in the house quicker because I mind the confusion more than because I'm concerned about the outcome. Who wins is not important to me. They have learned not to come in tattling. I say "Well if you can't get along with them, then play with somebody else, there are lots of other people in this world."

Q. Do you encourage her to fight back?

A. I have on occasions had to encourage her to fight back. As a rule she takes care of that little situation by herself. I have never allowed the children to strike each other. They fight back with words sometimes. I think they are foolish to fight with someone bigger than they are. They should get themselves out of the situation or out of trouble as an alternative. As a rule Gloria will hold her own pretty well, I think.

Orchard Town mothers often do not expect their children to obey them promptly, as the answers of these two women indicate.

Q. When you ask Linda to do something do you give her leeway?

A. I give her lots and lots of leeway. I think if she did something the first time I told her, I'd faint.

Q. What if she delays?

A. I don't know. I don't do anything; that's the trouble with her, I

guess. Most of the time when I'm desperate I do what I want her
to do myself. She's at that dawdling age, it drives me wild.

Q. Do you expect Bobby to obey at once, or do you give him some
leeway?

A. I give him a little leeway. If I call him to supper, if he doesn't come
right away, I call him about three times and then I act or my husband
does. Sometimes if there is five minutes more of the TV program, we
let him watch those five more minutes.

Q. How about following through?

A. We always follow through eventually . . . . Sometimes I let it ride,
other times, if he doesn't come or do what I tell him, I lick him.
Depends on what it is, sometimes I just say "To heck with it."

III ❖ Cross-Cultural Analysis of Socialization Practices Rating Scales

General Warmth of Mother

This scale measures the amount of warmth shown by the mother to her child and other members of her family, friends, and neighbors. Warmth may be manifested by playing with her child, enjoying him, doing things to please child and others, demonstrating affection in words and action. Routine caretaking and amusing the child as part of a schedule or as a matter of felt duty or responsibility are not to be considered as automatically indicating emotional warmth. The use of reward and praise as techniques of inculcation are not relevant to the scale *per se*. Signs of affection which are spontaneous with the mother should weigh more heavily in this rating than affection which comes only as a result of the child's or other people's solicitations.

7 Mother expresses much warmth and affection to others, enjoys people, is very friendly.

4 Mother is moderately warm and outgoing.

1 Mother is very cold and reserved; never expresses warmth.

Mood Variation of Warmth

7 Mother's warmth and affection are extremely variable and due to the mother's impulses rather than to any other reason.

1 Mother's warmth does not depend on her own moods. She either shows little variability in warmth or her variability is contingent on the situation.

Amount of Praise

This scale measures the degree to which the mother indicates by actions or comments that she is pleased with the child. This includes statements of praise made directly to the child, statements of praise made to others in the presence of the child, behavior such as smiling in admiration made

343

directly to the child, or appreciative winks and smiles made to others who are called upon to notice the actions of the child.

7   Mother praises child regularly and constantly admires him for good behavior.

1   Child is never praised or admired.

Frequency and Intensity of Physical Punishment

7   Mother frequently controls deviant behavior of child by use of painful physical punishment, e.g., frequently whips or beats child.

4   Mother often slaps child; infrequently beats child.

1   Mother never uses physical punishment.

Rewards for Using Aggression to Defend Himself against Peers (Reward for Retaliatory Aggression)

7   Mother would go out of way to reward.

5   Shows approval of rewards.

4   Lets it go.

3   Discourages.

1   Mother would go out of way to punish.

General Hostility of Mother

7   Mother expresses much anger, irritableness with others. Often scolds, nags, fights with others.

1   Mother never angry, irritable, or quarrelsome.

Mood Variation of Hostility

7   Mother's hostility is extremely variable and due to the mother's impulses rather than to any other reason.

1   Mother's hostility does not depend on her own moods. Either she does not show her dissatisfactions or her variability is contingent on the particular situation.

Amount of Time Mothers Care for Babies (A Baby Is Defined as a Child Who Is Not Yet Walking).

0   No answer

1   Never

3   Sometimes

5   About half the time

7   Usually

9   Always

Amount of Time Fathers Care for Babies.

As above

Amount of Time Adults Other Than Parents Care for Babies.
As above

Amount of Time Older Children Care for Babies.
As above

Amount of Time Mothers Care for Children.
0 No answer
1 Never
3 Sometimes
5 About half the time
7 Usually
9 Always

Amount of Time Fathers Care for Children.
As above

Amount of Time Adults Other Than Parents Care for Children.
As above

Degree to Which Mother Is Aggressive When Child Is Angry or Aggressive to Her.
1 Mother is never aggressive to child under these circumstances, she nurtures or distracts.
3 Mother scolds mildly.
5 Mother spanks or gives other formalized punishment.
7 Mother retaliates with extreme aggression.

General Permissiveness-Strictness of Caretakers.
7 Adults are consistently strict and punitive with children.
4 Adults are sometimes strict and sometimes permissive with children with about equal frequency.
1 Adults are consistently lenient and permissive with children. Children are very seldom punished.

Total Number of Chores.
0 No answer
1 One chore
2 Two chores
3 Three chores, etc.
9 No chores

Total Frequency of Chores.

Estimate from all chores how often children do some kind of work. Use a sum rather than an average estimate, i.e., if children have two jobs that they do several times a week, score as daily.

0 No answer
1 Never
2 Less than once a month
3 Less than once a week, more than once a month
4 Weekly
5 Several times a week
6 Daily
7 Several times a day

Frequency of
care of siblings
help cook
clean house
carry water
gather wood
feed or water animals
pasture animals
help in fields and gardens
run errands
gather food
other
regularity of school attendance.

These individual chores are rated on the same scale as total frequency.

Index